A WOMAN'S LIFE-WORK:
LABORS AND EXPERIENCES
OF
LAURA S. HAVILAD

First published in 1881

Published by Left of Brain Books

Copyright © 2023 Left of Brain Books

ISBN 978-1-396-32372-0

First Edition

PUBLISHER'S PREFACE

About the Book

A Woman's Life Work [Labors and Experiences] by Laura Smith Haviland.

About the Author

Laura Smith Haviland (1808 - 1898)

"Laura Smith Haviland was one of the most important women in the history of the Underground Railroad. She helped guide thousands of fugitives to freedom. She wrote:

"It is due to my parents to say, if I have been instrumental, through the grace of God, to bless his poor and lowly of earth, by adapting means to ends in relieving suffering humanity, it is largely owing to their influence."

Laura Smith Haviland was born on December 20, 1808 in Kitley Township, Ontario. Her parents were Daniel Smith (1785-1845), an approved minister in the Society of Friends, and Sene Blancher Smith (1787-1845). She grew up in the Society of Friends, also known as Quakers. In 1815, they moved to Cambria, Niagara County, in western New York state."

(Quote from wikipedia.org)

CONTENTS

PREFACE

IN presenting the following pages to the public, without the trace of an excellent scholar or eloquent orator, I fully realize my inability to compete with writers of the nineteenth century. With this incompetency in view, I have hesitated and delayed until three-score and thirteen years are closing over me. Yet as I am still spared to toil on a little longer in the great field so white to harvest, praying the Lord of the harvest to arm and send forth more laborers, because they are too few, I ask an indulgent public to allow my deep and abiding sympathies for the oppressed and sorrowing of every nation, class, or color, to plead my excuse for sending forth simple, unvarnished facts and experiences, hoping they may increase an aspiration for the active doing, instead of saying what ought to be done, with excusing self for want of ability, when it is to be found in Him who is saying, "My grace is sufficient for thee, for my strength is perfect in weakness."

LAURA S. HAVILAND.

OCTOBER, 1881.

EARLY LIFE

AT the earnest solicitation of many dear friends I have consented to leave on record some of the incidents that have fallen under my personal observation during three-score and ten years.

My father, Daniel Smith, was a native of Eastern New York, and for many years an approved minister in the Society of Friends. He was a man of ability and influence, of clear perceptions, and strong reasoning powers.

My mother, Sene Blancher, was from Vermont; was of a gentler turn, and of a quiet spirit, benevolent and kind to all, and much beloved by all who knew her, and was for many years an elder in the same Society.

It is due to my parents to say, if I have been instrumental, through the grace of God, to bless his poor and lowly of earth, by adapting means to ends in relieving suffering humanity, it is largely owing to their influence.

Soon after their marriage, they removed to Kitley Township, county of Leeds, Canada West (now known as Ontario), where I was born, December 20, 1808. I well remember the perplexities and doubts that troubled my young mind in trying to find the whys and wherefores of existing facts; yet I was naturally a happy and playful child. Some remarks made by my parents over a portion of Scripture father was reading, in which was the sentence, "and they are no more twain, but one flesh"-- "that is a close relationship; twain is two, no more two but one flesh"--struck me with wonder and amazement. "Yes," replied mother, "that is a oneness that is not to be separated, a near relation between husband and wife; 'no more twain, but one flesh.' 'What God has joined together let not man put asunder.'" It seemed as if every word fastened upon my mind a feeling of awe at the new thought, that father and mother were one person. "Then they think just alike, and know all about the other, if true; father and mother believe it, and they found it in the Bible, and that," I thought, "must be true. Now for the test--If father and mother are one, they must know each other's thoughts and whereabouts." After father had been out a few minutes I asked mother where he was. "Not far off; may be he's gone to the barn." But he was not there. At my report she said, "Perhaps he's gone to David

Coleman's, or some of the neighbors." This settled the matter in my mind, that they were not one. But I gave the same test to try father, which also proved a failure. But not quite satisfied without further investigation, I asked mother for permission to go to David Coleman's to play an hour with his little girls. Little did she know that the object of her little five-year-old skeptic was to present the test to their father and mother, to see whether they were one, and found the same result each time.

This settled the question in my mind that one thing in the Bible was untrue. Father and mother were mistaken in that part of the Bible that said husband and wife were no more two, but one. For a long time after this, whenever the Bible was referred to as authority, I would think, "It may be true, and may not, because I tried one thing it said that was not true."

Another mystery was hard for me to solve. In asking mother where we should go if we should jump off the edge of the world, she replied, "There is no jumping off place, because our world is round, like a ball, and takes one day and night to roll around, and that makes day and night." After the little child of six years had studied over this mysterious problem a short time, she returned with the query, "Why don't we drop off while under-side? and why don't the water spill out off Bates's creek and our well?" She replied, "Water, as well as every thing else, is always kept in place by a great law, called gravitation, that our Heavenly Father made when he made the world," and she said I would understand more about it when older. But this did not satisfy me; I wanted to know all about it then. As soon as father came in queries were repeated, but he closed as mother did, that I must wait until I was older, which made me almost impatient to be old enough to know how these things could be.

Another subject occupied my childish mind a long time, and was investigated to the extent of the miniature ability I possessed. And that was the interesting fact that I discovered one bright evening while looking at the stars, that our house was just in the middle of the world; and when we went to grandfather's (a distance of seven miles), as soon as it was night, I was out in the yard measuring the distance by stars, but to my surprise, grandfather's house was just in the middle. For I tried it all around the house, and went to the barn with my uncles, and could discover no variation. Consequently I must have been mistaken at home. But on our return I could not find by the stars but that we were just in the center of creation. Whenever I went with my parents to a neighbor's for an evening's visit, my first and foremost thought was to see how far to one side they were. But I always found myself just in the center of this great world; just as grown-up children are prone to think their own nation is ahead in arts and sciences, of all other nations--their own State ahead of all other States in moral and intellectual improvements--their own town or city, like Boston, the "hub of the universe." In fact, we are about the center; our pets more knowing, and our children smarter, than can be found else-where. But as the study of astronomy gives ability to look upon the vast universe of thousands of worlds much larger than our own, revolving in their orbits, it develops our intellectual faculties, and enables us to view the concave appearance of the ethereal blue from a standpoint widely differing from the occupancy of the center. And when supreme self is melted away by faith in the blood of the covenant, our spiritual vision becomes clearer and our miniature minds are expanding, and we learn to make due allowances for the acts and opinions of others, that we have called peculiar, because they do not quite accord with our own usages and tastes.

In 1815 my father removed with his family to Cambria, Niagara County, Western New York, then a wilderness. Soon after we were settled in our new home, we lost my baby brother Joseph, which made a deep impres-sion upon my young heart, and gave me great uneasiness in regard to my own future happiness, should I be taken away. I found great relief, one day, while listening to a conversation between father and grandfather, as to what age children were responsible to their Creator. Father gave his opinion that ten years, in the generality of children, is the age that God would call them to an account for sin. Grandfather said that was about the age he thought children were accountable, and all children that die previous to that age are happily saved in heaven. "Yes," said father; "where there is no law there is no transgression." At this great relief to my troubled heart, I ran out to play with my brother Harvey, to tell him how long we would be safe, if we should die, for father and grandfather said children that died before they were ten years old would go to heaven, and I would be safe almost two years, and he would be safe a good while longer (as he was two years and a half younger than myself). "Oh, yes," said he; "and Ira will be safe a great many years, 'cause he's little, if he should die as little Josie did." This earliest conviction of sin vanished like the morning cloud. This idea was so deeply embedded in my young mind, that whenever I heard of a child's death, my first inquiry was for its age.

If under ten, I was at ease over its safety; but if over ten years, I was distressed unless I could hear of some words from the one taken away, that would indicate a preparation for the change of worlds. The vividness of those early childhood impressions are frequent reminders of the importance of giving clear explanations to children, in regard to important religious truths, as their young hearts are much more impressible than is generally conceded.

EARLY IMPRESSIONS OF SLAVERY AND RELIGION.

During the first six years in our new home, there was no school within three miles of us, and all the privilege we enjoyed of this kind was a spelling lesson given daily to three of us, the two little girls of our nearest neighbor and myself. Our mothers pronounced the words for us alternately, at their house and ours. In this way we spelled our book through a number of times. This privilege, with four months in school previous to leaving Canada, proved a great blessing. As I possessed an insatiable thirst for knowledge, I borrowed all the easy readers I could find in the neighborhood. I was especially interested in memoirs of children and youth, which increased my frequent desire to become a Christian. I wished to read every book that came within my reach. I read a few of father's books, designed for more mature minds. I became deeply interested in John Woolman's history of the slave- trade, of the capture and cruel middle passage of negroes, and of the thousands who died on their voyage and were thrown into the sea to be devoured by sharks, that followed the slave-ship day after day. The pictures of these crowded slave-ships, with the cruelties of the slave system after they were brought to our country, often affected me to tears; and I often read until the midnight hour, and could not rest until I had read it twice through. My sympathies became too deeply enlisted for the poor negroes who were thus enslaved for time to efface.

The third or fourth I had ever seen of that race was an old man called Uncle Jeff. He seemed to serve any one who called upon him for chores, in our little village of Lockport, that grew up as by magic upon the Erie Canal. Uncle Jeff was frequently employed by merchants to cry off their stale articles on the street. At one time the old man, whose head was almost as white as wool, was crying, "Gentlemen and ladies' black silk stockin's of all colors for sale," holding them up to view as he passed along the street, followed by a group of boys crying out, "Nigger, nigger," and throwing grass and clay at him. At length he turned to these half-grown boys, looking very sad, as he said, "Boys, I am just as God made me, an' so is a toad." At this the boys slunk away; and I felt very indignant in seeing the men who were standing near only laugh, instead of sharply reproving those ill-behaved children.

Another colored man, named Ben, came to our town with a family who opened an inn. He was employed mostly in the kitchen, and while Ben was asleep on the kitchen floor, some rude boys put a quantity of powder in the back of his pants, and placing a slow match to it left the room, but watched the process of their diabolical sport through a window, and soon saw their victim blown up, it was said, nearly to the ceiling. His hips and body were so badly burned that he was never able to sit or stoop after this wicked act. He always had to walk with a cane, and whenever too weary to stand, was compelled to lie down, as his right hip and lower limb were stiffened. Yet little notice was taken of this reckless act, but to feed and poorly clothe this life-long cripple, as he went from house to house, because he was of that crushed and neglected race.

RELIGIOUS IMPRESSIONS AND EXPERIENCE.

In the Autumn of my thirteenth year, with our parents' permission, brother Harvey and I attended a little prayer-meeting at our Uncle Ira Smith's house, near by. Here was singing, experiences given, with prayer and exhortations, in which young people, as well as those more advanced in years, took part. All this was new to me, having never attended any other meeting than of Friends, usually called Quakers. My father being a minister and mother an elder in that denomination, they were very conscientious in training their children in all the usages, as well as principles, of that sect. At this Methodist prayer-meeting a young girl, but little older than myself, related her experience, and prayed so earnestly for her young associates, that it took a deep hold on my mind; and on my way home, on that beautiful evening, I resolved to seek the Lord until I could know for myself that my sins were forgiven. Oh, how I wished I was a Christian, as was Hannah Bosworth. She was so young, and yet she told us how earnestly she sought the Lord, and found Jesus so precious in the forgiveness of her sins. It was said in that meeting that God was no respecter of persons, and that I had read in the Bible; and then Jesus had said, "Suffer little children to come unto me, and forbid them not;" "and now, this very night, I will begin to seek the Lord, and I never will give up trying, if it takes as long as I live, until I receive an evidence that I am the Lord's child. I want to realize that peace and joy those men and women expressed in that meeting." As all had retired, I placed a candle in my brother's hand, and hurried him to bed, that I might know positively that no human ear could listen to my first attempt to address my Heavenly Father.

I knelt for the first time in my life, in the rear of our corn crib, but no words could I find for prayer, and a feeling of fear came over me, and I arose to my feet. I looked all around me, but no one was in sight; naught but trees and shrubs of the garden below, and the ethereal blue, bedecked with the beautiful moon and sparkling stars, above. Is it possible that He who created this beautiful world can notice a little girl like me? And the thought occurred that I had better wait until I was older. But the remarks to which I had just listened came vividly before me, and I renewed my resolve to pray to Him who had said, "Suffer little children to come unto me," and again knelt for prayer; but that feeling of fear increased, until it seemed as if some one was about to place a hand upon my shoulder, and I again found myself on my feet. But as no one was in sight, I queried whether this was not the enemy of my soul, to keep me from prayer, and fell upon my knees a third time, determined to remain in the position of prayer until my first petition to my Heavenly Father was presented. And the prayer of the publican was repeated over and over again, "God be merciful to me a sinner." These words above all others seemed just for me. I was a sinner, and mercy was what I wanted. I returned to the house with a still more fixed resolve to continue asking, with a firmer purpose never to give over until the evidence of pardoning love was mine. As I retired, I knelt by my bedside, and repeated the same prayer, with a few additional words, imploring the aid of the Holy Spirit to teach me the way of life, and penitential tears began to flow. Before I slept my pillow was wet with tears, and was turned for a dry place. As I was reading the Bible through by course, it became more of a companion than ever before.

The next prayer-meeting was attended, and as they knelt during the season of prayer I felt an impression to kneel with them. But the cross was very great and I did not yield. I thought if I did so it would be reported to my parents, and they would probably forbid my coming to these little meetings, which I so highly prized. But this was unprofitable reasoning, increasing the burden instead of bringing the relief sought. I wept on my way home, and in my evening supplication renewed my promise to be more faithful, let others do or say what they would, if the like impression was ever again experienced. With permission I attended the next prayer-meeting at my uncle's, and, as if to test my faithfulness, two young women of my intimate associates came in, and sat one on each side of me. At the first season of prayer, as I did not have that impression, I felt quite at ease, and thankful to my Father in heaven for excusing me. But the next united supplication, I felt that I must unite with them in kneeling, and while one tried to pull me up by the arm, with saying "I'd be a little dunce if I was in thy place," the other sister pinched the other arm, "Now, Laura Smith, be a little Methodist, will thee? I'd be ashamed if I was thee; every body will make fun of thee." But I kept my position and made no reply, but secretly prayed for strength in my great weakness. But my fears were fully realized. It was at once reported that Laura Smith would be a Methodist if allowed by her parents. And for a long time no permission was given to attend those little prayer-meetings, my parents assigning this reason: "This Methodist excitement is unprofitable, especially for children. They have an overheated zeal, that is not according to knowledge, and we do not think it best for thee to attend; we want our children at a suitable age to be actuated by settled principle, not mere excitement." This reasoning by my dear father strongly tempted me to give up my resolutions altogether. Until I was eighteen I felt no liberty whatever in unburdening my troubled heart to my dear parents. They were unacquainted with the longings of my poor soul. Like the lone sparrow upon the house-top, I mourned many weeks, sought the solitary place for reading my Bible, and prayer; often watered my pillow with tears, and longed for the day, and during the day longed for the night, in which I might pour out my sorrows to my Heavenly Father out of sight of human eye. I was conscious that my sadness was troubling my dear parents. Oh! how I prayed for light to dispel this darkness and doubt-- sometimes ready to conclude that, as it was my duty to obey my parents, the Lord would excuse me in waiting until I was of age. Yet in reading the many precious promises of the Lord Jesus, "Come unto me, all ye that labor and are heavy laden, and I will give you rest;" "Seek, and ye shall find," I found fresh courage. But why do I not find this rest for this weary heart? Why do I not find the way to seek for the hidden treasure I so much longed for? These queries were continually revolving in my mind, without a satisfactory solution. Sometimes I almost concluded that God was too good to send the beings he created for his own glory to perdition to all eternity, and all would ultimately be saved; at other times, I could not reconcile universal salvation with the parable of Lazarus and the rich man, and was ready to conclude that salvation was for the elected few, and there were those who could not be saved, and I was among the lost. In one of these seasons, of almost despair, I ventured to attend a Methodist meeting held in a private house, in company with my uncle. Being at his house, I did not go home for permission. The minister was a plainly dressed man; the opening hymn was new to me, but every line seemed especially for me:

> "God moves in a mysterious way,
> His wonders to perform"

It was read and sung in an impressive manner. The fourth stanza seemed specially suited to my case:

> "Judge not the Lord by feeble sense,
> But trust him for his grace;
> Behind a frowning providence
> He bides a smiling face."

This gave new light, new courage, and fresh hope sprang up, like streaks of the morning sunbeam in the Eastern sky, preluding the full blaze of the orb of day. The prayer and the text upon which he based his remarks were all flowing in the same channel. The exhortation was to the discouraged and despairing soul to remember that the darkest time of night was just before the break of day, a remark I had never before heard. I returned home stronger than ever before, and ventured to tell mother of the good sermon preached by Isaac Puffer. But she was again troubled, and reminded me of those we read of in Scripture, who would compass sea and land to gain one proselyte, that when gained, "were twofold more the child of hell than themselves." She also said that my uncles would be well pleased to have me go with them. I assured her that neither of my four Methodist uncles had ever intimated a word to me on the subject. "But," said she, "actions sometimes speak louder than words." This was not designed to discourage me, but darker than ever was the cloud of unbelief that filled my heart. Was Isaac Puffer a child of hell? then there is nothing in religion, with any body. It was all a farce--all mere "overheated zeal, not according to knowledge." All mere "religious excitement." I well-nigh distrusted all religion, and father's and mother's religion was the same as others, of no value. I had groped my way in midnight darkness, trying to find the true way, when there was none. In this despairing state, while on my way to my grandfather's on an errand, I halted to listen to the mournful notes of the forest birds at my left; I looked upon the field of waving grain at my right, and burst into a flood of tears as I exclaimed, Oh, what a sin- stricken world is this! Every head of wheat is bowed in mourning with poor me! Is there no balm in Gilead? is there no physician there to heal this sin-stricken world, this sin-sick soul of mine? Like a flash the answer came, Yes, Jesus is that balm; he shed his own precious blood for me on Calvary, that I might live now, and for evermore! Yes, the healing balm is applied, and I am saved! Oh, what a fountain is opened for cleansing! My peace was like an overflowing river. It seemed as if I could almost live without breathing--my tears were brushed away by the breath of heaven. I stood a monument of amazing mercy, praising God with every breath. All nature praising, instead of mourning as it did a few moments before. O, how changed the scene! The birds now sent forth their notes of praise! The leaves of the forest clapped their hands for joy, and the branches waved with praise! Every head of wheat was now bowed in sweet submission. O, what a leveling of all nations of the earth was this baptism. I had been prejudiced against the Irish people, as I never had seen one of that nation until they came to our town, Lockport (as it was then called), by hundreds, to work on the Erie canal, that ran through a part of father's farm; and as they were frequently passing our house drunk, I was afraid of them. But now every soul seemed so precious, I thought I could toil all my life long if I could become instrumental in bringing one soul to the Savior who died to save sinners, though they might be the greatest drunkards in that or any other nation. Jesus shed his blood to redeem all who would by faith accept salvation so freely offered. The African and Indian races were alike objects of redeeming love. That was a fathomless fountain. After spending a little time in this reverie, I went from this hallowed place to accomplish my errand, and met a neighbor, who looked at me earnestly and said, "Laura, what's the matter? are you sick?" "O, no; I'm not sick," and hurried on. And the first greeting I received from grandfather was the same query, who received the same reply. I left for home as soon as the errand was accomplished, but as I was passing out of the door I met my Uncle Americus with the same query, who also received the same answer. Oh, how I wished father and mother could understand me, and the overwhelming sorrow I had waded through in search of this satisfying portion.

If any little differences arose among my younger brothers and sister, all melted away with a word from me. This unalloyed peace remained with me a number of days, and when the time arrived for the appointed prayer-meeting at Uncle Ira's, I had a great desire to attend it, and I hoped, by asking for permission to go, mother might ask for my reason. In this I was disappointed with a denial. However, I continued to pray to Him who owned me as his child, to prepare the way in his own time. My anxiety increased to do something for my dear Savior, who indeed was chief among ten thousand. I could drop a few words here and there, but with great timidity, but nothing of my experience in this new life; that was hid with Christ in God. I was anxious to attend that little prayer-meeting, where my mind first was arrested on the subject of my soul's best interests. I often dreamed of earnestly praying or exhorting in that prayer-meeting, and would awaken myself in the exercise. I had a longing desire to invite to this gospel feast others, especially my young associates.

As Isaac Puffer had an appointed meeting at a brother Crane's, half a mile distant, on Sabbath at four o'clock P. M., I asked father for permission to attend, hoping thereby to find liberty to open my pent-up feelings to my dear parents, who so little understood me. But my hopes were vain. Father said, in reply, "Laura, I want thee never to ask me to go to a Methodist meeting again."

O, what a blow was this for my trembling frame! The door closed more tightly than ever before. Not one word could I utter. I left the room, to find my old resort in the grove, to weep bitter tears of disappointment. But widely different was this burden, now resting upon my heart, from that mountain weight of sin and transgression borne a few weeks previously. I read a few days before of the baptism of the Lord Jesus, our perfect pattern. But he came to fulfill. Then I read of Philip and the apostles who baptized after his ascension; and to my young and limited understanding I accepted the water baptism as an outward acknowledgment of the saving baptism of the Holy Ghost. I fully believed I had received the spiritual baptism, but I greatly desired to follow the Lord Jesus wherever he might lead. I read "Barclay's Apology" on that subject; yet my childhood mind dwelt much on what I read in these Bible examples. But to no human being did I present these impressions. And I also found the example of singing, that I believed was vocal, as I read, "And they sang a hymn and went out." And it seemed right, for the present, for me to unite with the Methodists, were it not for the opposition of my parents, that I felt sure would not exist could they but understand me. It also seemed clearly impressed upon my mind that, if my mind should become clear to unite with that branch of the Christian Church, it would be for eighteen or twenty years at longest. But why not always be my place, if it is my duty now? was a query that I much dwelt upon. I earnestly prayed that God would send Caleb McComber to us, an intimate friend of my parents, and a noted minister among Friends.

Within a week my heart leaped for joy at the announcement by my father that Caleb McComber was in the neighborhood.

"What has brought him here at this time? His brother (Dr. Smith) is all right; he has made no trouble of late in drinking," responded mother.

"I do not know, I am sure, what has induced him to come here at this time, as there is no meeting of business on hand, for him to take this journey of nearly a hundred miles to attend," rejoined father.

Ah, the Lord has heard and answered prayer! He has heard the cry of this poor child "Bless the Lord, O my soul, and forget not all his benefits." I could, with David, praise him with a full heart, and sought a lone place to return thanksgiving and praise to him who had so signally answered my petition, and was confident that the same All- seeing Eye and Directing Hand would prepare the way for the desired interview.

The following day being the Sabbath, we listened to a sermon by Caleb McComber that was thought very singular at that day for a Friend. His text was 1 Corinthians xii, 6 and 7; "And there are diversities of operations, but it is the same God which worketh all in all." He referred to the diversities of denominations, that were as families composing the one true Church. And in this diversity of operations there were those whose impressions of duty were clearly given in regard to complying with outward ordinances, water baptism and the Lord's-supper; and if these impressions were not complied with, a loss would be sustained in spiritual life. And he exhorted to faithfulness in obeying our Lord and Master. This discourse appeared as directly addressed to this trembling child as did that of Isaac Puffer.

At the close of the meeting, said one of the elders to another, "Did thou ever hear just such a sermon from a Friend? I thought it sounded like a Presbyterian discourse." Said another: "What ails Caleb to-day. I thought he preached like a Methodist." While these remarks were made I felt confident we had listened to a message from the Great Head of the true Church by his servant.

As he dined with our nearest neighbor, in company with his half- brother, Dr. Isaac Smith, and wife, we all walked in company nearly to our home, and the two young women invited me to call. I accepted, with the excuse, for a drink of water (hoping for an opportunity of telling that good man that I desired to have a talk with him, and for that purpose would call after dinner).

But while waiting for the glass of water, said Caleb McComber, "Child, how old art thou?"

The reply was, "Thirteen."

"I want thee to tell thy father and mother to come I here at three o'clock this afternoon, and I want thee to come with them."

I gladly performed my errand, and at three P. M. we were there. After a little space of silence he addressed the heads of families present, then directed his remarks to us (the two young women and myself), at first rather general. Then he said: "I want to say to one of you that thou hast passed through an experience far beyond thy years; thou hast known what it was to ask for deliverance from sorrow and darkness, and thou hast also known what it was to receive the answer of peace from thy Heavenly Father that the world knows not of. Hold fast that thou hast received, that no man take thy crown. Be faithful in the little, and more will be given. Bear in mind that little things are little things, but to be faithful in little things is something great."

With exhortations to faithfulness and encouragement, this was to me an undoubted evidence that He whose ear is ever open to the cry of his children had most signally answered prayer in this clear and definite searching of my heart. Very near and dear was that faithful nursing- father brought to this little child's heart. With all freedom, I could have related to him the obstacles that appeared in the way of duty with me. But at that hour my feelings were too deep for utterance. Instead of remaining longer, as was my impression, I returned home with my parents, with the view of returning for a more private interview when I could better command my feelings.

When about to return, I began to reason over the propriety of going back. Certainly that good man had said all I could ask, both in his sermon and in the religious opportunity in the family. And now there might be danger of going too far. And there are those two young women, who made sport of me in that prayer-meeting, where I knelt while others led in prayer. Now they would make more sport than ever, as there are so many there I could not speak to him without their knowing it, and I shrank from going. I feared John Bunyan's "lions in the way;" but if I had been faithful I would have found them chained, as were his. For it was hard for me to give up the more private interview, as I was very anxious to secure an interview between that minister and my dear parents, as I was sure he understood me much better than they. But I neglected my duty in this. O, how weak was human nature!

I had previously thought I would never again offend my loving Savior, but would follow him through evil as well as good report. O, how precious his cleansing blood appeared to me! It seemed as if the drops that fell in his agony in the Garden of Gethsemane possessed power to cleanse a world of sin and pollution. Yet I was not faithful in the little. Although my parents never after forbade my going to a Methodist or any other meeting, yet I saw it grieved them as I frequently attended those prayer-meetings, but never to the neglect of our own, and was often impressed to speak or offer prayer, but did not yield. I found, to my sorrow, that these omissions produced poverty of soul, and often cried, "O, my leanness! my leanness!" In secret many tears were shed over the loss of that joy that had been my experience.

Little by little the candle of the Lord that shone so brightly became dim, and at the close of one year I sought the society of the gay and mirthful, more effectually to drown my bitter regrets for having turned aside from the path so clearly marked out for me. I fully realized that the dark cloud overshadowing me was the result of disobedience.

In company with a few of my companions, I attended the funeral of an infant in our town. The service was conducted by a Baptist minister, who had just come into the place. There was nothing in his remarks that attracted my special attention. After the meeting closed, and people were leaving, the minister passed on a little distance, and turned back, as if something had been forgotten. Pressing through the crowd, he ascended the porch, and came directly to me, looking earnestly at me, as he reached his hand for mine, saying:

"I felt as if I could not leave this place without asking this young woman a few questions. Have you ever experienced religion?"

This came upon me like a clap of thunder, he, being an entire stranger, asking a question I never had occasion to answer. I hesitated, as I had never intimated a word of my experience to any human being. My first thought was to deny, but like a flash came the words of Jesus, "He that denieth me before men, him will I also deny before my Father and his holy angels. No; I can not--I will not, though I die. With this thought I frankly replied:

"I think I have."

"Do you now enjoy it?"

"I do not"

This relieved me from the dilemma of being a disgrace to the cause of Christ, as a number of my gay companions were with me, also those Christian young people to whom I had listened with interest in prayer and exhortations. But searching remarks from him followed. Still holding my hand, he said:

"You have known of earnest pleading for the pardon of sin; and you have known what it was to rejoice, as your prayers were answered. You have known your duty, and did it not, and have brought yourself into darkness. Do not occupy this dangerous ground longer. Return to jour first love. Do your first work over; and He who is abundant in mercy will again accept you. May God grant his blessing upon you! Good bye."

And he left me bathed in tears.

These earnest words reopened the many wounds that many neglected duties had made. I could not doubt but Elder Winchell was as truly sent from God to deliver this message as was Caleb McComber, for whom I prayed in my distress. But now the Holy Spirit had sought me out, unasked for, to warn me of the danger in the effort to occupy neutral ground, as I had concluded to do until I was of age. I saw more clearly that I was responsible to my Savior, who had done great things for me, whereof I did rejoice with exceeding great joy.

Again my Bible became my daily companion, with prayer for my Savior's directing hand. But my parents were again troubled, as those first impressions returned in full force. I intimated my condition of mind to my parents, but, with my natural timidity, not as freely as I ought. They still attributed these impressions to the influence of my Methodist uncles, and considered their duty was to place these restraints upon their child. Father and mother had requested to become members of the Friends' Society while three of their children were under seven years, and requested for us, making us equivalent to birthright members, according to the usage of our Society. From the time of my Christian experience, I was never in sympathy with the system of birthright membership. I believed it to be a source of weakness, instead of spiritual life in this or any other Christian body, and that all members of the Church militant should become united by a heart-felt experience. I fully realized the loss I was warned to shun by yielding to the earnest desires of my dear parents, who were conscientious in their restraint. They said, in after years, that they were laboring under a mistake, as was their timid child, in not more faithfully following those early impressions of duty. I was not faithful in the little, consequently more was withheld. My great mistake was the lack of faith, in not fully returning to my Father's house, where the little wandering prodigal would have been received, and the new best robe again granted, and the rough way would have been made smooth, and the impassable mountain that seemed to rise so high would have melted away before the life-giving beams of the Sun of righteousness. But I yielded to my timidity, and the conclusion was reached to live a quiet Christian life, with my Bible and secret communing with my dear Lord and Savior in secret prayer, as I could not give up a strictly religious life. But dimly did die lamp of life burn, compared with its former brightness.

The greatest source of retrograding in the divine life is unfaithfulness in the performance of known duty. Many of the clouds that overshadow us we bring by withholding more than is meet, and it tends to poverty of soul. The talent committed to our charge is to be occupied, and is always doubled when occupied by its possessor; but, as I saw many, in whom I had confidence as living a quiet Christian life--and this was more congenial to my natural feeling--I reached the conclusion to make my Bible and secret prayer my companions as long as I lived, and a Christian life in the Society of my parents' choice.

At the early age of sixteen I became acquainted with Charles Haviland, Jr., a young man who was acquainted with the Savior's pardoning love, whose father and mother were both acknowledged ministers in the Society of Friends. From him I accepted a proposition of marriage, and on the 3d of

11th month, 1825, our marriage was consummated at Friends' Meeting, in Lockport, Niagara County, New York, according to the usage of Friends. The following Spring we commenced housekeeping in our own home, in Boyalton Township, nine miles east of Lockport, and my dear parents and family removed to Michigan Territory. Although parting from them was severe, yet with my young and devoted husband I was contented and happy as was possible to be, with so many reminders of the cloud that rested over me in my spiritual horizon, with all my constant striving for its removal. Phoebe Field, an eminent minister among Friends, appointed a meeting in our neighborhood, in which she dwelt upon the necessity of receiving daily nourishment from the true and living Vine to become fruit-bearing branches, and remarked that there were those whose religious experience seemed divergent from the manner in which they were brought up, and through unfaithfulness had well-nigh lost sight of the highway of holiness, in the mistaken view of neutrality, when there was not an inch of such ground all the way from years of responsibility to the grave. We are gathering with Christ or scattering abroad. This earnest discourse so clearly defined my own condition, that I renewed my many broken vows, and was almost persuaded to yield the unsubdued will, and hope was indulged that the Father of unbounded mercy, in his illimitable love, would again reveal himself in breaking the bread of life.

September, 1829, we removed to Michigan Territory, and settled in Raisin, Lenawee County, within three miles of my parents, brothers, and sister, with our two little sons, to share with others the privations of a new country, as well as advantages of cheap land. As there were a number of our Society in this vicinity, a Friends' Meeting was organized, in which we all had an interest, and endeavored to maintain it in the usual order of our Society. But no true peace was mine, I was still a wanderer from the true Church militant. I once knew the good Shepherd's voice, but was now too far away to recognize it. In these sad remembrances I sought a subterfuge behind which to hide in a false rest. Eagerly I read a book on that subject, and drank its plausible arguments without stint. It was a panacea, a temporary opiate to quiet the vacillating condition of a restless mind; yet my Bible was not laid aside, and many portions of Scripture were vigilantly brought to prove this specious error to be a radical truth; and two years in this dead faith I lived a dying life. But I found my investigations were not for the whole truth, but was dwelling upon the love and benevolence of God to the exclusion of justice as an attribute of the Lord, as well as mercy, and decided to accept the whole truth, and abide its searchings; and sought for it in the written Word diligently, as for hidden treasures In reading Paul's epistle to the Hebrews, chapter vi, I found, "It is impossible for those who were once enlightened and have tasted of the heavenly gift, and were made partakers of the Holy Ghost, and have tasted of the good Word of God, and the powers of the world to come, if they shall fall away, to renew them again to repentance, seeing they crucify to themselves the Son of God afresh, and put him to an open shame." Oh, how these words thrilled my whole being! Again and again they were reviewed. No Hope! no hope for a lost soul like mine! were like burning coals upon my poor heart. I was once enlightened and tasted of the heavenly gift; but how dark have been these years. Oh! how soon did the lamp of life become dim through disobedience. I can never again drink of that fountain of love that once filled my soul to overflowing. But I had fallen away, and could never again be renewed, having crucified to myself the Son of God afresh, and put him to an open shame, by not honoring such a glorious Redeemer, as was my own personal Savior. O, what delusion to have indulged in the vain hope that I was serving him in a silent, quiet life, and then cover over all this unrest with the idea that God was too abundant in mercy to cast off any for whom he died to save. Day and night this terrible thought followed me for months, "I am a lost soul! irretrievably lost. No hope! Eternally lost!"

As I had never intimated to my dear companion the vacillating condition of mind, and the effort in finding rest, neither should he be troubled with the knowledge that his wife was a lost soul; neither should our little ones on arriving to years of religious understanding ever know that their mother was a lost soul. The midnight hour often witnessed many bitter tears of regret over the awful thought. So near perfect despair, I looked upon beast, bird, or even the most loathsome reptile, and grudged their happiness of living and dying without responsibility. These sad forebodings seriously affected my health, and my anxious husband and parents feared some serious disease was preying upon me. I sometimes thought the sooner I sank into the grave the better, as my doom must be met. O, that I could but claim the privilege of the prodigal, in returning to the Father's house, and of being accepted, though a great way off. O that I never had been born! O that I had followed that loving Savior's voice, so often clearly heard. It is now too late, too late! O that I had returned to my first love when within my reach. But I rejected the teaching of the Holy Spirit, and justly am I now rejected. In this distressing despair I opened a little book--the Christian experience of one whose exercises of the mind traced through my own experience, even to my present despairing state, as nearly as I could have related it in my own words. Through the instrumentality of a similar experience in another, who was restored and was long a useful Christian, I was encouraged to return, and found the healing balm. Never can I forget the thrill of joy that ran through my whole being as I laid aside that little book. I saw that I had misapprehended the meaning of the passages of Scripture that seemed to describe my condition, and that served to confirm my despair. I saw that those referred to, had so far fallen, and so often rejected the Holy Spirit's teachings, as not to realize their condition, and therefore lost sight of the necessity of a Redeemer. This was not, nor ever had been, my condition. Then I read Esau's seeking the blessing, "carefully with tears," that I had also long dwelt upon as my condition. Here, too, was a vivid thought, that he sought the lost blessing to subserve self, instead of glorifying God. Here the bright star of hope pierced through the cloud. Is it possible that I can go with confidence to that Father who has so long borne with this unbelieving, doubting, rebellious child? Why has he not cut off this cumberer of the ground long ago? His long-suffering and unbounded mercy, O how free! how unfathomable! With many tears of gratitude, mingled with new hope, new aspirations, the bright beam of day radiating from every promise, I could now fully accept the Lord Jesus as my mediator and restorer. By faith, I could fully trust the poor prodigal in his hand. O, what losses we sustain through unbelief. I have felt most easy in leaving my experience on record, as a warning to young Christians to shun the depth of despair into which I tank through unfaithfulness and unbelief. "By grace ye are saved, through faith." Increasing faith, strength, and peace, with restored health, was my rich experience.

ANTI-SLAVERY WORK.

Our family, with others, united with Elizabeth Margaret Chandler, who organized in our neighborhood the first anti-slavery society in our State. This was unsatisfactory to the ruling portion of our Society, as it had cleared its skirts many years ago by emancipating all slaves within its pale. Elizabeth M. Chandler was of the Hicksite division of Friends, and as Presbyterians and other religious denominations came into our anti-slavery society, meetings were frequently opened with prayer, and that was thought to be "letting down the principles of ancient Friends." And the subject of slavery was considered too exciting for Friends to engage in, by many Friends of that day. I began to query whether it would not be a relief to me, and also to my friends, to become disconnected with that body, as I saw clearly my path of duty would not be in accordance with the generality of our Society. After making it a subject of earnest prayer, I became settled as to the course to pursue, and concluded to unburden my heavy heart to my parents as I had done, to my beloved companion, which I did after our Sabbath meeting. We mingled our tears together. Father referred, to the same proscribing spirit they exercised over me in my early experience, that was now exercised over them. Father and mother wished me to defer sending in my request to become disconnected with our Society, as they, too, might think best to pursue the same course. This was a severe trial for each of us. Father had been an acknowledged minister of the Gospel nearly thirty years, and mother occupied the station of an elder nearly the same time. We, too, had become active members in this branch of the Christian Church. But the conclusion was fully reached within two months after our little conference over this important step, and the following letter of resignation was sent to our business meeting:

"We, the undersigned, do say there is a diversity of sentiment existing in the Society on the divine authority of the Holy Scriptures, the resurrection of the dead, and day of judgment, justification by faith, the effect of Adam's fall upon his posterity, and the abolition of slavery, which has caused a disunity amongst us; and there being no hope of a reconciliation by investigation, ministers being told by ruling members that there is to be no other test of the soundness of their ministry but something in their own breasts, thus virtually denying the Holy Scriptures to be the test of doctrine;--we, therefore, do wish quietly to withdraw from the Monthly Meeting, and thus resign our right of membership with the Society of Friends."

This resignation was signed by Daniel Smith, Sene Smith, Charles Haviland, Jun., Laura S. Haviland, Ezekiel Webb, Sala Smith, and fourteen others. A few returned, but the greater united with other Christian bodies, A few months after this there was a division in the Methodist Episcopal Church, on account of slavery. They were called Wesleyan Methodists. As this branch of our Father's family was the nearest our own views, we were soon united with them. Our testifications from Friends were said by other denominations to he sufficient to be accepted as Church letters, as our offenses named therein were "non-attendance of meetings for discipline, and attending meetings not in accordance with the order of our Society." This was the import of nearly or quite all who were disowned of our company. At that day, all were dealt with as offenders, and were regularly disowned, as our discipline at that time made no provisions for withdrawals. About a year after this, the yearly meeting of Friends in Indiana divided on the subject of slavery. No slavery existed in the society; yet its discussion was deemed improper, and created disunity sufficient for severing that body for a number of years, when they were invited to return, without the necessity of acknowledgments.

About this time we opened a manual labor school on our premises, designed for indigent children. With that object in view, we took nine children from our county house (Lenawee), and I taught them, with our four children of school age, four hours each day. The balance of the day was divided for work and play. The girls I taught house-work, sewing, and knitting. The boys were taken into the farm work by my husband and brother Harvey Smith. As our county superintendents of the poor gave us no aid, we found our means insufficient to continue our work on this plane. After one year of this work we secured homes for the nine children, except two invalids, who were returned to the county house. We then placed our school on a higher plane, on the Oberlin plan of opening the school for all of good moral character, regardless of sex or color. At that day (1837) there was not a school in our young State that would open its door to a colored person. And as my brother, Harvey Smith, had attended the Oberlin Institute, he united with us in this enterprise, and sold his new farm of one hundred and sixty acres, and expended what he had in erecting temporary buildings to accommodate about fifty students. The class of students was mostly of those designing to teach. Our principals were from Oberlin during the first twelve years of the "Raisin Institute." The first three years it was conducted by P. P. Roots and his wife, Anna B., who were excellent Christians. When they left, to open a similar institution at West Point, Lee County, Iowa, John Patchin became their successor, and conducted the school with equal ability three years. After uniting in marriage with a teacher in Oberlin, he was assisted by his wife. These thorough teachers earned for our institute the name of being one of the best in our State. Students were sought for teachers in our own and adjoining counties. Although our abolition principles were very unpopular at that day, as we generally had from one to three colored students in our school, yet the thorough discipline given in the studies drew the young people of the best intellect from the surrounding country. There were those who came from fifty to one hundred miles to prepare for teaching or for a collegiate course. Hundreds of young people who enjoyed the privileges our school afforded came to us with their prejudices against colored people and our position in regard to them; but they soon melted away, and went they knew not where. It was frequently said if we would give up the vexed abolition question, and let the negroes alone, Raisin Institute would become the most popular school in the State.

As a sample of many others, I will notice a young lady from Jackson County, who was brought to us by her father to become qualified for teaching. But her sensibilities were so shocked at meeting in her grammar-class a colored man that she returned to her room weeping over her disgrace, and resolved to write her father to come and take her home immediately. But the other young women persuaded her to attend the recitations assigned her, when to her surprise the same young colored man was in the advanced arithmetic class. And while impatiently waiting for her father to come and take her from this "nigger school" (as she and many others called it), a letter came from him advising her to remain, as he had expended so much in fitting her for two or three terms there; although if he had known that a negro would have been allowed to attend her class he would not have taken her there. She soon became reconciled, and before a half-term closed, when she threatened to leave at all events (as she read her father's letter), she came to that colored man to assist her in intricate parsing lessons. Before the close of the first term she as frequently applied to James Martin, her colored classmate, for assistance in solving difficult problems in mathematics as to any of the others. She was one of our best students; but this deep-rooted prejudice went, she knew not how, as with very many others.

As to religious privileges in our school, our prayer-meetings were held bi-weekly, Sabbath and Wednesday evenings, and ministers of various denominations frequently appointed meetings in our school on the Sabbath. While the Rev. John Patchin had charge of the institution he generally preached Sabbath evening, instead of the prayer-meeting.

In the third year of our school our two older sons made a profession of religion, with a number of other students, which was cause of great rejoicing. Surely, we were blessed above measure. Within two years after we were blessed with another shower of divine favor in the conversion of our two older daughters. Not unfrequently were these four children's voices uplifted in vocal supplication at the family altar. We were surely repaid more than a hundred-fold for all our toiling, and heavy burdens borne in founding Raisin Institute. As the fleeing fugitive ever found a resting-place and cheer in our home, we richly earned the cognomen of "nigger den;" yet Heaven smiled and blessed our work. We had many sympathizing friends in the Society from which we were disconnected as members, even with those who had deemed us too radical. There was unity with us in our work that brought us together in after years.

BEREAVEMENTS

OUR last chapter left us rejoicing in success, but how soon did deepest sorrow take its place. A dream seemed sent to prepare me for the severe ordeal so near at hand. I thought I was standing in our front yard looking eastward and an angel sitting on a bay horse appeared in the place of the sun's rising, coming to earth on some mission, gliding over the tree tops toward our house, where were father, mother, my sister Phoebe, and my husband, who held in his arms our little babe. I started to inform them that an angel was coming to earth on some errand, when his advance was so rapid I was likely to lose sight of him, and halted to watch his flight. He seemed to alight in our yard near me, and smiled as he said, "Follow thou me." "I will," I responded, as soon as I bid Charles and our folks farewell. The beautiful personage assumed a firmer tone, as he said, "Let the dead bury their dead, but follow thou me." At this command I responded, "I will," and followed him to the graveyard, where he left me. And I awoke with that angelic figure, with that sweet, yet solemn, voice ringing in my ear.

I related the dream, with its clear impression in my mind, to my husband, who replied, "That is a significant dream, and I think indicates death. I think we shall be called to part with our infant daughter Lavina; and it is quite evident that consumption is fast hastening our sister Phoebe to her long home." She was my own sister, who married my husband's brother, Daniel Haviland. He continued his remarks, by making suggestions as to the course we would feel it best to pursue about a burying-place for our little daughter, in case of a refusal of Friends to allow a plain marble slab, with her name and date of birth and death in their burying-ground; and suggested the corner of our orchard as a pleasant place, to which I assented. After spending half an hour in this conversation, he went out to his work. I prayed for my Savior's hand to lead me in whatever trial it was necessary for me to pass through.

Little did I think of the heavier stroke which was first to fall. A few days after this dream I was charging myself with being visionary; yet a few of these most impressive dreams, I believe, have been designed for our instruction. My husband was seized with a heavy cold, accompanied by a severe cough, that was increasing; yet he was able to be about the house and barn, giving directions, as to outdoor work, but nothing appeared alarming, when I was aroused by a startling dream of a coffin being brought into our front room by four men, of whom I inquired who was dead. The answer was, "A connection of yours." "I want to see him, for that coffin appears to be for a small man," was my reply. "He is a small man," was the rejoinder, "and you shall see him." Upon this, the closed coffin was brought to me, and I arose and followed the pall-bearers to the graveyard. As the people were standing around the open grave to see the coffin lowered, I saw a little child standing on the very edge of the grave opposite to me. I exclaimed, "Do take that child away, for it will cave into the grave after its father!" At that instant the light sand under its feet gave way, and, as it struck the coffin, the loud, hollow sound awoke me, trembling as with a fit of ague, and with the strong impression that I was soon to part with my beloved companion and infant daughter, although both were sweetly sleeping by my side. With this thrill through my whole being, I resorted to prayer for their restoration to health, if consistent with the divine will.

Although my husband had enjoyed good health a number of years, and had not for seven years previously called upon a physician, yet I now resolved to persuade him to call for one at once. As the clock struck four, and as I was leaving the bed to light the fire, my husband awoke, and said he had enjoyed the most refreshing sleep he had had since taking this cold, and felt so well he thought he soon should be rid of it. Whenever I spoke the chattering of my teeth revealed my agitation, and he expressed fear lest I should be ill from the hard chill. But little did he understand the upheavings of my troubled heart. Soon a severe paroxysm of coughing gave the opportunity to suggest the idea of sending for a physician. At length he consented, as he said, to please me, as he thought this cough would soon give way. But while I went to our boy's study room to awaken our son Harvey to go for the doctor, a severe pain in the region of the lungs was cutting every breath.

The doctor was soon with us, but he thought there were no discouraging symptoms apparent. I seat for Father Haviland, who also thought, as did the doctor, that I was unreasonably troubled; but during the following night he expressed doubts of recovery himself, and requested his will to be written, which was done. As his fever increased, great effort was made to control our feelings in his presence. At one time, as he awoke, he discovered fast-falling tears, and said: "Do not weep for me, my dear wife; remember those beautiful lines:

> 'God moves in mysterious way,
> His wonders to perform.'

We are not to

> 'Judge the Lord by feeble sense,
> But trust him for his grace;
> Behind a frowning providence
> He hides a smiling face'

Our separation will be short at longest. Then we shall be reunited where there is no sorrow--no more dying--in that glorious home. Two days ago there seemed a little cloud; but prayer was answered, and the cloud was all removed. The overshadowing now is that of peace and love." He called for the children. Looking upon us all, he said, "O, how dear you all are to me!" Calling each by name, he gave advice and exhortations as none but a departing husband and father could leave with his family--a legacy more precious than all the golden treasures of earth. Then he added: "I want you, my dear children, to promise me that you will meet your father in heaven. Will you meet me there?" Taking our little babe in his hands, he kissed it and said, "Dear little Lavina will soon be with her father," and closed with the prayer: "O Lord, I commit my dear wife and children into thy bands. Thou art the widow's God, and a loving Father to fatherless children."

The words of the dying Christian, beginning

> "What's that steals, that steals upon my frame?
> Is it death-is it death?"

were sung by his bedside, and as the last line,

> "All is well-all is well,"

was reached, he raised his hands, and repeated, "O, hallelujah to the Lamb!" Then, turning to me, be added, "My dear, I want these lines sung at my funeral." His last words were, "Come, Lord Jesus, thy servant is ready," and with a sweet smile his happy spirit was wafted home, March 13, 1845.

His disease was inflammatory erysipelas, at that time entirely new, and not understood by our physicians. It passed through our portion of the State, a sweeping epidemic, in the Spring of 1845, and proved fatal in most cases. My dear mother, who was with us during this week of sorrow, was taken home with the same disease, and in one week her happy spirit took its flight to God who gave it. She, too, left us hi the triumphs of faith. She had not left us an hour before brother Daniel came for me to go to his dying wife, as she was calling for mother, and he did not dare inform her that mother was dangerously ill. I took my little emaciated babe upon a pillow, and went to my dear sister, who was so soon to leave us. Her first query was, "How is our dear mother?"

"Mother is a happy spirit in heaven," was the reply, "and sister Phoebe will soon meet her there."

Her reply was: "It is well; but I had hoped to meet her once more in this world--yet we'll soon meet, to part no more forever. She soon followed brother Charles; but I trust we will all meet one day, an unbroken band. O how I wish I could see brother Ira!" an absent brother for whom she had often expressed great anxiety in regard to his spiritual and everlasting welfare.

The same burden of soul for the same brother had also rested on the heart of our sainted mother, whose funeral took place two days later. Within one week sister Phoebe died in peace. Here was the third wave of sorrow rolling over us.

From this house of mourning I was removed to my home with the same disease that had taken my husband and mother; and a number of our neighbors Were going the same way. My father and father-in-law thought me dangerously ill-chills and fever, with stricture of the lungs, that made respiration painful. They were very anxious to have the best help that could be obtained at once; "for," said father, "what is done for thee must be done quickly" I told him that every one who had been taken with this disease had died, as physicians of each school did not understand it. But I would return to my home, as they suggested; but felt most easy to trust myself with water treatment, and would like to take a shower-bath every two hours, and try that treatment twelve hours. This was done, and every bath brought relief to respiration, and my lungs became entirely free, though my neck and throat were still badly swollen and inflamed. Cold applications, frequently applied, soon overcame that difficulty, and in three days the disease seemed entirely conquered.

A relapse from taking cold, however, threw me into a stupor; but I was aroused by an expression of a neighbor, as he said: "She is not conscious, and never will be, unless something is done; and if she were a sister of mine a doctor would be here as soon as I could bring him."

"I will see if I can get an expression from her," said my brother Harvey.

"If we can only learn mother's wish it shall be granted," said my anxious son Harvey.

As I heard their remarks a strong impression came over me that if I were placed in charge of a physician I should not live two days, but if I could tell them to shower my head and neck often I would recover. As I looked upon my anxious fatherless children around my bed I made an effort to speak, but my parched and swollen tongue could not for some time utter a word. The answer to earnest prayer came from Him who numbers even the very hairs of our head. As my brother took my hand, saying, "If you wish a physician press my hand, or if you wish water treatment move your head on the pillow," I could not move my head in the least, and my only hope was to say no. When asked if I wished a doctor sent for, I prayed that my tongue might utter words of direction for the sake of my fatherless children, and said, "No."

"Do you want cold compresses, or shall we gently shower over a thin cloth on the swollen and inflamed portion of your neck and head?"

"Shower."

"Cold or tepid?"

"Well."

"If you mean well-water, how much?"

"Big pitcher."

"How often?"

"Twenty minutes."

Said my son Harvey, "It shall be done, if I sit by her every minute to-night"

I felt a positive impression that my Heavenly Father had answered my prayer directly, and granted an assurance, in the token of recovery, and I praised the Lord for his "loving kindness, O, how free." With this assurance I fell back in a stupor, except a dreamy consciousness of their showering, which was faithfully done, with the assistance of my brother. At twelve o'clock I awoke, and inquired where all the people were that filled the room a little while before, and was surprised to learn the hour of night. They said, as my breathing became more natural, the neighbors had left and the children retired.

I could speak easily, and the purple appearance of the skin had disappeared. In the morning the pain was entirely gone, but the soreness was still severe. But with frequent changes of compresses during the day, the swelling very much subsided. I wondered why father did not come, as he had not been to see me since sister Phoebe's funeral. My brother informed me that he had a chill during the funeral, and had not been able to leave. As he had a few fits of the ague some weeks previously, I supposed it was a return of that disease. The day following brother Sala came, and in reply to my inquiry after my father, said he was no better, but sent me a request to be very careful of myself, and hoped I would soon recover, and left in seeming haste to see brother Patchin. But I sent for him to come and tell me more about father. He soon came with brother Patchin and brother Dolbeare. He then told me that father had the same disease that had taken my husband and our mother, and he also said that it was father's request that for the sake of my large family of children, who were recently bereft of their father, that I would give up the idea of coming to see him.

But I could not be satisfied without going to see my dear father once more, and yet, the pleading of my dear children was almost too much to forego. "We have just lost our father; now what should we do if our mother should be taken from us?" "But if I am rolled in quilts and laid on a bed in the wagon, I am confident I can be taken to father's house safely"--distant nearly three miles. In this way I was taken to my dying father, though unable to walk across the room without assistance. As soon as he learned of my coming, he directed them to lay me on the bed until I was rested. In a few minutes he sent them to bring me to him. As my son and brother led me to his bedside, he placed the cold purple fingers over my pulse, and said, "I am so glad to see thee, but I feared it would be too much for thee to bear. There is a little feverish excitement about thee yet. I am more concerned for thee than for the rest of my children, on account of thy large family, that will so much need their mother's counsel and care. I want to say to thee, Look up to the widow's God for guidance, for wisdom from him is so much needed, with the heavy responsibilities now resting upon thee. Do not allow these bereavements to crush thy feeble frame. I have feared they had already seriously affected thy health. I know thy anxiety to bring up thy children in the nurture and admonition of the Lord. And he will grant ability to lead them to the Lamb of God, who shed his precious blood for us all." With other advice, he became weary, and said, "Now take her back to the other room, and lay her on the bed until rested." And during the few hours he lived he frequently sent for me to talk a few minutes at a time, watching my pulse each time, until within a few moments of the last farewell to earth.

There were six of his children present, to whom he gave his farewell blessing, leaving a bright evidence that all was well with him. "In me there is no merit. I am fully trusting in the merit of my crucified Savior, who shed his own precious blood for my redemption. I can say with Job, 'I know that my Redeemer lives,' and because he lives I shall live also." His last words, almost with his last breath, were, "Here she comes," and left this tabernacle for the building not made with hands, eternal in the heavens. Father and mother were lovely in their lives, and in their death were only two weeks divided. It seemed that my last earthly prop was gone. Three weeks later my youngest child followed her father and grandparents to the spirit home. Within six weeks, five of my nearest and dearest ones were taken from me.

There was hardly a family within two miles of us but was bereft of one or two loved ones by this epidemic. Five widows (myself included) at one time were standing around the death-bed of a near neighbor. Our female principal at that time, Emily Galpin, was taken with this epidemic, and died after three days' illness. A few hours previous to her death she requested a season of prayer, in which her husband, Rev. Charles Galpin, led. Her prospect was bright, and, clearly foreseeing the ransomed throng she was soon to join, said she, "Oh! how vain, how transitory, does all earthly treasure appear at this hour--a mere bubble upon the water." About a half an hour before she left us, she said, "Hark! don't you hear that beautiful music? Oh! what music; I never heard anything like it! Don't you hear it?" "No, we do not hear it." Being in an ecstasy, she exclaimed, "Look at that heavenly choir. Don't you see them? Don't you hear that sweetest of all music?" "We do not see them nor hear them." "There--they have left." A few minutes before her happy spirit took its flight, she again looked up very earnestly. "There they are again. Oh, how sweet! how beautiful!" And taking leave of her husband and two children, sister and brother-in- law, and of all present, committing her dear ones to the keeping of the Lord Jesus, with the request that the two lines,

> "Rock of Ages, cleft for me,
> Let me hide myself in thee,"

be placed upon the marble slab to mark her resting place, she fell asleep in Jesus.

Such fatality never before, nor since, visited Raisin as is 1845. In those days of sorrow commingled with the rest of faith, that brought peace and joy even in affliction, my only reliance was the widow's God, for wisdom I so much needed in the double responsibilities now resting upon me.

After the death of my sweet babe, twenty-two months of age, and my restoration to health, I looked over amounts of indebtedness with dates when due. I made an estimate of costs of harvesting and marketing the twenty acres of wheat and other grains, and what must be retained for family use; and found I would be able to reach only about half the amount due the following Autumn. I called on all our creditors within reach to inform them of probabilities, unless I could find sale for a portion of the stock. But none of the creditors wanted any of it. Said one, to whom the largest amount was due, "You do not think of taking your husband's business and carrying it forward, do you?" I replied, "I thought of trying to do the best I could with it." With a look of surprise, he said firmly, "You are very much mistaken, Mrs. Haviland; you can not do any such thing; you had much better appoint some man in whom you have confidence to transact your business for you." I informed him I had seven minor children left me, and I found seven hundred dollars of indebtedness, and it would cost money to hire an agent Then, I ought to know just where I stand, to enable me to look closely to expenditures. "Well, you can try it, but you'll find your mistake before six months have passed, and you'll see you had better have taken my advice." I knew I was not accustomed to business of this sort. All the other creditors whom I had seen spoke very kindly. Although these words were not unkindly spoken, yet they were saddening to my already sad heart.

I was too timid to go to the probate judge with any sort of ease for instruction. In looking around me for some female friend to accompany me, I could find but very few who were not undergoing like trials with myself, consequently I must submit to these new experiences, as whatever was right for me to do was proper. I depended upon an all wise guiding Hand, who is ever ready to reach it forth to the trusting child. I wrote to one, a few miles distant, to whom was due eighty dollars the ensuing Fall, that forty dollars would be all I should be able to meet. He called in a few days, and introduced himself saying that he had received a statement from me that I could only pay him the coming Fall fifty per cent on the eighty-dollar note he held against my husband. Said he, in a hurried manner, "I called to let you know that I must have it all when it is due, as I have a payment to make on my farm at that time, and I have depended on that" I told him I would gladly pay him every penny of it the coming Fall, but it would be impossible, as there were other demands equally pressing. "Very well, that is all I have to say, madam; I can not accept any such arrangement; I shall put in a way to bring it. Good-by."

He left in haste for me to ponder all these things over, in doubts as to my ability to meet all these rough places of outside life. Perhaps I had better leave this business with some man to deal with men. But prayer to the widow's God and comforting promises were my companions. Here was my only refuge and shelter in these storms. As I retired with a burdened heart, that I was endeavoring to cast at the feet of my Savior, the widow's burden-bearer, I had a sweet dream of an angelic host, that filled my room with a halo of glory, settled on every face, and those nearest my bed appeared in the form of persons dressed in beautiful attire; others were sweet faces that looked upon me with smiles of peace. As one took my hand, a familiar feeling sprang up, that gave me confidence to ask for the name. "My name is Supporter." And looking at the one standing near, "And what is his name?" "That is a woman, and her name is Influencer-of-hearts." Pointing to another still more glorious in appearance, "And who is that one?" "That is Searcher-of-hearts." "Then you all bear the name of your missions to earth, do you?" "We do," replied Supporter. As I looked over this host that filled my room I burst into a flood of tears for joy. I exclaimed, "Oh! what missions are yours! so many wayward hearts to influence, so much of sin and wickedness that reigns in this world to search out." At this said Searcher of hearts, "Support her, for she needs it" "I do," and he reached for my other hand, and as both of my hands were held by Supporter, I realized a wave of strength to pass over me, filling my soul. I awoke in an ecstacy. Yea, I will cast my care on Jesus and not forget to pray. Calm and sweet was this confidence in being cared for, and supported by an almighty arm.

A few days after I saw the exacting man coming through my gate, which, for a moment, caused a dread; but the second thought was, all, all is with my Savior. I met him with the usual greeting, and said, "You have called to see about that claim you have against me." "Yes, I have called to inform you that I shall not want any thing from you next Fall, and perhaps shall not want more than half next year, as I have received one hundred dollars that I had supposed was lost, and as I was coming within two miles I thought I would call and let you know of my conclusion." While I thanked him for the favor, secret praise ascended to Him who melts away the mountain that seems impassable, making a way where there seemed no way.

This may seem a small matter, but for me at that time it was a reason for rejoicing at this unexpected turn of affairs. It was but one of many similar cases, and none can more fully realize the blessing of these reliefs than the widow of nearly two-score years, who never previous to widowhood knew the burden of outside work in providing for a large family, which was now added to continued care of the Raisin Institute. Many night plans, for day execution, were made. I soon found sale for forty acres of the one hundred and sixty, which relieved me of the most pressing demands.

At times responsibilities were so great, and burdens so crushing, that I was almost ready to falter. My greatest anxiety was to guide my dear children aright. The four older ones had resolved to follow the dear Redeemer, but the slippery paths of youth were theirs to walk in. The consideration of these multiform cares at one time seemed of crushing weight. I questioned whether the burden I had so often left at the foot of the cross I had not taken up again, and whether I had as fully consecrated self, with my dear children, to the Lord as he required. I was endeavoring fully to yield all into my Redeemer's hands for safe-keeping. This was my constant prayer, yet this heavy burden during a few days seemed unfitting me for the every-day duties devolving upon me. In family devotion I opened to the fifty-fourth chapter of Isaiah, where I found precious promises that I accepted for my own, and the heavy burden for my children was uplifted. Never did I experience greater liberty in prayer, or exercise a stronger faith. Surely the silver lining to this cloud appears. "All thy children shall be taught of the Lord" were precious words. I was afflicted and tossed with tempest, but a sweet promise followed. All the way through that chapter the Comforter appeared with rich promises. With these before me I could freely leave all my burden with the Lord. I saw by the eye of faith all my seven children made acquainted with their Creator in the days of their youth. Although I never ceased asking, yet there has seemed an accompanying assurance. When from ten to sixteen years of age, my seven children yielded by living experience to the Savior's loving invitation, "Come unto me," that hour and day was victorious through faith. That weight of burden never again returned! The entire yielding all into the care and keeping power of Him who doeth all things well, at that hour was complete. I could say, "He leadeth me," without a, shadow of doubt.

As fugitive-slaves were still making their resting-place with us, I hired one of them, named George Taylor, a few months through hay- making and harvest. He had made his escape from a Southern master who was about to sell him farther south. Once before he had made an unsuccessful attempt at freedom, but was captured and placed in irons, until they made deep sores around his ankles. As he appeared very submissive, the sorest ankle was relieved. Being so badly crippled, he was thought safe. But supplying himself with asafetida, which he occasionally rubbed over the soles of his shoes, to elude the scent of bloodhounds, he again followed the north star, and finally reached our home. His ankles were still unhealed. He had succeeded in breaking the iron with a stone, during the first and second days of his hiding in the woods. He was an honest Christian man of the Baptist persuasion.

MARRIAGE OF TWO CHILDREN.

On June 6, 1846, my oldest son, Harvey S., was married to Huldah West, of Adrian, and my oldest daughter, Esther M., was at the same hour married to Almon Camburn, of Franklin, both of our own county. The mother's earnest prayer was, that these children might prove each other's burden-sharers, thereby doubling the joys, as well as dividing the sorrows, of life. My daughter's husband was one of our students, and in some of her studies a classmate.

We were fortunate in again securing brother Patchin to finish the academic year in our institution. Though the cloud looked dark that overhung our institution, by the sudden deaths of my husband, and sister Emily Galpin, which caused her bereaved husband to leave as soon as his place could be filled by a successor, we had the consciousness that our school was taking a deep hold on the minds of the community at large, as well as exercising a marked influence upon the young people who were enjoying its privileges. We found an increasing interest in abolition principles throughout our community. In this we praised God and took courage.

ANTI-SLAVERY EXPERIENCES

THIS chapter introduces the reader to representatives of a large proportion of slave-owners of the Southern States, who were perverted by a system well-named "the sum of all villainies."

Willis Hamilton, an emancipated slave, the hero of this narrative, who fled to Canada with his slave wife, Elsie, to seek for her the protection of the British lion from the merciless talons of the freedom-shrieking American eagle, was emancipated three years previous to the date of this chapter, together with nineteen others (the reputed goods and chattels of John Bayliss, a Baptist deacon, near Jonesborough, Tennessee). Slaveholder though he was, John Bayliss evidently thought his black people had souls as well as those of white skins, for he allowed his house servants to remain in the dining-room during evening family worship, thus giving them instruction which, as the sequel will show, made the slave the teacher of the master; for one morning, as "Aunt Lucy," an old and privileged servant, was passing through his room, she said:

"Massa John, I's bin thinkin' a heap o' dat ar what you read in the Bible t' other night."

"Ah, what's that, Aunt Lucy?" said the deacon.

"It's to do oder folks as you'd want 'em to do to you, or somehow dat fashion. I tell you, Massa John, 't would he mighty hard for you white folks to work great many years and get noffin'. Den, if you dies, whar'd we go to? I specks we'd go down de riber, like Jones's poor people did las' week."

"Well, well, Aunt Lucy, that was too bad; but Jones was in debt, and I suppose they had to be sold"

"O yes, I s'pose so; but dat you read in de Bible sort o' sticks to me--I can't help it," said this faithful old mother in Israel, as she went out to her work.

In a moment or two Mrs. Bayliss entered the room, and the deacon said:

"Wife, what kind of a text do you think Aunt Lucy has just given me?"

"Text?"

"Yes, text."

"What's got into her head now?"

"She says she's been thinking about what I read in prayer-time the other evening, referring to the golden rule, and that it sort o' sticks to her. She spoke, of the excitement over Jones's black people who were sent down the river the other day; and I tell you, the way she applied her text, it 'sort o' sticks' to me."

"O hush!" indignantly exclaimed Mrs. Bayliss. "Aunt Lucy's mighty religious, and has so many notions of her own she's not worth minding, any how."

"But she asked me what would become of my black people if I should die, and if I thought they would ever be torn apart as Jones's were. I tell you, wife, I have witnessed such scenes too often to feel right in risking a contingency of that kind," said the deacon, gravely.

"Don't be a fool, now, John Baybss," angrily exclaimed his wife, "about Aunt Lucy's fuss over Jones's niggers."

"Well," said the deacon, "I don't wonder at her feeling grieved; they belonged to her Church, and many of them were her relatives."

Here, for the time being, the conversation ended; but the soul of John Bayliss, awakened by the simple, straight-forward speech of his bond-woman, refused to be quieted, and he made this the subject of earnest prayer until the path of duty became so clear before him that he could not do otherwise than manumit his twenty slaves, although bitterly opposed by his wife (who refused to free the three held in her own right).

Elsie, the wife of Willis Hamilton, belonged to a neighboring planter. She was sold to a drover for the Southern market, and was being torn from her husband and two little daughters. Willis, in his agony, went from house to house, imploring some one to buy her, so that she might remain near her family. Finally one Dr. John P. Chester, who was about opening a hotel, agreed to purchase Elsie for $800, if Willis would pay $300 in work in the house, and fare the same as the other servants in board and clothing. With these conditions Willis gladly complied; but after they had spent a few months in their new home Deacon Bayliss examined their article of agreement and found it to be illegal. He told Willis that Dr. Chester could sell Elsie at any time, and he could establish no claim to her, even had he paid the $300, which, at the wages he was receiving, would take him nearly nine years to earn, with the interest, and advised him to leave Dr. Chester and work for wages, as he had done since his manumission. This advice was immediately acted upon, Willis being permitted to spend his nights with his wife. Every thing passed off pleasantly for a few weeks, until one of the house-servants told Elsie that she overheard Master John sell both her and Willis to a slave-trader, who would the following night convey them to the river with a drove ready for New Orleans. Frantic as the poor woman was with terror and grief at this information, she managed to perform her duties as usual until supper- time; and when all were seated at the table she slipped out unobserved, ran through a corn-field into the woods, sending word to Willis by a fellow-servant to meet her at a certain log. The moment Willis received the message he hastened to her with flying feet; and here the wretched husband and wife, but a few days before so full of plans for a pleasant future, held their council in tears.

Willis, in his sudden fright and excitement, could only exclaim: "What shall we do? Where shall we go?" Elsie, cooler and more composed, suggested going to Deacon Bayliss for advice. This Willis quickly did, and soon returned, it having been arranged that he should bring Elsie there and secrete her in the attic until the excitement of the hunt was over. After this they assumed the names of Bill and Jane, a brother and sister who answered to their own description of color and size on Willia's free papers-- the whole list of the twenty slaves emancipated by Deacon Bayliss being recorded on each paper.

After five weeks hiding at the southern terminus of the "Underground Railroad," they took up their line of march for Canada. In a Quaker settlement in Indiana they found friends to whom they revealed their true relationship, and here they spent a year with a Quaker family named Shugart. But the slight protection afforded by the laws of Indiana did not tend to give them a feeling of security, and so they started again for the promised land with their infant daughter Louisa. On this journey they were assisted on their way, and made easy and comfortable compared with their hasty flight from Tennessee, from whence they walked with swollen and blistered feet, and every nerve strung to its utmost tension from the fear of pursuit by their Southern persecutors.

As times were hard in Canada, Elsie consented to come to Michigan with her husband if be could find a Quaker neighborhood. In their search they found our house, and my husband, Charles Haviland, Jr., after learning their condition, leased Willis twenty acres of ground, mostly openings, for ten years, for the improvements he would make thereon. Here they lived for three years, when one day Elsie saw a strange man peering through the fence.

Her first thought was "a Southerner," and snatching her two Little ones she ran for our house, only a few rods distant. The man pursued her, and she called for help to a neighbor in sight, at which the skulking sneak took himself off to the woods. This incident so thoroughly aroused their fears that they took another farm, a few miles distant, for three years; then a farm near Ypsilanti for a few years; from whence they removed to Monroe, where they induced a friend to write to Willis's old friend and master, Deacon Bayliss, making inquiries after their two daughters, who were left behind in slavery. They received a prompt reply, purporting to come from Bayliss, informing them that their daughters were still living where they left them. He would see them, he said, by the time he received their next letter, which he hoped would be soon, that he might be the happy bearer of glad news to the children from their father and mother. He professed great joy at hearing from them, wished them to write all the particulars about themselves, but cautioned them to write to no one but him, and all would be safe. He requested them to inform him in what town they were living, as he noticed their letter was dated in one town, mailed in another, and he was directed to address them in a third. Their friend, however, strictly cautioned them not to reveal their definite whereabouts, but to answer all other queries. Willis wrote that as his farm lease had expired there, he would have to seek another farm, and did not know where he would be, but to address a letter as before and it would be forwarded to him.

Their next move was to return to their first Michigan home on my premises, a few months after the death of my husband, taking up their abode in the little log-house built for them a few years before, and working my land on shares. Another letter was soon received from their friend

Deacon Bayliss, as they supposed, and they urged me to reply; but I firmly refused to write to any one in the land of the slaveholder, lest the message should fall into the hands of enemies, and advised them to leave their daughters in the hands of the Lord, who would yet provide a way of deliverance for them as he had for their parents. In their great anxiety, however, to hear from their children, from whom they had been separated so many years, their plea was strong and persistent: but I remained immovable to all their entreaties, and told them of a slave family, who, after living twenty years in Indiana, had but recently been captured and returned to hopeless bondage. Upon this they yielded to me for the time being, but in a few weeks came again with pleadings made eloquent by suffering. As they had felt the vice-like grip of the peculiar system on their own hearts and lives, they realized too keenly the fate that might any time overtake their daughters. But I still resisted all their entreaties, and in a few days after they applied to J. F. Dolbeare, one of the trustees of Raisin Institute, who, thinking there was no danger, wrote all they desired, telling the supposed Deacon Bayliss all their past life in the free States and all their plans for the future. This they kept from me for a time, but Elsie's heart refused to be quieted, and she finally told me about it, first telling her husband she believed it their duty "For," she says, "I have thought more about it since Aunt Laura told me she dreamed of three poisonous green vipers which she poked so near the fire that their sacks were burned to a crisp and the poison all ran out, so that she thought them powerless for harm, but they still kept their threatening attitude; and who knows but these vipers may be slaveholders?" Willis said he had felt like telling me all the while, and both came to me with their story.

I much regretted this unwise step, but forbore all criticism, and told them we would hope for the best. A few days after a stranger appeared at our gate and inquired for a stray horse, which he said left him at Tecumseh. None having been seen he made similar inquiries at Hamilton's.

He also asked for a glass of water, and while receiving it, says to Elsie: "Auntie, where does this road lead to, that crosses the river east?" "To Palmyra," she replied, and frightened at being addressed as "Auntie," in the Southern style, hastened into her house.

The second night after this, at eleven o'clock, a carriage drove up to a log-house on one of the cross roads, and three men appeared simultaneously, two at the front and one at the rear window, but quickly disappeared. They had evidently mistaken their place, as it was a white family up with a sick child. It was a dark night, and there was a dug way ten feet deep perpendicular, near the fence to which their team was hitched, which the valiant and mysterious trio did not discover, and when they re-entered their carriage and attempted to turn around they tumbled into it, horses, carriage, and all. This little incident so disarranged their plans that they were until daylight returning to Adrian (only six miles distant), with their broken trappings and bruised horses. They told the liveryman, Mr. Hurlburt, that their horses took fright and ran off a steep bank, and begged him to fix the damages as low as possible, as they were from home, belated, etc. Mr. Hurlburt assessed them thirty dollars; but he afterwards said, had he known their business he would have doubled it.

Three days after this fortunate mishap Willis Hamilton received a letter inclosing three dollars, purporting to be from John Bayliss, who had come up into Ohio on business, and was on his way to visit them when he was suddenly taken very Ill, and was pronounced by the physicians in a critical condition--in fact, they gave him but little encouragement for recovery, and he desired Willis to come and visit him, and bring his wife and children, as he might want him for two weeks. He closed by saying:

"Whether I get better or die, I am resigned, and can say the Lord's will be done. I shall have every train watched until you come. God bless you

"Respectfully yours, JOHN BAYLISS"

Of course I was given this letter to read, and I suggested the utmost caution in obeying this request, for, as the old rat in the fable said, there might be "concealed mischief in this heap of meal" I called for the other two letters, and found they were written by the same hand Willis says: "Oh! I know the old boss too well, he's true as steel; he won't have anything to do with trap business. Besides, I've got my free papers, and I'm not afraid to go, but I wont take my wife and children" I proposed that Mr. Dolbeare or some neighbor go with him That pleased him, but Mr. Dolbeare could not go. As my son Daniel and I were going to Adrian, I proposed to get either Mr. Backus or Mr. Peters, both strong anti-slavery friends in the city, to accompany him to Toledo. As we were about starting, Joseph Gibbons, a neighbor, came with the suggestion that Willis remain at home, and James Martin, who was about his color and size, go in his stead; as Gibbons agreed with me in believing there was a deep laid plot. To this all parties agreed, and Willis gave me the letter and the three dollars towards the fare of whoever should go with James, who was an intelligent young colored man in our institution. Everything being in readiness we now started for Adrian, where we arrived just in time to jump on board the train, and consequently had no leisure to seek out and make the proposed arrangements with our above mentioned friends, but sent word back to Willis that we would return the following morning.

Once fairly settled on our journey the responsibility so suddenly thrust upon me made me cry out in my heart for wisdom beyond my own, and I prayed for a guiding hand to direct our actions in case we should find ourselves in the camp of the enemy, face to face with traffickers in human souls and bodies, who considered no scheme too vile or desperate for them to undertake, the success of which would in any way subserve their own interests.

We arrived at Toledo at 7 P. M., and as we left the cars James was, addressed by a man with the question: "Is your name Willis Hamilton?" (and without waiting for a reply), "Is your wife with you?"

"No, sir," said James.

"Perhaps I am mistaken," said the questioner, who was the porter of the Toledo hotel.

"Who do you wish to see?" said James.

"Willis Hamilton is the man I am sent for, by his old friend John Bayliss, who is at the Toledo hotel, so ill that he is not expected to live."

"Where is this Mr. Bayliss from?" said James.

"Tennessee, I believe."

"Very well, if there is such a man here I want to see him."

"Come with me, and I'll take you to his room," said the porter.

While this conversation was passing between the porter and James we were following in the rear, but apparently paying no attention to them. Our plan was for Daniel to keep James in sight if possible, and whatever he heard of the sick man to report to me in the parlor. We entered the hotel nearly together. I was shown into the parlor and James was taken up a flight of stairs from the bar-room. Daniel was following, when the porter told him the bar-room for gentlemen was below. He said, "I am taking this man to see a friend of his who is very sick, and no strangers are allowed to enter the room." Of course, my son could do nothing but return, so no further observations could be taken by us until the reappearance of James. For two long hours we neither saw nor heard anything of him, and becoming very anxious and restless I told Daniel to ask for James Martin, as he had business with him. Twice he made this request, but the porter only said, "Yes, yes, you shall see him in a minute," and dodged from room to room to keep out of sight.

Growing desperate, I finally told my son to tell the porter "if that young colored man is not forthcoming at once, a writ of habeas corpus will be served on him in fifteen minutes, as we must see him immediately. Also tell Mr. Woodward, the proprietor, that your mother is here with a message for Mr. John Bayliss, who we understand is very ill at this house." Mr. Woodward instantly summoned the porter, and we heard him say in an excited undertone: "There's trouble ahead unless that young black fellow comes down immediately; tell them to send him down at once." In a moment the porter, three gentlemen, and James made their appearance, evidently to the surprise of twenty half drunken Irishmen who had been chattering all the evening, but were now so still you could have heard a pin drop, to see Hamilton (as the sequel shows they supposed) brought down so publicly and without fetters. It afterwards transpired that Willis Hamilton, upon coming down stairs, was to have been put into a close carriage, sent away, and his family then sent for under the plea that he was detained with his sick friend, and this was the intelligent crowd who were to aid in the success of the plan.

I had seen a carriage stand fifteen or twenty minutes at the bar-room door and finally leave without a passenger, and Daniel saw the same carriage at the rear door equally long, which also left there empty. Upon coming down James Martin evidently took in the situation at a glance, for, giving my son a pinch, he said: "Mr. Haviland, let us go into the dining-room and call for supper." This was to give the drunken rabble time to leave so that he could relate his adventures with the Southerners after supper. But by this time the porter came to me to inquire if I wished to see Mr. Bayliss, the sick man. I replied in the affirmative, upon which he said: "He is very low; no stranger has been allowed to enter his room for three days, but his doctor is here. Would you like to see him?" "I would," I replied. A tall gentleman now entered the room and addressed me: "Madam, are you the lady who wished to see me?" "I am, if you are the physician who has charge of John Bayliss of Tennessee, who we learn is very ill, by a letter which Willis Hamilton received yesterday."

"I am Dr. Taylor of this city, and have the case of Mr. Bayliss in my care. His son-in-law is here taking care of him, and they are all greatly disappointed at not seeing Hamilton this evening, as Mr. Bayliss has sent for him and his family, and they can not imagine why he does not come."

"Well, I can tell you why. We feared a trap, as Willis's wife was formerly a slave."

"I don't see," said the doctor, "how you could suspect any thing wrong in that letter, as I understand they have written them before, and you should have compared the letters to see if they were written by the same person."

"We did so, and found they were written by the same person. But there are other points to consider: 1st, John Bayliss stands somewhat in the relation of a slaveholder, as in a former letter he spoke of three aged slaves living with him, and wished Hamilton and wife to stay with him two weeks if he lived, which was doubtful, and wished them to be sure and bring their children, though we all know that four little noisy children are not agreeable companions in a sick-room."

Here my learned doctor gave his head a vigorous scratch, and said: "Well, madam, Mr. Bayliss is probably childish from age, and his severe illness makes him more so. A nervous temperament like his, affected by disease, often enfeebles the mind, as body and mind are in close relationship philosophically. Now, he is just childish enough to want to see those children playing around his room, and he says he would make them handsome presents; and as money seems to be plenty with him and apparently no object, I judge they would be well paid for coming."

I did not appear to question this view of the case, but inquired how long Deacon Bayliss had been ill.

"About seven days, madam," replied the doctor.

"What seems to be the nature of the disease?"

"It was at first a violent attack of bilious fever, but for the last three days it has assumed a fearful form of typhus."

I told him that Hamilton and his wife were both very anxious about their old friend, and wished me to see him personally, and give him their reasons for not coming.

"I should be glad," said the doctor, "to allow you to see him, were it not for his extreme nervousness, but I dare not risk it. It seems hard to think the dying request of this poor old man can not be granted. He seems to consider this family almost next to his own."

"Yes," I said, "it is also hard and humiliating to humane and patriotic Americans that a system of human bondage exists in this country which causes these horrible fears and suspicions to loom up like specters before the mental vision of this persecuted and down- trodden race."

"That is very true," said Dr. Taylor; "slavery is the darkest spot on our national escutcheon. But in this case there is no cause for suspicion; for I am sure there is no plot with regard to the Hamilton family, and I call God to witness that every word I tell you is truth. As to the three slaves you spoke of, he told me during the first of his sickness that he emancipated all his slaves, twenty in number, but that his wife had three in her right, which she refused to free, and these have always remained in the family. He manumitted his slaves from purely conscientious scruples; and I believe that if there is a Christian that walks God's earth he is one, for he has manifested such patience and resignation during his severe illness that he has entirely won my affections. Now, don't you think you can induce Hamilton to bring his family here? I do not believe he will live three days."

"I will be honest with you," I replied. "Although you have talked like a candid man, I do not believe I could transfer sufficient confidence to the family to induce them to come unless I should see him, as they charged me over and again."

At this my tender-hearted Aesculapius sighed deeply, and said: "I am sorry that they or their friends should entertain any distrust, as I fear he may not be conscious two days longer. A council of physicians was called this afternoon, and three out of the four gave it as their opinion that he could not survive, at the longest, beyond three days; and I believe him liable to drop away within twenty-four hours, although it is barely possible he may live a week."

"Well," I replied, "one cause of suspicion, both with my neighbors and myself was that, although the letters from John Bayliss were all written by the same hand, the last one was equally well written as the others, although he was represented as so very low, with little hope of recovery."

Here my ready-tongued doctor very thoughtfully placed his hand to his forehead, but in a moment replied: "I will tell you how that was. His fever was off at the time, which enabled him to carry a steady hand."

"Well, of course," I replied, "we do not know that any plan exists to remand these people back to slavery, but we only judged of the possibilities. And for my part I do not believe in regarding the wicked enactments of men which contravene the laws of eternal right given by God, who made of one blood all nations who dwell upon the face of the earth, and of Christ, who left the realms of glory to bring blessings to mankind, and a part of whose mission was to unloose the heavy burdens and let the oppressed go free. And in view of the golden rule given by the great Lawgiver, I would not for my right hand become instrumental in returning one escaped slave to bondage. I firmly, believe in our Declaration of Independence, that all men are created free and equal, and that no human being has a right to make merchandise of others born in humbler stations, and place them on a level with horses, cattle, and sheep, knocking them off the auction- block to the highest bidder, sundering family ties, and outraging the purest and tenderest feelings of human nature."

"That is all right," said the doctor, "and I understand your feelings. Slavery is the greatest curse upon our otherwise happy country. But in this case there need be no fear of any conspiracy to injure your colored friends; and I did hope, for the sake of Mr. Bayliss, they would come and visit him, and gratify his dying request."

He then gave me some of the alarming symptoms of his patient, enlarged on the sympathy he felt for him, and finally proposed to go up and consult with his son-in law on the propriety of allowing me to see him in his present exceedingly nervous state. He said if he was not spoken to perhaps I might be allowed to look at him, as he was kept under the influence of opiates, and was to-night in a heavy stupor, and not disposed to talk to any one.

"Would such an arrangement be any satisfaction to you?"

I replied that, while it was immaterial to me, it would probably satisfy the Hamilton family; and, after a few minutes' consultation in the sick-room, be returned with the conclusion that I might enter the room, but that no loud word must be spoken, nor the sound of a footfall permitted.

"But you can not see his face, as it is covered with cloths wet in vinegar to draw the fever out, and he is now in a doze, and I do not wish to disturb him."

He then described the terrible paroxysms, bordering on spasms, suffered by his patient, in which it took four men to hold him, and was eulogizing his wonderful fortitude and Christian patience, when the son-in-law suddenly came rushing into the room in his shirt- sleeves and stocking-feet, and exclaimed:

"Doctor, doctor, do come quick; father's got another spasm, and I don't know what to do."

"Yes, yes," said the doctor, "I'll come; don't leave your father a moment;" and jumped up, apparently in great excitement. But at the door he halted to tell me that these spasms indicated mortification, when the son-in-law again opened the door with a bang and the exclamation:

"Doctor, why don't you hurry? Father is vomiting again, and I'm afraid he is dying."

At this they both rushed frantically up-stairs. In about fifteen minutes the doctor returned, saying he had given his patient a double dose of an opiate, and would let him rest awhile. He then launched out into a description of his treatment of Mr. Bayliss; how he had blistered him, and performed a surgical operation on him which had given him great pain; said he was attending him to the neglect of his other patients, and after exhausting a large amount of eloquence on the subject returned to the sick chamber. In a few moments be came back with the information that I could now be admitted, and conducted me to the room.

As soon as we stepped within the door the doctor halted, but I stepped to the center of the room, as if I had forgotten that I was only just to enter, and gazed at the bed and then at the lounge opposite. The doctor stepped to my side and said, "That is he on the bed yonder." I stood a moment and took a mental inventory of the sick man, who appeared full six feet tall and very slender, not at all answering to the description of the short, heavily built John Bayliss, of two hundred pounds avoirdupois. Of course, a fit of sickness might reduce a man's flesh, but it did not appear to me as especially likely to increase his height. As his face was covered with wet cloths I could not see the round physiognomy of John Bayliss, but passing my hand over the face I found it long and thin featured. I whispered to the doctor that I would like to notice his pulse. He said I could do so on the jugular vein. I did so, and found the skin of this fever-stricken man to be the natural temperature, but I whispered to the doctor that I was not so accustomed to noticing the pulse in that locality as at the wrist. After some resistance by the sick man, who finally yielded with a long undertone groan, I found his wrist, and the full, strong, regular pulse of a well man. There was now no doubt in my mind that I was alone at this midnight hour, far from home, in a room with three slaveholders.

As I stepped from the bed the doctor asked me if I was satisfied. The thought flashed through my mind that I had always contended that deception was lying, and that no circumstances could justify it But other thoughts also came, and I replied that I was satisfied.

At this the son-in-law, who had apparently been sleeping on the lounge, roused himself and commenced rubbing his eyes, and looking at the doctor, said, "Oh, doctor, do you think father is any better?"

"I can not conscientiously give you any hope," replied the doctor.

"Oh, dear!" he exclaimed, "what shall I do? I am almost sick myself, taking care of him day and night. If I had only known that they were near Tecumseh, where I lost my horse, I would have seen them; but I hoped to have found him better when I returned, instead of which he was much worse,"

At this I stepped towards him, and said: "If you are the gentleman who was inquiring for a horse in our neighborhood a few days ago, you called at Hamilton's house and asked for a drink of water."

"What, that place where a black woman brought me a glass of water?"

"Yes; that was Hamilton's wife."

"Is it possible! that little log house where there was a pile of pumpkins in the yard?"

"Yes," I said.

"Oh! if I had only known it," he exclaimed, "we would have had them here to help us. What trouble we have had. I reckon father will die, and I shall have to go home alone. God knows we have had a bad trip of it."

The careful doctor now began to fear we would disturb the patient, and we were about leaving the room when he suddenly exclaimed, "I want you to see what black bilious matter Mr. Bayliss vomited a while ago;" and, stepping back, be brought me a white bowl two-thirds full of what might have been the contents of a coffee-pot, with a bottle of black ink thrown in, and a few spittles floating on top. This, he told me, indicated mortification. We now passed into the parlor, where we could talk without disturbing the patient. "Now, madam," as you are fully satisfied with regard to Mr. Bayliss's illness, can't you do something to get the Hamiltons here?"

"I am willing," I replied, "to do all in my power, but see no better way than to inform them of the state of affairs upon my return, and the train will leave for Adrian at eight o'clock to-morrow morning." The doctor went up stairs to see what word they wished to send, and soon returned with the request that I should write to Hamilton to come immediately, and the porter would go with the letter for ten dollars, and his father would send another ten dollars to Willis. I still insisted that my original plan was the best, as the road through the cottonwood swamp was almost impassable.

The son-in-law now entered, and after walking across the floor a few times, with sighs and groans and bemoaning his dire calamities, said his father wished the letter written.

He returned to his father and the doctor went for writing material. They closed the door behind them for a consultation, I supposed.

The reader will remember that during all this time I knew nothing of the experience of James Martin with this afflicted trio, but had been compelled to grope my way blindly. As the doctor and son-in-law went out my son came in. He had overheard something about the writing, and said, excitedly: "Don't write, mother; there is no sick man here. That tall man is Elsie's master, and they threatened James's life when they" had him up stairs."

"Daniel, I know there is no sick man here," I said; "but they do not think I dream of any plot. It is now midnight, and it is not wise to let them know that we distrust them. Sit down and let us talk naturally."

The doctor now returned with writing material, and I sat down to write while he conversed with my son on the weather and kindred topics. Now my intention in writing to Hamilton was to serve these slaveholders by defeating them. I knew, too, that disguising my hand-writing was not enough to reveal to the Hamilton's that the letter was a sham, and whatever I wrote would be subjected to the perusal of my employers before it was sent. At this hour, too, a messenger could not probably be secured, even for twenty dollars. But as I seated myself at the table and took my pen in the manner in which I could appear to serve the slaveholders, but in reality defeat them, it came to me like a flash, and I cheerfully wrote all they dictated, not omitting the fact (?) that a council of physicians had decided that John Bayliss could not live to exceed three days; and after handing it to the doctor and son-in-law to read, I requested permission to add a few lines on my own responsibility, which was readily granted, as I explained to them that Elsie would not be prepared with regard to clothing, either for herself or children, to be away so long, and I could easily loan her sufficient garments.

This, of course, was as happy a thought for them as for myself, and was so received. "Indeed, madam," said the son-in-law, "that will be very kind in you. They can get ready so much quicker." So I added to my letter to Willis as follows: "Tell Elsie to take for herself the black alpaca dress in the south bed-room, and the two pink gingham aprons and striped flannel dresses in the bureau in the west room for the little girls. To come to Adrian, take the double team and farm wagon." I signed my name and handed the letter to the delighted stranger. He then gave my son a lighted sperm candle to light us over to the Indiana House, at that time the best hotel in Toledo, and kept by Salter Cleveland and wife, anti-slavery friends of ours. This light, however, served them to follow us, as well as guide us to our haven of safety.

After settling ourselves with our friends to tell our adventures I had a chance to hear James Martin's story. After the failure of my son to follow James and the porter/ up stairs, James was of course entirely in the hands of the enemy. At the head of the stairs they were met by an elderly gentleman with a lamp, who offered to conduct James to the sick room, and he was told to enter the first right hand door. On opening the door he found no one inside. "Oh," said his guide, "they have moved him to the next room, as was suggested by the council of physicians this afternoon; we will find him there; and opening the door the stranger assumed an attitude of command and told him to go in." James, however, replied: "I shall not go in, sir; you can see as well as I that the room is empty." The stranger gave a surprised look at the interior of the room and said: "Oh, I guess they moved him to the farther room, as some one suggested, after all. As there is no other room he can be in, you will certainly find him there."

By this time, of course, James began thoroughly to distrust his conductor, and hesitated about going farther; but desiring to make all the discoveries possible, and thinking if violence was attempted he could run down stairs to us, he passed on to the third door, and throwing it wide open found this room also empty.

He was about turning back when two other men suddenly appeared through a door at the left, and the three surrounded him, one leveling a revolver at his head, another at his breast, and the third pointing a dirk at his side, all indulging in an indiscriminate volley of oaths and threats. Said his grey-haired guide (who afterwards proved to be John P. Chester, Elsie's master, the same who had enacted to me the role of the sympathetic physician), "If you stir or speak one word we'll kill you. Go into that room, or you're a dead mail." In this position they entered the room and locked the door. "Now, Hamilton, we've got you, damn you."

"My name is not Hamilton, but James Martin," was James' reply.

"Damn you," rejoined Chester, "I know you; you were once a slave in Tennessee."

"No, sir, I never was a slave, nor was I ever in a slave state. I was born and brought up in the State of New York."

"Then you're a d----d spy, and I've a great mind to shoot you this minute," said Chester.

"If you call me a spy because I came here to see Mr. John Bayliss for Mr. Hamilton, then you can do so, for this is why I am here, and I came here with no intention of harm to any one, I am entirely unarmed, I have not so much as a penknife with which to defend myself, but I tell you, gentlemen, I have friends here in this house."

At this they dropped their weapons as by an electric shock, and Chester exclaimed, "You shan't be hurt! you shan't be hurt!" Then turning to his son: "Tom, put up your pistol."

"But," says Tom, "I propose to search him and see whether he's clear of arms."

"No! you shan't do it. I reckon it's as he says."

James, seeing that they were thoroughly intimidated, now felt at his ease. The Southerners, of course, did not know but a posse of armed men awaited their actions instead of one little woman and a lad of seventeen. Chester now addressed James in a subdued tone and manner, asking him to sit down, "and I'll tell you all about it Mr. John Bayliss is here and he is very sick; he is not expected to live. But I am Elsie's master; my name is John P. Chester, and I bought her out of pure benevolence to save her from going down the river with a drove. Willis was going from house to house begging for some one to buy his wife, crying and taking on like he was nearly crazy, and I felt sorry for him, and told him if he would help me buy her by paying three hundred dollars in work for me, I could do it, and he entered into a written agreement with me that I was to feed and clothe him the same as my other servants, and give him a good price for his work; but before he had been with me a year he took my property and ran away with it, and now I want to get it back."

"Why don't you go and get it then?" said James.

"Oh, there's such a set of d----d abolitionists there I can't do it," said Chester. "Hamilton wrote to me that he had put in ten acres of wheat this fall on shares on a widow lady's farm, and that he had a yoke of oxen, two cows, pigs and chickens,"

"Yes," said James, "that is all true."

"Well," said Chester, "you can have all he has there, besides any amount of money you please to name, if you will assist me in getting him and his family here. Will you do it?"

James replied, very carelessly, "Well, I don't know but I will for enough."

"You see," said Chester, "if I can get them here, I can get help from one place to another in Ohio, and when I strike Kentucky I'd be all right." In laying plans and making arrangements they consumed two hours' time, and, as the reader will remember, I became nervous and sent for James, after which I had my experience with the doctor and the sick man.

After finding ourselves quietly seated with our friends in their private parlor, before we had fairly finished relating our adventures, the night watch came in with the report that three men were pacing around the house at about equal distances, whom he suspected to be burglars. Orders were given to keep the outside rooms lighted, and if any attempt was made to enter to ring the alarm bell and assistance would be forthcoming. Morning light, however, revealed to the watchmen that their suspected burglars were the three Southerners, who had stopped at the Indiana House a few days, but not finding co-operation probable in their slave-hunting business, had changed their quarters to the Toledo Hotel. I recognized my doctor and the son-in-law; and the other, a tall, slender young man, of twenty-two, was my sick and suffering deacon, who an hour previous had been so near death's door. Their object, of course, in guarding the house, was to see that we sent no messenger to defeat the letter I had so kindly written for them. But on this matter I gave myself no concern, as Elsie was as well acquainted with my wardrobe as I was, and would know at once that it contained no such articles as I mentioned; also, that the house had no south bedroom, and no bureau in the west room, neither was there a double team nor a farm wagon on the place. Consequently I had no fears that the letter was not faithfully fulfilling its mission.

A few minutes before we left the hotel for the 8 o'clock train to return home a colored man came to James, evidently quite excited, and said: "We have just heard there is a colored man here having trouble with slave-holders; if this is true, there are enough of us here to do whatever is necessary." James did not reply, but looked inquiringly at me. I replied, "There is trouble," and taking him into a back room, gave him a brief sketch of James's experience. I told him I did not think it probable that violence would be offered in daylight, but as Mr. Cleveland and son were both ill, we would like to know who our friends were at the depot. He assured me we should have all the aid we needed. "While at the depot," said he, "we shall watch both you and the slave-holders, and whatever you desire us to do, madam, say the word, and it shall be done." I thanked him, but did not think there would be any difficulty.

The three Southerners were at the depot as soon as we were. In the ticket office James gave up going, as he thought they intended going with us. But this I did not care for, and told James he must go now, as there was no other train until night, and there was no telling what they might do under cover of darkness. When we got to the cars the doctor and son-in-law jumped aboard, but the sick man was determined to take his seat with me, and followed my son and myself from coach to coach, and whenever we showed any signs of seating ourselves prepared to seat himself opposite. I looked at his snakish eyes, and concluded to leave my sick deacon to see James, who still lingered in the ticket office.

I again urged him to go with me, as I should take another coach when I returned and get rid of the Southerners. When I returned I ran past the coach I had left, and Daniel beckoned to me, saying, "Here, mother, this is the car we took." "Yes," I said, "but I see a lady ahead that I wish, to sit with." At this the sick man jumped up and exclaimed, "I'll be d----d if I don't take that seat then." But Daniel pressed his way past him, and noticed his heavily-laden overcoat pocket. By the time my son reached me there was no room near us for the sick deacon, so he returned to his first seat.

During all this time about a dozen men, black and white, were watching us closely. I beckoned the one who called on us at the hotel to come to our apartments, and told him to tell James to come immediately to my door. He came, and I opened the door and told him to enter, as the train was about moving. When he was inside he says: "I am afraid we will have trouble." Just then the conductor passed, and I said to him: "I suppose we will be perfectly safe here, should we have trouble on our way to Adrian." "Most certainly," he said (raising his voice to the highest pitch). "I vouch for the perfect safety and protection of every individual on board this train."

Near Sylvania, a small town ten miles from Toledo, the train halted to sand the track, and our chivalrous friends got off. Chester and his son Thomas, the sick deacon, stationed themselves about three feet from us; and Chester, pointing to James, said in a low, grim voice: "We'll see you alone some time;" and, turning to my son, "You, too, young man." Then directing his volley of wrath to me, he roared out: "But that lady there--you nigger stealer--you that's got my property and the avails of it--I'll show you, you nigger thief;" and drawing a revolver from his pocket, his son doing the same, they pointed them towards my face, Chester again bawling out, "You see these tools, do you? We have more of 'em here" (holding up a traveling bag), "and we know haw to use them. We shall stay about here three weeks, and we will have that property you have in your possession yet, you d----d nigger stealer. We understand ourselves. We know what we are about."

"Man, I fear neither your weapons nor your threats; they are powerless. You are not at home--you are not in Tennessee. And as for your property, I have none of it about me or on my premises. We also know what we are about; we also understand, not only ourselves, but you."

Pale and trembling with rage they still shook their pistols in my face, and Chester, in a choked voice, exclaimed: "I'll--I'll--I won't say much more to you--you're a woman--but that young man of yours; I'll give five hundred dollars if he'll go to Kentucky with me."

Just then the conductor appeared and cried out: "What are you doing here, you villainous scoundrels? We'll have you arrested in five minutes." At this they fled precipitately to the woods, and the last we saw of these tall and valiant representatives of the land of chivalry were their heels feat receding in the thicket.

Of course, this brave exhibition of rhetoric and valor called out innumerable questions from the passengers; and from there on to Adrian, though already terribly fatigued, we had to be continually framing replies and making explanations.

Among the people of Sylvania the news spread like wildfire, and it was reported that over forty men were at the depot with hand-spikes and iron bars, ready to tear up the track in case the Hamilton family had been found on the train bound for Toledo.

When we arrived at Adrian my oldest son, Harvey, and Willis were there to meet us; and when we told Willis that Elsie's old master and his son had but an hour previously pointed pistols at our heads and threatened our lives, he could hardly speak from astonishment. Harvey said my letter arrived before sunrise, but that no one believed I had any thing to do with it. However, as the porter swore he saw me write it, Professor Patchin and J. F. Dolbeare were sent for; but they also distrusted its validity and the truthfulness of the bearer.

Elsie had no faith in it at all. "If," said she, "the old man is so very sick, as he hasn't seen us for years, they could bring him any black man and woman, and call them Willis and Elsie, and he'd never know the difference; and as for that letter, Mrs. Haviland never saw it. I believe the slave-holders wrote it themselves. They thought, as she was a widow, she'd have a black dress, and you know she hasn't got one in the house. And where's the pink aprons and green striped dresses? And there's no south bed-room in this house. It's all humbug; and I sha'n't stir a step until I see Mrs. Haviland."

Said another: "These things look queer. There's no bureau in the west room."

The porter, seeing he could not get the family, offered Willis ten dollars if he would go to Palmyra with him, but he refused. He then offered it to my son Harvey if he would take Wills to Palmyra.

"No, sir; I shall take him nowhere but to Adrian, to meet mother," was Harvey's reply.

After their arrival in Adrian the porter again offered the ten dollars, and Lawyer Perkins and others advised Harvey to take it and give it to Willis, as they would protect him from all harm. But when I came I told him not to touch it; and the porter, drawing near, heard my explanation of the letter, and the threatening remarks of the people, who declared that if slave-holders should attempt to take the Hamilton family or any other escaped slave from our city or county they would see trouble. He soon gave us the benefit of his absence, and we went home with thankful hearts that public sentiment had made a law too strong to allow avaricious and unprincipled men to cast our persecuted neighbors back into the seething cauldron of American slavery.

All that day our house was thronged with visitors, eager to hear the story which was agitating the whole community, but about midnight I told my friends that rest was a necessity, for never in my life was I so thoroughly exhausted from talking; but, as the next day wan-the Sabbath, I would in the evening meet all who chose to come in the Valley School-house (at that day the largest in the county) and tell them the whole story, and save repeating it so many times.

When the evening came we met a larger crowd than could find standing-room in the school-house, and report said there was a spy for the slave-holders under a window outside.

I related the whole story, omitting nothing, and was followed by Elijah Brownell, one of our ablest anti-slavery lecturers, with a few spirited remarks. He suggested that a collection should be taken up to defray our expenses to Toledo and return, and fourteen dollars was soon placed in my hands.

From a friend of our letter-carrier, the porter of the Toledo Hotel, we learned that the plans of the slave-holders accorded with those given James Martin in the sick-room. After getting the Hamilton family in their clutches they intended to gag and bind--them, and, traveling nights, convey them from one point to another until they reached Kentucky. This was precisely on the plan of our underground railroad, but happily for the cause of freedom, in this case at least, not as successful.

The citizens of Adrian appointed a meeting at the court-house, and sent for me to again tell the story of the slaveholder who had so deeply laid his plans to capture, not only his fugitive slave Elsie and her four children, but also her husband, who was a free man. Other meetings were called to take measures for securing the safety of the hunted family from the iron grasp of the oppressor, whose arm is ever strong and powerful in the cause of evil; and so great was public excitement that the chivalrous sons of the South found our Northern climate too warm for their constitutions, and betook themselves to the milder climate of Tennessee with as great speed as their hunted slave, with her husband, hastened away from there fifteen years before.

It may be asked how the Chesters discovered that Hamilton and his wife were in Michigan. We learned afterward that John P. Chester was the postmaster at Jonesborough, and receiving a letter at his office directed to John Bayliss, he suspected it to be from friends of his former slaves, and opened it. His suspicions being confirmed, he detained the letter, and both corresponded and came North in the assumed character of Bayliss. His schemes miscarried, as we have above narrated, and Bayliss probably never knew of the desperate game played in his name.

About two weeks after the departure of this noble trio I received a threatening letter from John P. Chester, to which I replied; and this was followed by a correspondence with his son, Thomas K. Chester (the sick deacon). From these letters we shall give a few extracts.

In a letter received under the date of December 3; 1846, John P. Chester writes: "I presume you do not want something for nothing; and inasmuch as you have my property in your possession, and are so great a philanth-ropist, you Hill feel bound to remunerate me for that property.... If there is any law of the land to compel you to pay for them I intend to have it."

In my reply, December 20, 1846, I wrote:

"First, convince me that you have property in my possession, and you shall have the utmost farthing. But if Willis Hamilton and family are property in my possession, then are Rev. John Patchin and wife, principals of Raisin Institute, and other neighbors, property in my possession, as I have dealing with each family, precisely in the same manner that I have with Willis Hamilton and family, and I do as truly recognize property in my other neighbors as in the Hamilton family. Prove my position fallacious, and not predicated on principles of eternal right, and they may be blown to the four winds of heaven. If carnal weapons can be brought to bear upon the spiritual you shall have the liberty to do it with the six-shooters you flourished toward my face in Sylvania, Ohio....

"As for my being compelled to pay you for this alleged property, to this I have but little to say, as it is the least of all my troubles in this lower world. I will say, However, I stand ready to meet whatever you may think proper to do in the case. Should you think best to make us another call, I could not vouch for your safety. The circumstances connected with this case have been such that great excitement has prevailed. A. number of my neighbors have kept arms since our return from Toledo. I can say with the Psalmist, 'I am for peace, but they are for war.'

"At a public meeting called the next evening after our return from the Toledo trip, fourteen dollars was placed in my hands as a remuneration for the assistance I rendered in examining your very sick patient. I found the disease truly alarming, far beyond the reach of human aid, much deeper than bilious fever, although it might have assumed a typhoid grade. The blister that you were immediately to apply on the back of the patient could not extract that dark, deep plague-spot of slavery, too apparent to be misunderstood,"

I received a long list of epithets in a letter, bearing date, Jonesboro, Tennessee, February 7, 1847, from Thomas K. Chester, the sick deacon:

"I have thought it my duty to answer your pack of balderdash, ... that you presumed to reply to my father, as I was with him on his tour to Michigan, and a participant in all his transactions, even to the acting the sick man's part in Toledo ..., True it is, by your cunning villainies you have deprived us of our just rights, of our own property.... Thanks be to an all wise and provident God that, my father has more of that sable kind of busy fellows, greasy, slick, and fat; and they are not cheated to death out of their hard earnings by villainous and infernal abolitionists, whose philanthropy is interest, and whose only desire is to swindle the slave-holder out of his own property, and convert its labor to their own infernal aggrandizement.

"It is exceedingly unpleasant for me to indulge in abuse, particularly to a woman, and I would not now do it, did I not feel a perfect consciousness of right and duty.... Who do you think would parley with a thief, a robber of man's just rights, recognized by the glorious Constitution of our Union! Such a condescension would damn an honest man, would put modesty to the blush. What! to engage in a contest with you? a rogue, a damnable thief, a negro thief, an outbreaker, a criminal in the sight of all honest men; ... the mother, too, of a pusillanimous son, who permitted me to curse and damn you in Sylvania! I would rather be caught with another man's sheep on my back than to engage in such a subject, and with such an individual as old Laura Haviland, a damned nigger-stealer....

"You can tell Elsie that since our return my father bought her eldest daughter; that she is now his property, and the mother of a likely boy, that I call Daniel Haviland after your pretty son. She has plenty to eat, and has shoes in the Winter, an article Willis's children had not when I was there, although it was cold enough to freeze the horns off the cows.... What do you think your portion will be at the great day of judgment? I think it will be the inner temple of hell."

In my reply, dated Raisin, March 16, 1847, I informed the sick deacon that my letter to his father "had served as a moral emetic, by the mass of black, bilious, and putrid matter it bad sent forth. You must have been exercised with as great distress, as extreme pain, that was producing paroxysms and vomiting, that you had in your sick-room in the Toledo hotel, when your physician was so hastily called to your relief by your son-in-law, as the matter that lies before me in letter form is as 'black', and much more 'bilious,' and nearer 'mortification' than that I saw there."

"We thank you for the name's sake. May he possess the wisdom of a Daniel of old, although his lot be cast in the lions' den; and, like Moses, may he become instrumental in leading his people away from a worse bondage than that of Egypt.

"According to your logic, we are not only robbing the slaveholder, but the poor slave of his valuable home, where he can enjoy the elevating and soul-ennobling privilege of looking 'greasy, slick, and fat'--can have the privilege of being forbidden the laborious task of cultivating his intellect--is forbidden to claim his wife and children as his own instead of the property of John P. Chester."

I pitied the young man, whose bitterness of hate seemed incorrigible, and gave advice which I deemed wholesome, although I yielded to the temptation of dealing somewhat in irony and sarcasm.

But the next letter from the sick deacon was filled and running over with vulgar blackguardism, that I would neither answer nor give to the public eye. It was directed to "Laura S. Haviland, Esq., or Dan." As it arrived in my absence, my son Daniel handed it to Rev. John Patchin, who became so indignant in reading the list of epithets that he proposed to reply.

The first sentence of his letter was:

"Sir,--As John Quincy Adams and Henry Clay were seated in Congress, they saw passing on the street a drove of jackasses. Said Henry Clay, 'There, Sir, Adams, is a company of your constituents as they come from the North.' 'All right; they are going South to teach yours,' was the quick reply. And I think one of those long-eared animals has strayed down your way, and your ma might have sent you to his school-- I think, however, but a few weeks, or your epistolary correspondence with Mrs. Haviland would have been vastly improved."

From the report my son gave me of the short epistle, it was filled with sentenced couched in the same spirit throughout; "for," said he, "that rabid fire-eater has been treated in a manner too mild. He needs something more nearly like his own coin."

I shortly after received a few lines from Thomas K. Chester, informing me that he had my last letter struck off in hand-bills, and circulated in a number of the Southern States, "over its true signature, Laura S. Haviland, as you dictated and your daughter wrote it; for, as strange as it may appear, I have the handwriting of every one of your family, and also of Willis Hamilton. I distribute these hand-bills for the purpose of letting the South see what sort of sisters they have in the North." We learned from a number of sources that to this circular or hand-bill was attached a reward of $3,000 for my head.

As for the letter that Chester had richly earned, neither my daughter nor myself had the privilege of perusing it, as it was mailed before my return home. But I presume the indignant writer designed to close the unpleasant correspondence.

SECOND EFFORT TO RETAKE THE HAMILTON FAMILY.

After the passage of the famous Fugitive-slave Bill of 1850, turning the whole population of the North into slave-hunters, Thomas K. Chester, with renewed assurance, came to Lawyer Beacher's office, in Adrian, and solicited his services in capturing the Hamiltons, as he was now prepared to take legal steps in recovering his property. Said he:

"I ask no favors of Adrian or Raisin, as I have my posse of thirty men within a stone's throw of this city. All I ask is legal authority from you, Mr. Beacher, and I can easily get them in my possession."

"I can not aid you," said Mr. Beacher; "it would ruin my practice as a lawyer."

"I will give you $100, besides your fee," rejoined Chester.

"You have not enough money in your State of Tennessee to induce me to assist you in any way whatever."

"Will you direct me to a lawyer who will aid me?"

"I can not; I know of none in our State who could be hired to assist you. And I advise you to return to your home; for you will lose a hundred dollars where you will gain one, if you pursue it."

At this advice he became enraged, and swore he would have them this time, at any cost. "And if old Laura Haviland interferes I'll put her in prison. I acknowledge she outwitted us before; but let her dare prevent my taking them this time, and I'll be avenged on her before I leave this State."

"All the advice I have to give you is to abandon this scheme, for you will find no jail in this State that will hold that woman. And I request you not to enter my office again on this business, for if it were known to the public it would injure my practice; and I shall not recognize you on the street."

In a lower tone Chester continued, "I request you, Mr. Beacher, as a gentleman, to keep my name and business a secret." With a few imprecations he left the office.

My friend R. Beacher sent a dispatch to me at once by Sheriff Spafford, to secure the safety of the Hamilton family at once, if still on my premises, as my Tennessee correspondents were probably in or near Adrian. I informed him they were safe in Canada within six months after the visit from the Chesters. Mr. Beacher also advised me to make my property safe without delay, but this had been done two years previously. On receiving this information my friend Beacher replied, "Had I known this I would have sent for her, for I'd give ten dollars to see them meet." Mr. Chester heard that the Hamilton family had gone to Canada, but he did not believe it, as he also heard they had gone to Ypsilanti, in this State, where he said he should follow them.

We learned in the sequel that he went to Ypsilanti, and took rooms and board in a hotel, while calling on every colored family in town and for two or three miles around it, sometimes as a drover, at other times an agent to make arrangements for purchasing wood and charcoal. During four weeks he found a family that answered the description of the Hamilton family in color and number. He wrote to his father that he had found them under an assumed name, and requested him to send a man who could recognize them, as they had been away over eighteen years. The man was sent, and two weeks more were spent in reconnoitering. At length both were agreed to arrest David Gordon and wife, with their four children, as the Hamilton family, and applied for a warrant to take the family as escaped slaves. The United States Judge, Hon. Ross Wilkins, who issued the warrant, informed one of the most active underground railroad men, George De Baptist, of this claimant's business. He immediately telegraphed to a vigorous worker in Ypsilanti, who sent runners in every direction, inquiring for a Hamilton family. None could be found; and the conclusion was reached that they were newcomers and were closely concealed, and the only safe way was to set a watch at the depot for officers and their posse, and follow whithersoever they went, keeping in sight. This was done, and the place they found aimed for was David Gordon's. On entering the house the officer placed hand-cuffs on David Gordon, who in surprise asked, "What does this mean?"

Said the officer, "I understand your name is Willis Hamilton, once a slave in Tennessee."

Gordon replied, "No, sir, you are mistaken; I never was in that State; neither is my name Hamilton, but Gordon, and I have free papers from Virginia."

"Where are your papers? If they are good they shall save you."

Pointing to a trunk, "There they are; take that key and you'll find them."

While the officer was getting the papers, Chester went to the bed of the sick wife, placed a six-shooter at her head, and swore he'd blow her brains out in a moment if she did not say their name was Hamilton. "No, sir, our name is Gordon." Their little girl, standing by, cried out with fear. He turned to her, with pistol pointing toward her face, and swore he'd kill her that instant if she did not say her father's name was Willis Hamilton.

At this juncture, the officer's attention was arrested. "What are you about, you villain? You'll be arrested before you know it, if you are not careful. Put up that pistol instantly, and if these papers are good, I shall release this man, and return the warrant unserved."

He examined them and said, "These papers I find genuine." He then removed the handcuffs from David Gordon, and with the discomfited Thomas K. Chester and Tennessee companion returned to the depot for the Detroit train.

While on their way they met a colored man that Chester swore was Willis Hamilton. Said the officer, "You know not what you are about; I shall arrest no man at your command."

On returning the unserved warrant to Judge Wilkins, Chester charged him with being allied with the "d----d abolitionist, old Laura Haviland, in running off that family to Malden, to keep me out of my property."

"I knew nothing of the family, or of your business, until you came into this office yesterday," replied the judge.

In a rage and with an oath, he replied, "I know, sir, your complicity in keeping slave-holders out of their property, and can prove it." He threw his hat on the floor and gave a stamp, as if to strengthen his oath.

The judge simply ordered him out of his office, instead of committing him to prison for contempt of court; and with his companion he went back to his Tennessee home, again defeated.

Thomas K. Chester wrote and had published scurrilous articles in Tennessee, and in a number of other Southern States. They were vigorously circulated until the following Congress, in which the grave charge was brought against the judge, "of being allied with Mrs. Haviland, of the interior of the State of Michigan, a rabid abolitionist, in keeping slaveholders out of their slave property." A vigorous effort was made by Southern members to impeach him, while his friends were petitioning Congress to raise his salary, Judge Wilkins was sent for to answer to these false charges. Although they failed to impeach him, yet on account of these charges the addition to his salary was lost.

When these false accusations were brought into Congress, and the judge was informed of the necessity of his presence to answer thereto, he inquired of Henry Bibb and others where I was. They informed him that I was absent from home. On my return from Cincinnati with a few underground railroad passengers, I learned of the trouble Judge Wilkins met, and I called on him. He told me of the pile of Southern papers he had received, with scurrilous articles, designed to prejudice Southern members of Congress against him. Said he, "Although they failed in the impeachment, they said they would come against me with double force next Congress, and should effect their object." Said the judge, "I want your address, for if they do repeat their effort, with the explanation you have now given, I think I can save another journey to Washington. The judge was never again called upon to defend himself on this subject, as their effort was not repeated; neither did their oft-repeated threat to imprison me disturb us."

DEATH OF THE CHESTERS

In the third year of the Rebellion, while in Memphis, Tennessee, on a mission to the perishing, I found myself in the city where my Tennessee correspondents lived a few years previous to their deaths. From a minister who had long been a resident of that city, and had also lived near Jonesboro, where they resided during the correspondence, I learned the following facts: A few years prior to the war John P. Chester removed with his family to Memphis, where he became a patroller. His son Thomas transacted business as a lawyer. I was shown his residence, and the office where John P. Chester was shot through the heart by a mulatto man, whose free papers he demanded, doubting their validity. Said the man, "I am as free as you are; and to live a slave I never shall." He then drew a six-shooter from its hiding-place and shot him through the heart. He fell, exclaiming, "O God,

I'm a dead man." The man threw down the fatal weapon, saying to the bystanders, "Here I am, gentlemen, shoot me, or hang me, just as you please, but to live a slave to any man I never shall." He was taken by the indignant crowd, and hung on the limb of a tree near by, pierced with many bullets. I can not describe the feeling that crept over me, as I gazed upon the pavement where John P. Chester met his fate, and which I had walked over in going to officers' head-quarters from the steamer. Oh! what a life, to close with such a tragedy!

Thomas K. Chester being a few rods distant ran to assist his dying father, but his life was gone ere he reached him. A few months later he was brought from a boat sick with yellow fever, and died in one week from the attack in terrible paroxysms and ravings, frequently requiring six men to hold him on his bed. He was ill the same length of time that they falsely represented a few years before in the Toledo hotel. Said the narrator, "Thomas K. Chester's death was the most awful I ever witnessed. He cursed and swore to his last breath, saying he saw his father standing by his bed, with damned spirits waiting to take him away to eternal burnings."

After a long walk one day, I called at the former residence of the Chester family, and was seated in the front parlor. It is hard to imagine my feelings as I sat in the room where those two men had lain in death's cold embrace--men who had flourished toward my face the six-shooter. It was by this kind of deadly weapon the life of one was taken; and as nearly as words can describe the feigned sickness, the last week of the life of the other was spent. No wonder the blood seemed to curdle in my veins in contemplating the lives of these men, and their end. It is beyond the power of pen to describe the panorama that passed before me in these moments. The proprietor of the Toledo hotel lost custom by his complicity in their efforts to retake their alleged slave property. A few months after the hotel was burned to ashes.

AN OHIO SCHOOL-TEACHER

IN the Autumn of 1847 a gentleman of evident culture called for early breakfast, though he had passed a public house about two miles distant. I mistrusted my stranger caller to be a counterfeit; and told him, as I had the care of an infant for a sick friend, he would find better fare at the boarding hall a few rods away. But introducing himself as an Ohio school-teacher, and accustomed to boarding around, he had not enjoyed his favorite bread and milk for a long while, and if I would be so kind as to allow him a bowl of bread and milk he would accept it as a favor. He said he had heard of our excellent school, and wished to visit it. He was also acting as agent of the National Era, published at Cincinnati, in which he was much interested, and solicited my subscription. I told him I knew it to be a valuable periodical, but, as I was taking three, abolition papers he must excuse me.

He was also very much interested in the underground railroad projects, and referred to names of agents and stations, in Indiana and Ohio, in a way that I concluded he had been on the trail and found me, as well as others, and perhaps taken the assumed agency of the Era for a covering. He said it was found necessary in some places in Ohio and Indiana to change the routes, as slave-holders had traced and followed them so closely that they had made trouble in many places, and suggested a change in Michigan, as there were five slave-holders in Toledo, Ohio, when he came through, in search of escaped slaves. I replied that it might be a good idea, but I had not considered it sufficiently to decide.

Continuing his arguments, he referred to a slave who was captured by Mr. B. Stevens, of Boone County, Kentucky. He saw him tied on a horse standing at the door of an inn where he was teaching. In surprise, I inquired:

"Did that community allow that to be done in their midst without making an effort to rescue the self-made freeman?"

"O yes, because Stevens came with witnesses and papers, proving that he legally owned him; so that nothing could be done to hinder him"

"That could never be done in this community; and I doubt whether it could be done in this State."

"But what could you do in a case like that?"

"Let a slave-holder come and try us, as they did six months ago in their effort to retake the Hamilton family, who are still living here on my premises, and you see how they succeeded;" and I gave him their plans and defeat. "Let them or any other slave-holders disturb an escaped slave, at any time of night or day, and the sound of a tin horn would be heard, with a dozen more answering it in different directions, and men enough would gather around the trembling fugitive for his rescue. For women can blow horns, and men can run. Bells are used in our school and neighborhood; but if the sound of a tin horn is heard it is understood, a few miles each way from Raisin Institute, just what it means."

Looking surprised, he answered: "Well, I reckon you do understand yourselves here. But I don't see how you could retain one legally if papers and witnesses were on hand."

"Hon. Ross Wilkins, United States judge, residing in Detroit, can legally require any fugitive so claimed to be brought before him, and not allow any thing to be done until the decision is reached. And there are many active workers to assist escaping slaves in that city, who would rush to their aid, and in ten minutes see them safe in Canada. I presume if the slave claimant should come with a score of witnesses and a half-bushel of papers, to prove his legal right, it would avail him nothing, as we claim a higher law than wicked enactments of men who claim the misnomer of law by which bodies and souls of men, women, and children are claimed as chattels." The proprietor of the boarding hall desired me to allow him to inform the stranger of our suspicions, and invite him to leave. But I declined, as I had reached the conclusion that my visitor was from Kentucky, and probably in search of John White, whose master had sworn that he would send him as far as wind and water would carry him if he ever got him again. Professor Patchin and J. F. Dolbeare called to see him, and conversed with him about his agency for the Era, etc.; and brother Patchin invited him to attend the recitations of the classes in Latin and geometry. The second was accepted, as mathematics, he said, was his favorite study.

By four o'clock P.M., the hour of his leaving, the tide of excitement was fast rising, and one of the students offered to go and inform John White of the danger we suspected, and advise him to take refuge in Canada until these Kentuckians should leave our State.

We surmised that the five slave-holders he reported in Toledo were his own company, which was soon found to be true. One of my horses was brought into requisition at once for the dispatch-bearer; but he had not been on his journey an hour before we learned that our Ohio teacher inquired of a boy on the road if there had been a mulatto man by the name of White attending school at Raisin Institute the past Winter.

"Yes, sir."

"Where is he now?"

"He hired for the season to Mr. Watkins, near Brooklyn, in Jackson County."

This report brought another offer to become dispatch-bearer to the hunted man. The following day found John White in Canada.

Two days after George W. Brazier, who claimed John White as his property, and the man who had lost the woman and five children, with their two witnesses, and their lawyer, J. L. Smith, who recently made me an all-day visit, entered the lowest type of a saloon in the town near by, and inquired for two of the most besotted and wickedest men in town. Being directed according to their novel inquiry, the men were found and hired, making their number seven, to capture John White. The field in which he had been at work was surrounded by the seven men at equal distances. But, as they neared the supposed object of their pursuit, lo! a poor white man was there instead of the prize they were so sure of capturing. They repaired to the house of Mr. Watkins, and inquired of him for the whereabouts of John White. The frank reply was:

"I suppose he is in Canada, as I took him, with his trunk, to the depot, yesterday, for that country."

At this Brazier poured forth a volley of oaths about me, and said he knew I had been there.

"Hold on, sir, you are laboring under a mistake. We have none of us seen her; and I want you to understand that there are others, myself included, who are ready to do as much to save a self-freed slave from being taken back to Southern bondage as Mrs. Haviland. Mr. White is highly esteemed wherever he is known; and we would not see him go back from whence he came without making great effort to prevent it."

At this Brazier flew into a rage, and furiously swore he would yet be avenged on me before he left the State."

"I advise you to be more sparing of your threats. We have a law here to arrest and take care of men who make such threats as you have here," said Mr. Watkins.

With this quietus they left for Tecumseh, four miles distant from us.

While at Snell's Hotel they displayed on the bar-room table pistols, dirks, and bowie-knives, and pointing to them, said Brazier, "Here is what we use, and we'll have the life of that d--d abolitionist, Mrs. Haviland, before we leave this State, or be avenged on her in some way." The five men then in haste jumped aboard the stage for Adrian. As the authorities were informed of these threats, and Judge Stacy was going to Adrian on business, he proposed to leave with a friend he was to pass the import of these threats, fearing they might quit the stage while passing through our neighborhood, and under cover of night commit their deeds of darkness. I received the note, and told the bearer I accepted this as the outburst of passion over their defeat, and did not believe they designed to carry out these threats, and requested the excited family to keep this as near a secret as possible, during a day or two at least, to save my children and the school this exciting anxiety. But I could not appear altogether stoical, and consulted judicious friends, who advised me to leave my home a night or two at least. This was the saddest moment I had seen. I felt that I could not conscientiously leave my home. "If slaveholders wish to call on me they will find me here, unless I have business away." They insisted that I should keep my windows closed after dark, and they would send four young men students, to whom they would tell the secret, with the charge to keep it unless disturbance should require them to reveal it. We received information the following day that the five Kentuckians took the cars for Toledo on their arrival at Adrian. Their threats increased the excitement already kindled, and neighbors advised me not to remain in my house of nights, as there might be hired emissaries to execute their will. Some even advised me to go to Canada for safety. But rest was mine in Divine Providence.

The following week I accompanied an insane friend with her brother to Toledo. The brother wished me to go to Monroe on business for them. He soon informed me that the five Kentuckians were in the same hotel with us, and he overheard one say that I had no doubts followed them to see whether they had found any of their runaways, and that one of their party was going wherever I did to watch my movements. This friend also saw them consulting with the barkeeper, who sat opposite at breakfast table, and introduced the defeated stratagem of the Tennessee slave- holders at the Toledo hotel a few months previously. Said he, "I believe you are the lady who met them there. Some of us heard of it soon after, and we should have rushed there in a hurry if there had been an attempt to take a fugitive from our city. They might as well attempt to eat through an iron wall as to get one from us. I am an abolitionist of the Garrison stamp, and there are others here of the same stripe." And in this familiar style he continued, quite to my annoyance, at the table. He came to me a number of times after breakfast to find what he could do to assist me in having the hack take me to whatever point I wished to go.

"Are you going east, madam?"

"Not today."

"Or are you designing to go south, or to return on the Adrian train?"

"I shall not go in either direction today."

Leaving me a few moments, he returned with inquiring whether I was going to Monroe, and giving as the reason for his inquiries the wish to assist me. I informed him I was going to take the ten o'clock boat for Monroe. I learned in the sequel that they charged me with secreting the woman and five children, and aiding their flight to Canada; but of them I knew nothing, until my Ohio teacher informed me of their flight, and while I was suspected and watched by their pursuers, we had reason to believe they were placed on a boat at Cleveland, and were safe in Canada.

We learned that their lawyer made inquiries while in my neighborhood whether my farm and Raisin Institute were entirely in my hands. When they became satisfied of the fact they left orders for my arrest upon a United States warrant, to be served the following Autumn, if they failed to recover their human property. About the expiration of the time set George W. Brazier went with a gang of slaves for sale to Baton Rouge, Louisiana, and died suddenly of cholera. There his projects ended, and John White soon returned to his work in Michigan.

These circumstances delayed my prospect of going to Cincinnati and Rising Sun to learn the condition of his family, but as money had been raised by the anxious husband and father and his friends, I went to Cincinnati, where I found my friends, Levi Coffin and family. The vigilant committee was called to his private parlor, to consult as to the most prudent measure to adopt in securing an interview with Jane White, John's wife, whose master, Benjamin Stevens, was her father, and the vain hope was indulged that he would not make an effort to retake the family should they make a start for freedom. The committee proposed that I should go to Rising Sun, and, through Joseph Edgerton and Samuel Barkshire and families, obtain an interview with Jane White, as they were intelligent and well-to-do colored friends of John White's in Rising Sun.

Accordingly I went, and called on Joseph Edgerton's eating-house. On making my errand known, there was great rejoicing over good news from their esteemed friend Felix White, as John was formerly called. In conferring with these friends and Samuel Barkshire, they thought the errand could be taken to Jane, through Stevens's foreman slave, Solomon, who was frequently allowed to cross the river on business for his master, and was looked for the following Saturday. But as we were disappointed, Joseph's wife, Mary Edgerton, proposed to go with me to Benjamin Stevens's, ostensibly to buy plums. As there was no trace of African blood perceivable in her, and the Stevens family, both white and colored, had seen her mother, who was my size, with blue eyes, straight brown hair, and skin as fair as mine, there was no question as to relationship when Mary introduced me to Jane and her sister Nan as Aunt Smith (my maiden name). It was also known to the Stevens family that Mary was expecting her aunt from Georgia to spend a few weeks with her. When we entered the basement, which was the kitchen of the Stevens house, twelve men and women slaves just came in from the harvest-field for their dinner, which consisted of "corn dodgers" placed in piles at convenient distances on the bare table, made of two long rough boards on crossed legs. A large pitcher filled as full as its broken top would allow of sour milk, and a saucer of greens, with a small piece of pork cut in thin slices, were divided among the hands, who were seated on the edge of their table, except a few who occupied stools and broken chairs. Not a whole earthen dish or plate was on that table. A broken knife or fork was placed by each plate, and they used each other's knife or fork, and ate their humble repast with apparent zest. I have given this harvest dinner in detail, as Benjamin Stevens was called a remarkably kind master. It was frequently remarked by surrounding planters "that the Stevens niggers thought they were white."

As we were informed they had no plums for sale, Mary proposed filling our "buckets" with blackberries, as there were an abundance within a short distance, and asked Jane if she or Nan could not go and show us the way. "I'll go an' ask Missus Agnes," replied Nan, who soon returned with the word that Jane might go, as she wanted to make another batch of jam. "But she says we must get dinner for Mary and her aunt first." A small tablecloth was placed over one end of the table, and wheat bread, butter, honey, and a cream-pitcher of sweet milk was brought down for us. Not a child of the nine little ones playing in the kitchen asked for a taste of anything during or after our meal. All that was left was taken up stairs, and we were invited to call on Mrs. Agnes, who received us cordially. She was teaching Jane's oldest daughter, of seven years, to sew. After a few minutes chat with the mistress, we left for blackberries.

When out of sight, I told Jane I was the one who wrote a letter for her husband, Felix White, to her, and directed it to Samuel Barkshire, who told me he read it to her, but did not dare take it from his house, but took the braid of his hair tied with blue ribbon, sent in the letter. She looked at me in amazement for a moment, when she burst into a flood of tears. As soon as she could command her feelings she said her master had told her that he had heard from Felix, and that he was married again, and was riding around with his new wife mighty happy. When I gave her the errand from her husband she was again convulsed with weeping. Said she, "I would gladly work day and night, until my fingers and toes are without a nail, and willingly see my children work in the same way, could we only be with Felix." Poor heartbroken woman, she sighed like a sobbing child. But two of her children were out a few miles with one of the Stevens married children, to be gone two months, and she sent a request to her husband to come on the sly to assist in bringing their children away after the return of the absent ones, so that all might go together. I assisted her in picking berries, as she had spent so much of her time in talking and weeping her mistress might complain. I gave her a little memento from her husband, and left the poor heartstricken, crushed spirit.

The daughter and grandchildren of the master withheld them from going to their natural protector, yet he was called one of the best of slave-holders. Here was a woman and sister whose widowhood was more desolate than even death had made my own. And her poor children were worse than fatherless. I returned to my home and anxious children and friends.

But the grieved husband felt confident his intimate friend William Allen, who would have left for freedom long ago but for his wife and child, would assist Jane and the children could he know from him how many warm friends there were in the North to assist them. His friends, as well as himself, were anxious to make another trial without the risk of his going into the lion's den. Means being provided, three mouths later found me again in Rising Sun. After a little waiting to see William Allen, I took a boat and went four miles below on the Kentucky side, and called at the house of his master to wait for a boat going up the river within a few hours.

As they were having a great excitement over counterfeiters, and were making great efforts to find the rogues, and looking upon every stranger with suspicion, I was believed by my host to be one of them in disguise. Within an hour after my arrival the sheriff and a deputy were brought into an adjoining room. The lady of the house appeared excited. Her little girl inquired who those strange gentlemen were; she replied the sheriff and his deputy. I looked up from the paper I was busily reading, and entered into conversation with the lady of the house, when I overhead one man say, "I don't think there is anything wrong about that woman." This remark led me to suppose I might be the object of the undertone conversation among the gentlemen in the adjoining room. Soon after the three gentlemen came into the room, with whom I passed the usual "good afternoon." One, whom I took to be the sheriff, made a few remarks over fine weather, etc., and all three returned to their room. Said one, in a low voice, "I tell you that woman is all right; she's no counterfeiter." My excited hostess became calm, and quite social, and made excuses for having to look after the cooking of her turkey, as she allowed her cook to spend this Sabbath with her husband in visiting one of their friends. "And I always burn and blister my hands whenever I make an attempt at cooking. But my cook is so faithful I thought I would let her go today."

As I gave up the idea of seeing William Allen, I was about to go to the wharf-boat and wait there for the five o'clock boat. But she urged me to take dinner with them, as I would have plenty of time. After dinner they directed me across a pasture-field that would shorten the half-mile. Just out of sight of the house I met William Allen, with his wife and little girl of ten years. As they were so well described by John--or Felix, as he was here known--I recognized them, and gave the message from their friend, from whom they rejoiced to hear. He said he longed to be free, and thought two weeks from that day he could go over to Samuel Barkshire's to see me. During this time he would deliver the message to Jane. At present, he said, it would be very difficult crossing, as there was great excitement over men that passed a lot of counterfeit money in that neighborhood, and they were watching for them. I told him it was not safe for us to talk longer there, as they were slaves, and I was not free to be seen talking with them, and gave them the parting hand, informing them that many prayers of Christian people of the North were daily ascending for the deliverance of the slave. "May God grant the answer!" was the heartfelt reply.

During the two weeks Mary Scott was introduced, who had recently bought herself, with her free husband's aid. She related to me the sad condition of her sister, Rachel Beach, who was the slave of Mr. Ray, the brother of Wright Ray, of Madison, Indiana, the noted negro catcher. She was the kept mistress of her master, who held her and her five children, who were his own flesh and blood, as his property. After her sister Rachel's religious experience, she was much distressed over the life she was compelled to lead with her master. She had often wept with her weeping sister. When she thought of escaping, she could not leave her five little children to her own sad fate. As I was informed that Mary Scott was a reliable Christian woman, I gave her a plan, and names of persons and places of safety, with a charge not to stop over the second night--if possible, to avoid it--at the first place named; for it was too near her master's brother, Wright Ray, as he would make great efforts to retake them.

This plan was adopted. But they were kept two days at Luther Donald's station, which brought them into great difficulty. He was so well known as the slave's friend it was unsafe to secrete fugitives on his own premises; and he placed them in an out-house of one of his friends. On the second night of their flight, when they were to be taken to the next station, Wright Ray was on their track, and entered the neighborhood at dark twilight, filling it with excitement on the part of both friends and foes. The cry of a child brought a neighbor to their hiding-place, who told her she was unsafe; but he would take her and the children to his barn, where they would be perfectly secure. Soon after her new friend left her she felt in great danger, and when her children were asleep in their bed of stalls she ventured to place herself by the road-side. Here she heard horses coming, and listened to hear the voice of their riders, to see if she could recognize her first friends, as they had told her they were going to take them to another place of safety that night; but, to her grief, she heard the voice of Wright Ray, with his posse. Filled with fear of capture, she groped her way still farther back in the dark. After her pursuers passed she heard two men coming, in low conversation. She prayed for direction, and felt impressed, as she said, to tell these men her trouble. They proved to be her friends, who missed them as they went to take their suppers. As Ray and his company were known to be in town, they knew not but they were captured. Runners were sent to the usual resorts of slave-hunters, to see if any clew could be learned of the fate of the missing family.

"O, how I prayed God to deliver me in this my great distress!" she said, in relating her flight in my interview with her in Canada. She led her two friends to the barn, from whence her sleeping children were removed; but by the time they reached the road they saw the lantern, and heard rustling of stalks by her pursuers. As her new friend was a well-known friend to slave-hunters, she and her children were still in great danger. She was dressed in men's clothing, and her girls dressed like boys, and they were taken out in different directions. Rachel and the youngest child her guide took to a Quaker neighborhood, while two men took each two girls on their horses and took different roads to other places of safety; but no two of the three parties knew of the others' destination. Two days of distressing anxiety were passed before a word reached the mother from her children. Not knowing but they were back to their old Kentucky home, she could neither eat nor sleep for weeping and praying over the probable loss of her children. But her joy could not find expression when two of them were brought to her. At first sight of her darlings, she cried out, "Glory to God! he has sent me two more. But where, O, where are the other two?" The two men who brought these in their close carriage could give no tidings, as they had heard nothing from them since leaving Donald Station. Rachel continued weeping for her children because they were not. On the following day they were heard from, and that they would be brought on the following day, P. M.

A number of the neighbors were invited to witness the meeting. Among them was a strong pro-slavery man and his family, who had often said the abolitionists might as well come to his barn and steal his horse or wheat as to keep slave-holders out of their slave property; yet he was naturally a sympathetic man. This Quaker abolitionist knew it would do him good to witness the anticipated scene. The knowledge of the prospective arrival of the children was carefully kept from the mother until she saw them, coming through the gate, when she cried aloud, as she sank on the floor, "Glory; hallelujah to the Lamb! You sent me all." She sobbed as she clasped them to her bosom, continuing, in an ecstasy, "Bless the Lord forever! He is so good to poor me." The little girls threw their arms around their mother's neck, and burst into a loud cry for joy. "But the weeping was not confined to them," said our Quaker sister, who was present. "There was not a dry eye in that house; and our pro-slavery neighbor cried as hard as any of us."

After the excitement died away a little, said one, "Now, we must adopt a plan to take this family on to Canada."

The pro-slavery man was the first to say, "I'll take my team, and take them where they'll be safe, if I have to take them all the way."

Another said, "It is cold weather, and we see these children have bare feet; and we must see about getting them stockings and shoes and warm clothing."

And the little daughter of him who had so generously offered his services in aiding this family beyond the reach, of danger sat down on the carpet and commenced taking off hers, saying, "She can have mine."

"But, Lotty, what will you do?" said the mother.

"O, papa can get me some more."

"Yes, papa will get you some more," said her father, wiping his eyes; "and your shoes and stockings will just fit that little girl." And the mother could hardly keep her from leaving them. But she told her to wear them home and put others on, then bring them back.

Said our informant, "I will warrant that man will hereafter become a stockholder."

But the rescue of the Beach family cost Luther Donald his farm. He was sued and found guilty of harboring runaway slaves and assisting them to escape. But not one sentence of truthful evidence was brought against him in court; although he did aid the Beach family when a stay of three minutes longer in their dangerous hiding-place would have secured their return to a life of degradation. Friends of the fugitive made up the loss in part, and the God of the oppressed blessed him still more abundantly. He was diligent in business, serving the Lord.

While rejoicing over the safe arrival of the Beach family in Canada, heavy tidings reached me from home. In a letter I was informed of the illness of my eldest son. Before the boat arrived that was to bear me homeward a second letter came with the sad intelligence of the death of my first-born. Oh, how my poor heart was wrung with anxiety to learn the state of his mind as he left the shores of time. Why did not the writer relieve me by giving the information I most needed? And yet I was advised to remain until the weather became more mild. I had a severe cough that followed an attack of pneumonia, and physicians had advised me to spend the Winter in a milder climate. But this bereavement seemed impelling me to return to my afflicted children. But more than all other considerations was to learn the state of that dear child's mind as he was about leaving the land of the dying for the spirit world of the living. He had been a living Christian, but during the year past had become more inactive, and in a conversation on the subject a few days previous to my leaving, he expressed regrets in not being more faithful. He urged me to take this trip, yet I could not but regret leaving home. "Oh my son, my son Harvey would to God I had died for thee!" In this distress, bordering upon agony of soul, I walked my room to and fro, praying for an evidence of his condition. In the conversation above alluded to he expressed a sincere desire to return.

Said he, "I am too much like the prodigal, too far away from my Savior." How vividly did his words come before me! Oh, how these words ran through my mind in this hour of sore trial. Is this the Isaac, I dwelt upon as I was leaving my home, that I may be called to sacrifice? I had in mind my son Daniel, who was fearful I would meet trouble from slave-holders, as he remarked to his brother Harvey, "Mother is a stranger to fear, though she might be in great danger."

"That fact, seems to me, secures her safety," replied Harvey.

As I overheard this conversation I shrank from the trial of leaving my home circle, in which death had made such inroads, and for the time being doubted whether I was called upon to make the sacrifice. But prayer was now constant for an evidence of my son's condition, whether prepared for exchange of worlds. He who spake peace to the troubled sea granted the answer of peace, with an assurance that my prayer was answered, and that in his own good time he would make it manifest.

I took the boat for Cincinnati, and on the morning after my arrival at the home of my valued friends, Levi Coffin and wife, I awoke with a comforting dream, which but for the circumstances I would not record. I find in the written Word of divine truth that God, at sundry times, made himself known to his faithful servants in dreams. And he is the same in all ages, in answering their petitions and meeting their wants. In the dream I thought I was living in the basement of a beautiful mansion. Being rather dark, damp, and cool, I looked for some means of warming my apartments, when I discovered the windows conveyed beautiful rays of sunlight sufficient to dry and warm apartments designed for only a temporary residence, as my future home was to be in the splendid apartments above, which I was not to be permitted to enter until the work assigned me in the basement was done. While busily engaged in sweeping my room, and arranging my work, I saw my son Harvey, descending from the upper portion of this limitless mansion, which I thought was now his home. I hastened to the door to meet him. As the thought struck me that he had been a slave, I cried out, "My son Harvey, art thou free?"

"Oh yes, mother, I am free; and I knew your anxiety, and I came on purpose to tell you that I went to my Master and asked if he would grant my pardon? And he looked upon me and saw me in my blood as I plowed in the field, and he said I should be free and live."

"Oh, what a relief is this glad news," I replied.

"I knew you desired me to go for my freedom long ago, but I did not know that my liberty would be so easily granted--just for asking. I am now free, indeed."

This message delivered, he ascended to his glorious home above. I awoke with the words of this message as clearly impressed upon my mind as if vocally spoken. I opened the Bible at the head of my bed, and the first words that met my eye were these: "I saw Ephraim cast out in the open field; I saw him in his blood, and I said live; and he shall live." With promises given by him with whom there is no variableness or shadow of turning, my heart was filled with praise and thanksgiving for the Comforter who grants peace such as the world knows not of. Very soon a letter came with the detailed account of the last hours of my son Harvey, in which he left a bright evidence of his preparation for the future life. He sent for Rev. John Patchin, of Raisin Institute, of whom he requested prayer; at the close of which he followed in fervent prayer for himself and loved ones. Then brother Patchin inquired if perfect peace was his at this hour? "It is," he answered; "I am ready to go," and he soon fell asleep in Jesus.

I remained a few weeks longer; but the close search for counterfeiters made it difficult for William Allen to cross.

The request was repeated by John White's wife for him to come for them. I returned home with the consciousness of having done all that I could in delivering the messages as requested. The husband and father could not feel reconciled to give up his family to a life of slavery, and went for them, and brought them a few miles on the Indiana side, above Rising Sun. They secreted themselves during the day in the woods, and with the aid of his friend and Solomon Stevens's slave, previously alluded to, who was also attempting to escape with the family, he made a raft upon which they were about to cross a creek to reach the team on the opposite side. Suddenly six armed men pounced upon them, and captured the family, with Solomon. To save John from the hazardous attempt to defend his family, his friend held him back in the thicket, knowing the effort must fail. As he was not allowed to move he sank back in despair in the arms of his friend. He had risked his own life and liberty in his attempt to rescue them. He learned that George W. Brazier swore he would chop him into inches if he ever got possession of him again. After his unsuccessful effort in Michigan he offered six hundred dollars for his head, dead or alive. Benjamin Stevens also offered six hundred dollars reward for his daughter and his five grandchildren, with Solomon. He afterwards sold them all for the very low price of one thousand dollars, with the proviso that they were not to be sold apart.

But poor Jane was not left long to grieve over her disappointed hopes. She died of cholera. We heard she went rejoicing in that hope that reaches beyond the vale. They were taken to Lexington, Kentucky, but the grieved husband and father again made his way northward. He was two weeks in reaching a settlement that was said to be friendly to fugitive slaves. Forty miles distant from his old Kentucky home he assumed the name of James Armstrong. The family upon whom he ventured to call appeared very kind, and the man told him he would take him the next day to a Quaker settlement, but he suspected he was reported to Wright Ray and posse, who came into the house and bound him. Placing him on one of their horses, they took him through fields and back roads until they crossed the Ohio river, and lodged him in the Woodford jail, a short distance from the river, nearly opposite Madison, Indiana. Wright Ray had no idea of having in his possession John White, who had so recently eluded his grasp in his unsuccessful trip with Brazier in Michigan. He found among his papers in which were advertisements of escaped slaves, Henry Armstrong advertised as belonging to the widow Armstrong, of Maysville, Kentucky. With her Wright Ray had an interview, hoping to arrange for the reward, which she refused to give, for he had been away so long, he would be of little use, as Henry was willed free at her death. But she told him if he could get enough from him to pay him for his trouble, he might do so. Consequently he made him an offer to release him for four hundred dollars, and encouraged him to write to his friends in Michigan to aid him to that amount. He wrote to a son-in-law of Mr. Watkins, so as not to mention a name of persons the men had to do with in Michigan, and the letter was brought to us. We all understood the writer to be our friend John White.

A few friends were consulted as to the measures to be adopted. It was proposed that I should go to Cincinnati, and there make such arrangements as the friends might think proper. As they proposed to bear my expenses, I said, "If you send me, I shall go to-morrow morning."

"But," replied the bearer of the letter, "as it is the Sabbath, I suppose I should hesitate."

"It was lawful on the Sabbath to lift a sheep out of the ditch in the days of Moses, and is not a man better than a sheep?"

"I can not answer you. All I have to say is, follow the dictates of your own conscience."

I took the stage at Toledo, and in three days I was consulting the vigilance committee in Levi Coffin's council chamber. As it would not do for me to transact business with Wright Ray, Micajah White, nephew of Catherine Coffin, offered to go as soon as the money was obtained. Levi Coffin introduced me to Dr. Judkins, of whom I hired the money, but hoped to lessen the amount if possible, in the arrangement with Wright Ray. I urged on the nephew the necessity of taking the first boat for Madison, as every hour endangered the safety of John White. Whatever was done for him must be done quickly. Wright Ray was found very willing to accept three hundred and fifty dollars, which was placed in the hands of the clerk of the boat until his prisoner was delivered to his friends in Cincinnati, when Micajah White agreed to see the money paid to Wright Ray. This was done, and within three weeks from the time I left home I returned with John White. The day after John's release Brazier appeared at the jail, having heard that he was there. But he was too late.

A few months after John White's release from Woodford jail George W. Brazier went to Baton Rouge, Louisiana, with a gang of slaves for sale, and suddenly died of cholera, just before the time fixed for his return. It was said he intended to make a second effort to capture John White, or to arrest me with United States warrant. Time rolled on, and John F. White married a young woman in Canada, his home a number of years. After the late war he removed to Ann Arbor, Michigan, to educate his children. When we last heard of his first children, his oldest daughter was married to Solomon, the ex-slave of Benjamin Stevens. We rejoice that brighter days are dawning. Ethiopia is stretching out her hands to God.

THE UNDERGROUND RAILWAY

AS my married children had charge of the farm, and the younger ones were in school, and well provided for, I spent a few months in mission work and nursing the sick. My dear friends, Levi and Catherine Coffin, had given me a very cordial invitation to make their house my home whenever I was in Cincinnati. Soon after my arrival, at early dawn, nine slaves crossed the river, and were conducted to one of our friends on Walnut Hills for safety, until arrangements could be made to forward them to Victoria's domain. I called on them to see what was needed for their Northern march, and found them filled with fear lest they should be overtaken. As there was a prospect before them of being taken down the river, they concluded to "paddle their own canoe." They had with them their five little folks, that seemed as full of fear as were their trembling parents. A little girl of five years raised the window-shade to look out. When her mother discovered her she exclaimed, in a half-smothered voice, "Why, Em! you'll have us all kotched, if you don't mind;" and the little thing dropped behind a chair like a frightened young partridge hiding under a leaf at the mother's alarm of danger. While making our plans, we were greatly relieved, to find that the well known Quaker conductor, William Beard, was in the city, with a load of produce from his farm. This covered market-wagon was a safe car, that had borne many hundreds to his own depot, and was now ready for more valuable freight before the city should be filled with slave-hunters. But few weeks elapsed before we learned of the safe arrival of these two families that we fitted for their journey to Canada.

One of our vigilance committee came early one morning to inform us that there were two young men just arrived, who were secreted in the basement of Zion Baptist Church (colored). As their home was only twenty-five miles from the river, it was necessary to make all possible speed in removing them before Kentucky slave-hunters should block our track. I took their measures, to procure for each a Summer suit, and went to our store of new and second-hand clothing, at Levi Coffin's, where anti-slavery women met tri-monthly, to spend a day in making and repairing clothing for fugitive slaves. In early evening I took a large market-basket, with a suit for each, and had them conducted to a safer hiding-place, until a way opened for them to go to a Friends' settlement, about eighty miles distant, where George chose to remain and work a few months. But James would not risk his liberty by tarrying, and censured George for running such a risk. "You needn't think your new name's gwine to save you when ole massa comes"

But little did James understand the deep-hidden reason that kept his friend George behind. He worked faithfully nearly a year, kept the suit I gave him for his Sunday suit, and used his old Kentucky suit for his work, patching them himself, until patch upon patch nearly covered the old brown jeans of his plantation wear. When warm weather again returned, without revealing his design of going back to his master in Kentucky, for he knew his abolition friends would discourage his project, he took the eighty dollars he had earned since he left his master, and wore the suit of clothes he brought away, and in the darkness of night went to his wife's cabin. Here he gave a full history of the kind friends who had paid good wages for his work, and said he was going to take all to his master, and tell him he was sick of freedom; "and you mus' be mighty mad," he went on, "'case I come back; and say, 'If he's a mind to make sich a fool of his self, as to be so jubus, 'case I talked leetle while wid Jake, long time ago, as to run off an' leave me, he may go. He needn't think I'll take 'im back; I won't have nothin' to say to 'im, never!' Ad' I'll quarrel 'bout you too; an' when all ov 'em is done fussin' 'bout me comin' back, I'll steal to you in a dark night, an' lay a plan to meet on Lickin' River; an' we'll take a skiff an' muffle oars till we get to the Ohio; an' I knows jus' whar to go in any dark night, an' we 'll be free together. I didn't tell Jim I's gwine to make massa b'leve all my lies to get you; for I tell you, Liz, I ain't got whole freedom without you."

Before eight o'clock A. M. George stood before his master, with his old name and old plantation suit, presenting him with the eighty dollars he had earned for his master since he had left his home, that he never wanted to leave again. For he had found "abolitioners the greates' rascals I ever seen. I wants no more ov' em. They tried hard to git me to Canada; but I got all I wants of Canada, An' I tell you, Massa Carpenter, all I wants is one good stiddy home. I don't want this money; it's yourn."

His master was well pleased, and told all his neighbors how happy his Tom was to get back again, and gave all the money he had earned since he had been gone. It was a long time before neighboring planters had the confidence in Tom that his master had, and they told him that Tom should never step his foot on their plantations; but he told them all that he had perfect confidence in Tom's honesty. "He came back perfectly disgusted with abolitionists; he said they will work a fellow half to death for low wages. And he even patched his old suit, himself, that he wore off. And I have found the reason why he left. He and Liz had a quarrel, and now he don't care a fig about her; and I heard yesterday that her master says he'll shoot him if he dares to come on his plantation. But he needn't worry; for you couldn't hire Tom to go near Liz."

Tom's master told him all the planters were afraid of him, and said he would play a trick on him yet.

"I'll stay at home, then, and won't even go out to meetin's, till all ov 'em will see I means what I says."

"That's right, Tom; they don't know you like I do. Bat I told them 't would do all the niggers good just to hear your story about the meanness of abolitionists. You know, Tom, that was just what I told you, that they pretended to be your friends, but they were your worst enemies."

"Yes, massa, I al'us bleved you; and if Liz hadn't cut up the way she did I never'd tried 'em."

All things went on smoothly with Tom. He was never more trusty, diligent, and faithful in all that pertained to his master's interest. Three months still found him contented and happy, and the constant praise he received from his master to his neighbors began to inspire them with sufficient confidence to permit him to attend their meetings occasionally, though he did not appear anxious to enjoy that privilege until his master proposed his going, and then he was careful to attend only day meetings. Neighboring white people often talked with him about his Northern trip, and all got the story he had told his master, until Tom became quite a pet missionary, as his reports went far and near, among both whites and blacks. After Lizzie's master became quite satisfied with her hatred toward Tom, he allowed the hound, which he kept over two months to watch for Tom, to go back to the keeper. Though Tom and Lizzie lived eight miles apart, they had a secret dispatch-bearer, by whom they reported to each other; but visits were very few and far between.

One day, in her "clarin-up time," Lizzie came across a bundle containing a Sunday suit, placed in her cabin when Tom left for the North, which she took occasion to have a good quarrel over. Taking them into her mistress, the master being present, she said, "Missus, that'll I do wid dese ole close Tom lef, when he get mad an' run'd off to spite me; now I'll burn 'em up or giv' 'em to de pigs for nes', I ain't gwine to hav' 'em in my way any longer."

"Oh, don't burn 'em up, can't you send 'im word to come and get 'em?"

"I sends 'im no word, if he never gets 'em; I'd heap better giv' 'em to de hogs."

Turning to another house servant, her mistress said, "Dil, you tell Page's Jim when he goes to that big meeting your people are going to have next week, to tell Tom to come and take his truck away, or Liz will pitch 'em in the fire for 'im."

But there was no hurry manifest, after he got the word. Tom's master told him he had better go and get his clothes or Liz might destroy them. Said our George, "One Saturday evenin' I went to have my las' quarrel with Lizzie. I called her bad names, an' she flung back mean names, an' twitted me with runnin' away to make her feel bad, when she didn't care a picayune for me; an' I tole her I never wanted to see her face agin, an' we almos' cum to blows."

A few months after this there was a holiday, and Tom was so faithful, his master gave him permission to visit his aunt, six miles distant in an opposite direction from Lizzie's home, and she too got permission to visit her friends five miles away, but not towards Tom's master. The plan laid in his midnight visit was to start after sundown, and go until dark in the direction of the place each had their permission to go, and then go for Licking River; and she was to go up the river, while he was to go down, until they met. He was to secure the first skiff with oars he could find to aid them down the river with all possible speed to the Ohio. They succeeded in making good time after they met, until day dawn overtook them, when they hid the skiff under a clump of bushes, and the oars they took the precaution to hide some distance away in case the skiff was discovered and taken away. They secreted themselves still further in the woods, but not so far but they could watch their tiny craft through the thicket. Much to their discomfiture a number of boys found their skiff, and had a long hunt for the oars, but not succeeding, furnished themselves with poles and pushed out of sight to the great relief of the temporary owners, so near being discovered during the hunt for the oars. At ten o'clock, when all was still, they crept out of their hiding-place, took their oars, and hunted two hours before they found another skiff. Though smaller and harder to manage than the one they lost, yet they reached the Ohio just at sunrise. Two men on the opposite side of Licking River hallooed, "Where are you going?"

"To market, sir."

"What have you got?"

"Butter an' eggs, sir."

As he saw them in the skiff and pushing toward them, he expected every moment to be overhauled, but he pulled with all his might for the opposite shore, and did not dare look back until they had reached the middle of the river, when, to their great relief, the two men had given up the chase and turned back, and had almost reached the place of their starting. He said Lizzie trembled so hard that the coat over her shook, so great was her fear. Said Lizzie, "I reckon the owner of the coat shook as hard as I did when you was pullin' for life. I specs you sent fear clare down into them paddles you's sweattin' over;" and they had a good laugh over fright and success.

With George there was no fear after entering the basement of Zion Baptist Church, his old hiding-place. As soon as the report came to us that a man and his wife had just arrived, I called to learn their condition and needs, and asked the woman who had charge of the basement to tell them a friend would call to see them, as new-comers were always so timid. A voice from the adjoining room was heard to say, "Come right in, Mrs. Haviland, we are not afraid of you;" and as the fugitive clasped my hand in both of his, I exclaimed, "Where have you seen me?"

"Don't you mind Jim and George you giv' a basket full of close to las' Summer? You giv' me the linen pants an' blue checked gingham coat and straw hat, an' you giv' Jim thin pants and coat and palm-leaf hat; and don't you mind we went out in a market-wagon to a Quaker settlement?"

"Yes, but how came you here again?"

"It was for this little woman I went back." Then he went over his managing process, as above related.

As I was soon to go to my home in Michigan, it was proposed by our vigilance committee that this couple, with Sarah, who made her escape over a year previously, should go with me. Sarah was to be sold away from her little boy of three years for a fancy girl, as she was a beautiful octoroon and attractive in person. She knew full well the fate that awaited her, and succeeded in escaping. She was an excellent house servant, and highly respected by all who made her acquaintance for her sterling Christian character and general intelligence. She had lived in a quiet Christian family, who gave her good wages, but she did not dare to risk her liberty within one hundred miles of her former home.

A few days after the arrival of George and wife a mulatto woman and her daughter of sixteen, bound South from Virginia, left a steamer and joined our company. While waiting for a certain canal-boat, the owner and captain being friendly to our work, another young man joined us. These we received at different points to avoid suspicion. Before we reached the third bridge we were overtaken by Levi Coffin with another young man, whom he had instructed implicitly to regard all the lessons I might give him. I gave them all a charge to say nothing of going farther than Toledo, Ohio, and talk of no farther back than Cincinnati.

While on our way George pointed at a wire, and told his wife it was a telegraph-wire, at which she dodged back, and for a moment seemed as badly frightened as though her master had been in sight. It was a lucky thing for us that no stranger happened to be in sight, as her fright would have betrayed them. Even an assurance from George that the wires could do no harm, could hardly satisfy her, until he appealed to me to confirm his statement, that it was the operators at each end of the wires that gave information.

The day before we reached Toledo one of the drivers left, and the steersman employed our boy William, with the consent of the captain. I told George to tell William I wanted to see him at the expiration of the time set for him to drive. He came into the cabin, while the other passengers were on deck, and told me all the hands seemed very clever, and the steersman told him he would find a good place for him to work in Toledo, and that he would see that he had good wages. He asked him various questions, that led him to disclose his starting point, Vicksburg, Mississippi. As he was so very friendly he answered all his queries, even to his master's name. This I had charged him not to give. As George and the other colored man saw the steersman and another man employed on the boat so very intimate, and careful to keep William with them, they began to fear for their own safety. There came up a sudden shower during William's time to drive, and he got thoroughly drenched; and as he had no change of garments, the steersman and the other boys of the boat furnished him out of their own wardrobe. It had now become difficult for me to secure an interview with William, on account of his close friends, and I became as fearful of the telegraph wires as was Mary, over whom we had a little sport.

But William began to fear all was not right, and regretted having told this man of his condition, and made an errand on deck, as he saw me sitting alone. He told me all he had said to the steersman. I told him to appear very careless, and say nothing, but to appear as if he was going with the steersman, as he had suggested. As we should be in Toledo in three hours, I would go into the city, and the women and George would follow me to a place of safety. Then I would return for my shawl, that I should leave on the boat. By that time, the passengers would all have left, and he and the other young man must remain about the boat. Then I would watch the opportunity, and when I went out, I should turn short corners, but give them time to keep me in sight. Accordingly, I returned for my shawl, but made no haste to leave until those close friends entered a saloon; then was our time; I gave them the wink and left for a place of safety.

After I had put one and two in a place, my next work was to solicit money to pay our fare to Canada, on a boat that was to leave at 9 A. M. the next day. Here were six fares to pay to Detroit, as Sarah had sufficient to pay her own. The friends in Cincinnati had paid their fare to Toledo. It was now nearly night, and I had but little time; but I succeeded by nine o'clock the next morning, leaving a colored man to conduct them to the boat; with hardly five minutes to spare I reached the boat, with my living freight.

Once out in the lake we felt quite secure. Yet there was a possibility of a telegram being sent to William's master, and danger of being overtaken by officers in Detroit. Knowing of their anxiety to see Canada, I waited until we were near enough to see carriages and persons on the road on the other side. When I said to George's wife "There is Canada." "It ain't, is it?" "It is, certainly. It is where no slave-owner can claim his slave." She ran to her husband to tell the good news. But neither he nor the balance of them believed her, and all came running to me. "That ain't Canada, is it?" Being assured that the land of freedom was in full view, with tears of joy they gazed upon their "House of Refuge," and within forty minutes we were there. And to see them leap for joy was rich pay for all my care in their behalf. George and Jake had both armed themselves with deadly weapons, in case of an attempt to capture them, resolving on liberty or death. I left each with fifty cents and returned to my own sweet home.

I found the large building unfinished. As the first buildings were temporary, they were unsuitable for students to occupy another Winter, which would be the eleventh Winter our school had been in successful operation. Brother Patchin, our principal, was called to another field as pastor and teacher, and would go if the new building was not ready for use by the following academic year. While these probabilities were under consideration, brother J. F. Dolbeare was taken from us, after a short illness. As he was an important trustee, and an active Christian worker, his loss was severely felt. We had a few months previously met with a similar loss in the death of another trustee, our valued friend and brother, Elijah Brownell, a minister of the Society of Friends. Surely dark clouds again overhung our favorite institution, in which many of our students were taught in the school of Christ, before they came to us, and many out of the hundreds who had enjoyed the privileges of our school, we had good reasons for believing, yielded their young hearts to the loving Savior's invitation while with us. With the undying interests of the youth so near my heart, it was a trial to have our school suspended a year; but what could I do? I must keep up the ten per cent interest on three hundred dollars of my indebtedness, and could not contract five hundred dollars more to finish the institution building erected on the acre of ground I had given for that object. It was enclosed, and a portion of the floors laid, and doors and windows cased. This had cost over one thousand dollars for a building thirty by fifty-six feet.

As the farm was still carried on by my married children, I concluded to return to Cincinnati and engage in nursing the sick during the cold season, as the cough to which I was subject was returning. All things considered, the conclusion was reached to suspend Raisin Institute one year at least. An Oberlin scholarship was presented me for my daughter Laura Jane, who decided to take a gentleman's collegiate course. Not only my financial pressure seemed to direct toward that more southern field, but the cause of those who were thirsting for liberty, and were almost daily leaving boats or crossing the river, was also a strong incentive to occupy a post near the Southern end of the road whose Northern terminus was in Queen Victoria's dominions.

Many of my friends thought me presuming to venture so near those who had threatened my life repeatedly, and in the hand-bills of the Tennesseans (report said) there was offered $3,000 reward for my head. Thomas K. Chester stated in a letter that he had sent them to a number of the Southern States, to let them know what sort of sisters they had in the North. But J. F. Dolbeare, on the night before his death, called me to his bedside, and, taking my hand in his, said, "Sister Haviland, you have passed through close and trying places in your work, and your anti-slavery mission is not yet finished. Your trials are not over. Greater dangers are for you to pass through--I see it. O, may the Lord prepare you for the work he has for you to accomplish! He has sustained you thus far. He will grant you his protecting arm. I know it." I have often had occasion to remember the words I listened to in that solemn hour, during thirty years that have since passed.

A slave-owner from New Orleans, with his wife, three children, and their nurse, Maria, were bound for Cincinnati. When at Louisville, he was told if he was going to spend the Summer in Cincinnati he'd be sure to lose his servant-girl, "as that city is cursed with free negroes and abolitionists." At this unpleasant information, Champlin and his wife concluded to make their temporary home in Covington, instead of Cincinnati, to the great disappointment of Maria, as she and her husband had been over two years in saving all their little silver pieces, until the amount was one hundred dollars, which was to be used in taking her to Canada.

As this "Northern trip" had been calculated two or three years before, and as they went to no place without their faithful nurse, the slave couple also made their plans. Her husband told her, as she would have a good opportunity to secure her freedom, he would manage to secrete himself on some through boat, and meet her in Canada; and he could go with less money than she could, and insisted upon her taking all they had saved. But after Maria found they were going to hire rooms and board in a hotel in Covington, she went to the trunk that contained her clothes and the children's, and to her great disappointment her hundred dollars, that she had so securely tied in a little rag and rolled in her garments, was taken out by her mistress, who never pretended to go to her trunk for any thing, having no care whatever of her children's wardrobe. But she must hide her feelings by putting on a cheerful face, though she felt as though all her hopes of freedom, of which she had so fondly dreamed, were blasted forever.

She found her task, as usual, was to keep the wardrobe of her mistress and the children in order, and care for the children day and night. A few days elapsed, and she asked her mistress if she would please give her money to purchase herself a pair of shoes, as she heard they were cheaper here than at home. She said she would either get her shoes or give her the money in a few days; but neither shoes nor money came. Two and three weeks passed, and Maria ventured to repeat her request; but the reply was, "Your shoes are good enough for a while yet."

While her master and mistress were over the river, she frequently took the children to the river, to amuse them in looking at boats and in picking up pebbles on the bank, when her longing look was noticed by a white man, who ventured to ask her if she would like to go across the river. She told him, if she did, she had no money to give to any one who would take her. After learning that her master's residence was in New Orleans, he told her, if she would never let any one know that he had ever said or done any thing about helping her, let what would happen, he would take her over without any thing, in the night, whenever she could get away; but if it was ever known there it would ruin him. She promised; and as no one was near, and the three children playing at a little distance, he pointed her to a large root on the bank, under which she could hide, and there wait until she heard a low whistle near the root, when she could come out and step into a skiff without saying a word, and he would muffle the oars so as not to be heard, and take her to a colored family he knew over the river, where she would be safe until they would send her on to Canada.

"But how can I go on, when I's got no money?"

"They know of a way to send such people as you without money. You'll get with those over there who will see you safe; never fear."

"I never can tell you," she said, in relating her story, "how strange I felt about sich good news as this, and wondered if it could be true. I jus' trimbled like a popple leaf all the evenin'. Master and missus was over in the city to a lecture on Fernology, and didn't get back till twelve o'clock. I kep' the chillen awake later'n common, so they'd sleep sounder. Then I tied my clothes up in a tight bundle, an' had my shoes an' hat whar I'd lay han's on 'em, an' put out the light. I was snorin', when missus looked in an' said, 'All's asleep--all right;' an' I waited till the clock struck one, an' all still. I crep' sof'ly out on the street, and down to the root, an' waited for a whistle. The clock struck two. O, how long! Will that man come? Chillen may cry, an' missus fin' me gone. Had I better wait till it's three o'clock? May be he can't come. He said, if any thing happen he couldn't come to-night, I mus' go back, an' try another night. An' 'bout as I began to think I better go back come the whistle. I stepped in, an' we went over; but the clock struck three before we got half across, an' he was mighty fear'd he couldn't get back afore daybreak."

News reached us during the day that a woman crossed the river early, and was so near it as to be dangerous for a hiding-place; and it fell to my lot to see her in a safe place as soon as the darkness of night would shield us from being detected by Champlin and his aids, who were already seen at street corners. I took a black Quaker bonnet and a drab shawl and a plain dress-skirt in a market-basket, with which to disguise our fugitive.

I found her in a dark room, where I fixed her up for a walk; and she told me of her loss of the hundred dollars, but I told her all would be well without it. I instructed her to take my arm as we went, and take good care to limp all the way, for we should pass plenty of Kentuckians. Thickly veiled, we walked half a mile, turning short corners to elude watchers, if any, from our starting-point. As we went up Central Avenue to Longworth, we passed through a crowd, one of whom said:

"I'm going to line my pockets to-night. Thar's five hundred dollars reward out."

Said another, in a low tone, "When did she cross?"

"Last night some time, they say."

My Quaker sister, limping at my side, was trembling, I sensibly felt, as she hung upon my arm, as we listened to these remarks from her pursuers. I took her to a very intelligent colored family on Longworth Street, who were well known to us as true friends.

Although I had passed her pursuers without fear, yet when Levi Coffin informed me that Ruffin, the greatest slave-hunter in the city, had just moved next door to Burgess, where I left Maria, my fears were almost equal to Maria's. "Laura, thou hast left thy fugitive with a good family, but in a poor place," said our venerable friend. "But wait until to-morrow evening, when thou hadst better give her another move, as I know they will use all possible care." The following evening Levi and friend Hughes were to be on Central Avenue near Longworth Street, and as I came out with my Quaker woman, they were to walk half a block ahead and turn on Ninth Street to his house, and if sister Catherine's sign appeared on the balcony of the second story, we were to ascend the outside flight of steps, and take her up to the attic in the fourth story.

Champlin had doubled the reward, and was raving with rage over the loss of their nurse. He said he would have her if he had to "set one foot in hell after her," cursing and swearing in a perfect foam; and said a thousand dollars should be doubled but what he would have her. As the streets were too well lighted, to give her the appearance of a white person through the veil, I called for a saucer of flour, with which I thoroughly powdered her face. Before her veil was adjusted she happened to look up and saw herself in the large mirror before her, and burst into a laugh over her white face and Quaker bonnet. I gave her a shake as I placed my hands over her shoulders: "Don't laugh loud, for your liberty's sake. Remember the next door neighbor would get his thousand dollars reward from Champlin, if he could know you are here." "I won't look at that glass ag'in, I looks so quare."

I took her on the front walk, and following our previous plans, at the invitation of the white cloth on the balustrade, we soon found ourselves in the attic. She remained here two weeks, not daring to move in any direction, as the wealthy New Orleans planter's biped bloodhounds were seen and heard from in almost every direction through the city.

As there was in this case an unusual excitement, the editor of the Cincinnati Commercial inserted a little note in his paper, of the escape of the New Orleans nurse from her owners, who were boarding at White Hall Hotel in Covington; and that the mistress had taken one hundred dollars from the nurse previous to their arrival at their destination. The day following this notice Champlin came to the Commercial office and demanded the authority the editor had for charging his wife with stealing from their servant. For whether it was he or any one else, it would prove a dear job to vilify his wife like this, for he'd have their life or $3,000; and swore nothing short would settle it. He told the editor he would give him till ten o'clock the next morning, when he should come prepared for the settlement (referring to his pistols, which he knew how to use). At once Levi Coffin received a call from the editor for advice, as he was his informant. During this interview, Catherine came into our room, saying, "Laura, they are in a tangle with that New Orleans slave-holder, and they want thee to help straighten it." Going in, I was introduced to the editor, and main proprietor of the Commercial, and they related the difficulty.

"Now," said Levi, "this young man has invested in this firm all he is worth, and Champlin will probably ruin his business if he fails to give his authority for stating Maria's loss of her hundred dollars; and as I gave him these facts, in case he gives my name as authority, he will then come upon me, and make trouble, as Champlin seemed determined upon vengeance."

After a little reflection over these statements and threats I told them I did not see but I came next, as I told Levi these facts, which I took from Maria and the family where she was first secreted. And as I had no property in Ohio, and the little I owned in Michigan I had arranged to keep from slave-holders, I would stand in the gap and our young friend might refer to me as authority, if compelled to give it, rather than lose his life, or property even.

Said Levi, "This is liable to terminate in a serious affair. It would lay thee liable to imprisonment if he is so disposed, and thy children in Michigan would feel very sad over such an event."

I replied that I did not fear of remaining long in prison, neither did I believe he was going to be permitted to put me there, but at all events I was fully prepared to allow my name to be given. With this conclusion our young friend left us, saying that if he could manage that exasperated man without naming me, he would do so. We were all anxiously waiting to see the result of the fearful meeting at the hour of ten the following day. Champlin was there at the hour, with the stern query, "Are you ready, sir, to give me your authority, or abide the consequences?"

"I am, sir. The colored family where she first stopped informed us."

"Do you take a nigger's testimony?"

"Certainly I do. They are respectable and honest, though poor."

After pouring forth a volley of oaths, and saying he wouldn't stoop so low as to notice what a nigger would say, for they were all a pack of liars, he left the office, to the great relief both of the editor and ourselves. Very soon he came to us with the pleasing report, how those pistols, so full of powder, flashed in the pan.

But the slave-hunters were still so numerous, it was thought best to dress her up for another walk, and I took her to a family near Fourteenth Street, and wrote a letter in Maria's name to her master, dated it ahead, and from Windsor, Canada West, and sent it enclosed in a letter to a friend at that place, with directions to mail it to the master at the date I had given. Maria informed her master Champlin that Canada was not the cold barren country he had always told her it was, for they raised great fields of corn, and potatoes, peas and beans, and everything she saw in Kentucky; and that she had found the best of friends ever since she left home, and signed her name.

In less than two weeks Kitty Darun's niece came in great haste to inform us that "Champlin had got poor Maria, and Aunt Kitty is nearly crying her eyes out over the sad news that a colored man brought over last night."

"That is all a mistake."

"Oh, no, it's no mistake, for that colored man worked near White Hall yesterday, and he said the report was just flying."

I hushed her loud words, and whispered, "I can take you to Maria in ten minutes, I know just where she is."

"Are you sure, and may I go tell Aunt Kitty?"

"Go and whisper it, for there are but few friends who know she is still in the city, because of the close search made for her, that is still kept up."

The next day she came to us with another story, "That he didn't get Maria, but got a letter from her in Canada. And that was the current report."

I told her, "I understood that too, and would tell her all within a few weeks."

The result of this letter was a withdrawal of all the hired hunters within twenty-four hours, and during three days' quiet two young men came from a few miles distant across the river, who got the privilege of a holiday, and of spending it nearly ten miles farther from the river than was their home. As they left the night before, they would have until the next morning before being missed.

As Cazy (one of our vigilance committee) came before sunrise to inform us of the new arrival, Catharine Coffin came to my bed-room and gave me a call: "Come, Laura, here are more runaways; Cazy is here and they want thee." In less than five minutes there were four of us to decide on the plan of securing the newcomers and the one on our hands. "What shall we do? Our funds are out, we haven't a dime in our treasury," said Cozy.

"We must get enough to take then; two young men and Maria out as far as the Stubbs settlement to-night," I replied; "for you see all is quiet now over Maria, and by to-morrow the city will fill up again with slave-hunters."

"That is what I told Cazy before thou came in; but he says he has a job on his hands he can not leave," said Levi.

"Where Is Hughes?"

"I don't believe I could get him to leave his work to see to it; but may be he'll go for you," wild Cazy.

"I'll try." And throwing on my shawl and bonnet, called on Hughes, and told him he must go and take Maria and two young men who had just arrived this morning.

"But what can we do without money?"

"I'll get it to-day. What amount is wanting?"

"It will take eight dollars to hire a close carriage and team to go thirty miles to-night, and I must be back to my work by eight o'clock tomorrow morning."

"I'll have that ready before night."

"Then I'll call at Uncle Levis's at noon, and see whether you are sure of success in getting the money; then I will call at the livery on my return to my work and engage the carriage and team, to be ready by seven and a half o'clock this evening."

When he called at noon I had four dollars in money and a traveling suit for Maria, and knew just where I could get the balance. Now for the plan of starting. I told him he must manage the two men and I would manage for Maria. "But there are two toll-gates that are closely watched for colored people, and I want you to go with us past those gates, as two white persons in front would pass the load; not seeing any colored people, they would make no inquiries. As Catherine's health was poor, and cholera was raging in the city, she was not willing I should remain away over night, and Levi secured William Beckley to follow us a little distance behind until we had passed those gates, when I was to return with him. The carriage, with our company, was to be driven up Central Avenue as far as the orphan asylum, and halt for Maria and myself; and as he passed the street she was on, Hughes was to take out his white pocket handkerchief and wipe his face, while William Fuller, at whose house Maria was secreted, was to walk on the street at the time appointed to watch for the signal; when discovered, as he turned toward the house, we were to step out on the street, and walk the half block where our carriage was in waiting."

But in this we found it necessary to adopt my old rule of being carelessly careful, as there were Kentuckians in their rented houses each side of William Fuller's, and they were overheard to say three days before, that they believed they had "niggers hid at Fuller's, for the blinds in the second story hadn't been opened in two weeks." The weather being warm, and the rising of the full moon, and their next door neighbors sitting on their front porches, all combined to bring us into full view. As we were watching for the moment to start Maria took up her bundle of clothes; but I told her the least appearance, aside from common callers, would create suspicion, and we must send them after her. "But they's all I got, an' I will never see 'em ag'in," said Maria, sorrowfully.

"But your liberty is of more value than a cart load of clothes."

"Oh, yes, I knows it; but I can't even change."

"Hand them to me," and they were opened and tightly rolled into the shape of a six months' baby in a trice; and, as I rolled it in a shawl, I said, "I'll carry the baby myself." The watchful wife says, "William is turning back, and I will walk to the corner with you." As we reached the gate, the neighbors in full view, sister Fuller's little girl called, "Mamma, I want to see the baby; I didn't know that woman had a baby." The frightened mother tried to hush her in a smothered voice, that I feared would betray her excitement. "Let her go with us, mother," said I. "But auntie hasn't time now to let little sis see the baby; wait till next time we call, because we are late, and our folks will be waiting for us." And as we leisurely walked along, sister Fuller invited us to come another time to make a longer call.

After turning the corner, our sister and little girl left us, and we quickened our pace to the carriage we saw in waiting. Friend Hughes stood by the hitching-post, but looked wild with excitement when he saw me turn to the carriage, as he knew there was no baby aboard; and as he had hitched in a darker place than near the entrance, he did not recognize us. But as I gave my baby a toss in the carriage, saying, "This is part of our company; take care of my baby," he recognized my voice. "O, yes; this is one of your tricks." Soon we were seated, and on our way. We passed the two fearful gates with a sharp look by each keeper, and half a mile beyond I proposed to return; but friend Hughes said there was a short piece of woods ahead to pass through, then the coast would be clear the balance of the way, and he would rather I would go through the woods with them. Just before entering the grove we heard the loud talking, singing, and laughing of ten or a dozen men we were going to meet.

As this boisterous company appeared before us, Hughes turned to the two men behind us, and said, "Are your pistols ready?"

"Yes, sah;" and each took from his own pocket a six-shooter.

"Boys, if those men attempt to take our horses by the bits, and I say, Fire! will you do it?"

"Yes, sah."

Said I, "Hughes, be careful, be careful. Your excitement will betray us if you are not very careful."

"We don't know what rabble we are going to meet, and I propose to be ready fur 'em."

"There is nothing known of this company, and I know we are safe."

"I don't know it; and if they make the first move to stop us, be ready, boys."

"All ready."

There were two six-shooters behind me, and one in the hand of Hughes, that I feared much more than all the slave-holders in Kentucky.

But we were soon relieved by the remark of one, as we were passing, "It was well we stopped that bent from falling, or't would have killed Smith as dead as a hammer." We found by this that they had been to the raising of a building, and a number of them were more than half drunk.

After going a mile or two farther, and our excitement was over, I took leave of our company, with a charge to keep quiet and all would be well, and returned to Levi Coffin's by twelve o'clock. The following morning we received a good report from our conductor, Hughes, of the safe delivery of this valuable freight in the Quaker settlement depot, where they were forwarded to Canada.

FUGITIVE SLAVES ASSISTED

THE exciting intelligence reached us that Clara and her three little ones were about to be captured by slave-holders in the city, on Pearl Street. I called on her at once, and found the house was surrounded the night before by strangers, who were followed to a hotel, and on the record the name of her master's son was found. Poor woman! She had passed through great suffering in making her escape with her two children; a third was born in Cincinnati--yet it too must share the antic-ipated fate of its mother. She had always been a house-servant, but found the death of her master was about to make great changes, he being deeply in debt. By the aid of a chambermaid she was secreted on a boat, and kept the two children drugged with opiates until she feared they would never come to life. But after her arrival, under the care of a skillful physician, they survived. She had found good friends among her own people and Church two years. I found her weeping, with the two youngest in her arms, the oldest sitting on a stool at her feet. With fast-falling tears she kissed her babes. "O ma's precious darlings, how can I spare you!" I told her if her master did not come for her until it was dark enough to conceal her, arrangements were made to come for her with a close carriage, to take them out of the city to a place of safety.

"I reckon you can't save us," she sobbed.

I told her we would pray the Lord, who knew all her deep sorrow, to open the way for us.

"Yes, I cried mightily to him to help me out o' that dark land back yonder, and it 'peared like he did bring me out; but if I had stuck closer to him I reckon he'd kep' me from this hard trial;" and fresh tears freely flowed.

With my hands on her shoulders, my tears mingled with hers. In broken sentences, she referred to the separation of her husband when he was sold and taken down the river.

I left her, with a heavy heart, yet strong hope that her young master (as she called him) would be defeated.

At twilight, I called to assist in getting them ready to jump into the carriage that our friend William Fuller would drive to the door within fifteen minutes; and being ready, we were in the carriage turning the first corner within a minute, and left them in charge of an underground railway agent, who took them on his train as soon as their clothing and pocket-money were forwarded to them, to the great relief of many anxious hearts.

A little past nine o'clock, her master and his posse surrounded the house, and lay in wait until the stillness of the midnight hour was thought most favorable to pounce upon their prey and hurry them to the river, where they had a boat in waiting for them. Then their force was increased, and an entrance demanded. The owner of the house (a colored man) refused admittance without legal authority, although threats of breaking down the door or windows were made; but they were resisted with returning threats of shooting the first man that dared to enter without proper authority. As they were expecting an attack, the women had left their home for the night. The watch was kept around the house until morning approached, when the marshal, with his official papers, was brought to claim Clara and three children. But to their great disappointment, in searching the house, no Clara or children were there. In great rage her master left, swearing vengeance upon him who had kept them in suspense all night when he had spirited them away, for he knew he had harbored his property in his house; but all the reply he received was, "Prove it, if you wish." They got no track of them until they heard from them in Canada.

A fugitive by the name of Jack secreted himself on a large steamer from the lower Mississippi, and left it on landing in Cincinnati. Being so far from his old home, he hired himself as a barber, in which business he was very successful about two years, when his master learned of his whereabouts. He made the acquaintance of a free colored man by the name of Robert Russel, who was an idle, loafish mulatto, sometimes working at little jobs in Cincinnati, and also in Covington. In the latter place he fell in with the slave-holder, who was watching for an opportunity to secure the aid of some one who would induce Jack to come to the river, where he would hurry him onto the ferry, and get him on the Kentucky side, when he could easily return him to the far South. As he found Robert Russel a man of no principle, he gave him ten dollars if he would decoy Jack to the wharf of

Walnut Street landing about noon, when men were generally at dinner. He succeeded, when the master with his Kentucky friends slipped hand-cuffs on poor Jack, and took him on the ferry for a thief. The more Jack protested, denying the charge, the louder they cried thief! thief! Some of his colored friends consulted their favorite lawyer, John Jolliffe, about arresting Jack's master for kidnapping, as he had taken him illegally, but they were told they could do nothing with him in Kentucky. They were compelled to leave their friend to his fate.

But the Judas who betrayed Jack ought to be brought to justice; but how could they do it? As I was at that time teaching a school of colored girls, in the basement of Zion Baptist Church, a number of colored men came to consult with me. I told them as Robert Russel was a renegade he was as liable to serve one side of the river as the other, and would as readily bring a slave to the Ohio side for ten dollars, as to decoy him back into the hands of his master for that money. They said Robert did not dare come into Cincinnati, fearing that justice would be dealt out in tar and feathers by the colored people. They learned soon after be came to the city that he ran away from Ripley to avoid being arrested for stealing. I advised them not to take the law of tar and feathers, as they had indicated, in their own hands; but to spoil the petting he was getting from the slave- holders across the river, by warning them against Robert Russel, for he would as readily play the rogue one side as the other; and this they could do in a little printed card that might be dropped on the sidewalk through a few streets in Covington, and they would run him out of their town in a hurry. This idea pleased them, and they wished me to draft the card, and they would print and circulate it. I told them I would take my noon recess to prepare it, and at 4 o'clock my school would be out, and they might come for it. I gave it as follows:

> Slave-Holders of Kentucky!
> BEWARE OF THE ROGUE, ROBERT RUSSEL!

Who absconded from Ripley, Ohio, to evade the strong arm of the law he richly deserved for misdemeanors in that town. This man is a light mulatto, and betrayed one of his race for ten dollars, in Cincinnati, bringing him into life-long trouble. He will as readily take ten dollars from any of your slaves to bring them to Cincinnati, and again take ten dollars to return them to you, as he has no higher purpose to serve than paltry self. A LOVER OF RIGHT.

This was printed on a placard of ten by twelve inches. They procured two hundred for distribution, but found it more difficult to get a distributor than they anticipated. I told one of them to go to Levi Coffin's and inform him and his wife where I was going after my school was dismissed, and that I would distribute them through Covington, but to let no one else know of it, except their committee who secured the printing, as it would produce increased excitement. I went a mile from the river before commencing my work, and left one or two in every yard, when no eye seemed directed toward me, I dropped them by the street side until I reached the ferry that returned me to my anxious friends in Cincinnati, just as the sun dropped behind the Western hills.

The following day report gave an account of the evening's excitement in Covington. A company of slave-holders met to consult over this placard, and the conclusion was reached to give Bob Russel until nine o'clock the following morning to leave the State or take the consequences. Two slaves had left them within a couple of months, and they charged him with taking them over the river. Some of the more excitable were for hauling him out of bed at the close of their meeting (ten o'clock), and dealing summary vengeance for their recent losses, but as he pledged himself to leave their State the next morning never to return, they left him to his own uncomfortable reflections.

A party consisting of four, from New Orleans, came to Cincinnati to spend the Summer, and made their home at a hotel. It was soon ascertained by the colored people that their little nurse girl of about nine years of age, was a slave, and as the master and mistress had brought her there, she was by the laws of Ohio free. They took the opportunity to coax her away and place her among their white friends, who they knew would take good care of her. Very soon there was great inquiry for Lavina. They said she was just a little pet they brought with them to play with and mind the baby, and they knew she was stolen from them against her will; but that if they could get sight at her, she would run to them, unless she was forcibly held back by some mean person. Diligent search was made among the colored people whom they suspected, but no clew could be found of her whereabouts. They were then advised to visit some prominent abolitionists, where they were satisfied she had been taken. So close to Elizabeth Coleman's were they watching, that she felt unsafe, fearing they might come in and find her alone with her little pet fugitive, so she took her to Samuel Reynold's by night.

The search continued. Samuel met the master on the street in front of his house, but had left orders to dress Lavina in his little boy's suit; and holding the master in conversation awhile, he said he would call for Jim, to bring them a glass and pitcher of water, having already told his wife to give Jim a few necessary instructions hew to appear very smart and active. As she came out to give them drink, Samuel gave the master and his two friends a few lessons in Ohio law, informing him that all slaves brought into the State by their owners were free. The master contended that it would be very cruel to keep Lavina from her mother (who belonged to him), and he knew if he could be allowed to see her it would be sufficient to convince them of her attachment to him, and promised to leave the child to her own choice. "But," said Samuel, "Lavina is on our underground railroad." This was as new to the New Orleans slave-holder as were the Ohio laws he had been explaining. After discussing the right and wrong of his claim, Samuel called to his wife to send Jim with a pitcher of water; and out came the little fellow. "Pour a glass of water for this gentleman, Jim;" and their heated discussion continued. The master took the glass from Jim, who looked him full in the face, with one hand in his pocket, while Samuel was serving the other two gentlemen with a glass of water. The women in the house were filled with fear, as they deemed Samuel rather imprudent. But Jim returned with pitcher and glass, and the master and his friends went back to the hotel none the wiser, either of Lavina's whereabouts or of the operation of this new kind of railroad. Lavina was well cared for, and her master and mistress returned to New Orleans with a new experience, minus a nurse girl.

Another fugitive, by the name of Zack, came across the river from Virginia into Ohio. He had lain in the woods by day, and traveled by the North Star at night, when it was clear, but in rainy or cloudy weather he found he was as liable to go South as North. There had been much rain to impede his progress, and he suffered much from hunger. He had advanced only a few miles from the river, when he found a family of true friends, who replenished his clothing, and was preparing food for his journey, when his master, with eight other men, found out where he was, and came with officers to search the house and take their prey. They came in the night and demanded entrance. "Wife, what shall we do? There are men under every window."

"Let them search the two lower rooms first, and while you go with them you tell Zack to slip into my room while you are with them, and I'll see to him."

"But I tell you he can't be got out of this house without being caught."

"Go on; I know that." And he left her and gave the frightened man his orders. But before he reached her room she rolled up the feather-bed and drew the straw mattress to the front side of the bedstead, and told Zack to jump in. Her oder obeyed, she threw back the feather-bed, and before the master and officer entered her room she was occupying the front side of the bed. The clothes-press, wardrobe, and under the bed were all closely scrutinized. The husband, pale with excitement, was expecting, in every place they searched, that poor Zack would be found. But they all left satisfied that he was not in that house, though so very sure they had found the right place. The noble woman said he shook with fear, so as to make the bed tremble during the search, knowing but too well his sad fate if he should again fall into the hands of his master. Every necessary measure was taken to hasten his progress to Canada.

In December, 1852, Calvin Fairbanks, who had served a term of three years in the Kentucky penitentiary for aiding slaves to escape, called at Levi Coffin's and informed me of a letter he had received, giving information that an interesting slave woman in Louisville, Kentucky, could cross the river, if a friend would meet her at Jeffersonville, Indiana, and take her to a place of safety; and he proposed to be the conductor. I advised him, by all means, not to go so near Kentucky, as he was so well known through that State. He said he expected we would oppose him. I advised him to consult with Dr. Brisbane, as Levi was absent. But he chose to keep the matter quiet, and went on his dangerous expedition. I was called away to College Hill as nurse, and in three weeks, when I returned to Levi's, he called me into the store, saying, "We have a letter for thee to read; somebody is in trouble, and Samuel Lewis, Dr. Brisbane and myself have been trying to find out who it is, but can make out nothing by the letter. The signature is of stars, that he says is the number of letters in the name, but we can make nothing of it;" and he handed me the letter, dated from Louisville jail.

As soon as I counted the six stars in the first name, I said, "Levi, it is Calvin Fairbanks! Read out the last line of stars, and we'll find Fairbanks."

At this point Dr. Brisbane entered the store.

"Doctor," said Levi, "Laura has found our riddle; she says it is Calvin Fairbanks."

Both were astonished, not knowing he was down the river. I told them of his call in Levi's absence, and of his errand.

"Poor man, how he will suffer, for they will soon find him out, and they are so very bitter against him, I fear he will die in their penitentiary, for they will have no mercy on him," said the doctor.

"He sends us an appeal for help, but I see no way we can render him assistance," responded Levi.

A few weeks later a colored man, who had been mistaken for a slave, was released from that jail. He came to us telling of the suffering the prisoners endured, having no bed but a pile of filthy straw in their cells; and that Calvin requested him to see his friends, and tell us he must perish unless a quilt and flannel underclothing were furnished him; and he also needed a little pocket money. No one dared to take these articles to him, for only two weeks previously a man by the name of Conklin had brought the wife and four children of an escaped slave into Indiana, and was captured in the night. All were taken to the river, and the poor woman and her children returned to their owner, without her meeting the husband and father, who had sent for them. Conklin was bound with ropes and thrown into the river, where he was found a few days after. Four weeks before Williams, from Massachusetts, followed two little mulatto girls who were stolen from their free-born parents by a peddler, and found them near Baltimore, Maryland. As soon as his errand was made known a baud of ruffians lynched him.

These two cases of murder, without the semblance of law, had produced much excitement in the North, and now the Fairbanks case was increasing the exasperation of the South. But here was a suffering brother in prison. A few days of earnest prayer determined me to go to Louisville jail with a trunk of bed clothes and under flannels. I looked for strong opposition from my friends, but to my surprise when I proposed the plan to my friends Levi and Catherine Coffin, they favored my project. Catherine did her full share in furnishing a trunk, a thick comfortable and pillow; others soon brought a change of flannels; and as Levi met friends and made known my project of going to Louisville, the mites were brought to the amount of fourteen dollars for Calvin, and enough to bear my expenses. Levi saw Captain Barker, who possessed an interest in the line of packets running to Louisville, and he offered half fare, and promised to send for me in time for the Ben Franklin, No. 2, to leave for Louisville the next day at 2 P. M.

Dr. Brisbane, on returning from an absence of a few days, told Levi not to allow so rash a move, and said that I must not go to Louisville in this excitement, for it was dangerous in the extreme; and he referred to Conklin's fate, that was just as likely to be mine. This so discouraged Levi, that he said, "It may be we have been too fast in giving thee words of encouragement." My reply was, "I find no geographical lines drawn by our Savior in visiting the sick and in prison."

Here was a suffering brother, who had fallen among thieves, and I felt it my duty to go to his relief. There seemed also a clear answer to prayer that I should be protected; and if time would allow me to call on Dr. Brisbane before I left for the boat, I would do so, as I desired to see him.

"If thou art going, I advise thee not to call on the doctor, as I know how he feels about thy going, and all thy reasons will not satisfy him in the least."

I told him if the doctor or any one else would go, I should feel easy to give it up, but otherwise I could not.

During this conversation Melancthon Henry came in, as he said, "with his mite" of three silver dollars for brother Fairbanks. He said, "You are going into the lion's den, and my prayer is that you may be as wise as a serpent and harmless as a dove. I know the venom of the serpent is there in power, but God will give his children the wisdom without the poison." Melancthon was a son of Patrick Henry, who had emancipated him with his slave mother. He was a member of the Wesleyan Methodist Church, to which I was at that time attached.

Soon after Captain Barker sent for me, and told me to refer Colonel Buckner to him in presenting my note of introduction, as he was favorably acquainted with the colonel and he should mention me as one of his friends.

Arrived at Louisville about day-dawn, I took a hack, and ordered the hackman to place the trunk on the porch of the front entrance of the jailor's residence. As the colonel's wife answered the door-bell, I inquired for Colonel Buckner. She stepped back to call him, when in an undertone I heard, "Who is it?" "I don't know; she came in the hack and is genteelly dressed, and I think came from the boat."

He "genteelly" met me, took Captain Barker's letter of introduction, and then introduced me to his wife and daughter, and to his wife's sister from Boston, who was there on a visit with her daughter, making quite a lively social circle. My errand was immediately made known, and the colonel excused himself for overhauling the trunk to take its contents to Calvin at once, as it was in the line of his duty as keeper of the prison to examine every thing brought in for prisoners; not that he expected to find anything improper for Fairbanks to receive. I told him I designed returning to Cincinnati on the same boat I came on, and it was going out at 4 P. M.

"Why go so soon?" he asked.

I replied, "My errand here is accomplished, when I see that these things are delivered to Calvin Fairbanks; and as I have a little pocket change, sent by his friends in Cincinnati, I would like to see Calvin, as I shall write his mother after my return."

"I will see if the sheriff thinks it best. There was a great excitement in the city when Fairbanks was arrested and brought here, and Shotwell, the injured man who lost his servant Tamor and her child, is very much enraged, and being a man of wealth and influence here, I dare not take you in to see Fairbanks on my own responsibility; but I'll see the sheriff, and if he says you can see him it is all right."

With a little note from me he took the trunk of things to Calvin, and brought back a receipt. As he handed it to me he said, "I suppose you will recognize his handwriting, so you'll know it's from him?"

I replied that I had seen a note of his writing, but was not familiarly acquainted with it, but was perfectly satisfied with the receipt.

He said he had been to see the sheriff, but he was absent, and would not return for two or three days, "and I think you had better wait," he continued, "and see him, as you can remain with us; it shall not cost you a cent."

I told him my friends in Cincinnati would be at the wharf to meet me the following morning; and as I had nothing further to accomplish, being satisfied that the things and money had been received by Calvin Fairbanks, I felt free to return. But he urged still harder.

"It will be too bad for you to return without seeing him, as you are the only friend that has called to see him since he has been here; and I know he wants to see you, for he asked if you were not coming in to see him, and I told him I was waiting to see the sheriff; and I think you had better wait till the boat makes another trip, as your stay here is as free as air, and we would like you to stop over; then you can see the sheriff, and I reckon he will not object to your going in to see Fairbanks, and yet I dare not take you in without his approval."

I at length consented. They were all very polite, and I rested as sweetly that night as if in my own room at Levi Coffin's, or in my own Michigan home. The next day the colonel was very free to talk of the false ideas of Northern people about slavery; spoke of Elizabeth Margaret Chandler's work on slavery, that I took from their center table; said his wife's Boston friends sent it her, but "it was nothing but a pack of lies."

I told him that she lived and died neighbor to me, and I esteemed her as a noble woman.

"But she never lived in the South, and had no right to judge of their condition without the knowledge of it."

I was introduced to a young man who he said had been suffering a few days' imprisonment under false charges, but on the examination, had that day, was found not guilty. As the family withdrew from the parlor, this young man seemed very anxious to deliver a secret message from Fairbanks to me; he said he had made a confidant of him, and told him to request me to see to forwarding Tamor's trunk of valuable clothing to a place of safety. He then told me the mark on the trunk, and the place in Louisville where it was waiting to be forwarded. I said that I had told the colonel I had no idea of Tamor's whereabouts, as I had supposed she was taken with Fairbanks until informed to the contrary; and that I had no business here whatever, aside from bringing a few articles for his present relief.

After being absent awhile, he returned with a note purporting to be from Calvin, inquiring whether I had made the acquaintance of persons therein named. I told the bearer I had not, and if he saw Calvin he could tell him so. He urged me to send Fairbanks a note, as the colonel or any one else should know nothing of it; but I refused, becoming satisfied that he was more of a dispatch-bearer for the colonel than for Calvin Fairbanks. I learned afterwards that this was true, and that he was released for the purpose of getting hold of additional evidence with which to convict him, and perhaps convict myself also.

In the evening a gentleman of their city made a call on the family, and to him I was introduced. He spent an hour or two in conversation with myself and the others. The jailer, Colonel Buckner, told me just before I left that their city papers--Louisville Courier and Louisville Commercial--inserted a notice to the effect that "Delia Webster, from Cincinnati, is here, and is quartered for a few days in the city." This little notice created much excitement; and as the gentleman alluded to knew Delia Webster personally, the colonel brought him in to make my acquaintance and report accordingly. As he passed out of the parlor, he told the colonel he might rest assured that lady was not Delia Webster, and they had nothing to fear from this Cincinnati lady, and he should set the editors right. All this excitement was carefully kept from me, as they wished to keep me as long as they possibly could, hoping to glean some additional evidence against Fairbanks, although the jailer told me they had sufficient evidence to convict Fairbanks for a term of twenty-five or thirty years at least, as this was the second offense, and he had no doubt but that he had been guilty of many others. The papers next day came out with a correction, "that it was not Delia Webster, but Mrs. Haviland, from Cincinnati; and, as abolitionists generally went in pairs, she had better keep a lookout, or she, too, would find an apartment in Colonel Buckner's castle."

Delia Webster was arrested near the time of Calvin Fairbanks's first arrest, and for the same offense, and sentenced to the same penitentiary, but in six weeks was pardoned.

The colonel was disposed to spend much time in discussing the merits, or rather demerits, of abolition principles, which seemed to be a new theme for this Methodist class-leader and jailor. He said:

"I want to convince you that you abolitioners are all wrong, for you go against colonization, and you can't deny it; and if there was ever a heaven-born institution it is colonization."

"Do you claim that God has conferred the prerogative to a man or set of men to draw a line, and say to you or me. 'You shall go the other side of that line, never to return?'".

"O no, that is a different thing. We belong to a different race."

"Whatever privilege you claim for yourself or I claim for myself, I claim for every other human being in the universe, of whatever nation or color. If the colored people choose to go to Africa. I have no word to say against their removal; it is their right and their privilege to go. And if they wish to go to any other part of our world they have the same right with me to go."

"O no, not to Canada; for you have no idea of the trouble it makes us. We expend thousands of dollars in preventing our slaves from going there."

"That is the defect in your policy. It is the existence of your system of slavery that makes you all this trouble." "As I told you of Miss Chandler, so it is with you, because you never lived in a slave State, and know nothing of their contented and happy condition. They have no care; if they are sick the doctor is sent for, and they are as tenderly cared for as our own children, and their doctor's bills are paid. I know if you would live here a few months you'd see these things very differently. You would see our slaves marching out to their work, singing their songs and hymns as merrily as if they'd never had a troubled thought in their heads. Here's my wife, born and raised in Massachusetts, and now she thinks as much of our institution of slavery as any of us who are raised here."

"If your slaves are so happy and contented, why do they make you so much trouble in their effort to reach Canada?"

"O, there's free niggers enough to be stirring up the devil in their heads; for their notions are not fit to mingle with our servants. And there's the good the colonization of these free negroes is doing. I know of one man that manumitted two of his slaves on purpose to have them go to Africa as missionaries; and there is the design of Providence in bringing those heathen negroes here to learn the Gospel plan by Christ, to save the dark and benighted heathen of their own country. We have reports from the two missionaries that I told you were set free for that object, and their master sent them off to school a year or more to fit them for their work."

"But why not give them all an opportunity of educacation, to enable them to read the Bible and books and papers. That would improve the race at home; and instead of sending them off, as you say, they would be preachers here among their people."

"I tell you that wouldn't amount to any thing, as there are but few that can learn any thing but work, and that they are made for. Their thick skulls show that they can't learn books; and if you knew as much about them as I do you'd see it too, but you are such an abolitioner you won't see it."

I told him I had seen colored people in the North who were well educated and intelligent.

"O yes, there are a few who can learn, but I speak of the race. They are different from us, you know. Not only their skin is black and hair curled and noses flat, but they stink so."

"But here is your house-servant, Mary, preparing your meals, setting in order your parlor and private rooms, and waiting on the persons of your wife and daughter--and her hair is as short and skin as black and nose as flat as any you'll find; and yet this disagreeable smell only troubles you in connection with the principle of freedom and liberty."

"You are such an abolitioner there's no doing any thing with you," he rejoined, and left the room.

He soon returned, and said:

"There's another thing I want to talk with you about, and that is amalgamation. If you carry out your principles, your children would intermarry with negroes; and how would you feel to see your daughter marry a great black buck nigger?"

"That is the least of my troubles in this lower world," said I. "But as far as amalgamation is concerned, you have twenty cases of amalgamation in the South to one in the North. I say this fearless of contradiction; it is a fruitful product of slavery. There are hundreds of slaves held as property by their own fathers. You'll find it wherever slavery exists. You find it here in your own city, Louisville."

Giving a shrug of his shoulders, he replied, "I will acknowledge this is a sorrowful fact that can not be denied."

This ended his talk on that subject.

After supper we were all enjoying a social chat before a blazing grate in the dining-room, and I was sitting near the kitchen door, that was ajar, where were their slaves in hearing. In their presence I had avoided answering some of his questions, but now a question was put within their hearing, which seemed to demand a square reply, and I gave it.

"I would like to know, Mrs. Haviland, where you abolitioners get your principles of equal rights. I'd like to know where you find them."

"We find them between the lids of the Bible. God created man in his own image--in his own likeness. From a single pair sprang all the inhabitants of the whole earth. God created of one blood all the nations that dwell upon the whole earth; and when the Savior left his abode with the Father, to dwell a season upon our earthly ball, to suffer and die the ignominious death of the cross, he shed his precious blood for the whole human family, irrespective of nation or color. We believe all are alike objects of redeeming love. We believe our Heavenly Father gave the power of choice to beings he created for his own glory; and this power to choose or refuse good or evil is a truth co-existent with man's creation. This, at least, is my firm conviction."

No reply was made, but, at his suggestion, we repaired to the parlor, where other conversation was introduced, but no reference made to Bible arguments.

During the time of waiting to see the sheriff the jailer's wife frequently spent an hour or two in social conversation. She said they never bought or sold a slave but at the earnest solicitation of the slave.

"Our black Mary was one of the most pitiable objects you ever saw. She was treated shamefully, and was put here in jail, where she lay three months, and was so sick and thin there wouldn't any body buy her. I felt so sorry for her I used to take her something she could eat, and I had her clothes changed and washed, or I reckon she would have died. She begged me to buy her, and I told Mr. Buckner that if she was treated half decent I believed she would get well. So I bought her and paid only four hundred dollars; and now you see she looks hale and hearty, and I wouldn't take double that for her. But there is poor black Sally, just four weeks ago today she was sold to go down the river in a gang, and I never saw any poor thing so near crazy as she was. She was sold away from her seven children. As I heard her screams I threw my bonnet and shawl on and followed her to the river, and she threw herself down on her face and poured out her whole soul to God to relieve her great distress, and save her poor children. Oh how she cried and prayed. I tell you no heart, not made of stone, could witness that scene and not melt. Many shed tears over poor Sally's prayer. A man standing by went to the trader and bought her, and went and told her that he lived only eight miles away, and had bought her, and she should come and see her children occasionally. She thanked him as he helped her to stand up, for she seemed weak. But in just two weeks from that day she died, and the doctors examined her, and said she died of a broken heart. They said there was no disease about her, but that she seemed to sink from that day, growing weaker and weaker until she died. That was just two weeks ago to-day."

Her eyes frequently filled with tears as she related this sad incident, and yet she could cheerfully say, "Oh, Mrs. Haviland, go with me into the kitchen to see my nigger baby." As we entered the kitchen there stood the mother by her fat, laughing baby, bolstered up in his rude cradle of rough boards. "There, isn't that a fine boy? he's worth one hundred dollars. I could get that to-day for him, and he's only eight months old; isn't be bright?"

"He is certainly a bright little fellow."

As I looked at the mother I saw the downcast look, and noticed the sigh that escaped a heavy heart, as she listened to the claim and price set upon her little darling. It's mother, Mary, was ebony black, her child was a light mulatto, which was in keeping with the story of abuse to which she was compelled to submit, or else lay in jail.

During the afternoon of Friday a Mr. Adams, from South Carolina, came to recognize and take his slave Jack. Said the colonel: "He was decoyed by an abolitioner, and now you can see what your principles lead to. There's Jack in the yard" (pointing toward the man). "His master has just been in jail with me and talked with Jack, and I let him out, and he's going around town with him to see if he can get his eye on the rogue that enticed him away. You see he's a great, stout, smart-looking fellow, and the rascal got sight at him, and saw him alone, and asked him if he wouldn't like to be free, and be his own master. He said he would. 'Then meet me at eleven o'clock by that big tree near the road yonder, and I'll take you with me to Canada, where you'll be a free man.' Jack met him at the place appointed, and they vent on till daylight, then hid till night, and traveled on. 'Now,' said this abolitioner if you will let me sell you in this little town ahead, I'll be around here till near night, then I'll go on to the next tavern (or I'll tell them so), but I'll stop in a little wood this side, and wait for you till eleven or twelve o'clock, and you can meet me, and I'll give you half I get for you, then well travel all night again, when we'll be out of reach of their hunting for you. Then we can travel by day-time, as you can call me master, and I'll call you my body-servant.' Jack was now fairly in his hands, and did as he directed. As he had divided the money with Jack he had confidence in this mean fellow, and thought he would take him on to Canada. He met him according to the plan, and, after traveling all night again, another proposition was made to sell him again, and he would again divide and give him half, which now amounted to a large sum for Jack. But this was not the end of sales; for he played the same game over and ewer, until they reached this city, when Jack was caught and put in jail. After he'd been here three days he told me all about it, and I took the money and wrote to Mr. Adams to come and get him. By the time that abolitioner got here he had sold Jack seven times, and divided with him every time. So, you see, that is just the fruit of your principles."

I patiently waited until he finished his story, with its charges, when it was my time.

"Colonel Buckner, I do not acknowledge this to be the work of an abolitionist, This was a selfish, unprincipled man; he was making himself rich, and probably was taking Jack down the river, and would have kept on selling him, and dividing, until he would have sold him for the last time, and then have taken from Jack all the money he had given him from these clandestine sales. I have no word of sanction to give to work like this; I should say his place was here in jail instead of Jack. If Jack had come to us hungry and naked, we should have fed and clothed him; and if sick with fatigue and footsore, we should have given him a ride toward Canada, if he wished to go there; but as for this man, I will not own him as an abolitionist. I repudiate his work altogether."

"Oh, yes, he told Jack he was an abolitioner."

"Then he was a hypocrite. I want to suppose a case for you to consider. Perhaps a fine appearing man comes into your city, attends your Methodist meetings, and calls himself a Methodist. He speaks well in your class meetings, speaks, prays, and sings in your prayer- meetings, and you became very favorably impressed with him as a Christian. He engages, perhaps, as clerk or bookkeeper in one of your large business houses across the street, and during three or six months appears so candid and punctual in all business transactions, that they confide to his care important business. But the opportunity arrives when he takes advantage of this confidence, and forges a draft of $3,000, and it is cashed, and he is off, never to be heard from again. Now as you learn of this dark deed, you have no idea of acknowledging that man as a Christian brother, have you?"

"Oh, no, certainly not; we expect and know there are hypocrites."

"So do we expect hypocrites in our abolition ranks; but because of counterfeit money we would not reject the true coin."

In the evening I was introduced to Mr. Adams, of South Carolina, with whom we all seemed to enjoy free and easy conversation. He was quite pleased to find his servant Jack, and a secret thought stole over me that he was also pleased to get with him two or three times his value in gold.

Sabbath morning Ben Franklin No. 2 packet came in, and I prepared to go to the boat, as the jailor said the sheriff had not yet returned from the country. Said the jailor:

"I don't like to have you leave without seeing Fairbanks, as you are the only friend who has called on him. I have a great mind to assume the responsibility of just taking you into the jail a few minutes before you go."

"I would thank you very kindly," I said, "if you think it prudent; but if not, I shall not urge you in the least."

"I reckon there can be no harm done. Come on, we'll go," and I followed him into the jail, and he called for Fairbanks.

I met him under circumstances that had caused such bitter prejudices against him that there was no shadow of probability that any thing like justice would be shown him. Besides, there were forty sad faces before me, of persons who, the jailer told me, had committed no crime, but were placed there for safe keeping, as they had been purchased in different places for the lower market. A gang was being prepared by a trader, and these were all shades, from the ebony black to those with fair skin, straight hair, and blue eyes, with hardly a vestige of African descent. With this scene before me, I could not restrain tears, neither were Calvin's eyes dry. As he held my hand in both of his, he said:

"Let us keep good courage. I think I shall be released after my trial. I want you to see my lawyer, Mr. Thruston; he says he will take my case through for six hundred dollars."

I told him I had no power to indemnify a lawyer. And after I received his note urging me to see him, I sent a note back by the keeper to that effect.

"But if you can see him, he may fall in his price two hundred or three hundred dollars. Don't leave without seeing him."

I told him I would have seen him if he had been in town on receiving his note, and yet I could see no important benefit in securing an interview with the lawyer, as his figures, unless greatly reduced, were beyond our reach in Cincinnati.

"Perhaps he may reduce them if you see him."

With these beseeching words, with tearful eyes that brought tears to the eyes of the colonel as well, the colonel said at once:

"I think you ought to comply with Fairbanks's request, and stay over one more trip. You can stop with us and be welcome. If you choose to call on

Dr. Field, as Fairbanks has suggested, you can do so; but I reckon it's your duty to see his lawyer."

Dr. Field was a practical abolitionist. Like Dr. Brisbane and James G. Birney, he emancipated his own slaves, and left Louisville on account of slavery, and made a home in Jeffersonville, on the Indiana side of the river.

As it was now ten minutes, double the time suggested by the jailer while we were on our way to the jail, I turned to the keeper, and told him as my interview was prolonged beyond its limit, I would go; and on taking leave of Calvin he pointed to four men standing a few feet from him, and said, "Do you know those men?"

I looked up and nodded to them a recognition. They were fugitives who had been recaptured by virtue of the fugitive slave law passed in 1850, some of whom had made their escape from slavery many years before. One, whose name was Baker, with whom I was well acquainted, had hair straighter and skin fairer than very many of our Anglo-Saxon race. These four answered to the nod, smiling through their tears. They had enjoyed a taste of freedom, and now were to be hurled back to a dark life of bondage more bitter to them than ever before. But not a word could I utter to them. The slight bow, as I was turning away, was all; and yet that was sufficient to set on fire a world of iniquity in the four officers in front of the iron grates through which we conversed with Calvin Fairbanks. These officers beckoned to the jailer as we were passing through to the outer gate, and upon his opening it, he said, "Will you please pass through the yard into our apartments alone?"

"Certainly," I responded; and turning to me, he remarked, "Those officers beckoned to see me a moment."

I drew my arm from his, that he had so politely tendered in going to and from Calvin. In passing through the yard I met their slave man, who said, in a low tone, "Did you see Fairbanks?"

I answered, in a like tone, "I did."

"Glory!" he cried, just loud enough for me to hear.

Near the door I was met by Mary, who said but little above a whisper, "Did you see him?" As I gave a nod, she said, "Good, good!" clapping her hands for joy.

I waited in the parlor for the return of the jailer, as he had said he would go to the river with me. He soon came in, pale and trembling with excitement.

"Mrs. Haviland, those officers are all boiling over with excitement. They wanted to know if I didn't see how just the sight of you was like an electric shock all over that crowd of slaves." "Didn't you see those four runaways cry at the sight of her?" said one of the officers. I told them my attention was all taken up with your conversation with Fairbanks, and noticed nothing of others.

"They say it is very evident that you are a dangerous person, and deserve to be here in this jail just as much as Fairbanks, and they are for arresting you at once; and I don't know, Mrs. Haviland, that it will be in my power to protect you. There have been threats in the papers every day since you've been here; and Shotwell has had his officers out hunting in every hotel for you; but we have kept it carefully from the public that you were with me, until now these officers are determined to arrest you."

Said I: "Colonel Buckner, should your officers come in this moment I have nothing to fear. The God of Daniel is here at this hour. Should I be arrested, you wouldn't keep me in your jail three days. I have no more fear than if I were in my own room in Cincinnati."

His trembling voice became quiet; and more calmly he said:

"Well, it is a glorious thing to feel like you do; but I reckon you'd better go over the river to Dr. Field's, and when Mr. Thruston comes into the city I'll send him over to see you. I advise you not to set foot on the Kentucky shore again, as I know it will not be safe. There is this morning a great excitement jail over town about you. So one of the officers told me. But I'll go to the river with you right soon."

We started for the door, when he halted: "I don't think I had better go with you now, as these officers may come out and make trouble, and I reckon you'd be safer alone."

"Very well, I have no hesitancy whatever in going alone;" and I bode him "good-bye."

As I was opening the door he reached his hand to return the "Good-bye -- God bless you!" and I left the jail and jailer.

I passed a large hotel, with perhaps fifteen or twenty men standing on the sidewalk in front. All seemed in a perfect buzz of excitement,-- When I saw this company of men, the first thought was to pass over on the other side. "But I will neither turn to the right nor the left, but pass through their midst," was an impression that I followed; and so busily engaged were they in their excited conversation that they hardly looked to see the little passer-by, the subject of their thoughts and words. Said one:

"Great excitement in town to-day."

"Yes, sir; you can see a group of men at every street corner."

I smiled to myself, as I thought, "Little do you think this is the little old woman you are troubling yourselves over."

I soon was in Jeffersonville inquiring for Dr. Field's residence, and was shown the house across the street, and upon its front porch stood a little group--the doctor and family, with two ministers--watching me; and as I opened the gate and inquired if this was Dr. Field's residence:

"Yes, I am the Jason," said the doctor. "We're been looking for you, Mrs. Haviland, every day since you've been in Louisville."

This was an unexpected salutation, and I felt at home again as I clasped their warm hands of friendship.

"How is it that you have knowledge of me?"

"Just walk in, and I'll show you the papers; haven't you seen them?"

I told him I had not, and knew nothing of it until just as I was leaving; the jailer told me there had been threats in the daily papers to arrest me. When I read these little scurrilous articles, calculated to inflame an already inflamed public, I wondered, as well as the doctor, that they had not found my whereabouts and made trouble. I hoped my Cincinnati friends had not seen this, as I had written them the reason of my delay, and sent the letter by the same boat that brought me to Louisville. I enjoyed sweet rest with these Christian friends, and attended with them their afternoon meeting. The minister who preached was as earnest an abolitionist as the doctor, and brother Proctor preached as radical an abolition sermon as I ever listened to; it seemed like an oasis in a desert.

The day following I sent a note to Lawyer Thruston's office, and received in reply the statement that his illness had prevented his leaving his room during two weeks past, and urged me to come and see him without delay, and he would stand between me and all harm. The doctor said, as he was a lawyer of influence in their city, he advised me to go; and as it was snowing a little, he gave me an umbrella, with which I might screen myself while passing the jail, as well as be sheltered from the snow. I found the lawyer very affable in his manners, and he said they would do the best they could for Fairbanks, and we might pay what we could. I returned without difficulty to our "Jason."

I wrote a little article under the caption of "Correction," and sent it to both the Commercial and Louisville Courier. It was inserted, with the following editorial note:

"Notwithstanding the pretended laudability of her errand to our city, we are still satisfied it was out of no good motive, as birds of a feather will flock together."

Most assuredly I was thankful to see the return of "Ben Franklin, No. 2," which took me from that nest of unclean birds to those of more congenial and harmless habits. My anxious friends in Cincinnati had not received either of any letters, and had read only these threatening cards in the Cincinnati Commercial, copied from Louisville dailies, that caused great anxiety. I sent a letter by both trips that this boat made during the week I was in Louisville, and Colonel Buckner took both and said he would sec them delivered at the boat.

While on the boat a gentleman and his wife among the passengers were returning to their Eastern home, with whom I formed a pleasant acquaintance. Among other topics of discussion was the value of hygiene and hydropathy, in which a Louisville physician joined, narrating his observations of the system during a practice of fifteen years in Louisville. As be seemed to be an intelligent and social gentleman, we all seemed to enjoy our new acquaintances. I remarked to him that there seemed to exist quite an excitement in his city during the week past, over an old lady who took a few articles of under- clothes and a quilt or two to Fairbanks.

"O, yes; were you in the city?"

"I was, and was surprised at the excitement produced by her presence."

"Well, I suppose Shotwell did make a great stir over his loss of a house-servant. I understand be spent three hundred dollars in his effort to find that woman, as be thought she knew where his slave was. I have forgotten her name."

"Mrs. Haviland, from Cincinnati, was the one threatened in your dailies," I replied.

"Ob, yes, that was the name. I heard you say you are going to Cincinnati; do you know any thing of that lady?"

"I do; I have been acquainted with her from childhood."

"You have! What sort of a lady is she?"

"Well, if you should see her, you wouldn't think it worth while to raise all this breeze over her, or any thing she could do. She is a little, insignificant looking woman, anyhow; and yet I think she is conscientious in what she does."

"There wouldn't have been such a stir but for Mr. Shotwell, who felt himself wronged in the loss of his house servant;"

"But he is considered one of your most influential citizens, I am told."

"Yes, madam; I reckon we'll have to excuse him, for he is quite nervous and angry over Fairbanks."

After quite a lengthy conversation on this subject, my new lady friend, to whom I had related a portion of my Louisville experience, was waiting for an opportunity to put a joke on the Louisville doctor, and called me by name. At this the astonished doctor said:

"I reckon this is not Mrs. Haviland, is it?"

"That is the name by which I am called."

"Is this indeed the lady we've been talking about, and of whose appearance you gave such a brilliant description?" And he laughed heartily. "Well, well, Mrs. Haviland, don't judge our city by this little flurry of excitement; for we have good, substantial people in our town, and I hope you'll visit our city again sometime, and you'll find it's true. I reckon if those excited men had arrested you, there would have rallied to your aid a different class of men; for your errand was perfectly proper, and you would have been borne out in it, too, by the more sensible people of our city."

But my Cincinnati friends were not so confident of my safety. Said Levi Coffin, as I met him, "Dr. Brisbane has said it was most likely that we should find thee in prison; and our friend, James G. Birney, is also very much discouraged, and said he was sorry thou went at this time of excitement, of both North and South, over the lynching of Williams near Baltimore, the binding of Conklin and throwing him into the river, and now the illegal capture of Calvin Fairbanks in Indiana, and taking him over into Kentucky and lodging him in jail there. But they have no regard or respect for law. As we knew all this, we have all been exceedingly anxious for thy safety."

It was a season of rejoicing with us all that our suffering brother in prison had received present relief; and no threats were put in execution in regard to myself. I realized an answer to prayer before I left for that prison, and not a moment while in Louisville did I in the least doubt the keeping power to be stronger than the power of darkness. Our friend, James G. Birney, being feeble in health, sent for me to spend a day in his family; and a rich feast I enjoyed in listening to the experience of that noble Christian man. Worthy was he to have presided over our nation.

Excitement does not cease, though the base is changed. Tidings came to us that fourteen newly-arrived fugitives were housed in the basement of Zion Baptist Church. I repaired at once to see what was needed for their journey, and found a very sick babe, two months old. The mother said it was very sick before they left, and she did not expect it to live, but their arrangements were made to go for freedom, and she would rather bury her child on the way than to stay behind till it left her. It died that night, and they were provided with a respectable coffin, and the company, with others, formed a funeral procession to the burying-ground. After the burial the thirteen fugitives were taken to the Quaker settlement, twenty-five miles distant, and from thence were forwarded to Canada. The colored members of our vigilance committee informed me that an infant died in that basement once before, and they took up a part of the floor and buried the child in the grave prepared for it, to avoid suspicion; for its parents were the slaves of a wealthy Kentuckian, who was making great efforts to capture the family.

CHRISTIAN AND EDUCATIONAL WORK

VERY many incidents of interest we must pass over; but, suffice to say, there was seldom a week passed without a slave or slaves leaving a boat or otherwise crossing the river in quest of freedom.

I met on the street a sister White, who was much distressed about her son, who was almost gone with consumption, and yet was unwilling to see any minister or religious person, to say any thing to him about a preparation for the change. "Do, please, go with me now to see my dying son Harvey. May he'll listen to you."

I went to her house, and found him too weak to talk much. The mother introduced me as her friend who had called on her. I took his emaciated hand, and said, "I see you are very low and weak, and I do not wish to worry you with talking, but you have but little hope of being restored to health I should judge from your appearance."

He turned his head on his pillow as he said, "I can never be any better--I can't live."

"Then your mind has been turned toward the future, and may the enlightening influence of the Holy Spirit lead you to the Great Physician of souls, who knows every desire of the heart, and is able to save to the uttermost, even at the eleventh hour." I saw the starting tear as he looked earnestly at me, while I was still holding his feverish hand in mine. "Will it be too much for you, in your weak condition, if I should read to you a few of the words of our Lord and Savior?"

"O no, I'd like to hear you."

I opened to John xiv; and upon reading a few verses I saw that the impression made was deepening, and asked if it would worry him too much if I should spend a few moments in prayer.

"O no, I'd like to hear you pray."

Placing my hand on his forehead, I implored divine aid in leading this precious soul to the cleansing fountain, and that his faith might increase, and in its exercise be enabled to secure the pearl of great price.

As I arose from his bedside, he reached out both hands for mine, and said, "I want you to come to-morrow." He wept freely; and I left with the burden of that precious soul upon my heart.

The mother and sister, who were both professors of religion, stood near the door weeping for joy over the consent of the dear son and brother to listen to the few words of reading and prayer.

The day following I met the sick man again, and as soon as I entered his mother's room she said, "O, how thankful we are to God for this visit to my poor boy! He seems in almost constant prayer for mercy. Early this morning he spoke of your coming to-day."

As I entered his room he threw up both hands, saying, "God will have mercy on poor me, won't he?"

"Most certainly," I responded; "his word is nigh thee, even in thy heart, and in thy mouth."

"Do pray for me," he requested.

I read a few words from the Bible, and followed with prayer, in which be joined with a few ejaculations. I left him much more hopeful than on the previous day.

The next morning his sister came for me in great haste, saying, "Brother Harvey wants to see you, quick."

It was not yet sunrise; but I hastened to obey the message, as I supposed he was dying. Not a word passed between us until we reached her brother's room. Upon opening his door he exclaimed, "Glory, glory to God, Mrs. Haviland! Come to me quick, I want to kiss you; for God brought me out of darkness this morning about the break of day. O hallelujah! Glory to Jesus! He shed his blood for poor me; and I shouted louder than I could talk for a good many days. O, how I wish I had strength to tell every body that I am happier in one minute than I ever knew in all my life put together!"

He became quite exhausted in shouting and talking, and I advised him to rest now in the arms of the beloved Savior.

"Yes, I am in his arms. Glory to his name for what he has done for me! I want you to see my cousin George; he is sick, and not able to come to see me to-day."

I told him I would within a few days, and left him, with his cup of salvation overflowing.

About two hours before he died he looked at his mother, smiling, and said, "There's Mary; don't you see her, standing at the foot of my bed?"

"No, my son, mother don't see her."

"O, how beautiful she looks! It seems as if you must see her," and he looked very earnestly at the object. "There, she's gone now." Fifteen minutes before he breathed his last he said, "Here she is again, and so beautiful! Mother, can't you see her?"

"No, son, I can't see her."

"Beautiful, beautiful she is. There, she's gone again." Just as the soul took its flight, he upraised both hands, with a smile, and said, "Here she is, with two angels with her. They've come for me;" and the hands dropped as the breath left him, with the smile retained, on his countenance.

The sister Mary, that died a number of years previously, was about four years old; and his mother told me she had not heard her name mentioned in the family for months before Harvey's death.

My time was fully occupied in caring for the sick and dying, as cholera had become very prevalent and fatal. Among the many who died with that disease were Levi and Catherine Coffin's daughter Anna, about ten years of age, and a lady, the mother of three children, whose dying request was that I should take charge of her children until the return of their father, who was in California.

A few weeks passed, and my promise to Harvey White was forgotten, until one morning it rushed upon me with such force that I trembled. I hastened to see him, and, to my surprise, he too was very near to death with consumption, and without hope. His mother was a widow, also an earnest Christian; but her son George would not allow her or any of the ministers of her acquaintance to talk with him on the subject of religion. But he was glad to hear that his cousin Harvey had died so happy; and she thought if I should tell him about Harvey he would listen to me. He could speak but little above a whisper, I told him of my reading to Harvey, and asked if he would like to hear me read the same to him. He said he would; and I read the same words, and told him how earnestly his cousin Harvey had prayed, and God, who hears and answers prayer, answered him, and he died a happy Christian. His feelings became tender, and I knelt by his bedside in supplication. As I was about to leave, he said:

"There is a difficulty in my way, and I think you can remove it; but I am more rested early in the morning, and if you can come to-morrow morning I will tell you what it is."

I told him I would be there if life and health were spared.

The following morning I met him more rested. He said:

"I have tried to pray to God; then it seems as if Jesus Christ stands there, and if I pray to Jesus it don't feel quite clear, because I want to go to head-quarters, and I am confused, and don't know where to go or what to do, and so I've given it all up; for it's all dark before me, and I've concluded to die in the dark."

This sorrowful condition of unbelief brought secret prayer for divine guidance in words to place the divinity of the Lord Jesus as clearly as possible before him. I read a few passages where he manifested his power by miracles, "that ye may know that the Son of man hath power on earth to forgive sins." He heard me attentively, and suddenly exclaimed:

"Now I see it; now I see it; now I've got a foothold. Now I can pray. I want you to pray for me."

He followed in earnest prayer. At the close he raised his clasped hands: "I've found him; I've got him. O, how I wish I could have voice and strength to tell you how happy I am! I want to go to my Savior; he is my all. But I can not tell it here; I will tell it in glory. It's all light now; the darkness, is all gone."

He seemed much exhausted, and took leave of his mother and mister, and sank into a stupor, and quietly passed away that afternoon.

I felt under renewed obligations to praise Him for his loving kindness in reminding me, so vividly of the promise I made to that dying young man, Harvey White. How careful we should be to attend, to every little errand as we are passing through our life-work. I felt to upbraid myself for being so inattentive to that request. Had that precious soul left the shores of time without hope in Christ, I could never have forgiven myself for my neglect. There are neglected duties that dot my life here and there with regrets, that have been lessons to teach the necessity of greater faithfulness in the Master's work.

The daughter of John Hatfield came to me with the word that there was a woman at their house who wished to see me. Her father being a member of the vigilance committee I went without delay, and found the woman in great distress of mind. She said she was a slave, but had the privilege of working in Cincinnati at house-cleaning, washing, or any jobs she could get, by paying her mistress three dollars per week. In this way she had managed to lay aside for herself over twenty dollars during nearly two years. She had a husband and nine children, "An' las' year," said she, "missus was gwine to sell my oldes' gal an' her baby to get money to keep her two gals in school Norf somewhars, an' she tuck her baby an' run off for Canada, an' now she says she's got to sell my Mary;" and her tears came as from a fountain.

"Why don't she come away as your other daughter did?" I asked.

"Oh, she can't; missus won't let one o' my family come but me. She let's me come an' do all her marketin' arter I gets all her work a- goin', so my man an' chillen goes on wid it; she lets me come to de city to work, an' I pays her three dollars every week. Now I'se full o' trouble over my Mary;" and she wept so freely that it was some time before she could give me this little sketch. I found they lived fifteen miles from the river, and she had placed her money in the hands of a colored man by the name of Bailey, to keep for her to use at some future time in going to Canada with her family. He had told her when the right time came he would have her money ready for her, and would help her. I told her I would gladly relieve her were it in my power; but all I could do was to advise her to bring her family in the covered market wagon, and throw a quilt or blanket over them; then the hay she always put in for her team over that, and a bag of apples, and another of potatoes, or any thing she generally brought into market, placed in front so as to present the appearance of a load of marketing. As she had been over so often, she said, the ferryman hardly ever asked her for her pass, for he knew her so well. "Don't you see you are the very one to bring yourself and family here? You could drive over and take your family to either of three places: to a colored family on Macallister Street, by the name of Hall; or to Levi Coffin's, on the corner of Ninth and Walnut Streets; or bring them here to John Hatfield's. At either of these places you are as sure of going through safe as if you were already in Canada." She listened with great attention, and her tears dried away as she looked up, with her face shining with hope, and said, "I do b'leve I can do it; I never thought o' that. I'll go to Bailey for my money fus thing, an' I'll go mighty soon." I charged her not to name to Bailey or any other human being this side or the other, the plan I had given her, except to her own family. She promised, and left with a much lighter heart.

A few days later I was requested to meet Mary French, who would be at John Hatfield's house at twelve o'clock. Her friend said, "She is nearly crazy, an' I coaxed her to see you. She's los' faith in every body I reckon, for 't was a good bit afore I could get her to see you agin. She said she did see you wonst, an' you couldn't do nothin' for her. She's bin house-cleanin' wid me, an' it 'pears like she's 'cryin' all the time, day an' night, an' me an' another woman got her to see you, if I'd git you to come to Mr. Hatfield's at noon." I found her wringing her hands and weeping bitterly. As I looked upon that poor, despairing woman that I had left so hopeful a few days previously, I felt that I could say or do nothing for her but to point her to the God of Israel, who is able and willing to lead his oppressed children. I said, "Were you ever a Christian?"

"I was three years ago, an' I lived a prayin' life a year; then the white folks did so bad, it 'peared like I couldn't live 'ligion, an' I giv' it all up. Missus sole my poor gal down de river, to sen' her two gals to de Norf to school now she's gwine to sell my Mary, kase they's runnin' short o' money; an' she missed sellin' my gal las' year. If I hadn't lef de Lord maybe dis hard trouble wouldn't come 'pon me." And again she began to wring her hands with convulsive weeping.

As I looked upon that poor, crushed spirit, the most frantic with grief of any person I ever saw, a feeling of confidence sprang up in me that she would become free. Said I, "You have known what it was to ask God to give you freedom from sin, and make you free from the bondage of Satan. Now go to him with full purpose of heart, and he will restore the joys of his salvation and again will set you free in soul. Then, I feel confident that the Captain of the soul's freedom will open the way for freedom from this chain of slavery that now binds you as a family. Now go to Jesus; he will do great things for you. You lose confidence in your friends, you lose confidence in yourself; but go to the Lord Jesus, and believe he will direct you, and he will do it. Let prayer be thy constant work, then faith will increase--that will not fail." At these few words she became calm, and said, as she looked up, "Can you tell me where my daughter is?"

"Certainly," I said, "I heard from her yesterday; she is in Carthaginia, Indiana. I had supposed she went directly to Canada, and I was sorry she stopped so near to the line--not more than one hundred miles off."

"I was tole she went through this city with her baby."

"It was true," I answered. I was astonished to see her wipe her tears away and become calm so soon, and converse with so much composure.

"If we come soon can you go a piece wid us?"

"It will make no difference whether I am here or not, if you go to either of the places I told you of. There are a great many safe places here, but I gave those places you know so well, and can find day or night I shall probably go to my home in Michigan next week, and it is uncertain when I return; but don't forget to carry your burden to the Lord by constant prayer for his directing hand; and whatever way he opens, take it; if it should be any other way than the plan I suggested, take it, regardless of what I have said, except to mind closely the impressions you feel confident come from an All-wise Director. Do this, and I have great faith in your success.

"Never have I had the strong faith that I have at this moment, that if you go to the Savior for his help in this time of your great need, he will lead you out of slavery. I advise you not to wait for Bailey. If you come here you can all be taken to Canada without a dollar."

This seemed to surprise her. She said she could get a few dollars, as she was earning good day wages.

"One thing more I would say," I went on, "and that is, wherever I may be, whether in my Michigan home, or here in this city, I shall not forget to implore divine aid in the deliverance of this family from slavery."

With this solemn interview we parted, and the burden of prayer followed me to my home. Hardly a day passed without presenting that poor family at a throne of grace for their preservation.

Two months later found me again in the exciting scenes of Cincinnati. My first inquiry was for Mary French. "Yes, I heard a few days ago that her mistress had forbidden her ever to come to this city again, and had threatened to sell the whole family down the river, and I suppose they are all sold by this time," said John Hatfield. He said she remained in the city three or four weeks after I saw her, to get money to start with, but she was too late. Her Mary was sold just before she returned home, and the poor woman grieved so for her poor girl, that he heard her mistress abused her, and threatened to sell them all. It seemed as if I could hardly endure the thought, when I had indulged such strong hope of her success, but I could not yet give her up, though I regretted exceedingly her delay, as I felt great confidence that He who notes the falling sparrow, and hears the young ravens cry, would have brought that family out of bondage.

While in charge of the sick, word was brought by a workman in a shop that there was an exciting report in town that a market wagon brought over a load of nine slaves early that morning, and that a reward of five hundred dollars was offered for information of their whereabouts. While my heart leaped for joy, hoping it might be Mary French and family, yet as I was in a pro-slavery family, my feelings were kept to myself. The man of the house said:

"What a pity to lose that amount of property! But according to your principles, Mrs. Haviland, I suppose you are glad of it."

"Certainly. As I told you the other day, the negroes have the same rights from their Creator that we have, and no man or class of men has the right to take them away."

"Now can't you set aside these notions of yours? You can easily find out where they are, and slyly report them, and here's your five hundred dollars."

"I would not for ten times that amount. Would you do it?"

"Certainly I would, and should think it my duty."

"I am astonished to hear this from one who professes to be a follower of the Lord Jesus, a part of whose mission was to unbind the heavy burdens and let the oppressed go free. It is pain to me to hear you advance the sentiments you do in the presence of your children; and a class-leader in the Methodist Protestant Church. I can not henceforward acknowledge you as a brother in Christ."

"Why, Mrs. Haviland! You are the most uncharitable person I ever met. This hurts my feelings more than anything you have said in presenting your radical position."

"I do hope and pray that the enlightening influences of the Holy Spirit may lead to a far different view from your present one. I am grieved to hear this from one who is looked upon as a leader to the Lamb of God, who shed his blood for the whole universe of man, regardless of color or nation."

His reply was, "I want to refer you to a few more Scripture arguments that I have not mentioned. To-night, from seven o'clock till nine, I want to talk with you on this subject."

I told him I would be ready, but I had one request, and that was to make this a subject of prayer, as I should myself, during the day. He said he would seriously look it over, and left for his business.

At nine o'clock my patient was comfortably cared for, and I had been talking of going to Levi Coffin's on an errand for a number of days. I asked permission of her to be absent an hour for that purpose, and her consent for two hours was given. On my way I called on John Hatfield, to know whether this company of slaves was not the Mary French family.

"Oh, no, that poor family has gone down the river. I heard some days ago that they were sold to a trader."

"The market-wagon was the plan I gave Mary, and I hoped so much that it was her family."

"Yes, but we should be just as glad for other slaves panting for liberty, as for her," and I accepted the remark as almost a half reproof for being more anxious for her than for other slaves.

As I entered Catherine Coffin's room I inquired whether she knew this morning's company of the nine slaves to be Mary French and family. "I know nothing of the name, but a woman and little child are up in our attic; but nobody knows it about this house but Levi and I."

"Please go up and tell her a friend is going to call on her, so as not to frighten her."

"Go on; she'll know we would let no one but a friend go up." I walked slowly up to the fourth story, and lo! on a box in the corner sat Mary French with her little grandchild sitting at her feet. "Is it possible that is Mary French?" I exclaimed. She sprang to me with outstretched arms, clasped me with tears of joy and leaning her head on my shoulder sobbed.

"O, my God has saved me so far, but my pore Mary was sole down de ribber, when I is here in de city to git a little money to start wid. When I gets into missus' door, I sort o' felt somethin' wrong, an' axt her, 'Whar's Mary?', She say, 'I sole her las' week,' an' I cried, 'O my God! save my pore chile Mary!' an' she kotched up de tongs an' beat me on my head 'til I loss my min', and when I come to I was layin' on de floor bleedin'. You see here is a sore yit" (pointing to her head). There was a gash that must have been three inches long by the appearance of the scar and sore, yet unhealed. "Missus said I never, the longes' day I live, should set foot in Cincinnati, 'case free niggers ruin me, an' afore she have such a fuss as dis, she put de hull of us in her pocket. I knowd what dis mean, and I tried mighty hard to cheer up afore her. But my tears was my meat and drink a few days. I 'membered your word to go to de Lord day an' night, 'case I couldn't come to you no mo'e. In three days he answered my prayer, an' jus' tole me I's gwine to be free, an' I tole my husban' so, but he couldn't git faith in me. I tole 'im to put faith in God, as I did now. But I did lose faith in my bes' frien' when Bailey tole me you an' Hatfiel' betrayed my gal Mary, an' got a hundred dollars reward; den I was mos' crazy. And when dat 'oman tole me to go to you, an' I tole her I did talk to you, and tole her what Bailey said 'bout you an' Hatfiel', she said he was a bad man, an' lied only to keep my mouey. She begged me so hard I tole her if you'd tell me whar Mary is, I'd have faith in you, an' when you tole me so quick, all my faith in you come back. How I wish you could see my man, for he's so sure they'll cotch us. I don't know whar he is, for we's scattered among de good people. O, what a time I had wid 'im to git 'im started. I loaded an' unloaded four times afore he'd come. At las' a pore white man tole me he hear missus say she gwine to sell us all to de firs' trader come along. I say, 'What shall I do?' He say, 'If I was you, I'd run away.' I say 'Here's my man an' chillen, can't go widout 'em.' He say 'All go, an' if dey cotch you 'twon't be no wuss dan to go to de trader, and if I can do any way to help you I will, for I feels sorry for you.' When I tole my man, he was so skeered he didn't know hisself scarcely. He was ready to do anyhow I wants 'im, au' I went to dis white man, an' ax 'im for his boy ten year ole, to go wid me to market, an' take all my family, an' I'd cover 'em up in de market wagon. 'An' I'll tell your boy I wants 'im to watch my team for me, an' I'll gib 'im a dollar.' 'All right, only tell 'im what you'll do, an' tell 'im to come an' ax me an' he musn't know I knows about it.' An' I tuk missus' young hosses, an' put my man an' chillen in, cover 'em up, den put a bag o' taters an' apples an' a basket o' chickens in front. An' I had dis little boy by de chickens, so if he cry or make a noise I shake de basket an' de noise of de chickens kill de noise of de boy. An' I drove de fifteen miles to de ribber by daylight, and drove back of Covin'ton till de smoke of de ferry boat rise; den I prayed God to keep de ferryman from axin' me for my pass. For I's mighty feared he would, 'case I hadn't been here in so long. An' jus' afore sun up my man crawled out de back of de wagon. I told de boy to hol' de hosses till I fix somethin'. I whispered, 'Get back quick, for Gods sake,' an' he whispered, 'Let's go back, I knows dey'll cotch us.' 'Go back! Man, its death to go back; we'd be in jail in no time waitin' for de trader.' An' he crawl back an' I tuck 'im up agin, an' we trimble like a popple leaf. Den de smoke jus' rise on de ferry-beat, an' I drove on wid de white boy by my side. I prayed dat de Lord wouldn't let de ferryman ax me for my pass. If he did I's gwine to say, 'Dis white boy my pass;' but he didn't say a word, an' I praise God for answerin' my prayer." I told her she had nothing to fear from the five hundred dollars reward; she was in good hands; all she had to do was to go when they were ready to take them; but I would write a few lines for her to take to the first stopping place after leaving the city, advising to go by way of Carthaginia. "Write me from that town, and tell your daughter to go on to Canada with you without fail."

I left her with a lighter heart, rejoicing with that rejoicing family, though yet trembling with fear. The time appointed for the two hours' discussion on the subject of slavery arrived. My pro-slavery friend was not disposed to open the conversation he desired in the morning. After waiting until one hour had elapsed, I asked if he was prepared to bring the Scripture arguments he had for my consideration at this hour. He replied that he had thought of but little else during the whole day; but on the whole doubted whether his reasons would stand the test, and declined saying any thing farther in defense of the position he had advanced. A few weeks later he died of cholera. I called on his widow, who said he died a happy soul, and often spoke of his confidence in me as an honest-hearted Christian, and she never heard him speak disparagingly of the colored people after the long conversation we had on that subject. I regretted the loss of an opportunity of seeing him after Mary French and family were safe in Canada. I wished to give him their history, as I felt sure it would have been "like a nail driven in a sure place." He had lived in the South, and the subject of slavery had never been placed before him in this way.

The reward for the nine slaves was doubled on the second day of their exodus. All the clew the hunters got of their whereabouts was from the boy they met at the ferry. He could not read the names on the streets, and could only point as near as he knew in the direction where they all left. He told them he didn't know there were any in the wagon but "black Mary," till they all got out; then she told him to go to Walnut Street ferry, and he drove two or three blocks when he stopped and cried, because he didn't know where to find Walnut Street. Then a man came and told him to stop crying and he'd drive him to the ferry. They went to Hall's, on Macallister Street, but not one was left there five minutes. They were conducted to different hiding-places, and not one was left within a half a mile to a mile from that part of the city. Slave-hunters were paid from three dollars to seven dollars a day for watching around those suspected streets and those leading northward. The family were dressed in disguise and taken out in three carriages, closed, and two white men in front, that gave an impression at sight of a load of white people. At noon-day, in this manner, they rounded the corners, where were standing some of their hunters who were receiving their seven dollars a day, as was ascertained by a scheme gotten up by the colored people.

The next evening after the nine fugitives were taken northward, they drove a double carriage into an alley near North Street, and the same number of colored people, so closely watched for, were hustled in with haste, and driven off with speed. The call to "Stop, HALT," was not heeded, until the police rushed at the increased cry, "Stop thief, STOP THIEF," and slackened their pace. But while the excited crowd gathered to see the police arrest the thieves, the colored man beside the driver demanded the reason why he and his ladies should receive this insult to hinder their pleasure ride. By throwing a light from their dark lantern in the faces of their pursuers, the hunters they had suspected were recognized, to their great annoyance. There were those among them who would not have been exposed, perhaps, for half the amount of the reward.

A few days subsequent to this little episode I received a letter from Mary, after their arrival at Carthaginia, where she met her daughter, who, with her child, made their party number eleven. They very soon reached the "land of the free." Nothing further was heard from them until I went with my two daughters to Windsor, Canada West, to attend their first of August celebration, in commemoration of West India emancipation. There were gathered a very large congregation in a grove, of both colored and white people. While listening to an eloquent oration delivered by Samuel J. May, of Boston, I was taken from my seat and borne away a few rods, hardly touching the tops of the bushes with my feet. I turned first one way and then the other, until I discovered the sable face of Mary French, with big tears rolling down her cheeks. Not a word was spoken until we were entirely away from the congregation, and I said, "Mary, haven't we gone far enough?" when she let me down, and caught bold of my bands and kissed them, while tears of joy were still falling. "O, how happy we is to be all free. Can't you go to Malden an' see all my family? I knows my man would come all dis way afoot if he knowed you's here." I told her I could not, as I must return the next day with my two daughters.

"Is dey heah?"

"They were sitting by my side," said I; "those two girls dressed in white are my daughters."

"Sweet creturs! de little angels; I mus' go see 'em. I's got two gals here, too, an' I'll bring 'em to see you." And soon her hands were placed on the shoulder of each, still weeping for joy as she said: "God bless you! You tinks it strange to see an old black 'oman come to you like dis, but you wouldn't if you know'd what your mother has done for me an' my family. If it hadn't been for her we should all been in slavery to dis day. I wants you to go out dar whar you see your mother standin' afore a great while. I'm gwine back to her now." She came with her two girls, who were also very demonstrative in shaking and kissing my hands; but they laughed instead of weeping as did their overjoyed mother. By the time my daughters came to us we were served with cake and ice cream. As she and her daughters had on the ground a little stand from which they made sales, their favors in this line were repeated.

Instead of one year's suspension, as we designed, we had deferred finishing our institute building in Michigan from time to time, until four years had elapsed. As the Ohio school law made provision to support a colored school in any town or place where there were as many as fifteen regular scholars, my daughter Anna and myself taught a school for them of one hundred scholars one term, in the basement of Zion Church, Toledo. The expenses were paid from the school fund.

With several fugitives, I started on my way to Toledo from Cincinnati, and spent a day at our friend William Beard's. From thence we were taken to Newport, Indiana, where was a meeting appointed in behalf of Calvin Fairbanks, in which I gave a sketch of my visit to Louisville jail in his behalf. I read the letter I had received from his lawyer on leaving Cincinnati, containing a proposition to do the best he could for him, and with that object in view he staved off the case to the next session of their court. At the close of the meeting fifteen dollars were raised, Bishop Quinn, of the African Methodist Episcopal Church, giving one-third of it. As there was a fall of snow a foot deep, the friends concluded to take us across a swamp, which would save a number of miles; and as there were indications of a thaw, one man offered his team and double sleigh if a certain colored man would go that night and drive it. We were soon well protected from the prospective inclement weather, with the buffalo-robe presented to me, and quilts around the balance of our load.

The shifting wind brought quite a snow-storm, that covered us over about three inches deep. My company being very cold, I advised to stop at a house, the dim light of which was so tempting to the shivering company. I went to the door and asked permission to enter, giving our number, and our object in going through the swamp before a break-up. The two old people granted the favor; but when the old lady saw the color of my company she became rather suspicious. Said she, "If these are slaves we don't want any trouble, because you know the Fugitive- slave Law makes a deal of trouble in some places." I assured her they would have none of that character on our account, for these young people were going with me to attend my school. When we were warmed and the horses fed, we left our kind friends to borrow no more trouble for fear of being disturbed with slave-hunters.

About three o'clock we came to a large half-finished frame house, brilliantly lighted, and the man seemed to be preparing his team for leaving. I called with our driver to see if we could warm ourselves and feed the team, giving our reason for crossing the swamp to save distance, and as there were indications of a thaw in the afternoon, we chose to come through that night. The man said that was his reason for going for a load of lumber so early--he fearing a break-up. They were very kind, and insisted on our resting till daylight, and taking a warm breakfast. The invitation was accepted with gratitude. I spent my time in conversing with our kind hostess, while my company slept an hour.

At nine o'clock we reached Carthaginia. The first one we met was a colored woman, of whom I inquired where we could find a place to tarry for a night, and find provender for our horses. She took in our situation at once, and pointed to a large frame house in sight, the house of Samuel Jones, half a mile distant. While she was giving this information, a man ahead of us, with his carriage, stopped and turned back, saying, "There is Mr. Jones now, coming to see you, I reckon." As he came to us, I told him of the inquiry I made for a resting-place. "And that is my house for you and barn for your horses," he said. After giving each of us a shake of the hand, he said, turning to me, "I know you, though I never saw you before, and I will tell you of a circumstance, after we get home, whereby you will recognize me." We followed him to his very comfortable home. We were soon seated at a luxurious table. Breakfast being over, he related a circumstance in which I had taken a deep interest, and by corresponding, the release from slavery of his relative was effected.

Brother Jones gave me ten dollars for brother Fairbanks, in the Kentucky prison. Here we took leave of our conductor, Henry Marshal, and a team and teamster were provided to take us on by way of Bellefontaine. The anticipated warmer weather overtook us, and with a wagon we left Carthaginia. Streams with floating ice made fording difficult, especially Mosquito Creek; but our driver and Simon measured the depth of water, and with rails pushed the floating ice from the ford, to enable me to drive through. Working as they did with all their might to keep the cakes of ice from running against the horses and from impeding the wheels, when we reached the swift current of the stream a cake blocked the wagon so as to stop the horses a few moments. One horse became discouraged and began to lie down. At this the three women jumped upon a large floating cake, from which they reached the shore with the help of the men. Our teamster found his way into the wagon; and by pushing and crowding this way and that he loosened the wheel, and with continued urging and Simon's wading to the horses' heads, they finally pulled through. We drove to a house, where the men changed their socks, and rubbed their horses with straw, they said, two hours, and then fed them. We pursued our journey without further difficulties to our school in Toledo.

Often did my whilom slave scholars refer to the excitement at Mosquito Creek ford. I found the prejudice here very bitter against a colored school; but the colored people had combined their weak forces and built a church, designed for school, as well as their occasional meetings. My school averaged nearly twenty scholars during the term, at the close of which we put in a petition for a support from the school fund. But a majority of two ruled against us; for, although the State law required them to support this school, they had already complied with the requirement.

Although I had designed to return home and re-open Raisin Institute, yet to press the board of education into its duty I reopened their school for the second term; and every time that board met I met with them with my petition, informing them, at their first refusal to adopt the school, that this petition of the importunate widow would stand before them until it was granted. They frequently inquired of the colored people how long I was going to teach for them. The answer every time was, as I told them, until the board of education took it. In their discussions in the board I understood it was frequently remarked by our opposers "that the end of that negro school would be when Mrs. Haviland left, and that wouldn't be long, for the negroes were too poor to pay her." But it was not for money that I taught their school, but to see justice meted out to them.

There were fifteen families of the lower class of Irish who lived in shanties near the canal that ran within a few rods of our school-house, and as the most of our school passed them, or would have to go half a mile farther, we got from one man in particular a systematic cursing; beginning with cursing my feet, and cursing every toe on them, and cursing every nail on every toe, and so on, to cursing my head, and cursing every hair on it. This regular set of curses were for me every time I passed when he was in his cabin, and frequently a number of others standing by would join him. But as he or some of the others were so often drunk, it was a long time before I could find the suitable opportunity to go to their cabins and have a talk with them, as I desired. As some of their company were so boisterously furious, the children did not dare pass them unless I was with them, for in addition to cursing they were stoned.

When the second term was two-thirds through I proposed a picnic for the school and its friends, and had the scholars declaim a few pieces. An eloquent speech delivered in the House of Lords, when immediate emancipation was discussed in the English parliament, was well committed and declaimed by one of the young men. A number of the colored people feared a mob, but the majority were willing to risk any measure I thought best to adopt. I trained them thoroughly in speaking, and they trained themselves in singing, and the school selected a little girl to be crowned as their queen of May, and on the 25th of May we marched through town to a grove, with two beautiful banners. The one borne by the young woman who walked by my side bore the motto, "God is love," and next to it all the girls followed in couples. Then followed the young men and boys in the same manner, headed by the banner, upon which was inscribed, "Knowledge is power." I instructed the children and young people to walk straight forward, and not even turn their heads to the right or left, and not to notice by look or word any remark that might be made, not even to talk to each other until we reached our little stand in the woods. Not a word of disrespect was heard, and some of the white people who drove out with their carriages told me they had not seen such order in marching in any of the May picnics that the white schools had had that Spring. They were highly delighted with our exercises. At the next session of the board my school was recognized as a public one, and the chairman, Rev. Dr. Smyth, was authorized to hire me to teach the next term. He met me on the street and said, "Mrs. Havilland, the importunate widow's prayer is answered; your petition is granted at last, and I am instructed to hire you for the next term."

"Then my work is finished with this term," said I. "My object is accomplished. I have business at home that I hoped to have entered upon when I closed last term; but as your board refused to do its duty I continued, although I have not averaged twenty-five cents a week during the six months, as a large majority of the colored people here are very poor."

"I know that, and I have contended from the first that they ought to have a school; but I am surprised at your not remaining in the school, as you shall have a fair compensation now."

I told him I would give him the name of a competent teacher, who was now working himself through college at Oberlin--John Mitchel--a worthy Christian young man of their own color, with whom they could correspond and secure his services. His parents were living in Toledo, and he would be pleased to accept the position. I thanked the board through their chairman for the favor they had granted in behalf of the colored people in Toledo.

It being the seventh day of the week, as I was passing my Irish friends, and all quiet, and a company sitting on the grass in the shade of their cabins, I accepted this as my long-sought opportunity to talk with them. Addressing a group of half a dozen women, I said: "I have long desired to talk with you, as I am confident you do not understand me in teaching this colored school. I have felt it my duty to aid the most neglected class of people. We are apt to indulge in prejudices against certain classes or nations of people. Some people are prejudiced against the German people. They'll say he's nobody but a Dutchman, he's not worth noticing; and others are prejudiced against the Irish, and will say, 'They are nobody but Irish people, they are not worth noticing;' and others are prejudiced against black people: 'They are nobody but negroes, and they are not worth noticing. And then there are some who are prejudiced against soldiers, or sailors, as classes of men. People are too apt to despise other nations and classes of men. All this is wrong; God made us all as it pleased him, and it is not for us to find fault with our Heavenly Father, who loves all the human family alike. As we acknowledge the fatherhood of God, we should also acknowledge the brotherhood of man in all nations and classes."

Said one man to his friend sitting by, "In faith, Pat, that's good doctrine." "Yes, indade, that's the doctrine Father Mathew prached, ye know." "Jamie, that's all right," said another. One of the women concluded she would know the truth of the reports they had gotten up among themselves.

"An' did ye not marry a nagur?"

"Why, no! my husband was a white man, who died a number of years ago."

"And was he a black man?"

"He was a white man, and he left me with eight children, all under age, and the youngest and the oldest have followed their father."

"In fath, ye've seen a dale of trouble, I'm sure; and we heard that black man we often saw comin' from schule with ye an' that yellow lass an' boy was your chilther."

"That mulatto girl and boy live near my boarding-place, and they generally come and go with me to school and return; and that black man is a young man who has never had the privilege of going to school and learning to read and write and the use of figures, until I opened this school. Now he can read, write, and can use figures to good advantage."

"But it's a pity we didn't know ye before. We've been hearin' all this about ye, an' not a bit of it true. Our people was about to set fire to your schule-house--in faith, they said they'd give ye a dressin' of tar an' fithers, an' our praste forbid it."

"I knew nothing of that," said I; "but I wanted you to understand me before I left, which will be in four weeks. Then they will have a fine young colored man from Oberlin College to teach their school."

"But what a pity that is, for I'm sure they'll not get another such a tacher as you. Indade, I'm sorry to hear you're to lave us; I'd like to have my little gal go to your schule, if ye'll take 'er."

The man who was the systematic curser came to his door: "Indade, missus, we didn't know ye; an' now we'll fight for ye, an' we are sorry we didn't know ye for so long."

When I left them I shook hands with them all, for by the time our conversation closed about all their little community had convened, and I took occasion to speak highly of Father Mathew, the great temperance reformer of Ireland; and my little congregation pronounced as strong blessings upon me as they had curses. Even my systematic curser was among my best friends after that, and my scholars, as well as myself, were treated with the utmost respect ever after, and two of them sent for me when very sick and not expected to live, one of whom died a few days after. As she was in great distress of mind, I read to her some of those precious promises of our Savior, from which she drew great consolation. It would seem to many like casting pearls before swine to turn aside to present the truth to such ignorant and disliking people, but it is ours to obey these little impressions, and leave the result with the All-wise Director.

During my work in Toledo I called on a colored woman to solicit a little change for a very sick man who was very low with consumption, and was being cared for by a very poor family, and as she gave me twenty-five cents a beautiful white girl was sitting by, who gave another quarter. After school I called again and inquired for that young woman who gave for that sick man, without giving me time to ask for her mite, and to my surprise, found she was an inmate of a house of ill-fame, and tried to make Mrs. Buck promise not to tell me where she was living; for if I knew it I would never speak to her. I sent for her to meet me the following day after school, at her house. I found her sitting in the parlor waiting for me. As I took her by the hand, placing the other on her head, I said, "My dear girl, you are an unhappy child." And she burst into a flood of tears, and as soon as she could sufficiently command her feelings to relate her history I found she was compelled by her stepfather to live away from home. She had lived a year or more with a worthy woman, who kept a boarding- house in Cleveland; and there came to board a few weeks a fine appearing young man, who professed great affection for her, and proposed marriage. He told her his father was a very wealthy merchant in Toledo, and he was there on business for his father. After he had won her affections he proposed to take her to Toledo, and place her in a boarding-house until she could make up two rich silk dresses and other clothing suitable for her, as he was not willing his folks should know he was marrying a poor girl. He could easily take a dress pattern from each bolt of silk and his father never know it, and any other goods she needed. As his father was going to New York for a new supply of goods, he would supply her with other goods to make up until his father's new goods came, then he would hire a dress-maker to make up her silk dresses. All this she fully believed, as from a true and faithful lover, to whom she had given her heart's best and purest affections. She said, "A number of days I hesitated, because I wanted to tell my mother all about it, but he persisted in leaving Cleveland secretly, and return on our bridal trip to surprise my mother and that cruel stepfather. At last I foolishly consented, to my ruin and sorrow, for I haven't seen one moment of peace since I was deserted by that man;" and again bathed herself in tears. Recovering herself, she continued, "I wouldn't have my mother know this for the world. She is a good Christian woman. She's a Methodist, and has seen a sight of trouble with my stepfather; and, if she knew this, it would break her heart." On further inquiry I found he brought her to this house as an excuse to keep her secluded until they were about to be married, when he would pay her board a few days in the finest hotel in the city. "The next day after our arrival he brought me a beautiful lawn dress- pattern and a package of other material for me to make up while waiting for his father's goods. And not till then had he offered in word or act any thing amiss from a perfect gentleman. It was the next day after our arrival in this city, and to this house, that he proposed to live two weeks as if we were married, as it would be about a week or two at longest when the goods would be here, and he would get one of two dressmakers to prepare me for my wedding. I cried two days over this proposition, and by this time I had learned the character of this house. Here I was, a stranger to every body, but still had confidence in my new friend; and again, to my bitter sorrow, I yielded. But day after day of anxious waiting passed until two weeks expired, and no new goods yet, but another lawn dress-pattern came for me to make for myself, and another two weeks rolled away with only hearing (he said) that the goods were on the way. But at the close of the third two weeks he was missing. Daily I waited his coming. At length I went on the street. I inquired for his name and the name of his father's store, when, to my utter astonishment, no such store or names were found in the city. Here in a strange place, deserted, ruined, and filled with shame, I had no heart to go to my friends." She had been here six months. I advised her not to remain in this house another twenty-four hours.

"But what shall I do? Mrs. Cassaday will lock me up if she knows I am going to leave her. She called me a fool for giving you that quarter; she says these Christians are down on us; and if any of us should die, there wouldn't one of them come to pray for us. I told her I believed you would," I told her to pack her trunk, and if she was down town near the time for the boat to leave for Cleveland, to call a drayman to take her trunk to the boat and follow it, if possible, before Mrs. Cassaday came in. I told her how to manage in going to her old employer, and to tell her you were deceived by that young man, but you found him untruthful. "As you say Mrs. Cassaday kept you sewing most of the time, you can tell her you were employed most of time in sewing; but do not, at present, tell her or your mother of the life you have lived, and place of your residence while here." She promised she would gladly take my advice, and leave for Cleveland the first opportunity. As we parted she leaned her head upon my shoulder, with fast dropping tears, and said, "I shall always thank you for acting the part of a mother in helping me away from this horrible place." The following morning she called to leave word with Mrs. Buck, that fortunately for her Mrs. Cassaday was out just in time for her to call a drayman, that had just gone with her trunk to the boat, and she was now on her way to Cleveland, happier than she had been in six months, and that she should do, in all respects, as I had advised. Here was a beautiful girl decoyed and led from the paths of virtue by an artful, designing, and licentious young man, who basely sought her ruin by winning the affections of an innocent girl. Hundreds and thousands of these girls are in like manner led astray, and might be saved if mothers in Israel would take them by the hand of sympathy and lift them from the mire of this moral pollution.

At another time a request was left with my hostess to go to see a very sick woman, who was thought nigh unto death; but for a little girl that heard the request I should not have received it. She said, these poor white trash would curse me in health, and when they thought they were going to die, they were ready then to send for me to pray for them; and, as I was tired enough to rest after teaching all day, she did not think I ought to go for their calls. I told her if she would be so kind as to deliver all errands of that character I would be very thankful, and hastened to the bedside of an old soldier of the cross, who, with her aged companion, were visiting their children. She said she did not expect to remain much longer in this world of checkered scenes; but her son had been here a short time only, and had not formed any acquaintances among Christian people, and their hired girl said "she was passing your school-house one morning and heard you opening your school with prayer, and I told her to find your boarding-place, and leave word for you to come after your school closed, as I wanted to hear the voice of prayer once more." I read a chapter and offered prayer by her bedside. She and her weeping husband and children thanked me for the call, and desired me to call the day following, after school. I found her somewhat improved, and the next door neighbor said Dutch Mary was in the adjoining room, and seemed much affected, and said that was the first she heard read from the Bible in seven years, and the first prayer she had heard in that time, and she would be glad to see me, but she would not disgrace me by coming to her house. Then the woman told her she would ask me to see her in her room, and send for her when I came to see the sick woman.

I met her in great distress of mind. She told me of the wicked life she had spent during the last seven years of her widowhood, and wanted to know if I thought there was any hope whatever for her. "Do you think God can forgive me? I have never so much as opened my Bible that lies in the bottom of my chest all these seven years, until yesterday I went home and took my Bible for the first time to read in these years; and I felt so condemned after I read awhile that I laid it back, and didn't know whether it was of any use; for I have lived such a wretched life so long I doubt whether God can forgive me, for I feel worse and worse. Do you believe he can?"

"Certainly he is able to save to the uttermost. It is the enlightening influence of God's Holy Spirit that is showing you the exceeding sinfulness of sin."

I read to her the readiness of the Lord Jesus to forgive sin. "How ready to bless the humble and contrite heart! Only believe this with all thy heart, and the blood of Jesus is sufficient to wash away every stain that sin has made. Though they be as scarlet, he will make them white as snow." We knelt together, and she too offered earnest prayer for strength to live the new life, which she firmly resolved to do.

I saw her a week later, and she said she informed those men with whom she had committed those darkest of sins of her firm resolution to live a virtuous life, and she locked her door; but they persisted in troubling her through the night, threatening to tear her house down or burn it.

"Three nights I suffered from them. But by constant prayer, believing God would take care of me, I was delivered from them. And I have plenty of washing, ironing, and house-cleaning to do; and I get along so much better than I expected I could. I do want to go to meeting; but so many know of my wicked life I am afraid to go inside of a church."

I told her to go to whichever Church she felt most at home, and the Lord would open the way for her, and enable her to bring up her little girl of eight years in the nurture and admonition of the Lord.

At the close of my school I left this field, so white to the harvest, to enter, as I supposed, upon a field of home missions. At the expiration of a year I visited Toledo, and inquired of one who occasionally employed Dutch

Mary, but knew nothing of my experience with her, how she was prospering. The cheering reply was, "Splendidly; I haven't heard a disparaging word of her for months, and there used to be hard stories about her." I heard she had united with the Baptist Church, and I think she is trying to live a Christian. If she had not left town on a visit to her friends I should have seen her, but the report I heard of her was heart-cheering. May God bless her, and all who are receiving life-giving power who were dead in trespasses and sin.

FUGITIVES IN CANADA

WHILE visiting friends in Detroit and Canada previous to reopening Raisin Institute, as I designed, I was earnestly solicited by Henry Bibb, Horace Hallack, and Rev. Chas. C. Foote, the committee authorized to employ a teacher, to open a school in a new settlement of fugitives, eight miles back of Windsor, where the Refugee Association had purchased government land, on long and easy terms, for fugitive slaves.

They had erected a frame house for school and meeting purposes. The settlers had built for themselves small log-houses, and cleared from one to five acres each on their heavily timbered land, and raised corn, potatoes, and other garden vegetables. A few had put in two and three acres of wheat, and were doing well for their first year.

After prayerful consideration, I reached the conclusion to defer for another year my home work, and enter this new field.

In the Autumn of 1852 I opened school, and gave notice that at eleven o'clock the following Sunday there would be a Sabbath-school for parents and children, after which a little time would be spent in other religious exercises, pursuing the same course I did in Toledo, Ohio. This drew a number of callers who had no children to see if any could come to my Sabbath-school; and when I told them it was for every body of any age who desired to come, my school-house was filled to its utmost capacity. Many frequently came five or six miles with their ox-teams to attend these meetings, with their families. Every man, woman, and child who could read a verse in the Testament, even with assistance, took part in reading the lesson, and liberty was given to ask questions. It was not strange to listen to many crude ideas, but a more earnest, truth seeking congregation we seldom find. An aged couple, past eighty, missed very few Sabbaths during the year I spent there. The man was a fugitive slave, and his companion was an Indian woman, converted under the preaching of a missionary among the Indians. She had taken great pains to talk and understand the English language, and was an interesting woman.

As there was an increasing interest both in day and Sabbath schools, I give liberty for all who wished to enjoy a sort of class or inquiry meeting, following half an hour's service for exhortation after Sabbath school.

One couple desired a private interview with me, as they had been married only after "slave fashion." They said "It is not right to live this way in a free country. Now we wants you to marry us."

"I am not legally authorized," I said, "but I will send a note to brother Foote, and he will come at once and marry you legally."

"We thought you preached, an' made notes for us, an' could help us out in dis matter too."

Charles C. Foote came, and we called at their house at the appointed time, with a few neighbors, to witness the solemnization of the marriage that would have been accomplished three years before had they looked at these things from the same stand point they now did.

A few days after another couple came on the same errand. Said this man "We wants you an' Mr. Foote to marry us, case we's bin troubled 'bout dis many days, case we wa'nt gwine to let nobody know it, but God knows all 'bout us, an' now we's free indeed, we wants every thing straight."

"But why do you put me with Mr. Foote," I asked, "to marry you?"

"Didn't you an' Mr. Foote marry dat brother an sister week afore las'?"

"No; only brother Foote."

"Brother Foote repeated the questions," they answered; "then he pronounced them husband and wife; then they were married according to law. But he axt you to pray after he said dem words."

In all this ignorance they were like confiding grown-up children, patiently listening to every explanation.

The unbounded confidence they placed in me was surprising; for they often brought their business papers for me to examine, to see whether they were right. One man brought me a note, as the employer could not pay him for his work in money. He said it was a note for groceries; but the grocer refused to take it, and said it was not good. I told him there was neither date nor name to it. I wrote the man a letter, asking him to rectify the mistake, which he did; but he gave his employee credit for only half the days he had worked. They were so often deceived and cheated in many ways, because of their extreme ignorance, that I did not wonder at the conclusion one escaped fugitive had reached. His master was a Presbyterian minister, but he had known him to whip his sister, the cook, after coming home from Church; and he said then he never would have faith in white folks' religion. Since coming to this colony he watched me a long while before he made up his mind that white people could have a pure religion. But now he believed "that the Lord hid his Spirit in the hearts of white people at the North; but it was a make-believe in slaveholders."

I was surprised one day to meet the mother of three of my scholars, who gave her thrilling experience in her escape from slavery; but she had little more than commenced her story before I found her to be one for whom I laid a plan with her sister, who had bought herself. As I named a circumstance, she exclaimed in surprise, "Why honey! is dis possible? God sent you here to larn my gals to read, an' we didn't know you," and tears began to drop thicker and faster, as she recounted the blessings that had multiplied since her arrival in Canada. She had in the three years worked for a little home. Her two older girls were at work, and they were all so happy in their freedom.

These fugitives often came five or six miles for me to write letters to their friends in the South, with whom they left a secret arrangement very frequently with white people who were their friends, but secretly, for fear of the ruling power, as were the disciples of Christ who feared the Jews. Their notes, or articles of agreement, were generally brought to me to draft for them.

In six weeks of steady attendance fifteen young men and women could read the second reader, and write a legible hand, and draft a negotiable note. I took a specimen of a number of my scholars' hand-writing to an anti-slavery convention in Cincinnati, Ohio, and left a few with the Rev. John G. Fee, whose life had been threatened if he did not desist from preaching a free gospel in his home State-- Kentucky. But the brave Cassius M. Clay told him to go on, and he would go with him. He went to one place from whence he had received repeated threats, and trouble was anticipated; but Cassius walked into the church by his side, and placed the Constitution of the United States on the Bible, and over both his brace of pistols, with which he informed the audience he should protect free speech. At the same time he cast a glance at the threatening group in a farther corner, who left one by one, until the church was cleared of all but eager listeners. Brother Fee said his object in requesting these specimens of the fugitives writing was to exhibit to those who were constantly asserting that negroes could not learn. He wished them to see the legible hand-writing of those who had only six weeks' training from their alphabet.

After spending a few days' vacation, I returned to the toiling day and night in my school. As there were twelve heads of families anxious to read the Bible and hymn-book, and this seemed to be the height of their ambition, I opened an evening school for that class. It was steadily attended four evenings in each week, and this, with one evening devoted to prayer-meeting, filled the week, leaving only one evening free; and frequently they came with their ox-teams to take me three miles to lead a prayer-meeting for them in an adjoining settlement.

The Winter was quite severe, and I frequently was awakened with the snow sifting in my face, and not unfrequently found the snow half an inch or more deep over my bed on rising in the morning; but my health was firm, and I often thought I never enjoyed a year of toiling better than the one I spent here.

There were in this colony a mixed religious element--Baptist, Methodist, Presbyterian, and Free-will Baptist--deeply interested in Sabbath schools and class-meetings, open to all who wished to enjoy them. An organization was proposed. The proposition came from the Methodist element, but I did not deem it wise to organize from any one denomination, as divergent opinions would create controversy that would bring harm to many tender minds. Consequently I proposed to organize a Christian Union Church, without disturbing the Church relationship of any one. I prepared an extract from Gerrit Smith's concise plan of organizing, on a liberal-scale, a Christian Union Church, with but little change, and read it to them; and, after a little discussion and explanation it was readily adopted. I think the number of new converts was thirteen, who expressed a desire to be baptized by immersion. I exhorted them to attend to their own religious impressions, as I was not there to present particular religious tenets, but to present the crucified, risen, and glorified Savior. Brother Foote came and complied with their wish.

I closed my evening school two weeks to hold a series of meetings, in which a young Baptist brother assisted. We all continued to work together for the highest good of all around us.

I noticed a settled sadness in the countenance of a young man of twenty-five years, recently from Missouri. During recess he took but little interest in any thing outside of his book or writing lesson. After attending my school a few days he invited me to go to his boarding-place to spend the night, as he wished me to write a letter for him. I found his history was a sad one. He was sold from his wife and four little children to satisfy a heavy debt. The master tried to reason with him, and the man he owed would not take any of his slaves but him. He called him aside to have further conversation concerning the proposed sale; his wife presented herself also to plead that they might not be separated. Both knelt before him, beseeching with tears to allow them to remain together. Said he, "I tole 'im I'd serve 'im faithfully all the days of my life, if he'd only let us live together; and he seemed to give way a little, and said he did not want to sell me, as I was his foreman, and he thought he would make other arrangements. I watched him closely as I had but little confidence in his words, and armed myself with a dirk. One day he called me to go to the woods with him, to show me the trees he wanted chopped. As I was going I saw the end of a rope under his coat-skirt. I kept at a reasonable distance all the way, and when we came to the tree he wanted I should chop, he attempted to come near me and I stood back; then he told me plainly I must yield. I said I never would permit myself to leave my family, and, if he was so determined, I should never be of any use to any one, for life to me was of no value if I am to be taken from my wife and four little children. At this he, with the other man, who came out of the bushes, ran towards me, but I outran them. About seven miles distant he overtook me with a number of his slave men, and told me I had to give up. I flourished my dirk and told them that I would kill the first man that touched me, or they should kill me. At this they all stood back except the master himself. He flourished his bowie-knife and I my dirk, for the space of a few minutes, when he made a rush upon me, and he met my dirk before I met his bowie-knife. As he fell back I ran for the woods. In the darkness of the night I made my last visit to my wife and little children."

Here he became convulsed with weeping. When he could command his feelings to pursue the sad story, he said:

"Oh, that was an awful parting! The moment I entered my wife's cabin she threw her arms around my neck, exclaiming, 'Oh, my dear Bill, don't stay a minute, for they say you've killed Master Riggs. They say he was dyin' this evenin', and he's dead afore this time, I reckon, an' they swear vengeance on you. Some said they'd chop you in pieces-- some said they'd burn you alive.' I told her if God would help me to Canada I would write after awhile to her father (he was free, having bought himself), and may be he could manage to send her and our children to me; and I tore her arms from my neck."

Again he was overcome with grief. I advised him not to write at present. I never saw a more grief-stricken man. He was boarding with Henry Bibb's mother, who said she knew he was a man of deep trouble, "for he looked so sad and groaned so much nights; but I couldn't bear to ask him, because I thought it would be harder for him to forget it." Having been a slave herself, she could easily anticipate the cause of his sadness. Notwithstanding this, he made fair progress in reading, writing, and arithmetic in one term. During this time vigorous efforts were put forth for his capture.

While I enjoyed my work so much with these people in the woods, in schools, in meetings, and in their improvements generally, I do not say I found with them perfection. There were causes for reproof as well as of encouragement. They made great effort to improve their homes by taking trees from their woods to the saw mills to be cut up into boards for better floors than split logs, and for partitions to make their little houses more comfortable. Perhaps their improvements could not find better expression than the report of one of our neighbors, in reply to an inquiry of a friend in Detroit, as to how they were prospering in their refugee colony, "Fine fine we've all come to life, an' are in a state to see who'll make the bes' house."

Frequent arrivals of their friends from slavery often produced much excitement. At one time a company of twenty seven arrived, brought by John Fairfield, a Virginian. He often went into the heart of slave holding States and brought companies away, passing himself as their owner until they reached a free State. He telegraphed some friends in Windsor, and a dinner of reception was provided in one of the colored churches, and a great jubilee meeting was held. One very old woman, between eighty and ninety years old, shouted as she jumped around among the people, "I's young again. Glory! glory! Jesus is our Master for evermore, honey," shaking hands with the new-comers. "Glory to Jesus! I's sixteen," and she clapped her hands as she gave another leap. Said John Fairfield, "This pays me for all dangers, I have faced in bringing this company, just to see these old friends meet."

Our young brother Campbell, the literate Baptist minister who had labored with us in our series of meetings a few months previously, returned, and with the three Baptist families in that community conceived the idea that as I was soon to leave, they could organize a Baptist Church, and induce nearly all in that colony to unite, and they went to work industriously to secure the individual consent of our Christian Union members; but the plan was, with one accord, rejected, except by our Baptist friends. As they said nothing to me concerning it, each day brought some complaints about their organising a Baptist Church "over our heads," as a number expressed themselves. But I told them "not to feel hurt over their desire to organize a Baptist Church. We will give way for them to occupy half the time." Brother Maglothin, who had just come with his family from Virginia, was an earnest Christian man and a licensed Wesleyan minister, and he was ready to take my place in keeping up our Sabbath-schools and meetings.

Rev. N. P. Colver, of Detroit, had appointed the Sabbath to meet the friends in our school-house, for the purpose of organizing a Baptist Church and of ordaining brother Campbell to take charge of it. I told all of our people to be sure and attend it with me. As I retired on the night previous to the proposed meeting, I read the sweet promise of the loving Savior, "I will be with you to the end," with an assurance of entire trust.

The hour arrived, and our house was well filled, but with many saddened faces. Brother Colver gave a short discourse, and ordained brother Campbell, who was left in charge of the Baptist branch of the little flock. At the close of the exercises I remarked that I hoped we would all manifest the same abiding interest in each other's spiritual and temporal well-being as we had heretofore done; that there was a fair understanding between the brethren and sisters that every other Sabbath was to be occupied by brother Maglothin, thus alternating with brother Campbell; and as the next Sabbath would be my last for the present with them, it would be my duty to explain the basis upon which our Christian Union Church was organized. My earnest and constant prayer was and ever would be, whether present or absent, that the love of the Lord Jesus Christ would ever dwell richly in each heart of his followers in that community, with whom I had spent a year that I could class with the most pleasant of my life.

The following-Sabbath found our house well filled. After singing an appropriate hymn, and prayer, I read 1 Corinthians iii, with remarks; after which I read the license from the Wesleyan Methodist Conference, acknowledging a qualification to preach the Gospel of our Lord Jesus Christ. In it was granted liberty to organize a company of believers into a Church; and I presented our articles of agreement to build each other up in the unity of the Spirit and in the bonds of peace, regardless of name, in this "Christian Union Church." To this we all assented without a jar, and some of our Baptist brethren present voted in favor.

At this their minister, arose with an acknowledgment that he had not understood the foundation of this organization before, and regretted very much what he had said against it, and would ask pardon of all these brethren and sisters and of myself. Before I had an opportunity to reply their deacon and another followed, asking pardon for what they had said, for now they saw the wrong. I replied that if feelings had been hurt by whatever had seemed unkind, they were now healed by the same love and unity that had so universally prevailed in our little band, that had given courage and strength all through the year. Here were sad faces brightened; and others followed me, manifesting the healing power of love. The Lord was in our minds reconciling to himself, and melting away every apparent root of bitterness.

I left them again united, but our little Baptist organization lived only till their fourth meeting. From their own choice it was discontinued; and, as the majority in that community were of Methodist proclivities, it has never ceased to be of that family name, being a few months after reorganized under the auspices of the Methodist Episcopal Church.

I had, previous to leaving this field, written to William Anderson's wife, Maria, directed to her father, and dated in Adrian, Michigan, and I instructed letters from her to be sent to that city in my care. Soon after my return a letter came from her father, as William had directed. I opened it, and found the very plausible plan of bringing William's wife and four children to him. Her father wrote of the loss of his own wife; and as the size and color of Maria answered to the description of his own wife, as recorded on his manumission papers, be proposed to take Maria and the children a few miles away in the night, where they would be kept secreted until the excitement of hunting for them was over, when he proposed to take them a night's journey northward. By that time he hoped that he could travel openly, with his free papers. I replied as William requested, in his name, and forwarded both the letter and a copy of my reply to him, with a renewed caution for him not to cross the Detroit River, as it was possible that all these plans were devised by his enemies, instead of the father-in-law and his wife. They had desired him to meet them on their way, and also inquired for names of places and persons who aided him, for the purpose of passing through safely to some point where they could meet to part no more until death itself should separate them. I wrote him to wait patiently the result, and not allow himself to become too much elated over this plausible plan, for I had written "that there were many friends who assisted him, whose names he had forgotten, neither could he call to mind the names of the many places he passed through, for he was taken from place to place in haste. They, too, would find no lack of friends; and if they brought his family to Adrian, Michigan, and inquired for Mrs. Laura S. Haviland, a widow, they would learn where he could be found."

Not many days elapsed before the answer came in the person of a Southerner, accompanied by Mr. Warren, of Detroit, with my letter in his hand and with the statement that I would know the where abouts of William Anderson. He said his family had arrived in Detroit with his wife's father and that they were in the family of a colored minister by the name of Williams.

I told him I was acquainted with the Williams family, and was very glad to hear of the arrival of William Anderson's family, over whom he had been very anxious, and inquired when they came.

"Yesterday, about four o'clock," was the reply. "There seems to be quite an interest in the family by the white people. Mr. Hallack gave me five dollars to pay William's fare to Detroit to meet his family, as I volunteered to come for him. And here's a letter he sent to his father in law, you can read for yourself."

I took it, and as I opened it recognized the letter I wrote for him. "Yes, this is all right, it is the letter I wrote for William."

Beginning to appear quite nervous, he said "You see in that there is a statement that you would know where he's at work, and," taking out his watch, "I see we'll have to hurry to get to Adrian by train time and if you'll be so kind as to tell me where to find him as they are very anxiously waiting for us, I shall be obliged to you. It would be a great disappointment if we should fail to reach Detroit when the next train goes in."

He walked to and fro across the room, first to the door, then to the window, in a hurried, excited manner, while I was purposely detaining him to see him tremble. I was quite satisfied that he was a bogus coin by the index of his face. When I told him, at length, that he was working in Chatham, Canada West, and that I wrote this direction to avoid any possible scheme or plot to return him to hopeless bondage, his face reddened and voice trembled as he replied "I don't know any thing about it, only what Mr. Hallack told me. That is every thing that I know in this matter."

I told him what Mr. Hallack had informed him was all right, and he could tell him to send the family on the first train from Windsor to Chatham, and they would meet William there. He bowed, "I thank you;" but looked as if his words very much misrepresented him.

By the time he was out of sight I had my horse and buggy ready, to follow him to Adrian, to telegraph Horace Hallack and George De Baptist to forward a dispatch to William Anderson, Chatham, Canada West, to leave that city without an hour's delay, as I was satisfied his enemies from Missouri were after him, and probably would take him as a murderer. The telegram was sent, and he obeyed its request.

Within two days my caller was there, inquiring for William, and was told by a number that he had been at work in town some time, but left a couple of days before, but knew not where he went. After a few days' search and inquiries in that town, he returned to Detroit, and for the first time called on Horace Hallack to inform him that he was in search of a colored man by the name of William Anderson, who was a free man, that had committed in the State of Missouri a cold-blooded murder of a Baptist deacon, for the paltry sum of five dollars, and he understood he had been quite recently in Chatham, Canada, but had left that city. He, would like advice as to what course to pursue to ascertain his whereabouts. Horace Hallack referred him to George De Baptist, who was well acquainted with leading colored men in many localities both in Canada and this side the river.

Our Missourian was now in good hands, as I followed my dispatch to them with a long letter, giving William Anderson's experience in detail. George De Baptist told him if he had been a slave, he would have taken every measure within his reach to protect him in his freedom.

But as he said he was always free, and such a high-handed murderer as he represented, he would go just as far to bring him to justice. "I will tell you what I will do; I will write to an intelligent colored man in each of the largest settlements of colored people, Chatham, Amhurstburg, and Sandwich, and will receive replies from each within four days, and I will give you the result of their inquiries." At the time appointed the Missourian returned for tidings.

Said George, "I have received answers from each letter, and from Amhurstburg and Sandwich they write they have known or heard nothing of a man by that name; but the man to whom I wrote in Chatham has known all about him, being well acquainted with him, and he writes that William Anderson had been talking of going to Sault St. Marys, and that he left two weeks ago, rather mysteriously, without telling him or any one else where he was going; but the greater probability was he went there."

He gave the letters to him, to read for himself. Consequently he hired Mr. Warren and another man, and took the trip to Sault St. Marys, where he spent a week inquiring for William Anderson; but be failed to get the least clew to his whereabouts, and returned to Detroit. He left a power of attorney with his friend Warren to arrest him in case be could be decoyed over the Detroit river; if that plan did not succeed, he was to telegraph him if he found his whereabouts in Canada. If these plans failed, he left directions to arrest me with a United States warrant. But about the time I was to have been arrested Mr. Warren, the man who was empowered to arrest me, died with cholera --a singular coincidence. Mr. Warren's brother expressed deep sorrow and regret to find the papers granting legal authority to transact such business in his brother's possession at the time of his death. He allowed George De Baptist to see them before they were destroyed. This was the second time cholera defeated my arrest.

Pursuit was still continued for William Anderson. Three years after I fell in company with D. L. Ward, attorney of New Orleans, in a stage between Ypsilanti and Clinton, Michigan. He was making some complaints about the North, which drew forth a few remarks from me. "Oh, I am glad I've got hold of an abolitionist. It is just what I have wished for ever since I left my home in New Orleans. Now I want to give you a little advice, and, as it will cost you nothing, you may accept it freely, and I hope you will profit by it; and that is, when you abolitionists have another Sims case, call on Southern legal gentlemen, and we will help you through. We would have cleared Sims, for that Fugitive slave Law is defective, and we know it, and we know just how to handle it."

"Why did you introduce a defective bill?"

"Because we made up our minds to bring you Northerners to our terms, whether it was constitutional or not, and we have done it, because we knew we could do it; not because we cared for a few niggers; for I say, if a nigger cares enough for freedom to run for it, he ought to have it. Now we knew that was an unconstitutional thing before we put it before Congress; but we put it there to let you know we could drive it down Northern throats, and we did it, too."

"I acknowledge," I replied, "that there is too much servility in our North; there is too much crouching and cringing, but I am prepared to say there are more than seven thousand that have never bowed the knee to your Baal of slavery, and never will. We never shall do homage to your Southern goddess, though you may cry loud and long in demanding its worship. You say if we have another slave case, if we come to you to help us through, you will do it, and that if a slave wants his freedom bad enough to run for it, you think he ought to have it?"

"Yes, madam, we will aid you, for we know just how to handle that thing."

"Supposing a man is about to be sold from his family, and he falls at his master's feet, and pleads in tears to remain with his family, and promises to serve him faithfully all the days of his life, if he will only permit them to remain together; but the master persists in the sale; the slave makes his escape; is overtaken by his master, yet, severely wounding him, he succeeds in gaining his liberty. Now what do you say in regard to this supposed case?"

Looking me full in the face, he asked my name, which was given. Said he, "I think I am acquainted with that case. Is it not William Anderson, a runaway from Missouri?"

"William Anderson's case is very similar to the one I have described."

"Oh yes, madam, and you are implicated in that affair, but as you are a lady I will not disturb you; but you are liable to great difficulty in that case, and I will tell you we are going to have Anderson by hook or by crook; we will have him by fair means or foul; the South is determined to have that man, and you'll find your House of Refuge will not protect him either."

"This is the way I perceive you Southern legal gentlemen will help us. But you will never get Anderson from Canada. Your determination will fail."

"We shall not fail, but I will tell you after I return from our filibustering tour, as we am going out next month. We are confident of success in that, too, for our fleet is in good condition. We shall then take Anderson, if not before, and let you see how much your House of Refuge will do to hold that man from the South."

I never heard from D. L. Ward from that day. I had written previous to this interview to the governor-general, Lord Elgin, of the first effort to retake him as a murderer. He replied that, "in case of a demand for William Anderson, he should require the case to be tried in their British court; and if twelve freeholders should testify that he had been a man of integrity since his arrival in their dominion, it should clear him." This information, however, I did not reveal to our Southern lawyer.

Three years later, in which time I had succeeded in finishing my Raisin Institute building, and reopened the institution in charge of a principal from Oberlin College, the sad tidings reached me that William Anderson was lodged in jail in the city of Toronto, under charge of murder committed in the State of Missouri. He was awaiting his trial, and Gerrit Smith was one of his legal advisers. I wrote immediately informing him of the previous efforts to search out his whereabouts, and that his pursuers at that date (1853) alleged that he was a free man, and had never been a slave. In reply, Gerrit Smith wrote:

"I am glad you have given me so much of his history. Poor Anderson! I visited him in jail. I will send you my speech in his behalf. I hope the friends will purchase his family. I have volunteered to do all I can for the poor man. Lord Elgin is removed; the present governor-general is a stranger to this case. God bless you.

"I am truly your friend, GERRIT SMITH."

A few days later, I received the thrilling speech of Gerrit Smith, like the man, full of pure and soul-inspiring thought; but I trembled with fear when two of the three judges were in favor of returning William Anderson to the State of Missouri, and that Riggs the claimant was liable to succeed; but through the efforts of his friends, and the opposing judge, the case was appealed to a higher court, and William Anderson was sent to England, where he remained in safety until the war opened, in which time the case was adjusted in his favor. The Missouri agent, Riggs, failed, and the friends of liberty rejoiced.

Three young men fled from Daniel Payne, Kentucky, and succeeded in reaching Canada, where they had proven themselves worthy of their hard-earned freedom. A few months elapsed, and their master came for them, and tried to hire them to go back with him, promising to make over to them manumission papers as soon as they returned. But he failed to inspire Alfred and his two brothers with confidence in his promise of freedom and fair wages for their work. He then secured the aid of a colored man to invite them to a dancing party in Detroit a few days after, but the boys mistrusted that their old master had the handling of this invitation, and did not accept it.

As they had been annoyed two weeks by the various plans of "Master Dan Payne," they concluded the next time he gave them a call to appear more social, and gave their plan to forty or fifty of their friends, who were to lie in ambush near the old barracks, where one of the brothers was to have a chill, and appear too sick to go over the river. But two days passed before the opportunity arrived that enabled them to carry out their plan. When Alfred informed the ex-master of the illness of his brother, of course he must hasten to the sick boy with a nice brandy-sling for the chills, and he purchased a good quantity for them all. While he was handing a glass of sweetened brandy to the sick man, a company of men rushed in and held him, while Alfred and two brothers stripped him of his coat, vest, boots, socks, and pants, and tied him with a rope in the same way the master had tied their mother, when he compelled her to be stripped, and tied her with his own hands, and whipped her until the blood ran to the ground. Alfred and his brothers applied dexterously the slave-whip, which they had provided for the occasion by borrowing a plantation slave-whip kept by Henry Bibb as a reminder of his slave life. Daniel Payne begged heartily for mercy. Alfred replied: "Yes, this is just the way my mother begged for mercy; but you had no mercy for her, and this is to show what she received at your cruel hands." They applied the lash until the forty stripes their mother had received at his hands had been given. Then they unbound him and gave him fifteen minutes to dress and leave Canada, and gave him a quarter to go with, keeping his watch and purse, which contained about forty dollars. He crossed the river within the given time, and sent an agent to call on the authorities, to whom he entered a complaint of being robbed of a gold watch and one hundred dollars, but made no complaint of the whipping. He affected to be too lame "with rheumatism" to return to his Kentucky home for a number of days, in which time the boys returned his watch, but kept the money. Alfred and his brothers said Mr. Payne was as untruthful about the amount of money as he was in calling his old silver watch gold. Suffice it to say, the young men were never after troubled or annoyed by Daniel Payne, of Kentucky. Although it was a course I would never have inaugurated, yet it was largely in human nature to requite the cruelties heaped upon their mother when it was beyond their power to protect her.

With very many pleasant remembrances, I left this laborious field of labor for home work, where I spent nearly three years looking after the best interests of my children, and making preparations to reopen Raisin Institute, for the moral, intellectual, and spiritual improvement of our youth.

RESCUE OF SLAVES

A family of six left their old Kentucky home in search of freedom. A young wife who was sold had made her escape three years previously. I noticed a stranger passing through my gate, and as he was a mulatto, I went out to see where he had gone. I found him sitting in the porch, waiting to see some one of whom to inquire whether he was at the right place. He handed a paper directed to me by an under-ground railroad ticket agent, who informed me there were six fugitives in his company. "Then there are six of you?" I asked; "and where are the balance?" "My two brothers are back a-ways," he replied, "'cause we's feared it wasn't the right place."

Being assured all was right, he went back for them. They had left their mother, with her two little grandchildren, in Carthaginia, until the boys could find a safe home for them, but they knew not whether they should go on to Canada or find the object of their search short of that place. They heard in Carthaginia that Michigan was the last place she had been heard from, and that was a short time after passing through that town. They were directed to me as being most likely to know the whereabouts of the young wife. They had been in my home a number of hours before the elder brother dared make the inquiry. I noticed the frequent heavy sigh and sad countenance, and I thought he was probably very anxious over the safety of his mother, and I assured him that she was in good hands, for I knew them to be true friends. While he assented, yet all my words of encouragement did not seem to cheer him, while the two younger brothers were happy. I went through my usual course of giving them new names. As they left that entirely with me, I gave as the family name Koss, and their given names Benjamin, Richard, and Daniel. But I came to the conclusion that the older brother was troubled over some friends he had left behind. At length, in a half hesitating and trembling manner, he ventured to ask if I knew any thing of a colored girl by the name of Mary Todd.

"Certainly I do," said I; "and did you know her?"

"Yes, ma'am," was his reply.

"Do you know whether her husband was sold? She worried a great deal about him."

"No, they talked of selling him lately." Then, after a pause, "She isn't married again, is she?"

"Why, no, she is a very steady, nice young woman. Every one in the neighborhood where she lives takes a great interest in her. Perhaps you are acquainted with her husband; why don't he come? He promised to follow her as soon as he could."

While his countenance lit up with joy, I had no suspicion of who he was until he said, "I am the man. I am her husband."

"Why didn't you tell me that before?"

"I was 'fraid of bad news if I got any."

"Afraid she was married?"

"Well, it's been mighty nigh three years, an' I couldn't go for a long time off the plantation, after she left."

As she was twelve miles from our school, and by this time it was nearly night, I hastened to inform brother Canfield, a Wesleyan minister, that the older brother of these fugitives was Mary Todd's husband. "Is it possible," he asked, "that Mary's husband has come at last?"

Soon, quite an excitement was produced in our neighborhood over the arrival of Mary Todd's husband. The next morning brother Canfield took him in his buggy to meet his wife and little son he had never seen; and a time of great rejoicing was in the whole neighborhood. As they were married after slave style, brother Canfield solemnized the marriage legally. The minister said we all forgot the black skin, when we saw that couple fly to each other's arms. Surely,

> "Skins may differ, but affection
> Dwells in black and white the same."

Mary had lived most of the time in the family of Fitch Reed, of Cambridge. They soon had a home for their mother, with her two little granddaughters, and were all happy, industrious, and highly respected.

One of the common trials of life, to mar our happiness in our family- like institution (February 23d) was the listless waywardness of some of our dear students, in a determined purpose to attend a dancing party under the guise of an oyster supper. How many delusive snares are laid to entrap and turn aside the youth into divergent paths. We found it necessary to suspend eight of our students for the remainder of the term. It is a painful duty of the surgeon to amputate a limb, yet it may be an imperative duty, in order to save the life of the patient, and restore the body to health.

This evening a very remarkable fugitive slave came from Tennessee. He had been five weeks on the way, in which time he had slept but one night, having traveled at night and buried himself in hay and straw in barns in the day-time to keep from perishing with cold, and to avoid detection. He says six years ago his wife and child were sold from him, which caused him days and nights of bitter tears. He then firmly resolved to make an attempt to gain his freedom by flight. He was captured in Illinois after a severe struggle. He showed us four pistol-ball holes in the arm he was most dexterously using in his own defense, and two large scars which he said were gashes made at the same time with a Bowie-knife, which enabled his enemies to capture him. After they secured him in jail he was advertised in papers, which his master saw, and came and took him back, and caused him to be whipped on the bare back until the flesh was so badly torn that he was compelled to lie on his stomach four weeks. During this time he was not able to turn himself. After recovering his master put him in the iron works, of which he was proprietor. "If I hadn't been one of his engineers he would have sold me instead of giving me that awful whipping that he thought conquered me; but he was mightily mistaken; for it only imbedded in my heart a more bitter hate than ever. I appeared contented and performed my work well. After a few months, he said one day, 'I've made you a good boy, Jim, and now I'll let you go to the big city with me.' I was very obedient, but he little knew of my determination to leave him as soon as I could make sure work of it. That is the reason I would not make friends with white people till I found Michigan, for we have heard that people in this State are friendly to us, and that it is next to Canada."

As this man was above mediocrity as to intelligence, his two days stay with us had a salutary influence over our school. He could not be prevailed upon to rest longer, as he could not be easy until he reached Victoria's dominions. His clothes were made comfortable, and I called on a few friends for a little pocket change, and sent by him a little note to the next station, where he was aided on to Canada.

Our Spring term opened with fair prospects. A number of our students who were suspended last term returned to us, they said, to redeem themselves, and they were as good as their word.

During our long vacation I attended an anti-slavery convention in Cincinnati, where I met a white slave man from Little Rock, Arkansas, who left his home in the night and by morning took public conveyance as any other white man would. On reaching Cincinnati he found friends of the slave to whom he revealed his condition. Levi Coffin advised him to go with me to Michigan. As he was in greater haste than I was, he proposed to go on at once. Consequently I wrote a letter of introduction to my friends, requesting them to furnish him with work. In two weeks I returned and found my young friend, Charles McClain, (for that was the name I gave him in Cincinnati) at work with a friend, who said it was a pity that I had introduced him as a fugitive slave, for they would not have believed it if the statement had not come from me.

He came to our school and improved very much upon what he had picked up from the white children who were going to school, and by the aid of a colored minister who could read and write, and by that means could read in the second reader and write a little. He was often seen in tears, and was very anxious to have his sister with him, who was as white as himself and, like him, had straight auburn hair, blue eyes, and perfect Caucasian features, without a vestige of African descent that could be detected. A deep sympathy was enlisted in his behalf. He was very anxious to convey intelligence to that sister of the ease with which he effected his escape, and that she too could free herself as easily. A number of the friends offered to aid, and one friend placed thirty dollars in my hands to bring about this result. I wrote to a colored minister in Little Rock, who replied, with a graphic account of their rejoicing at his success, and of his sister Ann's anxiety to come to him, but that she had no means. Charles wrote to her that he would send means with instructions. As I had for many years had a great desire to see more of the system of slavery in its own territory, as so many people of the North were insisting upon our exaggerations, and that we were judging the majority of slave-holders by the few unprincipled men we had seen, I concluded to become the bearer of this message.

With a well-defined plan of the streets and houses I left my home, in confidence that the God of Daniel would return me unharmed. After a little visit with my dear friends, Levi and Catharine Coffin, in Cincinnati, I resumed my journey. I felt a little disappointed at the leaving of a through boat an hour earlier than reported. Levi said, "Perhaps thou'lt find it's all for the best," and so it was. For the second day after leaving Cincinnati the vessel was burned and sunk, with great loss of property, and many of the passengers were seriously injured, and some fatally. As I soon after passed the wreck of partially burned furniture floating near the shore, and some hauled out lying on the bank, I was thankful for the disappointment.

At Napoleon I left the boat for another to go up the Arkansas river, and waited at the best hotel in the place, kept by the widow Reeves. She was probably a fair specimen of Southern women. The appearance of the people made me feel as if I was out of these United States. There was quite a company waiting to go up or down the river. Among them were six or eight young people--Colonel Thompson with his son and daughter, whom he was taking home from their school in Helena, Arkansas, and a young Dr. Jackson, who was very talkative and filled to over-flowing with affectation. With a twirl of his little cane, and half-bent bow, in a simpering manner he addressed the four young ladies sitting on the sofa before him:

"How did you rest last night, ladies?"

"Quite well, I thank you."

"Indeed, I am very happy to hear it, for I did not. I was dreaming all night of shooting and stabbing, and I had an awful time. I suppose it was owing to the awful time we had when I was here last over a nigger fight, or rather a fight over a nigger. It seems he had started to run away and they overtook him here, and he fought like a tiger. He had armed himself with a six-shooter, and I tell you he made the bullets fly lively, and they shot him before they could catch him. He shot one man dead and wounded two or three others, and I was called upon to extract a ball from the shoulder of one man."

During this conversation, and much more not recorded, I was writing a letter home, directed to a friend in Covington, Kentucky. There was an understanding, while in Cincinnati, that Levi Coffin was to take my letters from our Covington friends, and mail them home.

To my great relief, the small boat, "Rough and Ready," came in, and was to leave for Indian Territory, up the Arkansas River, in two hours; but a large boat was going up the next day. I went on both to see what they were, and I found the large boat looked more like an old slaver than a civilized craft, and made my choice without making known the reason. There was in the hotel an old lady going on the large boat, and she urged me to accompany her, and a young woman was going on the "Rough and Ready," who was anxious I should go with her, as she was alone, and going to her mother in Little Rock. The old lady said she was alone, and was going to her daughter, and asked Mrs. Reeves to intercede in her behalf. "Now, Mrs. Smith, I'll make a bargain with you. There is a rich widower on the big boat, and he's got lots of niggers and money. I'll give him to you if you'll go on that boat; and, I tell you, he's rich as Croesus." I had to enter somewhat into these familiarities, and told her I would not think of being so selfish as to take him from her.

I finished my letter-writing, and her Pomp was told to take my satchel to the boat with the young woman. There were Colonel Thompson and son and daughter, who made themselves quite too familiar to be comfortable. I soon noticed the captain seemed quite disconcerted, and made many excuses. His cabin help were set to cleaning and setting things in order, and his cook sent ashore for nuts, candies, and fruits. We hardly had started when Colonel Thompson charged me with being a reporter for some periodical. I assured him of his mistake.

Said he, "I knew you were a reporter; and when Mrs. Reeves was urging so persistently to have a dance, I whispered to my young folks not to have any thing to do with it, for you'd have us all in some newspaper."

I told him I was writing a letter to my folks.

Said he, "You need not think you are going to fool us in that way. I saw you write a few minutes, then stop, and listen awhile to Dr. Jackson and those young ladies, and then write again, then stop to listen to Mrs. Reeves, and then write again. I told my children they could see you had five or six pages for some paper; and you can never make me believe that was all for a letter. Now, if you will answer one question I'll release you. Haven't you written an article for a paper some time?"

I hesitated, for the next query would be, "What paper? At length I thought of the note of correction I wrote for the Louisville Courier, while in that city, in behalf of Calvin Fairbanks, while he was there in prison. I finally told him I would not say I had never written any thing for a paper.

"Now, if you will pardon me, just one more question, and if you will answer that I will be as good as my word, and trouble you no more on that score. What paper have you written for? I would like to know whether it was a Helena paper or any one in our State."

"No, not in this State," said I; "I did write a little card for the Louisville Courier."

"Ah, yes, that's it; that is a good Democratic paper. I am acquainted with the editor. I knew you were trying to cheat us all the while. I wish you would write an article for the Little Rock Democrat, If you will I will send the editor a letter of introduction; and I know he will pay you well for it."

But I declined, and was very much relieved when the Thompson family reached their home in Pine Bluff. Here I saw their slaves come to meet them for their baggage. They urged me to stop with them and spend a week or two, and they would take me out into the country to see some beautiful plantations, as they had an excellent carriage driver. The young woman said "Pa has owned him a number of years, and could always risk us with him anywhere. Our plantation is not a very large one, as pa has always had a store on his hands, but there are some very large and beautiful ones beyond us."

A sense of relief came over me as I saw them leave the boat, and we were the next day landed in Little Rock. Being after dark, I spent the night at the Anthony House. Before sunrise I was at the house of our friends, who were greatly rejoiced, and sent for the minister, with whom we consulted. After making all necessary arrangements, with the signs fixed upon whereby I might understand when the expected boat would arrive, whether any unfavorable indications were noticed, etc I inquired for a private and convenient boarding house where I could remain a few days waiting for tidings from a through boat. The family they named happened to be where the young woman who came on the same boat with me was boarding, with her mother and brother in law, who was keeping a tailor's shop. I inquired of this young woman and her mother if they thought I could secure board there a few days, while waiting for tidings from a brother. They thought Mrs. Shears might not have a convenient room for me but they would be glad to have me in their room. Soon the matter was settled. The son in law brought in sewing for his mother and sister in law, and I made myself useful by assisting them. The mother, Mrs. Springer, had a nice shally dress for me to make, that she said she couldn't have got made to suit her as well for eight dollars, and urged me quite hard to go in with herself and daughter in opening a shop for dress-making. I also did some sewing for Mrs. Shears, who also became quite social.

Mrs. Shears was very cruel to her slaves, and complained of the indolence of Jack, a boy of twelve years. "But I haven't got him fairly broke in yet. Don't you think, after I paid eight hundred dollars in gold for that nigger, and set him to shell a barrel of corn, he spent all that day in doing nothing? I was just ready to go away, when a nigger-drover brought a few he had left, and said he'd sell cheap, as it was the last he had on hand. He wanted nine hundred; but I told him I'd give him eight hundred in gold, and at last he concluded to take it. Well, as I told you, I set him to shelling on that barrel of corn, and I don't s'pose he shelled a dozen ears after I was gone. Don't you think, that nigger spent all that day in bawling after his mother--a great booby, twelve years old! He might have some sense in his head. I gave him one dressing, to begin with; for I found he'd got to know who was master. I've had him six weeks, and he isn't hardly broke in yet."

Poor motherless child! No doubt she too wept bitterly over the separation; but no word of pity, or even a sigh of sympathy, must be allowed here. I must listen to this, and a great deal more, with stoical indifference.

As Mrs. Shears had more company than usual, she came to me one evening, and asked if I would take her daughter's bed in her room, shielded with curtains, for the night. This was satisfactory to me. The following morning, at gray dawn, the two little boys, Jack and Jim, came in with fire from the kitchen, with kindling. The mistress rolled out of bed, and took her heavy-heeled shoe, dealing blows upon their heads and shoulders, and said:

"How come you niggers till this time o' day in here to build fires?"

"Aunt Winnie didn't wake us."

"I'll wake you up; here almost daylight, and not a fire built yet, when these four fires ought to have been built an hour ago. And didn't wake up, ha? I'll teach you to wake up."

And so she kept up the heavy blows, chasing them round and round the chairs, and the boys crying, "I will get up early, missus; I will get up early," till it seemed to me an unreasonable punishment.

Just as the two fires were going, and the little fellows went to light the other two, the son, Joe Shears, came in.

"What are these niggers about, that these fires are not all going long ago?"

"O, they had to sleep this mornin'; they say Aunt Winnie didn't wake 'em."

"I'll wake the young devils; I'll see whether they'll sleep till broad daylight. It's their business to have these fires going an hour ago;" and out he went.

At breakfast, I noticed Jim, the waiter, was missing, and Jack was not at his wood-chopping as usual. Soon after, as I passed through the rear porch, I saw the two little boys hanging, as I supposed, by their wrists, to a pole over the bay in the barn. The door was just opened by Joe Shears, to commence his day's work of whipping, as I soon heard the cries of one, then the other, alternating in stripes heard with their cries, by spells, until noon. During this time Joe Shears was sitting before the fire, playing cards and sipping his brandy between the whippings. Whenever he was out the whipping and cries were heard.

At noon little Jim was let down, very hoarse from crying, and his eyes red and swollen. By his walk I knew the little fellow had suffered intensely. But the little wood-chopper was not at his post. Soon after dinner the lash was again heard, with the hoarse cry of little Jack; and each time Joe Shears sat down to his card-table I looked for Jack, but after a game or two of cards he was out again, and the lash and cries resumed. I became so distressed that at four o'clock I took a walk on the street, ostensibly to rest by exercise after a day of sewing, but really to give vent to tears that had been all day pent up, for all appearance of sympathy must here be restrained. On my return I heard the battling of the paddle, with the cries of poor Jack, so hoarse that I could hardly have recognized it as a human voice had I not known what it was. I got no glimpse of the poor child until the next morning.

As the tailor, Joseph Brink, came in, the sister-in-law said, "We ought to have a lamp or candle lit before this time."

Said the mother, "We don't feel half thankful enough for this grate-fire. Just think, Joe Shears has been whipping those two little boys all this blessed day, and I should think they must be half dead to- night."

"What have they done?" said Joseph.

"I don't know; do you, Mrs. Smith?"

"Yes; you know I slept in Mrs. Shears's room last night; and the boys came in at nearly daylight with their pan of fire and kindling, and the mistress wanted to know why their fires were not all built before, and they said Aunt Winnie didn't wake them. And she whipped them with her shoe quite a while; then Joe Shears came in, and swore at them, and said he would wake them."

"And that was it? Only think," said Mrs. Springer; "you know Aunt Winnie was sick yesterday. And just because they hadn't these fires all built before daylight they've had them tied up in the barn all day; that cowhide Mrs. Shears keeps hung on her door-knob her Joe has swung over those two little niggers all day. I tell you, if the devil don't catch such people there's no use of having a devil."

Her son-in-law, in an undertone, said, "Be careful; don't talk so loud, or it will make a fuss here."

"Well, I don't care, I am mad. I tell you, Joe, hell is lined this very minute with just such folks as these."

"Well, I think they are more cruel here than they are in Georgia."

"I've seen just such work in Georgia and in Alabama, and it's all over. I tell you, there's more in hell to-night for treating niggers this way than for all other sins put together, and I know it."

"Be careful; they'll hear you, and it will make trouble. It's their property; it's none of ours."

"I don't care for that; they are human beings, and have feelings as well as other folks. There's that little nigger, Bob, they've hired of Dr. Webb, down street; they whip him and pound him about, and they'll kill him some day. And I think somebody ought to report to Dr. Webb how they are treating that young nigger. He is a mighty nice-looking boy. He is almost white, and they've got him all scarred up."

"Well, what of that? The doctor himself is no better. About three months ago his boy Tom was throwing wood in his cellar, and he did something he didn't like, and he kicked him down the cellar, then jumped down after him and took a billet of wood and was pounding Tom over his head when two white men were passing by and saw the whole affair; and as Tom fell the doctor came up out of the cellar and went down town and reported his Tom had a fit. But the two men went into the cellar after the doctor left and found him dead and his skull broken in. They reported what they saw and had a coroner's inquest over him, who found that Tom came to his death by too severe punishment. They arrested the doctor and put him in jail a few days, when his trial came off. The doctor was fined five hundred dollars, and he paid it and went free."

"Yes, that is the doctor we've been sewing for, is it?"

"Certainly."

"I tell you, hell is heaped with just such people."

She went on in that strain that reminded me of St. Clair's "cursing up hill and down" that almost frightened the New England old maid of "Uncle Tom's Cabin." I trembled myself, expecting every moment that some member of the family would hear her.

Two days later was washing-day, and the cook, Aunt Winnie, told her mistress she was too sick to do the very large washing for three boarders besides the family. I heard the mistress cursing her, and telling her she could if she had a mind to, and charged her with being lazy.

In came her son Joe. "What's all this fuss?"

"O, it's Winnie says she's sick and can't do the washing this week."

"Sick! I'll see how sick she is," and he took up a billet of stove wood and commenced beating her over her head and shoulders, and swearing that he would give her something to be sick for. Mrs. Springer called my attention to the quarrel of Mrs. Shears with her cook before Joe Shears came in. Then said she, "Poor Aunt Winnie will catch it now, I'll warrant. There, just hear those blows; they sound like beating the table; he'll kill her." And table, stools, and tin-pans or pails made racket enough for the whole kitchen to be falling down. The struggle with a volley of oaths lasted a few minutes.

Mrs. Springer, up to boiling rage again, "Hear that; what devils they are; don't you believe Aunt Winnie will die? Why, I can't hold still." In as careless a manner as I could command I said, "We can do no good by saying any thing. You know what your son said the other night."

"I know it; but there isn't a particle of humanity about them. I feel as if I want to pitch into the whole Shears family." Soon all was quiet.

"I believe Aunt Winnie is dead, don't you?"

"I think not."

"I am going in there to see."

As she got up to go to the kitchen she took the pitcher for water. While she was pumping the water near the kitchen-door, Aunt Winnie staggered to the door trying to wind a cloth around her bleeding head, and one eye was swollen shut. As she came in and reported how badly she was bruised up, she wanted me to take the pitcher and go to the pump for water; but I told her I would wait a little, for they might think we went on purpose to see Winnie.

"Poor thing, I know she came to the door on purpose to let me see her." And Mrs. Springer could not rest satisfied until I drew the next pitcher of water, when the poor woman reeled to the door with her hand on her head and the cloth around it saturated with blood. I could not sleep a wink after the day of the unmerciful whipping of those two little boys. Again the night after this unmerciful beating of this poor woman was spent in weeping, and prayer to Him who hears the cries of his oppressed children.

A few days after Aunt Winnie came to Mrs. Springer and asked her if she would cut and make a green delaine sacque for her, and cut a calico skirt, as she could make that in the night, and charged her not to let her mistress see it or let her know she had it, because her husband got it for her and gave her seventy-five cents to get Mrs. Springer to cut it; "for he is going to take me away three weeks from next Saturday night, 'cause the people are so hard here; he says I shan't stay here any longer." "I am so sorry for her, I told her to come in when her mistress and Joe Shears's wife are away making calls, and I would take her measure and cut and baste it: then for her to come in after they are all in bed and I would fit it and make it any time, keeping it under a sheet I've got to make, and in that way I can keep it out of sight; and I told her you and my daughter will say nothing about it. Said Winnie, 'I knows that by her face.' Do you know how quick these black people read faces?"

While she was sewing on Aunt Winnie's sacque, Joe Shears's wife came into our room a little while, and the daughter looked out the back window, where Jack was chopping, and said, "I don't think your Jack is going to live long."

"Why? I'm sure he eats hearty."

"He looks so bad out of his eyes; I've noticed it a few days past, and I've noticed he sort o' staggers sometimes, and he don't talk natural."

She jumped up and looked at him and hastened to her mother in law's room.

"Mother, Miss Springer says Jack is going to die."

"What makes her think Jack is going to die? I don't see any thing ails Jack, he eats hearty."

Miss Springer (laughing): "I thought I'd scare her out. I wish I could scare them to death, so they would treat their niggers like human beings."

"Well, you've got her out of the way long enough to get Winnie's sacque out of sight before our Joe comes in, for he's so mighty careful for fear we'll get into trouble; I know he'd scold if he knew it."

Strange position I was occupying, here among the most cruel of slave-holders. And they were calling me a superintendent of the underground railroad at home; and here was the starting-point on our underground railway, but a silent listener, and in surprise, I said, "Where can Aunt Winnie and her husband go? As you say, he is a slave." "I don't know, but they do go somewhere out of the way of their owners, though they keep up a mighty hunt for a long time; yet a good many of 'em are never heard from; and I don't know where in creation they do go, and I don't care, so they get away from these hyenas that have no more feelings for their niggers than a wild animal, nor half as much. I just wonder sometimes that the niggers don't turn upon 'em and kill such devils. I know I would if I were in their places." "Yet there are those who treat their servants kindly," I replied. I felt sometimes as if I was compelled to be indifferent.

My friend passed the window at which I was engaged in sewing. After a few moments I made an excuse to rest myself by taking a little walk, as each of us frequently did. I soon overtook this friend who informed me that Ann wished to see me after her tea was over, when she would be released for a half hour to walk out on the back way with a free mulatto girl, who was her intimate and confidential friend, and I was to go in a large yard of shrubs and fruit trees where I was to meet this friend who would call for Ann, with whom we were to take the proposed walk. At the appointed time and place I met the friend, who directed me to stand in a place out of sight of the street, or little cabin, the home of her very aged and decrepit parents, who were worn- out slaves, and as I understood were given their freedom. Their slave- daughter was permitted to step in and do little chores for them after her day's work was done.

While waiting in this lonely and solitary nook, three large bloodhounds came in sight. I remembered of hearing about their being let loose after sunset, to reconnoiter the premises, and I called to mind what I had heard and read in history, that however ferocious an animal is, a stern and steady gaze in the eye, by a human being, would disarm it of ferocity, and cause it to leave. This course I resolved to pursue with these three formidable enemies, that were already assuming a threatening attitude, with a low growl, showing their teeth, with hair on end--the leader as large as a yearling calf, the two following him slightly smaller. I fixed my eyes upon the sparkling eyes of the leader, that came within six feet and stopped; soon the growl ceased, the lips dropped over the long tusks, the hair smoothed back, and he quietly walked off with his companions. Soon came the girl, all out of breath: "Did the hounds come to you?"

"They did."

"Oh, dear! what did you do?"

"I stood perfectly still," I answered, "and looked in the eyes of the leader, and they soon became quiet and walked away."

"Oh, dear, that was the only thing that saved your life. If you had stirred a particle they would have torn you in pieces. I was so anxious to have Ann see you, I forgot the hounds until I started back, and I liked to have fainted, for I know they were awful. I liked to have screamed out 'God have mercy on that dear friend,' for I was 'most sure I'd find you killed."

"Oh, no, the Lord has preserved me, and I am not harmed." She was so badly frightened that it was some time before her voice ceased trembling; but He who is ever present with his trusting children was there.

Arrangements were made for Ann to go North, but if a word of suspicion was heard, I told her she must defer going to a future time; that she must go as her brother went, perfectly independent of any one, which she was confident of doing; but she wished to go on the same boat with me, if no one else was going from their city. I learned through her friend that she was overheard to ask a friend of hers for a shawl for a journey. I sent her word to abandon the idea of going then at once; that I should take the first boat for home.

She did not obtain her freedom until after her mother's death, two or three years later. I did not regard the trip lost, painful as it was. There was on the boat a sad couple, taken from a number of their children by a young beardless boy, perhaps eighteen or twenty, small and slender. I noticed them frequently in tears. They were noticed by a few of the passengers, who made remarks about the sad faces of those negroes. Said one heartless woman, "Look at that nigger cryin'. I don't see what she's cryin' about; she's got her young one and man to her heels." I carelessly watched for an opportunity to speak with one or both of these children of sorrow. As they sat on a pile of cable on the rear deck I caught the opportunity to inquire where they were going.

"We don't know; our young massa got to frettin', an' ole massa gib us to him and some money, an' tole him to go. We lef' three bigger chillun behin'; never 'spects to see 'em ag'in; I wish he'd buy a plantation somewhar, so we could go to work; 'pears like thar's no comfort for us poor people, only when we's got work, an' stops studyin' so much."

As the tears began to fall thick and fast, I took them by the hand and told them Jesus was the friend of the poor, and he had many followers who also remembered them in prayer. And he knew of their sorrow, and as they went to him he would comfort their sorrowing hearts. Pointing to his wife, he said, "She knows that, and I wish I did." I charged them to make no mention of my having spoken to them. For while they were slaves, I was not free. This young man with his heavy-hearted couple left our boat at Pine Bluff.

Surely I had seen enough of slavery in its own household. Three weeks was long enough to see and feel its virus. I met my old friends in Cincinnati with a glad heart, where I could draw a free breath. I could visit them but two days before I was on my way home, where were many glad hearts to listen in private circles to my experience in a slave State. More than ever they were convinced that the cannon and sword would, at no very distant day, destroy the monster.

Our institution was now in its second academic year, in charge of Joseph D. Millard, of Oberlin College. The stockholders had turned it over into my hands, making me sole-proprietor of the institution, with all its multiform cares and responsibilities. I had also frequent calls from fugitives in flight for freedom, whose claims were second to none other. But to see prejudice in our students melt away by an acquaintance with our work, richly repaid me for all my day and night toiling and cares, that seemed almost crushing at times. I purchased for the young men's hall a building that was erected for a water cure. That project failed, and the building that cost $2,000 to erect, was offered for three hundred dollars for my institution. I moved it one mile, and repaired it with fifteen rooms; and it was well filled the first year. This academic year of our usual three terms our students numbered over two hundred, mostly of those who had been teaching, or preparing themselves for teachers, or for a collegiate course. I served as preceptress, and was closely confined in school work. Realizing in a great measure the importance of molding the mind of youth for usefulness, these years of constant care passed pleasantly with the hundreds of young people of our own and adjoining counties.

A colored man, with a farmer's bag swung over his shoulder, approached two men at work on the railroad between Palmyra and Adrian, and inquired how far it was to Michigan.

"You are in Michigan, you fool you," was their reply.

"Then, will you please tell me how far it is to Canada?"

"You go to Adrian, about a mile ahead, and take the cars, and they'll take you to Canada in two hours; or, if you haven't money to go that way, you can go up that road till you come to the Quaker meeting- house, and go direct east two miles to the Widow Haviland's school, and she will tell you how to go to Canada, and it won't cost you any thing.' She is a great friend to your people."

He soon found me. I got my supper out of the way, and my men folks out again at their work. I then inquired who directed him to me, and he told me "two men six miles from this school said you was a frien' to my people; an' I thought if folks knew you six miles off I would be safe to come to you, 'case I wants to go to Canada right soon. I started once before, and traveled three nights by the North star; and as Indiana was a free State I thought I would stop and buy me some broad, an' the people was mighty kind, and said I could rest a week, and they would pay me for the work I did, to help me on to Canada. But firs' I knew my master come for me, an' I seed him pay them money-- s'pose 't was reward."

This time he was so cautious that he would make a friend of no one until he reached Michigan. They had always heard people were friends to colored people in this State. He was six weeks from Kentucky, and had not dared to make his condition known to any one, white or black, until he saw a colored man in the yard at Dr Bailey's, of whom he inquired for my house. I told him that his coat and pants were too ragged, and that I must repair them. As he had not a second shirt, I took one of my son's, and gave him a couple of towels, soap, and a pail of warm water, and told him to take off his coat for me to mend, while he went up stairs to the room over the kitchen to change his shirt. He hesitated about taking off his coat, until I told him he must. "I am not your mistress," said I, "and yet you must mind me." Tears started as he slowly drew it off, when the torn and bloody shirtsleeves revealed the long sears, and a few unhealed sores on his arms. Said I, "Are these the marks of the slave whip?"

He nodded assent, while tears were falling.

"When was this done?"

"Two nights afore I lef'."

"What was jour offence?"

"Dis was what I got for runnin' off, an' I fainted, an' master dragged me in my cabin, and didn't lock me in, 'case I's so weak. I reckon he thought I's safe. But I got an ing'on to rub over the bottoms of my shoes so dogs couldn't foller me, an' I got four loaves o' bread and a big piece o' boiled meat, an' crawled into de barn an' tuck dis bag an' buffalo-robe for my bed, an' dragged it into de woods, and tuck my bes' frien', de Norf star, an' follered clean to dis place."

"What did you do for something to eat?"

"I tuck corn in de fiel'. When I foun' log heaps an' brush burnin' I roasted a heap to las' a few days; but I was weak an' trimbly to start, an' kep' so all de way."

After this little history I made him take off his vest, which was also very reluctantly done. But what a sight! The back of his shirt was like one solid scab! I made him open his collar, and I drew the shirt off from his shoulders and from the appearance of the shoulders and back it must have been cut to one mass of raw flesh six weeks before, as there were still large unhealed sores. I told him he must sit here until I called in my son and son-in-law to see it. As they looked upon that man's back and arms, and walked around him, said Levi Camburn, my son-in-law:

"Mother, I would shoot the villain that did that as quick as I could get sight at him."

"But, Levi," I replied, "he is not fit to die."

"No, and he never will be; and the quicker he goes to the place where he belongs the better. Indeed, I would shoot him as quick as I would a squirrel if I could see him."

Joseph, my son, responded:

"I think Levi is about right, mother; the quicker such a demon is out of the world the better."

"I know this is a sad sight for us to look upon; but I did not call you in to set you to fighting."

Many of my friends, and my son-in-law Levi, had thought me rather severe in judging the mass of slaveholders by the few unprincipled men who had fallen under my special notice; but I never heard of any remark whatever from my son-in-law or neighbors, after this incident, that charged me with being too severe in judging slaveholders. I furnished the poor man with healing salve, and tried to persuade him to rest a few days until he would be able to work; but no, he must see Canada before he could feel safe. He was very loath to sleep in any bed, and urged me to allow him to lie on the floor in the kitchen, but I insisted on his occupying the bed over the kitchen. I gave him a note of introduction to the next station agent, with a little change; and a few weeks after I heard from my friend, whose name was George Wilson. The reporter said: "The first two weeks he seemed to have no energy for any thing. But then he went to work, and quite disappointed us. He is getting to be one of the best hands to hire in Windsor."

This was the second fugitive from slavery who slept in my home--mine being the first house they had dared to sleep in since leaving their old home. A few days later another fugitive came from Louisiana. He was a black-smith. I wrote to a wealthy farmer in Napoleon, Michigan, to learn whether he could not furnish business for one or the other of two new arrivals from slavery. To show the feelings of thousands of our citizens at this date, I will extract a portion of his letter:

"There are constantly in our moral horizon threatenings of strife, discontent, and outbreaks between liberty and slavery. The martyrdom of John Brown only whets the appetite of the monster for greater sacrifice of life. The continued imprisonment of Calvin Fairbanks and others are not satisfying portions. I read your letter to our Arkansas friend, and we are glad to learn that another has escaped from the land of bondage, whips, and chains. In view of the wrongs and cruelty of slavery, how truly may it be said:

'There is no flesh in man's obdurate heart;
It does not feel for man.'

"The natural bond of brotherhood is severed as flax that falls asunder at the touch of fire. Let the lot of bitter poverty be mine, and the hand of man blight every hope of earthly enjoyment, and I would prefer it to the condition of any man who lives at ease, and shares in every fancied pleasure, that the toil, the sweat, and blood of slaves can procure. Alas for the tyrant slave-holder when God shall make his award to his poor, oppressed, and despised children, and to those who seek a transient and yet delusive means of present happiness by trampling his fellow and brother in the dust, and appropriating the soul and body of his own crushed victim to the gratification of his depraved appetites and passions. I would rather enter the gloomy cell of your friend Fairbanks, and spend every hour of this brief existence in all the bitterness that the hand of tyrants can inflict, than live in all pomp and splendor that the unpaid toil of slaves could lavish upon man. Yours, etc.,

"July 27th, 1860.
R.B. REXFORD."

Our blacksmith, whom we called Charles Williams, proved to be an honest and industrious man.

We solicited over seventy dollars for a poor woman by the name of Jackson, from Marseilles, Kentucky, who had bought herself by washing and ironing of nights, after her mistress's work was done. During seven long years she did not allow herself to undress except to change. Her sleep was little naps over her ironing board. Seven years of night work brought the money that procured her freedom. She had a son and daughter nearly grow up, and to purchase their freedom she was now bending her day and night energies. Her first object was to purchase the son, as his wages would aid her to accumulate more readily the amount required for the daughter, as she had the promise of both of her children. But her economizing to purchase the son first for the sake of his help failed, as the master's indebtness compelled him to sell one of them, and market was found for the girl of sixteen. Nine hundred dollars was offered, and the distressed mother had but four hundred dollars to pay.

She had trusted in her Lord and Savior in all these years of toiling, and now must she see that daughter sold down the river? In her distress she went from house to house, to plead for a buyer who would advance the five hundred dollars, and take a mortgage on her until she could make it. At length she found a Baptist deacon who purchased her daughter, and she paid him the four hundred dollars. He was to keep her until the mortgage was redeemed by the mother, who was compelled to abandon her first project, and bend her energies toward making the five hundred dollars. After working very hard one year, she was able to pay but one hundred and fifty dollars to ward the mortgage, when her health began to fail. The deacon told her the money was coming too slowly, and that he could not wait longer than another year, before he would have to sell her to get his money back. "Weeping and prayer was my meat and drink day and night. Oh! must I see my poor chile' go after all my hope to save her?" A merchant in that town by whom she had been employed, told her he would give her a little secret advice, which was, to go to Louisville as she had done before, but not to stop there, but to go on to Cincinnati, and he would give her a good recommendation to his brother, Mr. Ketcham, who was a merchant and knew the abolitionists. They would aid her in raising the three hundred and fifty dollars; but she must not let it be known that he had advised her, or that she was going North. Mr. Ketcham introduced her to Levi Coffin and lawyer John Jolliffe, who gave her letters of introduction to friends at Oberlin, and other places, and by the time she was sent to me she had over two hundred dollars toward the release of the mortgage on the daughter. As her health was poor from constant overwork and troubles incident to slave life, to give her rest I took her papers, and while calling on the friends of humanity, did not slight some of my Democratic friends, some of whom had some years previously told me if I would go to work and purchase the slaves they would aid me.

Consequently I called on one who was living in splendor within his massive pile of brick, and reminded him of the promise he made me on a certain occasion. Now was his opportunity, as I was assisting a mother to purchase her daughter. I gave him the line through which I had received the best of endorsements as to her industrious and honest Christian character, and what the friends had done for her upon whom I had called, and but for her poor health would have brought her with me. After listening attentively to all my statements, he arose from his chair, walked nervously to and fro across his room, as if striving to his utmost to brace against sympathy, and said, "Mrs. Haviland, I'll not give a penny to any one who will steal slaves; for you might just as well come to my barn and steal my horse or wheat as to help slaves to Canada, out of the reach of their owners."

"Did I do right," I asked, "in rescuing that Hamilton family from the grasp of those Tennessee slave-holders?"

"If I had taken a family under my wing, of course, I should calculate to protect them."

"That is not the answer I call for. I want from you a direct reply; did I do right, or wrong, in that case? You remember all the circumstances."

"Oh, yes, I remember it well, and as I tell you, if I had undertaken to protect a family I should do it."

"I shall accept no prevarication whatever," said I; "I demand a square answer, and it is your duty to give it; did I do right or wrong in that case?"

He drew out his pocket-book, and emptied it in my lap. "There is hardly a dollar, and if I had more you should have it; of course you are right, and every sane man or woman knows it; but my political relations are such I wish you wouldn't say anything about it."

It is no new thing for politics to stand in the way of humanity. A few weeks later the glad mother returned and redeemed her daughter. I saw them together at Levi Coffin's, in Cincinnati, happy in their freedom.

Another woman was directed to me by William King, who, with Rev. C. C. Foote, had founded a colony a few miles from Chatham, Ontario, for fugitives from slavery. She managed to escape with seven children, and her husband's master offered him to her for six hundred dollars, two hundred dollars less than the market price. I went with her a few days, and received from the friends one hundred and thirteen dollars. Then the sight of one whom she recognized hastened her back to Canada, a proceeding which probably saved us the fate of the Oberlin or Wellington rescuers, who spent a few weeks in jail. A year after we heard the husband and father was with his family in Canada.

A few weeks elapsed when another woman from Cincinnati learned that her husband could be bought for a low figure because of a rheumatic difficulty. She had been freed three years previously, and by industry had accumulated three hundred dollars. She came well recommended by Levi Coffin and others. While making calls in her behalf in a store owned by a Democratic friend, upon presenting her claim to the proprietor and a few bystanders, a gentleman stepped into the door with, "I see you come to Democrats for aid."

"She knows her best friends," said our merchant.

"I slight no one," I answered. "I call upon my acquaintances regardless of politics.

"I will give you five dollars for every one you'll get from an abolitionist in this place," said the sparkling, black-eyed stranger.

At this quite a shout arose in the store.

"That speaks well for your abolition friends," was the ironical retort of another bystander.

"Who is that gentleman?" I inquired.

"Mr. Lyons, the banker on Main Street," was the reply.

"All right," I said, "I shall remember him." I stepped into Edwin Comstock's and mentioned this proposition.

"Very well; I will give five dollars for the sake of twenty-five dollars from Mr. Lyons," and I placed that in my book. I next met Stephen Allen on the street and I told him Mr. Lyons's pledge.

"All right," he said; "I will give four dollars, and that takes all I have in my purse to-day; but I am glad to give it for the twenty dollars we are to get from Mr. Lyons."

I called upon Anson Backus with my report and he said: "Here is five dollars for the twenty-five from Mr. Lyons." I then stepped into the Lyons's bank. "This, I believe, is Mr. Lyons, the proprietor, who pledged a few minutes ago five dollars for every one dollar I would get from an abolitionist in this place." His face flushed in reading the names with the fives and four dollar bills in the book I handed him.

"There is no abolitionist's name here."

"Isn't Edwin Comstock an abolitionist?"

"No, he isn't."

"Isn't Stephen Allen an abolitionist?"

"No, he isn't?

"Isn't Anson Backus an abolitionist?"

"No, he isn't."

"Then I ask you to define an abolitionist, for I call these men as radical abolitionists as we have in our country."

"Well, they are not."

"Please define them that I may know who they are."

"They are those who go down South and steal slaves away from their owners and report that they whip men and women and sell husbands and wives apart, and separate children from their mothers, and all that sort of thing, when it's all an arrant black-hearted lie."

"Mr. Lyons, you know all these flat denials are substantial truths. As you say you have lived in the South, you know in your own heart that men and women are cruelly whipped, and that families are separated, and these cases of cruelty are neither few nor far between. I will tell you what I have done for a woman who was a slave in Kentucky when she came to me for advice in Cincinnati, as she had a daughter to be sold, and her mistress was going to sell the whole family down the river. She was permitted to do her mistress's marketing in Cincinnati because she had confidence that she would not leave her family. I advised her to put her husband and children in that market-wagon and cover them with hay and bring them to a certain place I designated, and she would be aided in her flight to Canada. She took the plan I suggested, and her whole remaining family, nine in number, found themselves free in Canada. Was that the work of an abolitionist?"

"No, it isn't."

"Then I know not where to find one, for I see I too am out of the catalogue."

While this conversation was in progress he took three dollars from his desk and handed it to me; but as much as ever, I stopped to thank him, and told him the worst wish I had for him was that he would repent of his wicked position before the hour of death overtook him, and that he might find peace and pardon for these Satanic assertions he had made. He sat quietly listening while I gave out my indignation without stint. "Hand me back that three dollars," and it was as freely returned as I received it. He put it back in his drawer, took out five dollars and handed it to me, and hardly took time to nod "I thank you" for finishing my speech, which was not in the least interrupted, even with the increased subscription.

Poor man, I pitied him, for it was more than a year before I could get another opportunity to speak to him. His clerk left the bank as soon as he commenced his tirade. Although it is unpleasant to meet with such spirits, yet I never flee from them. If my cause is owned by the author of the Higher Law, none of these things move me. A few months after this we received a letter from Mintie Berry, the anxious wife, for whom we succeeded in raising enough to reunite the long separated couple, saying that their happy reunion was the result of favors from their many friends, to whom they returned grateful thanks, while they praised the Lord for the blessing.

I received a letter, July 4, 1859, from poor Calvin Fairbanks. Eight long years of the fifteen he had suffered in a Kentucky penitentiary. How sad are these lines, containing some of his prison reflections! He says:

"Speak kindly, ye muses, my spirit inspire,
Breathe softly and sweetly, sweep gently my lyre;
There's gloom in my harp-string's low murmuring tone,
Speak kindly, speak gently, to me here alone.

My spirit all broken--no soul-cheering ray
To warm, and illumine my cold dreary way,
No kind and beloved ones of days that are gone--
There's no one to cheer me, I'm alone, all alone.

From friends fondly cherished I'm severed away,
From the hills where I laughed at the bright early day;
And the morning of life like an arrow is gone,
Like a shadow, a moment, and here I'm alone.

The guardians of childhood, like the bright early flower.
Have blossomed with fragrance, and are lost in an hour;
And the cycle that brought them has eddied and gone,
And left me behind them, alone, all alone.

How solemn and dreary, how somber with gloom,
Are my lonely reflections, of the cold silent tomb,
The abode of a father once fearless and bold,
Of a sister once lovely, now silent and cold;

Of a mother lamenting her lost, lonely son,
Awaiting awhile, but a day to be gone,
And to mingle with spirits of blest early love,
And to rest in the bosom of Jesus above.

The thought of these loved ones, now silent for aye,
Or lingering and trembling, and passing away.
Breathes sadness on nature, most cheerful and gay,
And traces these numbers--we're passing away.

But cease my complaining, we'll soon be at peace,

> We'll rest from our labors, forever at ease;
> There's rest for the weary and joy for our gloom,
> For God is our refuge, in heaven our home.
>
> Yes, earth with her pleasures, and all that we love,
> We shall leave for the land of bright spirits above;
> No blasting nor mildew, nor soul-blighting care,
> No sorrow, no dying, no sin shall reign there."

The year 1861 opened full of excitement. Both North and South assumed threatening attitudes. Raisin Institute was affected by it; yet the work of the Lord prospered with us. Within three weeks fourteen of our students experienced the new spiritual life. But soon our ranks were broken. The seventy-five thousand men in arms called for at the first by President Lincoln were not sufficient to suppress the slave- holders' rebellion. Seventeen of our students enlisted for the bloody conflicts of civil war.

Our principal, F. M. Olcott, had purchased my institution, and I looked forward to a happy release of the $15,000 indebtedness that was resting over Raisin Institute. The room-rent was not sufficient to meet the interest and other incidental expenses, and the tuition fees were required to pay the teachers. This indebtedness rested upon my shoulders. But for the salutary influence it exerted in molding the characters of our youth, I should have failed.

The declining health of our dear brother F. M. Olcott brought increasing darkness over our future prospects, and the memorable battle of Bull Run increased the shock that startled the liberty lovers of our nation at the firing upon Fort Sumter. The cloud that hung over our nation also overshadowed our beloved institution. We closed this year with sad forebodings. Our beloved principal was fast hastening to his reward. He suggested a friend of his to fill his position the ensuing year, and died of consumption within six weeks of our vacation. He was a noble Christian man, and had endeared himself to all who enjoyed the privilege of his acquaintance. His loss was severely felt by his students, who enjoyed his faithful teaching, and especially by myself, as I had indulged the fond hope that he would become the efficient permanent principal.

The following year the institute opened with as fair prospects as could be expected, in charge of Edward A. Haight. Until the third year of the war our school was continued in successful operation. But during the last term of 1863-4, when the war had taken seventeen of our noble young men into the field, and the condition of our soldiers, daily reported as suffering and dying in camp and hospital, called for tender nursing, I offered myself for that work.

Leaving an excellent young woman as preceptress in my stead, I gathered from eighteen hundred to two thousand garments for freedmen, and hospital supplies for soldiers, and with papers from Austin Blair, governor of our State, from F. C. Beaman, member of Congress, and from others, I left my sweet home and the loved ones who still clustered around it. On my way to the depot I was met by Rev. P. Powell, who inquired how much money I had. "Fifteen dollars," was my answer.

"Why, Mother Haviland," he exclaimed, "you can never go with only that. Stop a day or two, and I'll get up eighty or a hundred dollars for you."

"But I have arranged for all my supplies to go on today. There are three or four boxes waiting for me at Hillsdale, and I wrote them I would be there to-night. I have not asked for money, but for supplies. I have a free pass to Chicago and return, and if I can get a pass free to Cairo and return, I think I can get along, and perhaps lives may be in peril in the twenty-four hours I might be waiting here for money."

"Will you telegraph me if you do not succeed in getting the passes in Chicago?"

"I will," I said, and went forward.

As I was taking leave of my son Joseph, and was about to enter the car, he held me by the hand, and said: "One promise I want you to make me, and make it so strong that your conscience will come in for a share; and that is, that you will stop, once in a while, to think whether you are tired or not. You are going among the suffering and dying, and I know you so well that you will go and go and do and do, until you will drop before you will think of yourself. If you will make me this promise I will feel a great deal better about you."

"Joseph," I said, "I will promise to do this," and we parted.

On visiting the sanitary rooms in Chicago I met Mrs. Hague, Mrs. Livermore, and others, who thought it very doubtful whether I could secure a fare free to Cairo, as President Arthur had shut down the gate on free, or even half-fare, passes. He had told them that associations might pay their agents enough to pay their fare. But I was under the auspices of no association. I was only a self- constituted agent, and I must try. Leaning on the arm of my guide, I went to President Arthur, and introduced myself by handing him my papers. On reading them he asked, rather sharply, "What do you want?"

"I am hoping to obtain a free pass to Cairo and return," I replied, "and free transportation for the supplies referred to in those papers."

"Are you alone, madam?"

"I am alone."

"Well, I think this is a heavy responsibility for a lady of your age. Are you aware of the responsibility you assume in this?" holding the paper up.

"I think I am aware of the responsibility. I do not know but the experience of age, however, may somewhat make up for the strength of youth."

"Well, I guess it will."

Settling himself back in his easy arm chair, he said again, "How long a time do you want it for?"

"I can not answer intelligently," I said, "I may wish to return for more supplies, within two or three months, and I can not say how long it will take to disburse these supplies judiciously."

"Very well," and he took my papers to his chief clerk, and soon brought me back passes, saying, "There are your passes, and they'll bring you back any time this year." He gave me also an order for free transportation. I left his office praising God for another victory.

I was met in the door of the sanitary rooms with "Did you succeed in getting a half-fare pass?"

"A free pass to Cairo and return," I said, "and free transportation for all my supplies from President Arthur."

The clerk clapped his hands, cheering: "You are a favored one; not one of us would have got that favor."

Not till then did they know of my leaving home with only fifteen dollars; yet it was sufficient.

A few hours more landed me in Cairo, where the wharf was lined with cannon, and piles of shells and balls. My first work was to find a soldiers' home, and visit hospitals. Oh, what scenes at once were presented to my view! Here were the groans of the wounded and dying soldiers. Some were praying--a few were swearing; and yet even these would patiently listen to reading the promises of Jesus and his loving invitations, and become calm.

HOSPITAL WORK

OUR last chapter left us in hospital world at Cairo. A portion of the freedmen's camp of three thousand the officers proposed to remove to Island No. 10, and wished me to take most of my supplies to that place. While waiting for their arrival I visited the United States Hospital at Mound City, a few miles up the Ohio River. Here, too, were dying soldiers, one of whom especially attracted my attention, as he was perfectly sane and rather unusually intelligent. I immediately addressed him: "My son, are you prepared to go hence?"

"Mother," he said, "that is a matter which I ought to have attended to long ago, but I did not, and now it is too late! I am dying."

"Oh, do not say too late! Remember the condition is, 'Believe and thou shalt be saved;' 'As thou hast believed, so shall it be unto thee.' These are the sure promises of our merciful Redeemer. Remember the thief on the cross looked at him with repenting spirit and living faith, and said, 'Lord, remember me when thou comest into thy kingdom;' and the quick reply was, 'This day thou shalt be with me in Paradise.' Can you not trust such a Redeemer?--such a loving Father as is our God, who saves to the uttermost all who ask with believing hearts?" He firmly held my hand and said, "I will try."

Our prayers were mingled in asking for the enlightening of the Holy Spirit, and while he was asking for the forgiveness of all his sins, that he might receive an evidence of acceptance, he seemed encouraged and gave me the names and address of his parents, for me to write them of his hope, in departing, of a better future.

There was also great suffering in the camp of freedmen. The officers wished me to aid them in persuading these people to go down to the island, as they were afraid of being returned to slavery at the close of the war, and desired to push as far into the free States as possible, and very loath to go back "an inch," as one of the officers expressed it. I took the names of these almost nude people, whom I instructed to come to my tent;

as the officers said I should have one for the purpose of giving out clothing to the most needy among them. They assured them that their freedom was a fixed fact; that they would never see the day again when they would be separated by being sold apart. This, I found, has a greater inducement for them to consent to the request of the officers to go to the island than all the clothing I could promise.

But one poor woman came to the captain weeping, saying, "My poor baby is dying' an' I can't leave him. He is my only child left me." In the great hurry and bustle of business the quick reply was, "Go back and I'll see to it." As she left the office he turned to me and said, "I don't know whether it is so or not; they get up all sorts of excuses." As she was not yet out of sight, I followed her to the slab hut and found it true. An hour later and the baby of eight years was in the spirit world.

"Now, missus, I can't go an' leave my dead baby for de wharf-rats to eat, an' de boat goes out at three o'clock."

I reported the death of the child and of the distress of the mother. "Tell her," said the officer, "we will see that her child is buried this afternoon, and I want her to go on this boat." I told the mother of the captain's wish, and that I would see that her child was buried.

"Ob, missus, it 'pears like I can't leave him so; they'll leave him here to-night, an' dese wharf-rats are awful. Da eat one dead chile's face all one side off, an' one of its feet was all gnawed off. I don't want to leave my chile on dis bare groun'."

The grief of this poor mother was distressing in the extreme. She knew not whether her husband and three older children, sold away two years previously, were still slaves or living, as she had never heard a word from them since they were taken from her. Those sad separations, she said, were much harder to bear than the death of this child. But she consented to go, on my promise to see that her child was buried before night. After she left for the boat I went to the captain to see his promise performed. He seemed very indifferent.

"What is the difference if that child shouldn't be buried this afternoon or whether wharf-rats eat it or not?"

"You promised to have it buried this afternoon," I said, "and I told that poor woman I would see that it was done; and I see no other way than to hold you to that promise, for I shall meet her on the island, and I must report to her."

Said the captain, "You won't allow such things as these to break your heart, after being in the army a little while and seeing our soldiers buried in a ditch, with no other coffin or winding sheet than the soldier's dress. For the time being we bury hundreds just in that way; and when from five to fifteen die in one day, as sometimes is the case in these large camps, we can not make coffins for them, but we roll them up in whatever they have. If we can get a piece of board to lay them on when we put them in their graves we do well." "But here you have lumber and plenty of carpenters, and you can have a plain coffin for the dead, and I do hope one will be made for this child. As I told the mother I would see that a coffin was made for her child and have it buried this afternoon, I will do it." He called the sergeant and gave the order for a carpenter among the soldiers to make it, and I saw the pine board coffin go to the burying ground with the child just before sunset.

Colonel Thomas and the captain doubted whether I could secure transportation from General Taliaferro, who was in charge of that post. They said he was a cross old bachelor, and had said he would not give another woman transportation to go into the army. "But," said Colonel Thomas to the captain, "she will be more likely to succeed if she goes herself without any word from us."

On the following day my car-load of supplies arrived, and I began to regret that I had not waited a day or two longer at home for the one hundred dollars that could have been placed in my hands, so that I could use it in an emergency if I should be refused transportation. With some misgivings I entered the general's office and requested an interview. I introduced myself by handing him my papers, which he looked over, and pleasantly asked what I wished.

"I am hoping," I said, "to secure transportation to Island No. 10, and to Memphis, Tennessee, for myself and the supplies referred to in those papers."

"Well, madam, I think your papers are worthy of attention, and I will grant your request."

This was said in such a pleasant manner I almost concluded the general had been misrepresented, but how changed his tone when he called his adjutant, who in an instant stood before him. "Go tell my clerk to come in." He hurried to obey his command, and returned with the report, "He is gone."

"Gone! where has he gone?"

"He went a few minutes ago to Church."

"Gone to Church! He has no business to go to Church, or anywhere else, without my permission; he has no right to leave his office without my order."

This he said in such a stern, vociferous manner that I wished myself out of his presence. But turning to me, in a mild tone, he said:

"Mrs. Haviland, you don't want transportation tonight. You come to-morrow morning at nine o'clock, and you shall have the papers."

With heartfelt thanks I left his office. On my return I found Colonel Thomas and the captain anxiously waiting to learn the result of my call on the general. They met me at the door of their office, and asked:

"What is the news?"

"The general grants transportation for myself and supplies to Island No. 10 and to Memphis," I said.

By their clapping of hands one would have thought they had got cheering news from the army. I found they too felt the weight of responsibility in this, as they had solicited my aid in getting these freed people to go to the island.

The following morning I found a boat was going to leave at half-past eight o'clock, but too early for the promised transportation, I told the captain of the boat of my wish to go with supplies to Island No. 10 and to Memphis, but had the promise from the general to have the papers at nine o'clock. A captain in the army, standing by, told him he could take me with supplies with all safety; for if General Taliaferro had promised transportation he could rest assured the general at Columbus, Kentucky, would be sure to give it.

"Very well," he said; "where are your supplies?"

They were pointed out, and he ordered them to be put on board at once.

On landing at Columbus I called on the general, and secured transportation from Cairo to places of destination. Now I thought all was straight; but as I handed my paper to the captain he said:

"This is an order for transportation. The captain-quartermaster is to fill it out, to be good for any thing."

I confessed my ignorance of army red-tape, and took back the papers to have them finished. He inquired for my pass from the provost-marshal. That, too, I knew nothing about; but the army captain came to my relief, taking my papers and getting the transportation filled, with a pass from the provost-marshal. These lessons I found important in all my after work.

We soon landed at Island No. 10, the area of which was two hundred and fifty acres of available plow land, with an excellent orchard of three hundred bearing apple and peach trees. Upon this island were seven hundred freedmen, who were making good use of the rich donations of twenty-five plows, with harrows, hoes, axes, rakes, and garden and field seeds, from Indiana and Ohio. Their superintendent, Chaplain Thomas, told me that he never saw a more willing and obedient people. They mostly lived in tents. Government had furnished lumber to erect a few temporary buildings. An old dilapidated farmhouse, and a few log-huts formerly occupied by the overseer and slaves, were the homes of Captain Gordon and Surgeon Ransom, with their families, who seemed to enjoy camp life as well as any I had seen. They had in charge four companies of soldiers. Their hospital assumed an air of neatness and comfort.

We took a stroll over the battle-ground, and saw the deep furrows plowed by the terrible shells, in which a horse might be buried. Here and there were interspersed "rebel rat-holes," as they were called, dug seven or eight feet deep, and nearly covered with planks and two or three feet of earth, in which they dropped themselves, after firing, to reload and be secure from flying shot and shell. I picked up a couple of cannon-balls about the size of a small tea-cup, of which a peck is used for a load. An officer told me that he saw twenty-five rebels killed with one discharge of these balls. O, what slaughter of human life!

Government provided a physician and dispensary for the freed people. Their hospital was a tent, like the majority of the regimental hospitals in the army. The first tent I visited was occupied by an aged pair, with two grown children, who appeared quite intelligent. Hard treatment and cruel separations had filled the greater portion of their lives. As I was making remarks on the wickedness of slavery, said the old man, with tearful eyes, "Please stop till I bring in my daughter and family from the next tent." They soon entered. "Please go on," said the father. While tears were coursing down the old man's furrowed cheeks, in undertone he ejaculated, "O Lord, I did not expect to live to see this day."

At the close of my remarks he arose to his feet, and in the most pathetic manner addressed his family as follows:

"My wife and children, have you thought we should ever see this? I fear we are not thankful enough to God. Do we prize this precious privilege as we ought? That dear wife was sold from me nearly twenty years ago; soon after my children were sold, and I thought my heart was broke. They punished me because I grieved so much, and then sold me to be taken another way. O, how I prayed for death to hide me from my troubles, for I thought none could see as much as I did. Many gloomy nights and days of sorrow I spent. I could hear no word from my wife, and nothing from my children. My master told me I should never hear from them again, because I made so much trouble over it; he would send me as far as wind and water would carry me, so I would never hear from them again. I remembered the words of my poor old father upon his death-bed, when he gave me this Bible: 'My son, the same God that made that Bible learned me to read it, and learned me to endure hard trials patiently. Remember, my son, the same God will do the same for you if you go to him for help;' and so he has. Praise be to the Lord forever!" He took from a box a Bible, all spotted over with mold, without and within: "This Bible has been manna to my soul for many years. God has learned me to read, as he did my poor father. He has been my support. I have prayed these many years for deliverance from bondage, and my faith told me it would come; but I didn't know it would come in my time. O, what a Savior is our Jesus! That dear wife was compelled to marry another man in these long years of separation. He was taken into the rebel army, and she came to the Union camp. A few days ago we met at Fort Pillow; and there we met our two long lost children; and here we found this daughter and family. O, how wonderful are God's ways! O, my wife, my children! let us live nearer that Almighty Deliverer than ever before, and praise his holy name forever." And the tall figure sat down, amid sobs and tears. The spirit of that family sermon I can never forget.

This noble man, Uncle Stephen, was but a few days before a slave; yet with the dignity of a patriarch he assumed his new relation. He was evidently a self-taught man, more intelligent, and using more correct language, than any I had met on the island.

On leaving my tent, tickets were given with explanations of my mission, which was both new and strange to them. In another tent I found a young man who had attempted to escape to our lines more than a year before, but was overtaken and shot by his master, shivering the bones six inches above the ankle, making amputation necessary. He was beginning to use his wooden leg. His master was taken prisoner by our men a few days before, and he, with one hundred fellow-slaves, fell into the hands of the Union army. He was fitted with a whole suit. This was done in but few instances, the general destitution forbidding it. It would have pleased the donors to see me with open boxes, taking out garment after garment, measuring and delivering, upon presentation of tickets previously given, to fifty or a hundred at a time; and to listen to the many thanks and hearty "God bless you!" as each garment was taken.

At breakfast the adjutant told me of five little boys belonging to some of the Fort Pillow families that were almost naked, and that he had given one little fellow a pair of his own pants. I told him to bring them to the commissary tent any time from nine to twelve o'clock, as I had arranged to meet the children to whom I had given tickets; and if he brought them or gave them a slip of paper with his name, it would serve the same purpose. Soon we were beside the boxes in our commissary tent measuring, fitting, and handing out, when up stepped the little fellow of eight summers with the tall man's pants, rolled over and over at the bottom, with one suspender tied around him, the other placed over his shoulder to hold them on. His eyes sparkled as a new suit was thrown over his arm; calling out, "See here, Johnnie, what I got!" "Yes, look at mine!" was the quick reply, while on the other side stood a little girl who exclaimed, in surprise, "Oh, Milla, my dress has a pocket, and see what I found," as she drew out a rag doll two inches long. Then a dozen other little girls instituted a search and found similar treasures, which I recognized as coming from certain little girls in Hudson, Michigan. All were on tip-toe with excitement, and these remarks were flying through this crowd of little folks when the adjutant came to the tent door. Laughing through tears, he said, "Have you ever thought of the Savior's words, 'Inasmuch as ye have done it unto the least of these, ye have done it unto me?'"

"That thought had come to my mind before engaging in this mission, and it is that which drew me from my Michigan home."

"Doesn't this pay you," he continued, "for coming all this distance, to see those sparkling eyes and light hearts dancing with joy?"

"Here is verified the declaration that it is more blessed to give than to receive," was my reply.

A woman came one evening with the following queries:

"Missus, whar all dese clo'es come from? Does gov'ment send 'em to us?"

On listening to my explanation, "An' don't gov'ment pay you for bringin' 'em to us?"

After all her questions had been disposed of she sat for a moment in a deep study; then said in surprise, "De Norf mus' be mighty, mighty rich to send so much money down here to carry on de war and send so much to eat, and den da send so many clo'es an' keep so many men here too; indeed da mus' be mighty rich."

They were preparing to open a school for them. Henry Roundtree, a missionary, was laboring among them, and would disburse clothing sent to that point.

After spending over a week on this beautiful island, on my way to the steamer, I was hailed by a female voice calling out, "Missus, missus, don't pass by dis yere way." Turning in the direction of the call, I saw a very old woman sitting on a log, clad in a man's coat, hat, and shoes, with an old patched negro cotton skirt. On approaching her I remarked, as I took the bony hand, "You are very old."

"Can't tell how ole I is, only I knows I's been here great while. You see dat white house over de river dar? Dat's been my home great many year, but massa drove me off, he say, 'case I's no 'count, gwine round wheezin' like an ole hoss, an' snap a gun at me an' say he shoot my brain out if I didn't go to de Yankees. An' missus come out an' say she set fire to my cabin some night an' burn me up in it. 'Go 'long to de Yankees; da wants niggers, an' you ain't no 'count no how.' An' I tole 'em, 'Wa'n't I 'count good many years ago?' But da say, 'Clar out wid you.' An' I seed some boys fishing' on de bank, an' da fetch me over."

Looking down at her stockingless feet she said, "Missus, I ain't had a suit o' clo'es in seven years." I told her if there was a woman's garment left she should have it. And I would tell the good people about her, and they would send her a suit of clothes.

"Tank you, missus; God bless you!"

And I left the giant-like old woman, whose head was bleached by the fronts of eighty or ninety Winters. While waiting on the gunboat for the steamer, I referred to the old woman I had seen, when one of the men turned to his comrade and said, "That's the same strange-appearing old woman we brought over," and he repeated the same story she related to me. Said one, "Such people ought to be made to bite the dust. Her master took the oath of allegiance to save his property; but he has no more principle than a hyena to turn out such an old white-headed woman as that to die like a brute."

Such are some of the incidents that gradually changed the politics of the army. They made our Butlers and Hunters by scores. They saw that man's inhumanity to man was the outgrowth of slavery. They clearly perceived that the iron rod of oppression must be broken, or the unholy rebellion would succeed.

At four P. M. I embarked for another field. On board the steamer were a number of officers and soldiers, and three women who were ex-slave owners. They had quietly listened to the conversation of the officers on establishing schools among the freed men, and taking them into the army as soldiers. I, too, had been a silent listener. After the officers had left the cabin, one of the women drew her chair near me, and in a subdued tone said:

"Do you believe it is right to set up schools among niggers?"

"Certainly I do," was my reply, "as they have as good a right to become intelligent as any other class of people."

"Do you think that it is right to make soldiers out of niggers?"

"Certainly, if it is right for any class of people."

After looking around to see whether any officer was in hearing, she added:

"And do you think it right to rob us of our niggers, as the Yankees are doing?"

"Certainly, if you call it robbery to allow the negroes to go where they please."

My replies were in my common tone of voice, yet it seemed to frighten her. She would take a look to see whether an officer was near. Then would go on with her queries in an undertone.

"I tell you it is mighty hard, for my pa paid his own money for our niggers; and that's not all they've robbed us of. They have taken our horses and cattle and sheep and every thing."

As I had my little Bible in my hand, I turned to the predicted destruction of Babylon in Revelation, and read, "Fine flour, and wheat, and beasts, and sheep, and horses, and chariots, and slaves, and souls of men." "You see here," I said, "are the very articles you have named. And God is the same unchanging Lord to-day."

"But I tell you, madam, its mighty, mighty hard."

In all this conversation she closely watched the officers, and often raised her handkerchief to her face while talking with me, as if to check the sound of her already stifled voice. How widely different were our positions, compared with six years before, when going down this river on an errand for a white fugitive from slavery. Then my thoughts could find no place even in a whisper, and slave-holders were cursing and threatening abolitionists. What a turning of tables! Now I could say all that was in my heart on the sin of slavery, and the slave-holder was now hushed. The coal-barge "L. S. Haviland," that I saw on my other trip tied up a little way above Memphis, was not now to be seen. I had not yet learned the fate of those Tennessee slave- holders who had so often threatened my life, and a number of my friends had advised me to keep a proper distance from them, as this might be the time for their opportunity. When I left my home I had no idea of going as far as Tennessee, or my children and friends would have feared for my safety; but, as for myself, I knew no fear.

In Memphis I found many hospitals filled with sick, wounded, and dying soldiers; and in better condition than I had anticipated, except the Jackson Hospital, which was one of the largest in the city. I asked permission of the guards to enter, but was informed their orders were very strict to allow no one to go in without permission.

"Very well," said I, "please inform me where I can find the clerk, and I will secure a permit."

The surgeon in charge was just passing out of the main entrance, and the guard introduced me. I informed him of my wish to visit his hospital. In a very surly manner he inquired:

"Have you a son here?"

"I have not," I answered.

"Then what do you want to go in here for? It is no place for a lady to step her foot over the threshold of a hospital."

"I perceive you and I differ widely in that; but if you doubt my fitness to visit your patients, you can examine my papers from the governor of my State and a member of Congress and others."

"If you have no son here, I don't see that you have any business here."

"Every soldier is some mother's son, and I wish to visit them, and here are my papers; you can read them if you wish."

Throwing out his hand angrily, he said:

"Go along, then; go along."

I went, but he took good care to bear me company.

As we entered each ward, every soldier who was able to bear his weight sprang to his feet, and stood by his cot during our stay in the ward. I saw at once that it was in pursuance of an order. I had made it a point to shake hands with every soldier that was awake and conscious, but the surgeon hurried through without giving an opportunity to speak to a half-dozen in the whole hospital. One poor skeleton of a man sat bolstered on his cot, eating his dinner, and had on his plate a spoonful of cooked onion.

"Where did you get that onion?" cried the surgeon.

"I paid my own money for it, doctor."

"Who said you might have it?"'

"Dr. Spears."

"Very well, then;" and passed on.

Here my disgust filled up to the brim. I cared but little for his attempt to browbeat me; but when he treated a helpless soldier like this I could hardly keep my indignation from boiling over. The first words spoken to me after entering the hospital were:

"Do you want to go into the kitchen?"

"I would like to pass through your kitchen," was my reply.

"Very unfavorable time, madam--very unfavorable; about dinner-time."

Very favorable, thought I, and went in. I could see at a glance that the large caldron of potatoes was boiled half an hour too long. Their bread looked well, and I suppose it was good. As we passed out, taking memoranda and pencil, I said:

"You have a very large hospital. How many will it accommodate?"

"Fifteen hundred, madam. Very few, very few at present, only four hundred and eighty-four."

"How many nurses have you?"

"Twenty-three."

"No female nurses?"

"No, madam. As I told you, a woman has no business to step inside of a hospital."

"As I told you, we evidently differ in that respect. Where I have found judicious female nurses it seems more home-like, and our soldiers feel more contented."

"Very few, very few judicious female nurses."

"They exist, notwithstanding. How many surgeons have you?"

"Only four at present."

"You are the surgeon in charge; please give me your name."

"My name is Surgeon Powers, of the Seventh Missouri Regiment."

His name and figures were too plainly recorded to be effaced. Here he turned a perfect somersault, if words could perform the feat. With an affected politeness, bowing himself almost double:

"Madam, I hope you will call again some time; call in the middle of the forenoon or afternoon--very unfavorable about meal-time."

"If I remain a week or ten days longer in the city," I replied, "I shall do so."

"I would he very happy to have you call again, madam; very happy to see you again."

I left with a heavy heart, and called at the sanitary rooms to ascertain the location of five unvisited hospitals. I found the room filled with officers and a few generals of high rank. I introduced myself, as usual, by handing Dr. Warrener, sanitary agent, my papers.

"Then you are visiting the hospitals, with supplies, etc., are you? I am glad to see you, as we have had no visitor from so far North. How do you find them?"

"I have found them," I answered, "more satisfactorily conducted than I anticipated, with but one exception."

"Have you visited the Jackson?"

"I have just come from there."

"To-day is not the visiting day. Did you see Surgeon Powers?"

"I did."

"Did you get into that hospital without trouble?"

"We had a parley."

"What did he say to you?"

I gave his objection and my reply in a low tone. To my annoyance, the doctor repeated it in a loud voice, and continued:

"You certainly could have given no better reason than that every soldier is some mother's son. What do you think of Surgeon Powers?"

I hesitated in view of all these officers; but my second thought was, no matter whether the President himself were present; and I frankly replied:

"I think he is a tyrant brandy-cask. Why do you allow such a man to occupy the responsible position of surgeon in charge of hundreds of the sick and wounded soldiers?"

"We tried once to get him out, and failed. You ought to see the medical director, who is in the city."

He gave me the location of the hospitals I desired, and I left. Remembering the promise I made my son Joseph, I returned to head- quarters, and spent the balance of the day in writing for soldiers and for myself.

The following morning I resumed hospital visiting. On the street I met an officer, who reached his hand with a smile, saying, "You do not recognize me, but I recognize you as being the lady in Dr. Warrener's office yesterday, after visiting the Jackson Hospital."

"I do not know but you thought me severe in my remarks concerning Surgeon Powers."

"Not at all--not by any means, for I had two sons under him six weeks, and they both declared they would rather die in the open field than be under the care of that drunken tyrant again."

"Why do you permit such a surgeon to have the care of the sick, wounded, and dying soldiers?"

"Well, it is difficult for us to do much with each other, but there is the medical director just ahead of us; you ought to see him; I'll introduce you. He is very much of a gentleman."

The first query of the medical director, after reading my papers, was "Have you visited the Jackson Hospital? And did you see Surgeon Powers?"

"I undertook to visit it yesterday," I said, "but was hurried through in such haste, by Surgeon Powers, that I could not speak to any of the soldiers, or stop to write for them to their home friends, if they desired."

"What do you think of Surgeon Powers?"

"I think he is an unfeeling tyrant. The white of his eyes had the color of red flannel, and the unmistakable brandy breath made standing near him very unpleasant. Besides, his ungentlemanly, morose treatment of helpless soldiers indicates his entire unfitness for the position he occupies. If the milk of human kindness is more loudly called for in one position than another, it is in the surgeon in charge of sick, wounded, and dying soldiers."

"We know, Mrs. Haviland, this is true, and we made an effort to displace him once and failed, because the medical director over the whole of us in this division, next in rank to Grant himself, is determined to hold him here. But if you will make out your report, with the recommendations from your governor and Congressman backing it, we can make that efficient. You may make your report as strong as you please."

I left him with cordial thanks, and soon the report was handed him. I visited all the hospitals in that post, and on my second visit to the Jackson found Surgeon Powers filled to overflowing with affected politeness; but it did not brighten the bleared eye, or straighten the zigzag gait of the surgeon.

A few weeks after I met a Memphis officer, who informed me that Surgeon Powers was relieved of hospital work altogether very soon after I left the city. A few months later he filled a drunkard's grave.

In one hospital in Memphis I found in one corner a female soldier, Charlie. She was in both Bull Run battles, and four others she named; besides, she had endured long marches. Here she was taken violently ill with typhoid fever, and for the first time her sex became known. She was large and rather coarse-featured, and of indomitable will. She said the cause of her enlistment did not now exist, and she wanted to go home as soon as able. She intimated that her betrothed had recently died, and she had no desire to remain in the army.

While in Memphis a telegram came from President Lincoln ordering four hundred colored men to be enlisted, and no more, until further orders. Colonel Eaton took this work for his breakfast spell. As he came in rather late for his morning meal he said, "I have enlisted the required number, and quite a company went away crying because they could not enlist. I comforted them by telling them that I presumed there would be another call soon." I had built a bed for myself in one corner of the commissary building, and as we were occupying the weakest point at the post, we were ordered to have no light in our tents, but before dark to have every needed article at our bedside, ready at a moment's warning to be conducted to Fort Pickering. Soldiers were kept in readiness for action, as the enemy was threatening to retake Memphis. At two, o'clock A. M. the loud cry, "Halt!" at the corner where I was sleeping, aroused me. This was quickly followed by a still louder "Halt! May be you don't know who I is; I holds a gun, an' her's off."

"Well-well, I only want to come to you; I don't want to go farther." The officer approached, saying, "That is right; if I had taken one step after you cried halt the third time, you should have shot me through, no matter who I am, if it was the President himself."

At the breakfast table Colonel Eaton remarked: "A number of our new colored soldiers were put on picket guard last night on trial, and not one sleepy head was found among them. Since we accept these men as soldiers I am confident it will do away the necessity of drafting men, as some think must soon be done."

I spent a few days in visiting hospitals, often reading portions of Scripture, and kneeling by the cot of the suffering and dying soldiers, imploring the Great Physician to heal the sin-sick soul. For some I wrote letters to their home friends, which I found was often very gratifying to poor homesick boys. One very sick with pneumonia wished me to write to his folks in Kent County, Michigan, that he was in the hospital from a little cold, but would soon be able to join his regiment again. I dared not write according to his directions, and told him I would finish his letter at head-quarters. When he asked my name, he wanted to know if I was a relative of Rev. D. S. Haviland, in Kent County, Michigan. When I told him he was my son, he held my hand in both of his and burst into a flood of tears, and said he had heard him preach many times, and thought he was such a good man. I saw his feelings were deeply affected, and I feared it would increase the fever, and I promised to come and see him again in a day or two. I sat by him with my hand upon his head and consoled him as best I could. When he became calm I left, and called on his physician for his opinion concerning him. He said he was still in a critical condition, but thought the disease was turning in his favor, and advised me not to write to his friends until two days more had passed, as he would then be able to judge better of his case. Two days later I called again and found him much better, but the doctor thought the excitement of my leaving him increased the fever during the afternoon. He was now a little stronger, and he said I had better not let him know that I designed leaving the city. I finished the letter with greater encouragement than I could have done conscientiously on my first visit.

As I was passing out one of the convalescents said, "Frank, here is that woman you wanted to see;" and he came on a run.

"Are you from Michigan?" I asked.

"Not quite," he said; "but I've been in Michigan. I am from Ohio, and that is its next neighbor;" and he seemed as glad as if he was meeting his mother. "O, how much you remind me of my mother! Your advice to us boys is almost in the same words my mother gave me when I left her;" and tears spoke louder than words of his appreciation of visits from his mother's representative.

I visited many camps of the freedmen, where there were two thousand, with daily additions. Forty came into Bethel Camp one afternoon. I went among them, and said to the man I met first:

"You concluded to use your freedom in coming into the Union camps?"

"Freedom!" looking up in surprise.

"Yes; you know President Lincoln has proclaimed all slaves free."

"Is dat so?"

"Certainly; you have heard about it, I suppose."

"No, missus, we never hear nothing like it. We's starvin', and we come to get somfin' to eat. Dat's what we come for. Our people home tell us Yankees want niggers to kill; an' da boils 'em up in great caldrons to eat, 'case da's starvin'. But all de white men gone into de army, an' lef' us all wid missus, an' da locks de bacon up for de sojers, an' gib us little han'ful o' meal a day, an' we's got weak an' trimbly. An' I tole my people we's gwine to die anyhow, an' we'd try de Yankees."

They were all so surprised at the idea of freedom that they could hardly credit the fact until their own people confirmed what I had told them.

Rations were given to that hungry company at once. I told them this did not look like killing off colored people.

"No, missus, dis 'pears like makin' alive, instead of killin'. God bless sich people as dese, if dis be Yankees."

A couple of young men followed me from tent to tent, as I was reading portions of Scripture, and advising them how to live in their new relation as a free people. I advised them to live soberly and honestly in the sight of all men; that our Heavenly Father looks upon all his children alike, and that our Lord and Savior died upon the cross for all alike, because he is no respecter of persons. The young men, asked to be excused for following me; "for," they said, "we never heard, white folks talk like you talks in our life. Da never talks fur our own good, an' dis is so new we wants to ax you please excuse us."

Our head-quarters were most of the time at Camp Bethel; but I spent a portion of my time in Camp Shiloh, which was in sight. On the Sabbath I attended a very large meeting in a grove of pecans, oaks, and magnolias. The minister was a colored man of considerable intelligence, could read quite well; and perhaps there were nearly or quite one hundred of our soldiers in attendance. I spoke to one man near the stand while they were singing, informing him that I would like to make a few remarks if their minister was willing. The minister said, before dismissing the congregation, he would give liberty for a white lady present to speak. "I do not know who she is. She may be here inquiring for some of her people; but we can tell better as to her object when we hear her;" and he invited me forward.

I saw at once the minister took me to be one of those slave-holders who were coming into their camp almost daily to persuade their slaves back, though not one of them ever succeeded. I told them my object was to inquire after the health of this people, body, soul, and spirit-- and my people were all who accept salvation through our Lord and Savior Jesus Christ; that our Heavenly Father made all the nations of the whole earth of one blood, and never designed that one race should hold another in bondage. I had hardly finished my first sentence before the minister and those near him were urging me to step to the top of their platform, as I had only taken one or two steps forward. "Come up here; our people all want to see you." I had to obey. Ten minutes' talk did not satisfy. The minister and others in that large congregation bade me go on; and ten or fifteen minutes more were occupied.

At the close a few hundred of those whose families had been broken up by cruel separations came to me, and many tears were coursing down the sable cheeks of many gathered around me to shake my hands, which were actually lame and swollen for three days after.

Said the disappointed minister, "It 'pears like an angel dropped down 'mongst us, in place of the slave-missus come for her people."

Said one woman: "My ole missus come las' week to get all fifty-five of us back again, and she tried mighty hard to get us to go back wid her. Den she went to General Grant, an' he say, 'If your people want to go back they may.' Den she try us again; but not one would go, 'case we knows her too well--she's mighty hard on us. Den she went back to the general, an' begged an' cried, and held out her han's, and say, 'General, dese han's never was in dough--I never made a cake o' bread in my life; please let me have my cook.' An' she tuck on so I jus' trimble; I's feared he'd tell me to go wid her. But all her cryin' didn't help her. General say, 'I can't help you, madam; if your cook wants to go wid you she can; but she is free, an' can do as she likes about it.' An' she went off cryin'; an' we could jus' kiss de groun' General Grant walks on ever since."

Among the most affecting scenes were meetings of members of families long separated. In passing out of this multitude my attention was attracted to a group who were singing, shaking hands, shouting, and reciting their afflictions and sore trials since they were parted. One woman found her sister, who was sold from her fifteen years before. They had not heard from each other till just here they met. "O sis' Susie, you know my two nice boys was sole from me two year afore I was sole off dat plantation down de river, an' it 'peared like my heart was broke; an' missus had me hit fifty lashes 'case I cried so much. An' de Lo'd has been my sun an shiel' all dis time. An' here I foun' my two boys; da's heap bigger, but da's my own dear boys. I's prayed long for freedom, an' God did come down and make us free. Glory, GLORY be to his name!" And they embraced each other in wild excitement during some minutes. Then they went to another part of the camp to meet some of their friends Susie told her of.

I hastened back 'to Camp Bethel, to witness the marriage of twenty couples that Colonel Eaton, who was a chaplain among them, was to marry with one ceremony. Many of the men were of the newly-enlisted soldiers, and the officers thought they had better be legally married, although many of them had been married a number of years, but only according to slave law, which recognized no legal marriage among slaves. At the appointed hour the twenty couples stood in a row, each couple with right hands clasped; and among them one young couple, that being their first marriage. All gave affirmative answers at the same time; first the men, then the women. After the ceremony Chaplain Eaton offered an earnest prayer; all kneeling. Then he shook hands with them to signify his congratulations, and I followed him in like manner. It was a novel scene, and yet solemn.

On the morning I was to leave Memphis I saw an old woman wringing the bottom of her cotton dress a few rods from the door. I inquired how her dress came so wet half a yard deep. "I come up in a leaky skiff las' night wid six boys dat do oberseer whip de Yankee out, he say; an' da say da go to Yankees now any how, an' I begged 'em to let me come, for da knows I has sich hard times. But da say, 'Aunt Peggy, de skiff leak so bad.' But I tole 'em I's comin' wid a basin, an' I reckon I dip fas' enough to keep us 'bove water. An' da let me come, an' it tuck all night to come seven miles up de river. Dar was forty of us on dis plantation. Massa is a big man in Secesh army, an' sent more'n a hundred of our people 'way off to de big plantation: an', missus, da all wants to come mighty bad, an' begged us to go see de big man right soon, an' tell him da wants to do any thing he wants 'em to do, if he will only let 'em come. For missus is mighty rich, an' don't need us, 'case she's got barrels of meal, an' flour, an' plenty bacon in de smoke-house, da keeps locked up, da say for de Secesh sojers. An' missus had us put a tin trunk of gole an' silver money, an' a big ches' of all her silver plate way up in de lof' few days ago. Missus, do please go tell de big man how da all begged us so hard to ax him, soon as we got here, if he 'll let 'em come."

I told her I would see the colonel, and inquired for the boys who came with her. She pointed to the six young men standing outside our door. I approached the young men, who were between twenty and thirty years of age, and shook hands with them, saying, "It seems your overseer didn't succeed in whipping the Yankee out of you night before last."

"No, indeed," said one; "he drove in the Yankee deeper every lick;" and another said, "I reckon he'll find out this mornin' how much Yankee he whipped out."

I informed Colonel Eaton of his new comers; and of the earnest appeal of the old woman in behalf of the remaining thirty-three, and how she backed her pleading, with enumerating the abundance of every thing her mistress possessed. He said he would see General Veach, and he might conclude to send a gun-boat for them.

On May 17, 1863, I called at Dr. Warrener's office on my way to General Veach's office for transportation to Cairo, but designed calling at Island No. 10 and Columbus, Kentucky. The doctor kindly offered to take my papers and get transportation and pass from the provost marshal for me, and allow me to rest the while. I was glad to accept the favor; but he soon returned, rather discouraged, and said, "I think the general rather cross today, and I don't know whether you'll get transportation or not. After reading your papers he asked where you were, and I told him you looked tired and were resting in my office, and I offered to do this errand for her, as it would save her a mile of walk. 'I'd like to see the lady,' he said, as he handed back your papers; and you'll have to go and see him." Here was another narrow place. I took my papers to General Veach in haste, as there was a boat which I was anxious to take going up the river that afternoon. I entered his office and handed him my papers, telling him I hoped to receive the favor of an order for transportation to Cairo, with the privilege of stopping at Island No. 10 and Columbus. He neither asked me a question nor opened my papers, but threw them to his clerk, with directions to give the order. Then he sent it to the quartermaster to fill. On my return I called on the provost-marshal and secured my pass. Said the doctor, "What did the general say?"

"Nothing," I answered; "he only looked at me when I gave him my papers, and passed them over to his clerk to make the order."

"I think he might just as well have sent them by me; but the general hadn't seen a Union woman for so long, he just wanted to take a look at one."

I was soon on the steamer that took me from this city of many exciting scenes. Here I learned the sequel of my Tennessee correspondents, formerly mentioned, and was shown the house where they had both lain dead men.

I found on the island many waiting for the remainder of my supplies. The number in camp had now reached about 3,000. I also spent a little time at Fort Pillow, where a company of ex-slaves, thirty-seven in number, had just made their escape from their old home. They had traveled all night to get to our lines. They took two mules and two carts to bring their bundles and little folks. Men, women, and larger children walked twenty-five miles, to get to Fort Pillow. "What time did you start?" I asked one of the tired women. "Early moonrise," was the reply. That was about 11 o'clock P. M., and they had made all possible speed to get to our lines, and seemed very much pleased to get clear of pursuers, as some in their neighborhood had been shot and killed in their attempt to come. The officers took charge of the mules and carts, and sent the people to Island No. 10. Here I took a steamer for Columbus.

After landing I saw a funeral procession of colored people, and a number of officers and soldiers. I joined the procession, and learned it was the only son of a slave mother who, two days previously, had left their plantation. He had heard that colored men were accepted as soldiers, and was exceedingly anxious to enlist. When they were nearly half across the river their young master reached the bank and bade them return or he'd shoot them; but the son pulled for the opposite shore, when a ball passed through his right arm, breaking the bone above the elbow. The mother took the oars and pulled with all her might, when a second ball entered the lungs of the son. They were met by a few of our soldiers, who took him from the skiff to the hospital, where he received the best surgical atten- dance, but without avail. Much sympathy was manifested in behalf of the bereaved mother, who was left with two little girls. Bereavement was no new trial for her. Her husband had been sold from her a few years before. I asked her if these three children were all her family. "O, no, honey; I had two big boys sold jus' afore the war. Don't know whar they went. An' now my poor boy is shot dead by that young massa I nussed with my own boy. They was both babies together. Missus made me nuss her baby, an' set her little girl to watch me, fur fear I'd give my baby too much, no matter how hard he cried. Many times I wasn't allowed to take him up, an' now that same boy has killed mine," and she buried her face in her faded calico apron until it was wet with tears. A soldier told me a large company of them were only waiting permission from their commander to go to that plantation and strip it. He said she seemed to be such a nice woman; that they all felt so indignant they hardly knew how to wait for orders.

From this sad scene, walking to the Soldier's Home, my attention was arrested on seeing a white man with a ball and chain attached to his ankle, with brick and his ball in the wheelbarrow, wheeling toward the soldier's camp, guarded by a black soldier. As I stood looking at the black soldier walking leisurely beside the white man in irons, an officer accosted me with, "Madam, that prisoner you see wheeling brick to our camp is a strong secessionist, and was a hard master over a large plantation with more than one hundred slaves, and he was taken prisoner, and all his slaves came into our camp. The younger men enlisted as soldiers, and that man made an attempt to escape and we put him in irons and set a black soldier, who had been his own slave, to guard him."

"What a turning of tables!" I said.

"Yes, you will find the same turning of tables within our lines all over the South."

At the door of a tent I saw a large, square block of iron, weighing sixty or eighty pounds, to which was attached a ring. I inquired of a colored man what it was for.

"That belonged to our plantation, and when master had a mind to punish us he ordered us locked to that block, and from one to a dozen of us sometimes were locked to it with a long chain; and when we hoed corn we'd hoe the chain's length, then the one next the block had it to tote the length of the chain, and so on till we did our day's work. Since we've been here we've seen nine of our masters chained to that same block and made to shovel sand on that fortification yonder. There were forty of us that belonged to our plantation standing in this yard looking on."

"How did you feel to witness such a scene?"

"O, I can't tell you, madam; but I cried like a baby."

"Why did you cry?"

"O, to think what great things God is doing. Man could never, never do it."

"Did the others feel as you did?"

"O no, some laughed, and one man said, 'Ah ha, you see now how sweet 'tis to tote the old block, don't you?'"

"Did he say that in his hearing?"

"O no, we's five rods off."

There were a number of houses burned down, May 28th, three miles beyond our lines. Mrs. Samantha Plumer inquired of Curlie, one of our boys of the home, if he would take us to that biggest house burning on the Moss plantation. No sooner was the suggestion made than Curlie got his ambulance ready for us, and we were soon in front of the smoldering mansion. The proprietor was raking over the debris for gold and silver or other imperishable treasure. Among the ashes; were hand-cuffs, chains, shackles, and other slave-irons. He was occupying one of his slave cabins, as the long row was vacated by seventy of his former slaves. He was said to be one of the wealthiest planters in Kentucky. One year previous to the war, report said he lost seven valuable slaves, and one from each of three adjoining plantations escaped at the same time. After a consultation over their loss they placed the blame of their escape on a carpenter from Illinois, who had been a few weeks working at his trade in their midst. To be avenged on the poor carpenter, a band of men came upon him in the night, took him out of bed, gave him a coat of tar and feathers, and treated him to a ride on a rail-horse. Then they furnished him with soap and lard with which to disrobe himself, and charged him to leave the State within twelve hours, never to be seen there again, or a calamity far exceeding this would be his portion. All his assertions that he knew nothing whatever of their slaves were of no avail. He left the State as requested, but wrote back to the chief leader, Moss, that if an opportunity ever presented he would be avenged on those who had heaped upon him these abuses. Mr. Moss said he saw that same carpenter a few days previous to the house-burning, with three other men, in soldier's dress, but he did not believe he was a soldier, but only in borrowed clothes, as he did not think a Union soldier would do so mean a thing. An officer remarked, however, that he was a hard master and a firm secessionist, but was now very tame. On our way back Curlie informed us that he had taken us three miles beyond our lines, and we were very near being caught just opposite the line at the firing of the sundown gun. But with Curlie's earnest pleading the guards consented to allow us to cross the line.

In one cabin there were two quite intelligent mulatto women, better clad than any I had met in the camp, one of whom was the mother of three fine-looking children. I remarked to one of them that they had a better chance for life than others I had seen, and inquired how long they had been within our lines.

One of them answered, "Only ten days. Thar was thirty-three when we left our plantation seven miles below Memphis, 'bout three weeks ago, but some of our people stopped at Memphis when we came up the river."

As I was interested in her recital, she became more excited in giving details, and said:

"Mistess got mighty feared of black smoke, an' watched boats mighty close. One day as she was settin' on the sofa she say, Mill, I reckon thar's a gunboat comin'; see de black smoke, an if they do come, I reckon they won't fin' that trunk o' money, an' ches' of silver plate you put up in the lof t'other day.' Lookin' out for the boat, 'Yes that's a gunboat sure. Now, if the Yankees do stop, you all run and hide, won't you?' I looked too, but didn't answer till I see the big rope flung on the bank. An' mistess got wild-like. 'Yes, they are stoppin'. Mill an' Jule run, tell all the niggers in the quarters to run to the woods an' hide; quick, for they kills niggers. Mill, why don't you go? I said, 'I ain't feared the Yankees.' 'Jule, you run and tell all the niggers to run to the woods, quick. Yes, here they are coming, right up to the house. Now, Mill, you won't go with them, will you?' As the men had started for the house I felt safe, and said, 'I'll go if I have a chance.' 'Jule, you won't go, will you?' 'I shall go if Mill goes.' She began to wring her hands and cry. 'Now, 'member I brought you up. You won't take your children away from me, will you, Mill?' 'Mistess, I shall take what childern I've got lef.' 'If they fine that trunk o' money or silver plate you'll say it's your'n, won't you?' 'Mistess, I can't lie over that; you bo't that silver plate when you sole my three children.' 'Now, Jule, you'll say it's yourn, won't you?' 'I can't lie over that either.' An' she was cryin' an' wringin' her han's, an' weavin' to an' fro as she set thar. 'Yes, here they come, an' they'll rob me of every thing. Now, 'member I brought you up.' Here come in four sojers with swords hangin' to their sides, an' never looked at mistess, but said to me, 'Auntie, you want to go with us?' 'Yes, sir,' I said, an' they look to Jule an' say, 'You want to go?' 'Yes, sir.' 'Well, you can all go; an' hurry, for we shall stay but a little while.' An' Jule jus' flew to the quarters, an' they all tied up beds an' every thing, an' tote 'em down, to the gunboats in a hurry. An' two sojers went up-stairs an' wa'n't gone but a few minutes, an' don't you think here they come, with that tin trunk o' money an' ches' of silver plate, an' broke 'em open an' tuck out a big platter an' water-pitcher an' a few other pieces an' say, 'See here, Tom, haven't we foun' a prize of solid silver for gov'ment,' an' he put it all back. An' another open the trunk,' O, see here, Jim; see what a mine of money we foun' for General Veach,' as he tuck up a han'ful of gole an' silver money an' sif it through his fingers, droppin' in the trunk, sayin', 'Ain't we got a pile o' money for gov'ment.' An' he han' it over to a sojer to tote to the gunboat. An' two ov 'em went down cellar an' come back with stone jars of butter, an' pezerves, an' opened 'em. 'Tom, see here, what a lot of goodies we got; won't we live well?' An' he cover'd 'em up agin an' toted 'em to the gunboat. Then they broke open the meal-room, an' rolled out barrels of meal and flour, saved for secesh sojers, an' rolled 'em down to the gunboat. An', last of all, they went to the smoke house, an' broke it open an' got a lot of bacon. 'Now, auntie, you all ready,' they say? 'Yes, sir,' I tell 'em. 'Here's a roll of linsey for our cloze, shall we take it?' 'Certainly, an' any thing else you'r a mine to.' As we started for the door mistess followed us cryin' an' wringin' her han's. 'Now, Mill an' Jule, I know you'll suffer when you leave me.' One o' the sojers turn to her and said, 'They won't suffer again as they have done with you.' An' this was the firs' words she spoke after they come in, an' the firs' they said to her. An' we all got on the boat in a hurry; an' when we's fairly out in the middle' of the river, we all give three times three cheers for the gunboat boys, and three times three cheers for big Yankee sojers, an' three times three cheers for gov'ment; an' I tell you every one of us, big and little, cheered loud and long and strong, an' made the old river just ring ag'in."

She became so excited she acted the part of her mistress admirably in the half-bent, whining, crying, and wringing of hands, as she followed them to the door.

"How did you feel about that silver plate that was bought with the price of your three children? Didn't you think you ought to have it?"

"O'no, I couldn't touch it. It was part o' my poor dear childern; but I didn't want mistess to keep it. I was glad to see it go to gov'ment."

The tears coursed down her care-worn cheeks as she related the sale of her three older children.

"I fell upon my knees afore master an' mistess, an' begged 'em not to sell my poor childern down the river, whar I could never see or hear from 'em any more. But master say it's none o' my business, an' I should stop my noise, or he'd have me punished. An' mistess say she won't have all this cryin' round her. 'Your childern belongs to us, an' you know it; an' it's not for you to make all this fuss over it, either.' I said, 'Mistess, wouldn't you grieve over your childern, if somebody take 'em from you?' 'You hush your sauce, or I'll have you punished. That's another thing; my childern's white.' An' then they had me punished."

Her husband was sent, with many others, to what they called the "big plantation," in the interior. She said her master was a "big man" in the secesh army. I found they called all officers big men. After she finished her story I told her I saw the seven she said went to Memphis, a few days before they left, and how Aunt Peggy begged me so hard to tell the big man that they all wanted to come. And to impress me with the idea that the mistress could do without slaves, she told me about the trunk of money and chest of silver plate; but I had no more idea of its being confiscated than had Aunt Peggy in her appeal.

My attention from this episode was arrested by another scene of a different character, but truly revolting--a young mother of only fourteen years, with a very sick infant, pale and emaciated herself; the grandmother of a very light complexion, and the great-grandmother a mulatto. All these four generations were the children of their old master, whose hair was white with age. He was the father of the great-grandmother, and of each generation to the fourth, and master, all in one. As revolting as this fact was, I was compelled to believe it, as his former slaves told me of his licentious character from his early youth to eighty years! He was never married, and was the owner of a large plantation, and his many slaves sought the first opportunity to make their escape. The condition of these women was truly appalling, and the history of their base and degraded master and father too revolting for the public eye or ear! I turned away with utter disgust at their recitals. The child soon died, and I thought it seemed a pity that its demented mother could not have gone with it; but I did what I could to relieve their wants.

The hospitals at this post were tolerably well cared for, except one regimental hospital, where were a number of sick and emaciated soldiers, who had no pillows but their haversacks, and no covering but their overcoats, and they piteously begged for milk. I went to their surgeon, and inquired whether boiled milk would not be allowed for those men who were so low with camp diarrhea, and whether I could not bring them quilts and pillows. "Madam, you can bring them milk, or any thing you've named; but I tell you, if you undertake to listen to all these soldiers' teasing, you'll have your hands full. As like as not, any way, they'll trade whatever you give them for whisky the first chance they have." I could not sleep until I secured the aid of two soldiers to go with me to carry milk, pillows, and quilts for those sick men. Their tears of gratitude, as I handed each his bottle of milk, and placed a pillow under their heads, and a quilt for those who had only an overcoat for a covering, paid me well. I returned to the Soldiers' Home quite relieved, but wearied and sick, with a severe cough, that had followed me for more than a month. I found it necessary to hasten home to rest.

I left this field of suffering and constant excitement May 30th, for dear home and anxious children and friends. A few days' rest restored health and strength, but we were not relieved from excitement. Our principal, E A. Haight, enlisted soon after closing the Spring term of our school. Preparation for another school-year was before me, beside the necessity of calling on friends in various places for supplies. I was informed by officers that I could now secure passes and transportation for an assistant as readily as for myself alone. My school vacation was fully occupied in preparing for the following academic year, and in looking for a congenial companion to share with me in this work,--one who was willing to sacrifice all upon our country's altar.

SANITARY WORK

WE found a necessity for organized work, and formed a Freed-men's Relief Association, in Detroit, with Captain E. B. Ward, president; Rev. William Webb, vice-president; Benjamin C. Durfee, secretary; and Francis Raymond, treasurer. These did what they could in gathering supplies in that city for me to take South the coming Autumn. Brother Aldrich was engaged to act as principal of Raisin Institute, and this gave me leisure to hold meetings in towns and county school-houses for soliciting help for my Southern work. During vacation our two halls were made ready for opening the Academic Year, as usual, on the first Wednesday in September, 1863-4. The school, though smaller than before the war, opened with fair prospects, and I felt at liberty to leave. The institution, being in competent hands, I obtained as a companion in labor one of the most devoted of Christian woman, my dear sister, Letitia Backus, of Pittsford, Michigan. With a car-load of supplies we left our homes for fields of greatest suffering, where least help was found. Well furnished with documents from our governor, Austin P. Blair, and two members of Congress, we secured passes to Chicago and return, then to Cairo and return, and from thence to Vicksburg, Mississippi. Waiting a few days at Cairo, for our supplies to reach us, we visited the hospitals and camps. Here we met a company of men who were called "Jay-hawkers." They were all tall, large men. One of these carried the treasure-bag, but I do not think he was a Judas to the government. A pillow-case was nearly half full of gold and silver watches, diamonds, and gold jewelry, which they said was confiscated for the government. They said wealth gave the rebellion strength, no matter in what it consisted.

After the arrival of our supplies we took a steamer down the Mississippi, and stopped a short time at Columbus. A little before landing I discovered an Irish woman had in her possession a six-quart tin pail of whisky, and a gallon jug that she seemed very careful to keep out of sight under the sofa; I took a seat by her side, and knew I could not be mistaken as to the contents of her pail and jug, and as I understood it was a forbidden article, I penciled on the margin of my official paper to the inspector to look well to the whisky the woman at my side had in her possession. As he came to inquire for my baggage to inspect, I told him where he would find it, and he would see by my papers what were their probable contents. Taking a look at the lady by my side, as he handed back my papers he remarked, "I think I'll not take the trouble to inspect your baggage, as I see you are all right." As we were going ashore, my red-shawled companion carefully gathered her pail and jug under her shawl at each side of her, and hurried to bury herself in the crowd. The inspector followed closely, and as he took hold of the pail to see what she had hanging on her arm, in her effort to get away from him it fell on the cabin carpet. As the cover came off we had quite a shower of whisky about our feet. At this the jug was seized by the inspector, amid shouts of "Good, good," and the laughter of the crowd, with muttering and swearing by the Irish woman. She hastened out of the crowd, leaving her pail and jug behind her.

At the Soldiers' Home we found Samantha Plummer and her excellent assistant. The following three days we spent in visiting hospitals. Hospital No. 2 was miserably cared for. The matron was a Southern woman, who had lost her husband in the Confederate army, but she professed to be a Union woman, and said her husband would never have gone on that side but for compulsion. Our officers seemed to pity her and her two daughters, and gave them a home in the hospital. The mother held the position of nurse, but not one of the three was a suitable person to be there. The sick and wounded soldiers did not look as if their beds or apparel had been changed in two weeks. The floor was filthy, and the scent was sufficient to sicken well people. From the appearance of the wash-boiler, running over with dried apples that were being boiled without care, I judged every thing to be done after the same style. I inquired of one of the convalescents in the yard when their supper hour was, and proposed to return to see how the brethren fared. Sister Backus was rather fearful I might make matters worse, as they might suspect we had an object in revisiting the hospital so soon; but we were on hand to see the burned and sour biscuits dealt out to those sick and wounded soldiers, with the half- stewed apples, and a choice given between rancid butter and a poor quality of black molasses. I hoped to see something better when the pail with a spout appeared, out of which was turned a substance half way between pudding and porridge, I asked if it was farina. "It's corn meal mush," and mush it was, running all through whatever was on the plate. I passed from one plate to another, tasting the biscuits and cutting pieces of apple to see if I could find one without an uncooked center, but with little success.

In going around I came to half a dozen of the boys trying to while the time away with a pack of cards. Having an armful of Testaments, I proposed to make an exchange. This was readily agreed to, as each of them had left his home with one, but had lost it in battle or storm. I gave them advice to commit at least one verse from their Testaments daily while in the army, and each promised to do so.

All this time of investigating their supper and making this bargain, sister Backus was busily engaging the attention of the matron. I left that hospital with a heavy heart, and spent a sleepless night. I told sister Backus I must remain there until that hospital was renovated. I wanted to go into it and "make things fly," right and left, if there was no other way. In the morning I found the medical director, and asked if he had visited Hospital No. 2 recently. He said he had not, but thought the surgeon having charge of that hospital a very clever sort of a man.

"I think there is not a single officer in that establishment," said I, "that is at all suitable to be there. Perhaps that surgeon is too clever. I tell you he is defective, or he would not allow such a hospital as that under his charge. But I find I am ahead of myself. You may take me to be some nervous mother, but I only claim to be a representative of common-sense women. Here are papers from the governor of my State, and from two members of Congress."

After reading them he said, "I will take up that hospital within two weeks, I think."

"Two weeks!" I exclaimed; "many of those soldiers will die before that time. I can not leave them for two weeks."

"Then I will tell you what I will do; I will bring the sickest ones here to this hospital, and put the rest on a boat and take them to Mound City, to the United States Hospital, and take up No. 2 within three days."

"That will do," I said; "I am satisfied with Mound City Hospital, and with this one. If you will do this I will go on to-day with our supplies for Vicksburg, Mississippi."

"Mrs. Haviland, it shall be done within three days," he replied, and I left him with a lighter heart.

We went on our way with a number of officers and soldiers on board. As we were on the boat over Sunday, I asked permission of the captain to talk to the soldiers. He gave me leave, saying it was a very unsuitable place for ladies on the rear deck, over cattle, sheep, and hogs, but they would prepare a place as soon as possible. While preparation was being made, a young man who had been studying for the ministry of the Cumberland Presbyterian Church, proposed to the captain to address the soldiers. As he was a minister the captain came and informed me that he had granted his request. I told him I supposed we could attend. "Certainly, certainly, if you like, only as I told you, it is an unpleasant place for ladies." Unpleasant as it was, we listened to a long sermon, and remained a few minutes longer to give the boys a mother's advice, as they were leaving their Northern homes, not to allow themselves to become demoralized by the many dangers and hardships they would have to endure.

About 8 o'clock the boat stopped a little below Napoleon, Arkansas, to wood. As it was very dark, our torches were lighted, and we saw a light advancing so fast on the bank that I thought it must be borne on horse-back. "No, it's too low," said a woman standing near me. But it went out as soon as it came to the landing, and our light was immediately extinguished, the cable was drawn back, the men leaped aboard, and the boat was wheeled so suddenly into the stream that there was great danger of bursting the boiler. We heard many inquiries as to what was the matter. But the fact ran quickly over the boat that there were guerrillas after us. The running lantern we saw was carried by an old white man, who overheard the talk of more than forty men, who were secreted in a clump of trees and bushes near the landing. They had planned to capture the first steamer that stopped to wood at that place, to take all on the boat as prisoners, strip it of everything on board, and let it float down the river. The old man told the men not to let it be known, if we were captured, that he had informed them of this, as it would cost him his life. Such a scene of excitement I never witnessed; men, as well as women, turned pale, and their voices trembled. Yet many of them flew to their card tables, expecting every moment to be shot into, and trembling with fear so as hardly to be able to hold their cards. The captain said if pouring tar into the furnace would send us beyond a bayou near by before they could overtake us, he thought we should escape. After passing that point our colonel came to me and asked after my companion. I told him as she was not well she had retired very early, and I thought she had better not know any thing of this excitement until morning, If we should escape; if not, it was time for her to become excited when we were taken.

"How do you feel in such an hour as this?" he asked.

"The God of Daniel lives at this hour," I answered, "and in him I trust."

"I see, you take it coolly," he replied, and looked surprised. I told him I pitied those card-players, for it was a hard play for them, while standing face to face with danger. "You see it is an effort," he replied, "to keep danger out of mind as much as possible."

"But see their pale faces and trembling hands. O, what a poor substitute they have for substantial trust in an Almighty Power! You see that gentleman and his wife sitting on the other side of the cabin. They are calm and perfectly composed; they, too, have their pocket Bible in hand. They are trusting children of the Most High, no doubt." He thoughtfully looked over that crowded cabin a moment, and walked away.

Very few retired before 12 o'clock, and those men and women were all that time making an effort to quiet their nerves at their card-table. The next morning our colonel called again with a little joke: "You meet danger so coolly, I think we had better take you with us to Texas for a general."

I was thankful for the improvement in sister Backus's health by a good night's rest, and that we had escaped. Without further trouble we reached Vicksburg, but learned that the loudest cry for aid was in Natchez, and we hastened there with our supplies. We were offered a home with Lieutenant Thirds and family, who had been invited to occupy rooms at Judge Bullock's. The judge was too strong a secessionist to take the iron-clad oath of allegiance, though solicited by his wife; for she feared they might lose their property by confiscation. To save it, he very blandly offered his parlor and best rooms in his large three-story brick house, where we found very comfortable quarters. Through Colonel Young, we obtained the use of a good-sized store on Main Street for our goods, and the surgeon of the freedmen's camp provided for us a small room near the camp, where were congregated four thousand freedmen in condemned tents. These tents were so leaky that, from exposure, after heavy rains and wind, we had from five to fifteen deaths in a day. Here we found constant work for head, heart, hands, and feet.

But few days elapsed at any time without hearing the roar of battle near by, and sometimes the cloud of blue smoke met our eye. One battle was fought within two miles by the negro soldiers, only a few days after the terrible Fort Pillow massacre. They fought desperately. One of their officers told me they had to command their soldiers to stop, and they obeyed only at the point of the bayonet; for they mowed the enemy down like grass, although they lowered their colors and began to stack their arms. Their officers told them to stop firing; but a number of soldiers replied, while reloading, "They hear no cry for quarter at Fort Pillow," and fired again. But when the enemy stacked their arms they were peremptorily ordered to stop. I didn't blame the boys for feeling as they did over that awful massacre. But strange as it seems, not one of our soldiers was killed, or even wounded. There was a white regiment in reserve, if needed; and the colored soldiers almost resented the idea that they needed any assistance whatever.

There was great excitement in the freedmen's camp that day over their victory. Said one woman, whose husband and two sons were soldiers in this battle:

"Why didn't you shoot away as long as one was lef'?"

"Our officers compelled us to stop."

"I don't care for that; they need killin', every one."

Said I, "You wouldn't kill the women, would you?"

"Yes, I would," she answered; "for they's wusser'n the men."

"Well, there are the innocent little children--you wouldn't kill them, would you?"

Hesitating a little, she said:

"Yes, I would, madam; for I tell you nits make vermin."

She and all her family had belonged to Judge Bullock's wife, and she was still living in her little cabin and doing the work for the family, as she had done heretofore, though she did not work so hard. She would take the time to do our washing for us. She said Judge Bullock was harder to please than her mistress; but he was afraid of our soldiers, and when Natchez was taken he kept hid in a thicket of bushes in the garden a number of days. They took his meals to him when no one was in sight, expecting the Yankees would kill every man they met; but as he found it otherwise he came into the house, and now he talked with us quite freely. Their slaves were mostly house-servants, and better treated than many others. Judge Bullock was formerly from the North, and married in the South, and his wife inherited the slaves. Their cook was a mulatto, of more than ordinary intelligence, and she told me of the most terrible scenes of barbarity that she had witnessed.

The marks of cruelty were in that camp so frequently seen--men with broken shoulders and limbs--that it was heart-sickening to listen to the recital of their wrongs.

One man I saw with a shred of an ear, and I inquired how his ear became torn like that. He hesitated to tell me, but one of his fellow- slaves said it was done by order of their master; that he was stripped and fastened by a large nail driven through his ear to a tree, and the overseer was directed to whip him on his naked body until his writhings tore his ear out, and that only ended the punishment. One man by the name of Matthew Lasley, living within two miles of this city, owned one hundred slaves, and was his own overseer. He worked his slaves early and late, and was proverbial for cruelty to them. They were not half fed or clothed. A few days after he had sold the wife and child of his slave Jack, they were burning log heaps and clearing off a few acres of new ground. They had worked until about midnight, and were preparing to "turn in." Jack had split an armful of kindling-wood, and was now ready to go to his lonely hut. Then his utter desolation rolled in upon his mind. When his master stooped over to light his cigar, the thought came to him like a flash to kill him, and then he too would die, and so would end his bitter days. No sooner was the thought conceived than the act was done. The ax was buried in Lasley's head; and he sank, a dead man, without uttering a word. Jack came immediately to the city, tapped on the window of Dr. Smith's sleeping apartment, the son-in-law of Lasley, and told him he wanted him to go at once to the new clearing with him. When the doctor went out Jack told him that he had killed his master.

"What did you do it for?"

"Master sole my wife and chile, an' I don't want to live any longer. Now, master, you may shoot me, or take me to jail, or do any thing you're a min' to."

"Well, Jack, I know you've had a hard time; but I shall have to take you to jail, any how, and see what the court will do."

After ordering Lasley's body to be taken care of, he returned to his wife and told her all, and added that he wondered he had not been killed long before, as it was what he had looked for. Dr. Smith employed one of the best lawyers in the city to plead Jack's case, and had all the Lasley slaves brought into court, not one of whom was without marks of cruelty--a broken arm or leg, an ear cut off, or an eye out. They were all in a nearly nude condition, three children under ten years of age entirely so. The daughter begged her husband to allow better clothes for them; but the doctor and the lawyer insisted upon their coming into court with just the clothing provided for them by their master The lawyer made an eloquent plea for Jack, and pointed to the hundred slaves, maimed and crippled and almost naked, and Jack was acquitted. Lasley's extreme cruelty had created a public sentiment in Jack's favor, so that unexpectedly to himself his life was saved. Jack was hunting for his wife and child among the multitude, but had not yet succeeded in finding them.

Week after week was spent in making personal investigations, measuring and preparing bundles for those nearly naked. As new refugees were daily coming in, the officers found it necessary to organize a new camp over the river, in the rear of Vidalia, Louisiana, on the Ralston plantation. As a few hundred were gathered there we went over and found them exceedingly destitute. There were twenty families, mostly of those recently enlisted as soldiers. Some of them were almost ready to desert. Said one, "They say we are free, and what sort of freedom is this, for us to see our families without a board, shingle, or canvas to cover their heads? We are conclud-ing to leave our regiment and build something to shelter our wives and children. They haven't got a place to sleep at night except in the open field." We told them we would make their families our first care, and advised them not to leave. Upon this they became more calm, and concluded to wait armpits, as I chose to keep my arms out in case of tipping over. Here came brother Reed, one of the teachers, offering to aid me; but he had no pass or transportation, and no time to get it. I called the attention of a passing general to my necessity for help, to be able to return before the firing of the sundown gun. He said if he was in command he would allow him to go with my load, and advised him to try it. On we hastened, but met an ambulance that Captain Howe had sent to the new camp for a sick woman with two small children. It was obliged to return, not being able to pass through the lines, as the provost marshal was not to be found. The supposition was very strong that the lines were closed, as it was the weakest point in the post, and the smoke of rebel fires was in sight on Lake Concordia. A battle had been fought a few days before, and another attack was-daily threatened. The driver and brother Reed were doubting the propriety of crossing the river. "For if the lines are closed," they said, "the President himself would not be permitted to pass." But I told them as they did not positively know that the lines were closed, we had better cross.

"It is your load, and if you say go we shall go," said brother Reed.

"I say go," was my decision.

Soon we were in front of the provost marshal's office. But he was not there, and no one knew where he was. After a long search, in accordance with my plea, some of the guards discovered and brought him back, reeling, with his head of long hair thoroughly decorated with feathers and straws. I met him in his office and read to him my papers, holding, them before his face as I would exhibit a picture to a two-year old baby. After explaining all, I made my request to pass his lines with my load of supplies.

"Who--who's there?"

I told him who he was that so kindly offered to aid me in disbursing these supplies just as I was starting; and that a general advised me to take him with my load, as he would pass him, if in command.

"Well, well, I don'--don't--li-like--this--whole--whole-sa-sale business."

But I pleaded for those suffering women and children with all the politeness I was capable of mastering, with disgust boiling over. With stuttering and mumbling his dislikes, and shaking his head, with the feathers and straws waving and nodding in every direction, he took his pen and scribbled a pass that was difficult to decipher. The next line of guards hardly knew what to do with it until I told them the provost marshal was drunk.

"O, yes, and it's no new trick; go on."

And without further difficulty we reached the group of sufferers, who were shivering as if in an ague fit. I threw to each family two blankets or quilts, and more than forty children were crawling between them within three minutes. I gave to each of those twenty women a suit of men's clothing that day to help them out of this intense suffering. I gave them also three rag-carpet blankets out of the four that were sent me by a woman who took up a new rag-carpet she had just put down, and cut it into four pieces after listening to the recital of the great suffering in these camps. She said she should put no more carpets on her floor as long as the war lasted.

Although I had seen so many marks of cruelty among these people, yet I said to myself, O that these poor people had remained in their old homes a little longer! Surely they can not suffer there like this. A little girl came for me to go to the old blacksmith-shop used as a temporary hospital, as her mother thought her brother was dying, and another brother was very sick. I entered that shop, and listened to the groans of the dying. I repeated to myself, O that they had waited a little longer! Four men and the little son of the distressed mother that sent for me were evidently dying, and four others were sick with pneumonia. The mother of these two sick boys was doing all she could for them all. I gave her ground mustard to make poultices, and ginger for those who had chills, and told her how to use them. I had a few pounds of each, and generally took a little package with me, especially after a storm. This miserable shelter leaked but little, but one side and one end were so open that we could throw a hat through the wall.

I saw a pile of irons by the door. Placing my foot on a queer double jointed ring, I said:

"I wonder what that queer sort of a ring could have been used for," looking toward the old dilapidated cotton-gin near by.

"That's a neck iron," said an old woman standing near me.

"A neck-iron! What do you mean?"

"Why, it's an iron collar to wear on the neck."

"But you are certainly mistaken," said I, picking it up; "you see these joints are riveted with iron as large as my finger, and it could never be taken off over one's head."

"But we knows; dat's Uncle Tim's collar. An' he crawled off in dat fence-corner," pointing to the spot, "an' died thar, an' Massa George had his head cut off to get de iron off."

"Is it possible for a human being to become so brutal as to cut a man's head off when he is dead?"

She looked as if she thought I doubted her word, and said: "It didn't hurt Uncle Tim when he was dead as it did when de iron wore big sores way down to de bone, and da got full o' worms afore he died. His neck an' head all swell up, an' he prayed many, many prayers to God to come and take him out his misery."

"How long did he wear it?"

"'Bout two years."

"Two years! It is impossible for any one to live that length of time with this rough heavy iron."

[Illustration: SLAVE IRONS IN POSSESSION OF THE AUTHOR]

"We work two seasons, any how, over in dat cotton-fiel'," pointing to the two-hundred-acre cotton-field at our right.

I took up another iron, and inquired, "What sort of an iron is this?"

"A knee-stiffener, to w'ar on de leg to keep 'em from runnin' off in dat swamp," pointing to the dark swamp bordering Lake Concordia, so fully draped with long Southern moss that in many places in it nothing could be discovered three feet in the thicket.

I went to the rear of the shop, with the ring under my shawl. Here stood a dozen or more of old and crippled men and women.

"Did any of this company," I asked, "live on this plantation before the war?"

"Yes, missus, six of us live here. I live here seven year."

I drew out the collar, and asked if any one could tell me what that was. One looked at another, and asked where I found it.

"In that pile of irons by the door," I replied.

One said, in a low tone, "Dat's Uncle Tim's collar."

"Yes, missus, dat is iron collar to wear on de neck."

"But you see it is fastened with heavy iron rivets."

"Yes, de way you see it is 'case Massa George Ralston order Uncle Tim's head cut off to get de collar."

"I want this collar," I said, "and another heavy iron a woman called a knee-stiffener. This plantation is confiscated, and these irons belong to you as much as to any body. Will you give them to me?"

Each seemed to wait for the others to speak, but the one to whom I had mostly directed my conversation at length replied:

"I reckon you can have 'em; for we's had all we wants ov 'em."

"I thank you; and if you can find any other slave-irons in that pile I wish you would pick them out for me to take home to Michigan, to show what sort of jewelry the colored people had to wear down here."

They turned over the heap, and found iron horns, hand-cuffs, etc., and explained how they were worn. They showed me also where the iron rod upon which was suspended a bell was cut off of Uncle Tim's collar.

Among the group was a crippled man walking with two canes, clad in tattered cotton clothes, that were hanging in frozen strings from his arms like icicles. I selected a whole suit for him, and a soldier's overcoat. He stepped in the rear of a cabin and changed, and came to me weeping.

"I come to show you," he said; "dis is de best dressin' I's ever had in my life. An' I thanks you, an' praise God."

As we were standing on the bank of the river waiting for the return of the ferry on her last trip that day, there were thirty or forty men waiting, who by their favorite gray appeared to be rebel citizens; but our many bristling bayonets kept them in subjection. The ferry soon took us over the river, and we were within our post before the sundown gun was fired.

As I had brought the sick woman and two little children that Captain Howe had sent his ambulance for in the morning, in one wagon, I must go to his hospital with them. This made us so late that the guard said I could not be allowed to enter the camp without a permit from the officer of the night. I told him where I had been all day without a fire; and as he knew the storm had continued until late in the afternoon, and this sick woman whom the captain had sent for could not get through the lines in the morning, I hoped he would read my papers. He held up his lantern to see them; but as soon as he caught sight of my old portfolio he said, "Go on, I know who you are; I've seen that before." I was permitted to leave my sick family in the hospital, and drove the two miles to our head-quarters by eight o'clock. Although very much chilled, I felt relieved, notwithstanding I had witnessed such scenes of suffering and dying during that eventful day.

One morning the little drummer-boy of twelve years of age marched into camp with seven men that he had taken prisoners, ragged and almost barefooted. The suffering men were glad to find comfortable quarters. Occasionally we found them tamely submitting to be taken, on account of their sufferings for want of food and clothing. One entire company, who suffered themselves to be captured, told our officers if they would allow them to wear out of sight some sort of a Union mark, so as not to meet with trouble from our soldiers, they would go and bring in their entire regiment, as they all wanted to come into our lines. They were furnished with a badge of national colors to wear under their coats. Soon the whole regiment were with us. One of our officers said they were among our most efficient helps. One of them told me if they had known the real object of the war they would never have gone into it; for more than half of them had never owned a slave, and those who did were better off without them. They were surprised to find an attendance of supplies. They had always been told that all the difference between the Northern people and their slaves was the color of their skin.

There was great excitement during the last presidential campaign. The slave passed through terrible experiences during 1860-61. It seemed to be accepted as a settled fact, that if Lincoln was elected it would result in war; and in many places regular drills were instituted. In Natchez the half-grown slave boys got together on Sunday afternoons, and drilled with sticks for guns. At first it attracted no particular attention, and the boys became as expert in handling their stick guns as were their masters. Two slave men were overheard repeating what their master said, that if Lincoln was elected he would free all the slaves, for he was a Black Republican; and they declared that if this was true they would go to the Yankees and help to free their nation. This talk was sufficient to raise the report of an insurrection throughout all that part of the State, and a large vigilance committee was organized to meet once a week and report what they might hear by listening outside the negro cabins. All slave men or boys who were overheard to pray for freedom, or to say any thing indicating a desire to be free, were marked; and in the discussions of this large committee of a hundred men, every thing that had occurred during a few years past, in efforts among the slaves to learn to read and write, was magnified and construed as pointing toward a long and settled purpose among the slaves to rise in insurrection. A majority of this committee decided by whipping and other torture to compel confessions from all these marked slaves, and then to hang them. A number of the committee resigned because they would not consent to these severe measures. Many negroes were dragged out of their cabins or yards without knowing the cause, stripped, tied to the whipping-post or taken to the calaboose, and given as many lashes as could be endured. At the close of each whipping the sufferer was called upon to make a full revelation of every sentence that he or she had heard in favor of liberty, or of the Yankees, among their people, either in conversation or prayer, and by whom, with a promise to be released from further punishment. Never was one released, but on Saturday generally ten or twelve of these sufferers were thrown into a wagon and conveyed to the gallows, where they were placed in a row, and all were hanged at the same instant.

Some hundreds were thus hanged in the edge of the city, and on an adjoining plantation. I carefully investigated the facts, and gathered the following statement from both white and colored citizens. I have good reasons for placing entire confidence in its correctness. A large number of slaves were hanged, owned by the following persons:

Frank Susetts, 26; James Susetts, 7; Dr. Stanton, 8; Dr. Moseby, 26; widow Albert Dunbar, 48; Mrs. Brady, 12; widow E. Baker, 28; Mrs. Alexander, 16; Dr. George Baldwin, 8; Stephen Odell, 5; G. Grafton, 5; James Brown, 3; Mr. Marshall, 1; Mr. Robinson, 2; Melon Davis, 1; widow Absalom Sharp, 3; Miss Mary Dunbar, 3; Joseph Reynolds, 2; Baker Robinson, 3; Lee Marshall, whipped to death 1; Mrs. Chase, whipped to death 1; a total of 209.

I was told by a number of persons, both white and colored, that there were over four hundred tortured to death in this reign of terror, before Natchez fell into Union hands, but I put in my diary only such as I found were proven to be facts.

Miss Mary Dunbar was very much distressed over the loss of one of her three slaves who were hanged, and offered the vigilance committee ten thousand dollars for his release, but to no purpose. Joseph Reynolds also offered the committee $100,000 for the release of his two, but was denied. One little boy of twelve years of age was taken to the calaboose and whipped, then taken with the wagon-load of other victims of their unrelenting cruelty to the scaffold, followed by his mother in wild despair, praying as she went through the streets, tossing her hands upward: "O, God, save my poor boy! O, Jesus Master, pity my poor child! O, Savior, look down upon my poor baby!" The woman who went with her to the scaffold said she cried these words over and over; "and when we got there," she said, "she fell on her knees before the head man, and begged for the life of her baby. But he kicked her on her head, and cursed her, and told her the boy had got to die. The boy exhorted his mother not to grieve so for him, 'for I'm going to Jesus; meet me in heaven;' and he, with eleven others, were swung off. The mother cried out, 'Oh, my God! my poor son!' and feinted." So perfect was this reign of terror that not even slave-owners, in many cases, dared to protest against this wholesale butchery. The repeated whippings mangled the bodies of many so badly that they were taken to the gallows in a dying state. One man died while being taken upon the scaffold; his sides were cut through to the entrails, and even a part of them protruded. I visited the calaboose, which had two apartments. The first entrance was large enough for two persons to be fastened to the strong iron staples. There was room for two men to each victim, one on each side, who, seated on a stool, could alternate the strokes upon the writhing sufferer. The floor of this calaboose was of hard wood, but it was so thoroughly stained with human gore that the grain of the wood could not be distinguished. Into the second room not a ray of light entered except on opening the middle door.

Frank Susetts was a millionaire in the city of Baton Rouge, Louisiana, and made his boast that he had no fear of Yankees, for he had gold enough to cover his front walk from the door to the gate, and could buy up any Yankee who might attempt to trouble him. "There are two things," he said, "they can never do: First, make me poor; second, make me take the oath of allegiance." He owned nine plantations, besides very much city property. Though hundreds of his slaves had left him, he felt himself secure in the abundance of his wealth. The government engineer, who had been casting about for the best place to locate a fort, had been looking over Frank Susetts's place and said it was the most elevated and desirable location he had found in the city, but he rather hesitated because of the magnificent buildings it would destroy. When Susetts's independent words reached his ear he at once decided, and took his men the second time to look over the ground. Standing near the palatial mansion, and within hearing of the owner, he said to his men, "Yes, yes, this is the place for our fort."

Frank Susetts approached him with the offer of thirty thousand dollars in gold if he would spare his place.

"I can not accept it, sir," said the engineer.

"I will give you fifty thousand dollars in gold if you will save it. It cost me one hundred and seventy-five thousand dollars to build this house and the out-houses."

"Should you offer all that you say it cost you, it would be of no consequence. We give you ten days to take away every thing movable from your premises, for this house will then be destroyed to make room for the fort. This is the site we have selected."

At the expiration of the time set, it was in flames. Frank Susetts and wife stood a block distant weeping. Two of their former slaves were looking at the conflagration.

"Ah," said one, "a little while ago it was massa Susetts's time, when he had so many of our people hung; now it is God's time. Praise de Lo'd, he's here to-day for sure. Glory to Jesus, massa Susetts's day is over; he can never have any more of our people hung."

It was now the 21st day of March, 1864. Many complained of these turned tables. Judge Bullock remarked that he couldn't even go to meeting without a "pass;" just what used to be required of the six thousand freed slaves who were then in this city of refuge. Painters were seen in various parts of the city dexterously using their brushes in wiping out standing advertisements for the sales of slaves. I saw a number of these white-washed signs. In some cases the paint was too thin to hide them. "Slaves, horses, mules, cattle, plantation utensils sold on reasonable terms." They knew these advertisements were not agreeable to Northern eyes. But I fear the covering of many of these hearts was as frail as the thin whitewashing over these advertisements.

On the Ralston plantation we visited families, gave tickets, and directed them to meet us at the place and hour appointed. Hundreds in squalid wretchedness were supplied. The following day, in the afternoon, all orphan children were to meet us. One hundred and twenty-two ragged children came. We placed them in two rows, the boys on one side and the girls on the other. Selecting each an assistant, we commenced measuring and distributing, keeping them all standing in their respective places until we had given every one something, but yet too little to meet their necessary wants. There were at that time twenty-seven teachers and missionaries in the city representing nine States. Six day-schools and three night-schools were established by them. Two other schools were taught by colored teachers; one of these was a slave woman, who had taught a midnight school for years. It was opened at eleven or twelve o'clock at night, and closed at two o'clock A. M. Every window and door was carefully closed to prevent discovery. In that little school hundreds of slaves learned to read and write a legible hand. After toiling all day for their masters they crept stealthily into this back alley, each with a bundle of pitch-pine splinters for lights. Milla Granson, the teacher, learned to read and write from the children of her indulgent master in her old Kentucky home. Her number of scholars was twelve at a time, and when she had taught these to read and write she dismissed them, and again took her apostolic number and brought them up to the extent of her ability, until she had graduated hundreds. A number of them wrote their own passes and started for Canada, and she supposes succeeded, as they were never heard from. She was sold after her master's death, and brought to Mississippi, and placed on a plantation as a field-hand; but, not being used to field-work, she found it impossible to keep up with the old hands, and the overseer whipped her severely.

"O, how I longed to die!" she told me; "and sometimes I thought I would die from such cruel whippings upon my bared body. O, what a vale of tears this was for poor me! But one thing kept me from sinking, and that was the presence of my dear Savior."

Her health so far gave way that she reeled with weakness as she went to and from her work; and her master saw she was failing, and gave her permission, to go into the kitchen a part of the time.

"O, how thankful I was," she went on, "for this promotion! and I worked as hard to keep it as any Congressman could work for some high office."

At length her night-school project leaked out, and was for a time suspended; but it was not known that seven of the twelve years since leaving Kentucky had been spent in this work. Much excitement over her night-school was produced. The subject was discussed in their legislature, and a bill was passed, that it should not be held illegal for a slave to teach a slave.

"All this time," said this dear woman, "I constantly prayed that God would overrule this to his own glory, and not allow those I had taught to read his Word to suffer, as we had been threatened. I can not tell you how my heart leaped with praise to God when a gentleman called to me one day on the street, and said he would inform me that I could teach my midnight school if I chose, as they found, no law against a slave teaching a slave."

This was accepted by that trembling teacher and scholars as a direct answer to prayer. She not only opened her night-school, but a Sabbath-school. I found more intelligence among the colored residents of this city than any other Southern city I had visited. Milla Granson used as good language as any of the white people.

We found many little incidents to cheer in all our rounds of pitiable scenes of sorrow. We sometimes met men and women among these Southerners of correct views on secession. One man said he never believed that slavery was right; all the arguments brought forward in its favor never convinced him. Although he held a few slaves by inheritance, he never could buy or sell one. His black people remained with him, and he paid them wages now that they were free by law, and he was glad of it. As he was nearly sixty years of age he had managed to keep out of the army, but had to keep quiet on the subject of secession. From the first he thought it the height of folly to resort to arms, as the Lord could not prosper their undertaking. I believe that man was a conscientious Christian; very different in spirit from Judge Bullock, who said one day in rather a careless mood, "I think you have one class of men in your North the most despicable I ever knew." Now, thought I, we abolitionists are going to take a blessing. "Who are they?" I asked. "They are that class you call Copperheads. They are too dastardly to come down here and help us fight, and they are too pusillanimous to fight for their own side."

Our daily work was very wearisome, having to walk from four to six miles each day. Fresh arrivals daily required our attention, and after wind or rain pneumonia and deaths were frequent. Bible-reading and prayer were also a part of our mission. One day, while sister Backus was opening barrels and boxes, and sorting and arranging their contents in our store, I went with a load, in a recently confiscated stage-coach drawn by mules. One of the mules the colonel said he was afraid to allow me to ride after; but I thought a little mule could do but little harm with the experienced driver, and I ventured the ride, taking in a poor crippled man on the way, who was just coming into camp. He was clad in a few cotton rags that he had patched with old stocking-tops and bits of old tent-cloth, to hold them together, and it was impossible to detect the original fabric. In passing down the "Paradise Road" to the camp in Natchez-under-the-Hill, the unruly mule pranced, kicked, and reared, until both of them became unmanageable, and the dust rolled up a thick cloud, hiding the way before us, as well as the galloping mules.

I believed that we should turn over at the short curve near the base of the hill, where was a number of large stumps; and that if we should strike one of them we should be dashed in pieces. But prayer for a guiding hand seemed in a moment to bring relief. We were overturned amid stumps, and were dragged a few rods on the side of the coach, when the canvas covering was detached from the wheels. Our driver was dragged a few rods farther, while the crippled man and myself were doing our best to crawl from under the canvas. By this time fifteen or twenty men reached us. I was out and hauling the canvas off the groaning man, whose head and face were covered with blood. I told one of the men to run for a pail of water, for I thought the poor man must be dying.

"O, no, it's all right,--it'll make me a better man," said he, while catching his breath, and wiping the blood from his mouth.

"You had better sit down yourself; you are badly hurt," said one of the men.

"O no, I am not hurt," was my reply.

But as I was getting a little child's shirt ready for the men to wash the crippled man's head, I found the front breadth of my dress torn across, and I had to throw back my bonnet to see; but I knew my limbs were all sound. Although it seemed as if we had turned many somersaults in a second, yet I never felt more vigorous. I knew the surgeon of that camp was within a few rods of us, and requested some one to go for him to care for my comrade. I saw a man carefully washing out the large gashes on his head, and I left for the surgeon, holding my torn dress-skirt in my hand. Just as I reached his office he was jumping on his horse, starting for me. He exclaimed in surprise, "Why, Mrs. Haviland! I've just this moment got the word that you were nearly killed, and I was going to see you."

"I am all right," I said; "but I wish you would go and see to that crippled man, for I am afraid he is nearly killed."

"Very well, but I shall look after you first."

By this time he was handling my arms, and pressing here and there on my body, I thought pretty harshly; for he either found or made some sore places. He ordered his ambulance, in which I was taken to head- quarters. As I was badly bruised, the surgeon urged me to take morphine. I was sure of not needing it, but promised to call for it if needed, and he allowed me to go without it. I found myself too lame to resume work for a couple of days; then I commenced again moderately, but carried marks of bruised flesh for a month or more.

About two weeks after this, while investigating a new arrival of a company of slaves, I learned that some of them were shot by their pursuing masters, and one woman's babe was instantly killed in its mother's arms; but the mother succeeded in passing into our lines, with her dead child in her arms, to be buried, as she said, "free." A woman and a little boy of three years, with dresses torn with briers to shreds, and feet and limbs swollen and bleeding with scratches, came in, from whom I was getting her sad history. Two gentlemen passing by, halted, and said one:

"This looks as if these would have been much better off at their old homes. Don't you think so?"

"I think this picture shows great effort in escaping from their old home," I replied,

"Do you live here?"

"I am only a temporary resident here. My home is in Michigan."

"May I ask your name?"

I gave it, and he continued:

"And so am I from Michigan. I've heard of you before, I thought this was some good Samaritan," giving his hand for a hearty shake.

"And who is this?" I asked.

"I'm Dr.----, from one of our Michigan cities. And what are you doing here?"

"I am doing just the work you see before us."

"Yes, and I saw a span of mules trying their best to kill her two weeks ago, when they came sailing down that Paradise Road up yonder; but they couldn't do it," said his guide.

I asked him what he was doing. He said he had just come to see if there was any thing he could do. I told him of the new camp on the Ralston plantation, and of this camp of four thousand. I hoped he would look after these, as we proposed to leave soon for other fields of labor below.

On March 24, 1864, I took letters to post-office, and found one from our dear friend, Addie Johnson, assistant matron of Soldiers' Home, in

Columbus, Kentucky. I went to General Tuttle for an order for transportation to Baton Rouge, and, as usual, introduced myself by handing my official papers. Being a very large man, he was in proportion consequential.

"What do you want?"

I told him I would like transportation to Baton Rouge.

"I don't know," he said; "that I am here to make the Government a great benevolent society, by giving every thoroughly loyal and earnest Christian man or woman transportation."

"Is there not an order," I replied, "from Adjutant-general Thomas, granting us transportation, rations, and quarters?"

"I have received no such order personally."

I bade him good morning, and left his office, fully determined to bring him an order, although I knew he must have seen one. My purpose was to take the first boat to Vicksburg, as General Thomas was then in that city, to see whether his order was to be honored. Passing Colonel Young's office, I called to see if he could grant the favor, and found that he could give the transportation desired, consequently I left the general without troubling him further. On my return I called at the other mission store, and met brother Burlingame and Isaac Thorne, who also wished to go below, but were doubtful whether General Tuttle would give them transportation They said they were waiting to learn of my success, and were surprised to find that Colonel Young had the power to grant it.

We took the steamer "J. H. Russell" for Baton Rouge. On March 27th Sunday morning, we passed the mouth of Red River, where was a gun boat, from which a few prisoners were taken aboard of our boat. A woman named Crosly was also taken on board, to go to New Orleans for the purpose of exposing those who had run through our lines contraband goods. There was a woman of property and standing on the boat, who still held her household servants, and made her boast that no one could even hire her slaves to leave her.

"I'd like to see any one offer my niggers a book," she declared. "I reckon they'd take it as an insult. They'd tell you mighty quick they'd no use for books or schools. The niggers never will be as happy as they have been. They'll soon die out. It's fearful to see them die off as they do in these camps. They know nothing of taking care of themselves. They are cared for by us as tenderly as our own children. I tell you, they are the happiest people that live in this country. If they are sick the doctor is sent for, and they are cared for in every way, they know nothing of care."

"If they are such a happy class of people, how was it that you had such a time of punishing and hanging them within the last two years?" I asked.

"O, that had to be done to save our lives, because they were about to rise in an awful insurrection."

"But what would induce them to rise in insurrection, when they are so happy and contented as you have described?"

"O, there is always somebody ready to put the devil in their heads," was her ready reply.

But Mrs. Crosly's report was of a very different character. She said, "There has never been the half told of this hell upon earth--the awful wickedness on these Red River plantations, where I have lived ever since I was fifteen years old. If you knew what I have passed through, you would not wonder that there is nothing but a wreck left of me. I married a plantation blacksmith when a young girl of fifteen, and left my people in Indiana, as my husband was hired by a rich slave-holder, Mr. Samuel Lay, who lived on Red River. We lived on his plantation many years, though he used to do a great deal in ironing negroes for neighboring planters."

I told her of the slave-irons I had found on a deserted plantation, to take to my Michigan home.

"Don't let the people here know it," she said, "or they will take them from you and drop them in the river; for they bury them, or throw them in the river or creek, to put them out of sight of Yankees. When the city was taken they sent painters all over the city, with brushes and paint-buckets, to paint over all advertising signs of slaves for sale, and hid all slave-irons they could lay hands on."

I told her that was done in Natchez, when that city was taken.

"And that is just what they did," she went on, "in Vicksburg. Among the slave-irons you found, were there any of those new-fashioned gags?"

I told her that there were not.

"You ought to get some of them. If I were at home I could get you two or three kinds; but you ought to see the new gags anyhow. They are made with barbs, as they make on fish-hooks, and they pierce the tongue if they attempt to speak or make a noise. They can't live many hours with one of them in their mouths, for the tongue swells up so. Mr. Lay had an old slave woman we called Aunt Hannah whipped, and gagged with that new gag, and left her all night in her cabin; and when I opened her door her tongue was swollen out of her mouth and looked so awful, I wouldn't have known her if she hadn't been in her own cabin. I told 'em she groaned so, I reckoned she was dying, and they sent for the doctor to come and cut the barbs out, and he told Mr. Lay she would have died in an hour longer. It was a long time before she recovered from it. But as near as she was to dying, the overseer left Ben all night with that kind of a gag; and they found him dead in the morning. You of the North have no idea of the perfect hell upon earth we've had down here. Mr. Lay brought Alice from Kentucky, and she'd been a kitchen-maid, and never worked in the cotton-field till she came here. The overseer was a mighty hard man, and he drew that long whip of his over her shoulders so often because she couldn't keep up with the other hands, that she ran away in the bush and was gone two days before they caught her. Then they whipped her awfully, and in two or three days they drove her out in the field. Within a week she ran away again, and was gone about two weeks. They caught her with the help of bloodhounds; and when she was brought in, her arms were torn by the dogs, and I trembled for the poor girl, for I knew they'd nearly kill her. Sure enough, the first I knew my husband had her at his shop, to iron her with a full set. There was a knee-stiffener, an iron collar with a bell, and a pair of handcuffs, with a chain between to allow her to use the hoe. When I saw the heavy irons I went to the shop and begged Mr. Crosly not to iron Alice like that, for it would kill her, as she was badly torn by the dogs. But he swore at me, and told me to go back into the house, were I belonged; this was his business. I went back and cried over it till it appeared I couldn't live; and I went out again and begged him not to put on all these irons; for he knew they were heavier than the law allowed, and he would commit murder, for she could not live in this way. But he only swore at me the more. At this Mrs. Lay came out in a rage, and said she would see whether any one could come in and interfere with the punishment of any of her slaves, and ordered another slave to cut across both of her feet with a pocket-knife, through the skin, so that blood was left in her tracks. I turned away, for I thought they would murder the poor girl before my eyes; and I cried myself sick and couldn't sleep, for I thought she must die before morning. The cotton-field was opposite my window, and after breakfast I watched to see the hands go to their work; and, sure enough, there was poor Alice hobbling out into the cotton-field. They had been at work but a little while when a heavy blow from the whip-handle on the back of her head brought her to the ground. 'O, my God!' I cried, to see that overseer hit her like that because she couldn't keep up her row. I prayed God that Alice might die at once and be out of her misery; and, sure enough, they brought her out of that field dead! I was glad of it. Poor girl! she could suffer no more under their hands."

"And did not her death call forth some action from the law?" I asked.

"Nothing of the kind was ever noticed on our plantation. I tell you it was a perfect hell on earth down here; you don't know anything about it; and yet, if these things are told, they'll deny it, and call them black abolition lies, when it's God's truth, and they know it. There was Uncle Jack, poor fellow! He ran away, and they brought him in with the bounds, after he'd been gone a week, and they made him strip and lie down on his face, and fastened his hands and feet to iron rings. Then a man sat on each side of him to do the whipping, alternating in their strokes from his feet to his head, then back to his feet, and so back and forth until they'd given him one hundred lashes. I passed by them, and saw his back cut up to a raw jelly, and the flesh twitched as you've seen newly killed beef. But this was not all. They took burning pitch-pine slivers and held them over his quivering flesh, dropping the melted blazing pitch from his head to his feet. After this awful torture, the two men carried him to his cabin, I thought, to die; and I had another all-night cry over Uncle Jack, He was not able to go out in the field again for two weeks."

Mrs. Crosly related many other incidents in her own experience, some of which are too shocking for the public eye or ear.

"My husband," she said, "bought two slave women, one of whom was the mother of two illegitimate children, that my children were compelled by their father to address as brother and sister. He also brought the mother to my apartments, and occupied my parlor bedroom with her for years--all to aggravate me. I didn't blame the woman Molly, for she couldn't help herself. She and I cried together over this state of things for hours, many a time. She often begged my husband to let her live a virtuous life, but it was of no use. He would only threaten to punish her. Poor thing! we felt sorry for each other, and she used to do all she could for me. I am so thankful she can now go where she pleases. She took her two children, and with the other woman went as soon as they could get through the lines. I am so glad all the slaves are free. Mr. Crosly has got our oldest boy with him in the army, and threatens to take my youngest boy of fourteen. But the Union officers say they will confiscate our property and make it over to me and my boys, so that Mr. Crosly can not take it from me."

The terrible scenes she had passed through, and witnessed, substantiated our oft expressed opinion that unlimited power on the part of slave-owners was equally degrading to the slave-holder and to the slave. Even more: it fostered the worst passions of a depraved nature. Her experience was no isolated one. Such cases in many localities were neither few nor far between.

On March 28th we learned, with surprise, that the bright light we saw the evening before, as we came from the soldiers' meeting, was the steamer "J. H. Russell" burning to the water's edge. No lives were lost, but all the baggage of passengers and many mules, horses, cattle, and sheep and other government supplies were destroyed. O, how thankful we were that we exchanged boats when we did, and were safely landed here in Baton Rouge. "Bless the Lord, O my soul! and forget not all his benefits," was my first thought. How many favors are often bestowed in disguise!

At three o'clock, P. M., I attended a meeting of colored people at the Methodist Episcopal Church, which was built by themselves, and upon invitation addressed them. I spoke perhaps twenty minutes, taking for my theme Psalm cxi, 12: "I know the Lord will maintain the cause of the afflicted, and the right of the poor." At the close of the meeting the colored people gathered around us, and gave us such a hand-shaking and "God bless you" as we seldom find outside of this oppressed people.

In the evening more than a dozen came to our lodgings and spent two hours recounting the trials of their slave-life, which were of thrilling interest. O, what a bitter draught was theirs, even to the very dregs! One poor man named Henry, owned by John Reese, near Baton Rouge, for the crime of visiting his wife and children oftener than once a month against his master's command, was ordered to be nailed to a tree by his ear, and whipped until it tore out. But even more awful scenes of persecution and outrage these people passed through, which we can not record. We closed our interview, after listening to their sad recitals, with prayer, in which all took part. A solemn season it was, to mingle our tears and voices with those who had passed through such scenes of suffering and were now praising the Lord for freedom.

On Tuesday, 29th, we visited the general hospital in the noble asylum for the mute and blind. Of the latter there were thirty inmates. They played on the piano and sang very sweetly, and we were interested in seeing the mutes converse with each other in their sign language. One little fellow was asked by the matron to give us their name for Yankee. He quickly passed his fingers through each other, and we all laughed to see ourselves with such an unstable name. All seemed much pleased to receive our visit.

We found here our sick and wounded soldiers with nothing but army supplies, boiled fat pork and bread. Surgeon Pole told us they were out of other supplies. We sent immediately to New Orleans for dried fruit, crackers, etc., and within four days they came rolling in by the barrel. We left this marble-faced edifice to visit a few camps surrounding the city of Baton Rouge. By request I attended a six o'clock meeting in the chapel for soldiers at the general hospital, accompanied by Rev. Joel Burlingame and Rev. Mr. Merryfield.

On Wednesday, 30th, we spent some time in visiting and distributing tracts and Testaments, and conversing with soldiers. We also visited a colored school of two hundred and twenty-four pupils. All were much engaged in study. We were invited to address them. Sister Backus and myself complied, and it seemed gratifying to them and satisfactory to us. We returned to our pleasant boarding place, wrote a letter, and made a number of calls. We found a woman who used to sympathise with Eliza Wilson in her slave-trials previous to her escape to the North. Through her we heard from Eliza's little girl, whom she left with her old master Bissel. A few days before she had come to her aunt, in Plaquemine, about nine miles, in the night, she heard that Yankee soldiers were in possession of that town. She had been told that a certain road led to Plaquemine, and took it in a moonlight night and found her aunt. Although she was only about ten years of age, and could not remember her mother, yet this woman said the child had heard I was going to take her to her mother, and that she was nearly insane over it. I had previously sent word to them by a soldier who was a dispatch-bearer, that the mother was very anxious to get her child if she was within our lines; and when he returned to Plaquemine he found the child and helped her to escape from Bissel with much less trouble than her mother had had seven years before.

About the close of the month we took a long walk to Fort Williams, where were three thousand sick and wounded soldiers. The scenes here were indescribable. The mingled language of acute distress, in prayer, groans, and occasional oaths from the profane, could be heard. One young man seemed too near death's door to survive. Said he: "If I die it will be suddenly, upon the amputation of this arm. It is too late for me now; but if I am spared I will seek an interest in Christ." But we had heard the cry of despair before, and could not give him up. The arm was taken off without causing instant death, as he was fearing. He then became an eager listener, and said he could now pray for pardon, and believed that the merciful Redeemer would grant the earnest desire of his soul. We found a few men, whose lives were given up by the surgeon, who were trusting, and possessed the comforting assurance of a glorious future. As we were about to leave, another soldier attracted our attention, who said he was not a Christian, but wished to be, and after repeating a few promises and praying with him we left. In tears, he requested us to see him again.

While we were waiting for a boat for New Orleans we again visited the hospital, and found both of those who were anxious at our previous visit rejoicing Christians.

I went to the office to inquire for a steamer for New Orleans, and on leaving was accosted by a young man with the query whether I was looking for a boat. As he saw that I noticed the feather in his drab hat, and star, with stripes on the sleeves of his gray coat, he remarked that he was an exchanged prisoner, and was on his way to his home at Atlanta, Georgia. Said I:

"You appear like a young man of intelligence, and I hope by the time you reach your home you will conclude to cast your net on the right side."

"We've been fishing on the right side these three years," he replied; "and we'll fight three, ten, or twenty years longer, if we live so long, but what we will have our rights--the right to hold our slave property without interference from Northern abolitionists. You need not judge of our strength because you have a little strip of this river, and our folks are rather discouraged here, and tired of war. If you could see our troops in Virginia, you'd see as hopeful and jolly a set of fellows as you ever saw. Give up? No, never! I tell you, madam, we are determined to have our independence if we fight till we die."

"I am sorry," I answered, "you can not be induced to adopt a course worthy of your zeal. Young man, the worst wish I have for you is that you may be prepared to die, for the fiat of the Almighty is against you. The sword and the boys in blue are going to bring you to terms. You will never again buy and sell men, women, and children like horses, cattle, and sheep in the market. The judgments of the Lord are upon you for these things."

"You needn't think God is on your side, for you've made our niggers our masters. Look! within, four rods of us stand nigger pickets, with their bayonets, and we can't pass those bayonets without a pass--and our own niggers, too. I tell you, madam, if I could have my way, I'd have a rope around every nigger's neck, and hang 'em, or dam up this Mississippi River with them;" and his black eyes flashed with fury. "Only eight or ten miles from this river slaves are working for their masters as happily as ever."

"We know that they are remaining on many plantations; but we know of a number of plantations that are worked by their former slaves because their former masters are paying them wages. But if they are as happy and contented as you describe, why do we see them daily coming into these camps, frequently for twenty to fifty miles, wading swamps and creeks, with swollen and bleeding feet? Why all this painstaking to get away from their masters, if they are so attached to them?"

"They are poisoned by the Yankees. You talk about the justness of your cause--any thing but justice to put arms in the hands of these niggers, to be our masters--to set our slaves over us with gun and bayonet. God Almighty will never prosper you--never."

"I see I can say nothing that will avail with you. I perceive that it is beyond the power of man. Hoping that a Higher Power may reach you, I bid you farewell."

With these words, I turned away; but had not advanced five feet when he called out:

"Madam, I hope we'll get the same boat. I'd like to see you again; for I like to meet people who stand up for their own principles."

Widely differing from this captain's spirit was another, who was the owner of a large plantation, with numerous slaves, yet a strong Union man, and his wife and daughters sympathized with him. Before the fall of Vicksburg he called all his slaves together, and told them this war would result in the freedom of every slave in the United States, and he wanted now to make an arrangement with them to work for him as heretofore. He promised to pay all the grown hands eight dollars a month, and board them with their families as he had done before, and to pay them at the close of each month. With tears of gratitude, they accepted his proposition. He told them that this arrangement must be kept secret, for their safety as well as his own; for they all knew there had always been a prejudice against him because he allowed them privileges that other planters adjoining them did not. They said to him, "Your niggers think they are white," because he never would have an overseer on his plantation, and would not have whipping and punishing among his grown people, and the families among his slaves managed their own children. He came into our lines as soon as he could, to save his life; and he told us he had not visited his home for a long time, except at night, as his life had been threatened, and that his wife and daughters, for their own protection, kept loaded pistols at their bedside. He had also armed a number of his servants, as they were likewise exposed to an attack. He was a noble-appearing man, and said, in conversation: "Mrs. Haviland, I have always held the same views on the subject of slavery that you do; but it was against the law to free them and allow them to remain here, and we could not send them away without breaking up some of their families. But I rejoice that it has come to an end; and I know of others who rejoice, but they do so secretly." His wife came to see him while we were there, and seemed to be a woman of sterling principle. She said they had to watch day and night, fearing their buildings would be burned, and perhaps some of them murdered.

We called on a widow and her two daughters who were in deep affliction on account of the bitterness of feeling toward them in consequence of their Union principles. They were a Christian family, and owned some property in the country, besides their residence in town. A number of our officers boarded with her. I was in her family a day or two, and as I left I took out my purse to pay her. "Don't open that," she cried; "I can't take a farthing. You don't know what we have to endure. I have two brothers in the rebel army, and when they came home, because I told them they were fighting against God in fighting against the Union, they swore at me and threatened to take my life; they said I was a Southern Yankee, and they were the worst of all. I expect they'll burn my house some night or get some one else to do it; and I know there are enough that would gladly do it. O, you can't tell how much good your prayer did us this morning. I do feel a daily necessity of looking to God to keep us. I want to make a request of you to remember us at God's throne, for we know not what a day may bring forth. Do plead for us in prayer, my sister." I left her and her daughters bathed in tears. We the took steamer Niagara for New Orleans, April 2d. It being dark, the captain concluded to wait till moonlight, when an order came to go up the river, near Port Hudson, for twenty soldiers and thirty thousand dollars in contraband goods with two men prisoners, who had been in charge of these goods for the rebels. While they were loading the goods sister Backus and myself took a long walk to the residence of John Buhler, aged seventy-five years, who lost a few weeks before one hundred and thirty slaves. The old man and his wife took us into their flower-garden, where were one hundred and twenty-five varieties of roses and many kinds of shrubbery, and the greatest variety of cactus I ever saw; many of them were six and eight feet high. One large pecan-tree was almost covered with a small yellow rose-climber in full bloom, presenting a beautiful appearance. They gathered nearly an armful of flowers for us, and took us into the room in which a bursting shell made sad havoc. They made many excuses for the weedy flower-beds in the yard and garden, as they now had no servants to keep them. Two drunken women came aboard the boat and were put off by our captain, but through the influence of their friends came on again. We turned from this scene, and took a stroll to another residence, where we found the former slaves of the owner the sole occupants. They had a hearty laugh when I asked if the "smoke-house key was frowed in de well?" "Yes, yes, missus," they answered; "we's got de managin'."

We returned to Baton Rouge (the place where we halted some time is called West Baton Rouge), arriving late in the afternoon. We walked up to our old boarding-place, and took supper with our dear friends.

On April 3d we arrived at New Orleans at nine A. M., in time to attend a colored Sunday-school. At its close I gave them a little talk. From thence we were piloted to the Bethel Methodist Church (colored) and found a quarterly meeting being held. Here we listened to a very interesting and intelligent discourse by Rev. William Dove. I made a few remarks on the comparison of present times with the former. At the close of the service many came forward to shake hands and tell us of the time when ministers and people were hauled out of this church of their own building and taken to jail. The free people were compelled to pay twenty-five dollars' fine, and slaves were punished with twenty-five lashes on the bare back, well laid on. This persecution the authorities deemed necessary in order to keep these poor people from rising in insurrection. They locked up their churches two years and a half, until the Union soldiers unlocked them. Though the authorities forbade their meeting at all, they often stole away two and three miles and held little meetings in deep ravines and in clumps of bushes and trees, to hide from their cruel pursuers; but they could not even there long escape their vigilant enemies. "Insurrection! INSURRECTION!" was constantly inflaming the guilty multitude. Imprisoning, putting into stocks, and all sorts of punishments seemed to be the order of the day.

A few months after the closing of their church the spotted fever broke out, slaying its thousands. An old pious colored woman said to one who was losing all his family, and called upon her to assist them: "Now, who is plotting insurrection? Who you gwine to take to jail now? Who you gwine to whip an' hang now? You can't take God out to jail." They heard that their enemies had concluded to stop their praying, for it was thought to be through the prayers of the colored people that all this trouble was sent upon them; for the plague was almost entirely confined to the white people. This class of accusers became even more bitter than before.

No one can look at this volume of history without calling to mind the hardness of heart of the ancient Egyptians.

MISSION WORK IN NEW ORLEANS

AT New Orleans, where we arrived April 6, 1864, our home was a very pleasant one. Beneath the windows of our room was a grove of fig-trees. We had the kindest of friends.

We visited ten colored schools in the city, filled with eager learners. One was taught by Mrs. Brice, who had in charge sixty scholars. She had been teaching here three years, under much persecution, and stemmed the torrent of opposition, sometimes in secret, before the war. Sister Brice and her husband had been struggling in this city nearly five years, through this bitter hate to the North, contending for Unionism everywhere, through civil, religious, and political life. We called on them, and spent two hours in eating oranges and listening to the fanaticisms and wild conceptions of this misguided people and terror-stricken multitude when the "Yankee" soldiers marched up the streets from the gun-boats. Schools were dismissed; the children cried as they ran home, telling those they met that the Yankees had come to kill them and their mothers. But there were those who cried for joy at the sight of the national flag. The starting tear manifested the deep feeling of these friends as they attempted to relate the scene, but said it was impossible, as it was beyond description. It seemed like an oasis in a desert to meet such kindred spirits. We left them, with their urgent request to make, another call before we left the city.

We were invited by the pastor to attend a love-feast meeting at half- past six o'clock, P. M., where we met a large congregation. The services were opened as usual.

Soon they were "breaking bread" with each other, shaking hands, and singing. Many were weeping. Some broke to each other the bread, exclaiming, "Praise God for this day of liberty to worship God!" One old man said to one of the ministers, as he placed his hand on his shoulder: "Bless God, my son, we don't have to keep watch at that door," pointing to it, "to tell us the patrollers are coming to take us to jail and fine us twenty-five dollars for prayin' and talkin' of the love of Jesus. O no, we's FREE! Yes, thank God for freedom!" Clapping his hands, his shouts of "Glory, glory, hallelujah!" were followed by others, until "Glory, hallelujah to the Lamb forever!" was heard from many voices. Men clasped the necks of their brethren, and shook hands with the sisters, singing, weeping, shouting, jumping, and whirling. Said one woman, as she clasped another, "O sister, don't you 'member when da tuck us over in dat jail dat night, an' said da would whip us if we didn't stop prayin'?" and then they both jumped and shouted, throwing up their hands in wild excitement. A half-hour was spent in these outbursts of long pent-up feelings; then they settled down into comparative quiet, and the pastor exhorted them to be brief in their remarks. Perhaps an hour was spent in the relation of experiences, and the meeting closed with singing:

> "The jubilee has come;
> And we are free, we are free."

Then there was again the shaking of hands, and another half-hour was spent in overflowing manifestations, as at the opening of their meeting. This long-oppressed people realized their great change beyond our conceptions.

At the Christian Commission rooms, No. 69 Carondelet Street, Dr. F. B. Smith, agent, we met brother Merrifield, of Baton Rouge, and brother Horton, who took us to visit a school of sixty pupils, taught by two colored men, Baptist ministers. They had opened it before the government or missionaries opened a school in this city for colored children. We had visited and addressed a number of other schools among these people of this city, one of which numbered over four hundred scholars, in a confis- cated college; but this in interest surpassed them all. Here in an old slave- pen, where hundreds and thousands had been cried off to the highest bidder, where the cries of parting mother and child had been heard and unheeded, where the pleadings of husbands and fathers were only answered by the lash, those many tears, sighs, and groans were exchanged for intellectual culture and religious instruction. Here were sundry Union flags waving and a large portrait of Abraham Lincoln hung on the wall behind the desk. The scene was inspiring.

After returning, two colored women, genteelly dressed, and quite intelligent, called on us and gave us a thrilling history of the past. They gave us some startling facts of the efforts made to return slaves, who had come within our lines to their masters, by making friends of our officers and soldiers. Men had enlisted from this State (Louisiana) and Mississippi as

Union soldiers from selfish motives. Their sole object was to assist in getting their slaves back, by taking them out of houses when employed by colored people, and from the street when sent to market, and placing them in jail. After orders were passed to give rations to the families of colored soldiers, one young girl, whose name was Rhoda, was doing well until she was overtaken with chills. Her brother gave her a paper certifying he was a soldier, and requested rations for her, but she was arrested on the street, and lodged in jail, where she remained three months, sick with chills and fever, and without change of clothing, although her female friends made many efforts to get food and clothing to her. At length a deliverer came, who found three hundred miserable, vermin-eaten prisoners, and set them free. A more grateful company was never found. Find fault who will with Benjamin F. Butler, this was just the work he did; and many lives were saved, and much suffering relieved, under his administration.

We dined with, a widow who had paid $1,800 for herself, and lived in good style by boarding her friends, who paid her extra board-bills to assist her. A Creole lady called to see us who could converse a little in English. The Creoles in New Orleans generally spoke French. This madam was a woman of wealth and position, and well pleased with the freedom of the slave.

We heard of a project devised by many masters to massacre all the blacks. One brought in three hogsheads marked sugar. A little slave girl, hearing her master say at dinner-table, that he had one filled with loaded pistols, another with dirks, and the third with bowie-knives, went and told her mother. She was directed to be careful and listen, while busy about the room, to all her master said, and report to her. In this way she heard the plans that her master and his friends designed to carry into execution, and informed her mother. The plan was to paint a large company of their men black, who should assume the attitude of fight; then all were to cry out "Insurrection! INSURRECTION!" and fly to every negro man, woman, and child, and kill them all off. The mother made an errand down-town with her little girl, and called on General Butler, to whom they told all. A party of officers and soldiers were dispatched at once, who visited that house, demanded the keys, and searched the premises. There they found the hogsheads, broke in the head of each, and found all as reported. The master was banished from the city, his family sent outside the lines, his property confiscated and his slaves set free. No wonder they disliked General Butler, when he defeated their base designs.

The convention which met in the City Hall to frame a free constitution for Louisiana created considerable excitement. Many slave-owners were confident they would have all their slaves back again, or get pay for them.

As there were no sanitary agents at Brazier City, and we learned of much suffering there, we called at the Christian Commission Rooms to make further inquiries, and found brother Diossy had just sent both an agent and a teacher to that point. "But if you are hunting for destitute places," he told us, "I wish you would go to Ship Island, in the Gulf of Mexico, as there are soldiers and many prisoners there, and they have no chaplain or agent to look after their sanitary condition" While I was inclined to go, sister Backus thought, in view of the very warm weather, and because we were so nearly worn out with several months constant toiling, we had better turn our faces homeward. I knew there was but little more than shadows left of us, yet I could not rid myself of the impression that it would be right to go; but I told her I would not draft her into service, or persuade her against her judgment.

I met at these rooms brother Merrifield and brother Horton, and the chaplain of the Michigan 6th Infantry. By their request we attended a soldiers' prayer-meeting. Near the close one soldier expressed his gratitude for the privilege of listening to the voice of mothers in counsels that reminded many of them of their own mothers far away. He could say no more for a moment, being overcome with emotion. "You may call me weak, and if this be weakness, then I am weak," he said. Another requested prayer for his sick soldier brother, and for the preservation of the Northern ladies who were laboring for them.

After this meeting I called at the office for transportation; but there was no encouragement that I could get it for a number of days, "perhaps two weeks," as General Banks had nearly all the boats up Red River, in his fleet. But as I was passing the gulf office I called and found the steamer Clyde going out for Ship Island in four hours, and at once secured transportation for us both. I returned to our boarding-house, and reported what I had done, and told sister Backus if she was willing to go the sea-breeze might do more to rest us than the labors would add to our weariness. She consented to accompany me, and we provided ourselves with half a bushel of reading matter at Christian Commission Rooms, and secured the aid of a couple of soldiers to carry our books to the street-car, from thence to a steam-car that landed us at the Clyde. As there was no berth for us we obtained a couple of blankets, but there being room for only one to lie down, we managed, by taking turns, to get considerable sleep. On April 8th, at ten A. M., we landed on Ship Island. It was of white sand, that resembled, at a distance, a huge snow-bank. We found a little sprinkle of brown sand, upon which grew a few scrubby trees and a species of cactus that spread out in clusters as large as a dinner-plate. The island is eight miles in length, and from one-fourth to three-fourths of a mile wide. The captain told us he should not leave until four o'clock, P.M., and we made use of our time accordingly. When we landed with our large market-basket heaping full of Testaments and other reading matter, the gunboat boys and prisoners gathered around us like hungry children. Prisoners in irons came holding the iron ball in one arm, while the other hand reached for a Testament, crying out, "Please give me a Testament, I lost mine in battle;" "Please give me one, I lost mine in a long march;" "Please give me something to read, I lost my Testament in a rain-storm." Many hands were reached over the shoulders of others, until thirty or forty hands at a time were extended. We soon exhausted our basket-supply. We had a few in our satchels, but we reserved them for the hospital and military prison. As we had disposed of the most of our books in an hour, we spent an hour on the beach gathering sea shells until noon, then took our rations, and spent the remainder of our time in hospital-visiting, and in learning from the officers what was needed to be sent on our return to New Orleans.

While engaged in other matters, we found our boat had left us, and was steaming away perhaps a mile from us. Sister Backus was greatly disappointed at being left, and gave way to despondency; but I assured her it was all for the best, and that as the Lord had heretofore provided for us, so he would provide for us now. We returned to the tent of Mrs. Green, a tidy mulatto woman, where we had left our satchels. As she met us and learned of our being left, and heard sister Backus lament over "not having where to lay our heads," she quickly replied: "Yes, you shall have a place for your heads. In that chest I have plenty of bedding, and I'll dress up this bed for you two. My husband can find a place with some of his comrades, and I'll make a bed for myself on the floor till the boat comes back." "There, sister Backus," I said, "the Lord is providing for us already." Tears filled her eyes. She replied, "I will not doubt any more."

Mrs. Green had a nice dinner prepared in the best style; table-linen of the finest damask, chinaware and solid silver spoons, pitcher, forks, and plated table knives, etc. I inquired how this came about, as I had not seen a table so richly set since coming into the army. Her reply was, that both of their fathers were wealthy planters, who made them free when they died. Her husband received by will twenty-five thousand dollars, and she also received from her father's estate a fine brick residence. They had it nicely furnished, and their property was valued at fifty thousand dollars. Her husband was making in his business from seventy-five to one hundred dollars a month, but he was so confident that this war would result in the freedom of their race that he, with others, enlisted in a colored regiment for seven dollars a month, under the rebel government, with a secret understanding among themselves that they would all go in with the Union army as soon as opportunity presented. The opportunity was furnished on the taking of New Orleans by Union troops. The regiment was officered by men of their own color, but the indignities they received at the hands of Union commanders caused their officers to resign their positions. One of the many was on one occasion of an order by one of their captains for shoes and blankets for his destitute men. It was not honored, and he went in person to inform the commander how needy his men were. The reply was that he need not expect negro regiments to be supplied the same as white soldiers. This was thrown in their teeth by Confederates: "You see what you get by going over to the Yankees. We never served you like that," said a Confederate.

We found Mr. Green an intelligent and pleasant man. Just as our dinner was ready, Captain James Noyce called to see us, and urged us to make our home with his family during our stay on the island. We told him of the kind offer of Mrs. Green. "I know," was his reply, "that Mrs. Green has the nicest things of any one on this island, but my wife and I want you with us." He said he should call for us in two hours, which he did; and we felt that our lots were cast in a pleasant place. There were two lieutenants boarding with them, both of whom, with the captain, appeared like men of sterling principle.

While enjoying a very pleasant social visit with our new friends, sister Backus espied the life of Orange Scott on their center table (a goods-box with a newspaper spread. In surprise she exclaimed: "Sister Haviland, here is the life of Orange Scott! Isn't this home-like? away here in the Gulf of Mexico!"

"Do you know any thing of Orange Scott?" inquired our hostess.

"I guess we do. We know all about him," replied sister Backus.

"You are not Wesleyan Methodists, are you?"

"Indeed we are, both of us."

She almost flew at us, placing her hands on our shoulders. "I don't wonder you seemed so much like relatives. Orange Scott is my father, and Mr. Noyce and I are Wesleyans," and she laughed and cried at the same time. The dear little homesick woman was overjoyed. She had been on the island a long time with her husband, and in poor health, sick and tired of army life, and longing for her Northern home. Yet she would not consent to leave her husband so long as he could stay in one place a sufficient time for her to be with him. But he was fearful it was impairing her health. On her account, as well as our own, we were thankful for the privilege of mingling with kindred spirits. The two lieutenants who boarded with them brought in their new mattresses to make a double bed for the captain and his wife, as they gave up their own bed to us during our stay. This left the lieutenants to sleep on the bare tent floor, with their blankets only. But we did not know of this arrangement until the day we left.

April 9th was very windy. We could not go out for the drifting sand, without being thickly veiled. I walked to the beach, near the soldiers' burying-ground, and stood two hours watching the waves as they lashed the bars of sand. Their briny spray bedewed the graves of soldiers, who had fallen far away from their kindred and their loved ones, in their Northern homes. I could not repress the tear of sympathy as these reflections came to me, and I listened to the solemn moan of the ocean. Yet here is the God of peace and love.

> "He plants his footsteps in the sea,
> And rides upon the storm."

This evening we listened to Lieutenant Kingsley's thrilling description of the cruel irons he filed off from a number of slaves, who were too intelligent to be held without severe measures. He said these men made soldiers who hesitated not to brave the greatest dangers. His experience reminded us of the words of another:

> "Beware the time when that chain shall break,

That galls the flesh and spirit;
When the yoke is thrown from the bended neck,
That is chafed too much to hear it
There's a God above, that looks with a frown,
To see how long you have trodden him down."

In distributing the remainder of our tracts and Testaments to prisoners we met a number of very intelligent men, who appeared to be men of Christian principles. I always made it a point to say nothing to a prisoner of the particular crime that placed him in confinement, but directed his thoughts to the Lord Jesus, the lover of sinners. As my sympathies became deeply enlisted in behalf of many of the prisoners in irons, I inquired of Captain Noyce, in whose charge they were, what crimes these soldiers had committed, that they should be confined in irons. "No crime," he answered.

"Then please tell me," I said, "why they are here?"

"For drunkenness, being late at roll-call, absence without leave, and selling government property, mostly exchanging rations for groceries, such as sugar and tea."

"Is this possible?" I exclaimed. "All these trivial offenses have been settled in their own regiments wherever else I have been."

"So they have wherever I have been, until I came here. But you seem almost to disbelieve my word. If you do, you can step into my office and examine the record for yourself. You will find these men sentenced from one year to thirty-eight for the offenses I have named."

"I have no reason to doubt your word, but I will thank you for the privilege of examining that record. Who pronounced these sentences?"

"Judge Attocha."

"Who is Judge Attocha?"

"He was a rebel captain, but after New Orleans fell into our hands he took the oath of allegiance, and General Banks promoted him by giving him the position of judge advocate."

"That man is a rebel still," I said. "He is doing for the rebel cause more than when at the head of his company, in the rebel ranks. You say a few over 3,000 have passed through your hands here and on the Dry Tortugas. We read in the paper, the day we left New Orleans, an order from President Lincoln to draft men, and here are three whole regiments laid upon the shelf. Are all these Union soldiers?"

"They are all Union soldiers. We had a Confederate here for murder, sentenced for a year. He was here only three months, when he was pardoned; and on your return to New Orleans you may see him walking the streets as independent as yourself."

"This is a flagrant wrong in holding these 3,000 men. Why don't you report Judge Attocha?"

"He outranks me, and should I presume to do it I would be put into a dungeon myself, and probably die there without an investigation."

Sister Backus and I went into the office, and the captain brought us a great roll, as large around as a man's hat. I unrolled a few feet, and read the name, regiment, company, offense, and penalty of each man, thus: For drunkenness, fifteen years hard labor with ball and chain, and all wages forfeited, except three dollars a month; for selling government property, eight years hard labor, with ball and chain, and all wages forfeited except three dollars a month. Some prisoners were sentenced to longer, others to shorter, terms; but upon all were imposed the same forfeitures, and all were put in irons. One man from near Battle Creek, Michigan, was sentenced for life. His offense was simply "suspicious character." No other reason for his sentence was given. I handed this fearful record to sister Backus, and we both read with heavy hearts. Every free State was represented. What can we do, we asked ourselves, for these poor men, some of whom are sick and dying with scurvy? This was a query hard to answer. I retired to bed, but not to sleep, wrestling in prayer to Him who hears the sighs of the prisoner to lead me to a door that would open for the 3,000 men in irons. The captain was a kind-hearted man, and told me that he had in many cases put the irons on so loosely that they could relieve themselves when out of his sight, but he charged them to be careful not to allow him to see them off. On account of the injustice of their sentences, he had favored them wherever he could do so, and keep his own record clear.

The next day, April 10th, was Sunday. The morning was clear and beautiful. Sister Backus said:

"You are sick, or very weary; for you groaned in your sleep so much last night."

"I am not conscious of having groaned," I said; "but I did not sleep a wink. I am distressed, and have spent the night in prayer for a guiding hand to open a door of relief for these prisoners, and I must see them before I leave this island. I am this morning bearing as heavy a heart as at any period of this deadly strife."

"Try and dismiss this subject if possible," she returned, "as they have appointed a meeting for us in the regiment, and I presume there will be an opportunity for you to see the prisoners."

As best I could, I dismissed the all-absorbing theme; and according to previous arrangement we met the regiment, with a few gun-boat soldiers and the officers. We enjoyed a favored season, and found a liberty of spirit our dear Redeemer only can give. After closing the services to the peace of my own mind, and to the apparent satisfaction of the large congregation, Captain James Noyce came to me and said:

"You are certainly too weary to visit the prisoners now."

"O no," was my reply, "if you will allow me that privilege."

"They are in very large barracks, and it is a very unpleasant place for a lady to visit; but if it is your wish, these gun-boat officers wanted me to ask you if you had any objections to their going."

"Not at all; all can go who wish."

Captain Noyce and wife took us to the barracks, where the prisoners were arranged in rows, six men deep, on both sides and at the end, leaving an aisle three feet in width between. In every berth there was a man in a horizontal position; and all were in irons, either in handcuffs with chain, or in a clog for the ankle, to which was attached the chain and ball. What a scene! The click of the irons at the least move greeted our ears. We walked midway of the long aisle, and looked over the sad faces before us. Upon the necks of those who stood near vermin were to be seen. Filthy and ragged were many of these poor boys. Some had been there a year, without change of raiment. I could say nothing of the injustice of their punishment; but I exhorted them to come forth from this furnace of affliction with higher, nobler, and holier aspirations than ever before, and to lift up their heads in hope of better days, although the heavens might then seem as brass and the earth as bars of iron. I spoke a few minutes, and as I closed my remarks I turned to sister Backus, standing by, and asked her to say a few words of encouragement, but she declined. She said that all she could do was to weep with those who wept. I knelt to pour out the overflowings of a full heart in prayer, and as I did so they all knelt with me, amid the clank and clatter of irons that made it necessary to wait a moment to be heard.

As we were leaving, two prisoners advanced a few steps toward us and said, "In behalf of our fellow-prisoners, we return to you our thanks for the kind words which you have spoken to us, and pray God to restore you safe to your Northern homes." We bade them adieu, with many tears. After leaving this place we visited other quarters equally large, with similar experiences.

I had become very much interested in a number with whom I conversed, who were very thankful for the Testaments we gave them. They gave evidence of possessing an earnest trust in God and of enjoying the cleansing power of the blood of his dear Son.

Accompanied by the captain and his wife, on Monday we visited the light-house, and ascended the flight of steps of sixty-four feet. The weather was clear and calm, and we had a fine view of the Gulf of Mexico on one side and the grand expanse of the ocean on the other. After dinner with the same party, accompanied by Lieutenant Kingsley, we took a ten-oar row-boat and went to see the burial-ground of four hundred deceased soldiers. The graves were all plainly marked with head-boards. These soldiers were mostly from Maine and New York, with a few from New Jersey, Wisconsin, and Michigan. This was another solemn place for reflection. The soldiers' grave-yard on this island differs somewhat from all others. Here their funeral dirge will never cease; the requiem of the ocean's surge will ever sound as if saying, "Sleep on undisturbed until the last trump shall wake the nations of the dead!"

We returned to our boat, and pursued our way to the extremity of the island. Here the picket-guards were much pleased to see us. They had been on the island about two years, ever since it was taken from the Confederates. We gathered a basket of shells, and our men gathered a quantity of crabs for breakfast. We were presented with some beautiful shells by one of the pickets. We returned home, having had a ten miles' ride. We passed the wreck of a ship burned many years ago, which gave this island its name. We could clearly see its charred cabin twenty or thirty feet below the surface. So clear was the water it did not seem more than eight or ten feet deep over the white sand, upon which beautiful shell-fish were crawling, as if to beautify the grand scene so new to us.

In a long conversation with Lieutenant Kingsley concerning his religious experience, he said he was not satisfied with his attainments in the divine life, and very earnestly requested to be remembered at a throne of grace. The moon rose full and clear on the sparkling face of the deep, reminding us of David's sublime thoughts when he exclaims in the eighth Psalm: "When I consider thy heavens, the work of thy fingers, the moon and the stars, which thou hast ordained; what is man, that thou art mindful of him? and the son of man, that thou visitest him? For thou hast made him a little lower than the angels, and hast crowned him with glory and honor."

After our return we enjoyed a season of prayer, in which Lieutenant Kingsley was earnestly remembered, and he expressed himself greatly encouraged. Leaving all those burdened souls with the Lord Jesus, who cares for all that he has redeemed with his own precious blood, I retired to rest.

The next day one of the prisoners came to inform me that their keeper had granted them the privilege of asking me if I would take a petition from them to General Weitzel, former commander of seventy of their number. They had heard he was then in New Orleans, and they thought if he could do any thing for their release he would, as he was a very kind officer. I cordially assented to his request, of course, and he thanked me with tears. In company with the captain and wife we visited the gigantic fort that had been two years in building, but was not yet completed. It was to cost two million dollars. The brick wall at the base is six feet thick, and about two hundred and fifty men were employed on it when we were there. It is constructed to mount forty cannons.

At supper I received a request from Lieutenant Foster, who was sick, to visit him. I found him in low spirits. He wished me to write a request to his wife to come to him, which I did. I read to him some extracts from an excellent little work, "The Soldier's Armor," and a chapter in the best of all books, closing with prayer. Lieutenant Foster seemed a devout Christian man, and expressed great satisfaction with this interview. The captain smiled on my return, saving I had "better remain with them and be their chaplain."

On April 13th we made a few calls, and two of the soldiers' wives came for us to dine with them. I made a copy of the record of the soldier prisoners, as a specimen of their alleged crimes, and the penalties imposed upon them. One of the prisoners brought me their petition, which reads as follows:

"SHIP ISLAND, April 12, 1864.

"MAJOR-GENERAL WEITZEL: Sir,--We whose names are affixed, prisoners on Ship Island; respectfully beg our release, and that we be allowed to return to our respective regiments. We are here for various military offenses, and for nothing criminal. Nearly all of us have participated in the engagements under your lead in this department, both on the battle-field and on the long, wearisome marches we have been called to undergo; and we have always followed cheerfully wherever you have led. We naturally feel that you are the proper person to appeal to to give us one more chance to redeem ourselves. And we solemnly assure you that we never will, by any unsoldier-like act, give you any occasion to regret any act of clemency that you may exercise toward us. Many of us have families dependent on us for support, and are suffering for our forfeited wages. Many of us are already suffering from that dread scourge--the scurvy-- which must increase to a fearful extent in this tropical climate as the season advances and sweep, us away. And now that the campaign is open and advancing, and men are needed, we hope we may be permitted to return to the field, and by future faithfulness in our country's cause be able to return to our homes with what all good men so highly prize- untarnished characters. Should you exercise your influence in our favor in procuring our release, rest assured you will ever be remembered with gratitude."

This petition was signed by "Moses Fuller," sentenced to three years' hard labor, with belt and chain, and forfeited wages, except three dollars a month, charged with selling government property, to wit: exchanging his surplus rations; but Judge Attocha would listen to no witness in the case. Sixty-nine other names were appended to this petition.

Our anxiously looked for steamer, the Clyde, came in view, but it was too windy for it to land until noon. It brought about thirty prisoners, who had come in with a flag of truce, mostly white refugees. One family was from Mobile. The woman said the suffering from the war was not much there, and all she knew any thing about had enough to eat and wear. "But I reckon poor people suffer," she said, evidently wishing us to understand she was not poor. She had two servants to wait on her and five children. But her servants seemed to think they were free here, and said they should leave her unless she paid them wages. There were a number of slaves who came here for freedom. I called on Colonel Grosvenor, the commandant of the post, who appeared like a kind-hearted officer, and he approved of the petition. The next day, April 14th, we took the Clyde for New Orleans, after being a week on the island. On our way to the boat a soldier came running to overtake us, with a message from another soldier that he had that morning found peace in believing. He would have come himself, only that he was on picket-guard and could not leave; but he wanted us to know that our mission was not in vain.

As Ship Island receded from view sister Backus, as well as myself, felt thankful that our Heavenly Father had ordered all things well in regard to our having been left "'way off in the Gulf of Mexico."

We reached our pleasant New Orleans home, at Elder Rogers's April 16th, and were as kindly received as if we had been friends of many years' standing. The next day, after a good night's rest, we made an effort to find General Weitzel, but failed. At two P.M., we attended prayer-meeting and had a rich season of communing with our Heavenly Father. There were present two chaplains, one of whom had been at various points in Arkansas, and he gave a thrilling account of some engagements his regiment had had with the enemy. The other was just from the dreadful fight at Alexandria, up the river. It is reported and believed by thousands that the rebel general came to General Banks with a flag of truce and informed him that, unless he withdrew his colored troops, he should take no prisoners and give no quarter. Report said further that they were withdrawn and were not permitted to advance on the enemy, as they desired, and the consequence was an awful slaughter of our Northern men. The colored troops complained of inactivity in the field more than any thing else. We found along the whole length of the river fortifications built, streets in cities cleaned, and the greater part of manual labor performed by colored soldiers.

We renewed our efforts to find General Weitzel, visiting all the offices of the army we could hear of. Some reported that he was up Red River assisting General Banks, but at length, with thoroughly blistered feet, I found him. I introduced myself, as usual, by handing him my papers from Governor Blair and F. C. Beaman, member of Congress. After looking them over, he asked:

"What can I do for you?"

"I hope you can do something," I said, "toward releasing three thousand of our soldiers now confined on Ship Island and the Dry Tortugas, seventy of whom have served under you; and here is a petition from them."

He took it, and read the petition, and not more than a half-dozen names perhaps, before he became too much excited to read further. "Mrs. Haviland," he said, "these are as noble soldiers as I ever had serve under me. I don't think Moses Fuller, or any of the others, is capable of doing a wrong act. They are the most conscientious men I ever knew. Judge Attocha has no right to give these sentences; he has no business in this department of the work."

"Can't you do something for their release?" I asked.

"If I were in command I would tell you very quick; but General Banks is the one you ought to see."

"I am aware of that; but he is beyond my reach up Red River. And they told me they sent him a petition similar to this three months ago; but they had heard nothing from it."

"I will do what I can toward getting up a committee to investigate and report these facts."

"Do you think you can accomplish any thing in their favor?"

"I fear it is doubtful, but will do what I can."

This was but little relief to me; but what could I do further? I called at the Christian Commission rooms, discouraged and weary, while sister Backus returned to our quarters. These rooms I found well filled with officers, among whom were generals of high rank, indicated by the eagles and stars on their shoulders.

"Here comes Mrs. Haviland, from Ship Island. And how did you find things there?" said brother Diossy.

"Sad enough," was my reply; and I handed him a copy of the petition that I gave General Weitzel, with the extract of the record of fifteen prisoners, detailing the offense and penalty of each. The officers gathered around to see and hear.

"This is too bad," said one.

"Can't you do something for these soldiers?" I inquired.

"I wish I could; but I can't leave my post."

Said another, "It is a pity some one doesn't."

I turned to him with, "Can't you do something for their release?"

"It is the same with me," he answered; "I can not leave my post."

"Some one ought to see to their release. Can not you see to their release?"

"I tell you, madam, it is hard to do much for each other."

"Gentlemen," I responded, "I have learned one thing thoroughly since being with the army, and that is, it is almost impossible to get one officer to touch another's red-tape. But position or no position, head or no head, these flagrant wrongs ought to be plowed up beam deep. Here comes an order from President Lincoln for drafting men, and Judge Attocha has laid three thousand on the shelf, when all they ask is to be permitted to return to their respective regiments. That man is serving the rebel cause more effectually than when at the head of his company in the rebel ranks, by decimating the Union army; and here you have it in a tangible form. I am informed that Judge Attocha was a rebel captain. He is a rebel still, and in the exercise of this authority is banishing your soldiers for trivial military offenses, in irons, with forfeited wages; for which their families are now suffering."

The thought struck me, What will these officers think, to see a little old woman talking to them like this? for I addressed them as I would a group of ten-year-old boys. I had lost all reverence for shoulder- straps, and cast a glance over my audience, when I saw a number in tears. Surely there are hearts here that feel, I thought to myself. I turned to brother Diossy, and said, "You can leave your position, and get another to occupy your place here?"

"Yes, I could, if it would avail any thing; but it would be impossible for me to accomplish what you have done on Ship Island."

"Why? The idea seems to me perfectly preposterous."

"I will tell you why. There is so much wire-pulling here in the army. I would be suspected of trying to displace an officer for the position for myself, or for a friend standing behind me. Consequently I could not have examined the record as you did."

"That is true," rejoined a general. "I presume there is not one of us that could have had access to those records that you had, for the reason that Mr. Diossy has given. They know you have no such object in view, but see you as a sort of soldiers' mother; and records, or any sort of investigation, would be opened to you when it would be closed to us."

I told them I had not viewed it from that stand-point.

One of the officers, a very large man, six feet and four inches tall, I should judge, stepped up to me in officer-like style. "What do you propose to do with facts you gathered on Ship Island?"

I looked up in his face, a little hesitating.

"I say, madam, what do you propose to do with these papers?"

"I can hardly answer intelligently," I replied; "but I will tell you one thing I do propose to do, and that is, to take these facts from one officer to another, over all the rounds of the ladder, until they reach the highest official at Washington, but what justice shall be done to those poor soldiers in irons."

He settled back, with softened tone. "Well, it ought to be done."

The commanding appearance and tone, with the changed mellow voice, of that officer is still vividly remembered.

There were two chaplains in this company who said they would unite with General Weitzel on the committee he proposed, and they could learn within a week whether they could accomplish any thing in their behalf. If favorable, Chaplain Conway said he would write me at Adrian, as we were soon to return to our homes, and would write, as I requested, by two boats in succession, as guerrillas were at that time frequently interrupting boats. If no letter was received within two weeks I was to accept it as granted that nothing could be done for them in that department.

At 2 o'clock we attended prayer-meeting, where we met many soldiers and two chaplains. I was called upon to give a sketch of our Ship Island visit, and at the close a frail and spoke encouraging words to them, in passing through this transition state. From them we went to the river bank to see five hundred prisoners of war, captured up Red River. Many of them were citizens of New Orleans.

On returning we went to a meeting of the colored people, where we found Uncle Tom's spirit waiting confidently for the "better day a- coming." A number of white soldiers present encouraged us with kind words. After refreshments we attended another meeting, and listened to an instructive sermon by a colored chaplain, of the Second "Corps d'Afrique," as the colored regiments were called in that part of the country. He was the first colored man who received an appointment from the government.

At 4 P.M. we visited the colored Sabbath-school of seven hundred at the Medical College. Chaplain Conway superintended. Colonel Hanks, General Banks's wife, and a number of other visitors were present. Dr. John P. Newman addressed the school, and gave a thrilling narrative of his visit to the Holy Land, exhibiting the native scrip, sandals, girdle, goat-skin bottle, a Palestine lantern, and sundry other curiosities. After a few encouraging remarks by Col. Hanks, the superintendent unexpectedly called upon me to address the school. After the session closed I was introduced to Mrs. Banks, who wished me to write out the sketch of the facts I had gathered on Ship Island for her to send to her husband. This I did. She said that Judge Attocha promised General Banks that he would do all in his power for the Union cause, and now in this way he was paying him for his promotion.

After giving my statements to Mrs. Banks, and the petition to General Weitzel, I felt that I could leave for home on the first boat going North; yet we had but little hope of success in behalf of the 3,000 prisoners in this department. We took passage on the hospital transport Thomas, bound for Cairo, with eighty wounded soldiers from the Red River expedition, all discharged or furloughed for home. Medical Inspector Stipp kindly gave us a state-room. We were grateful to our Heavenly Father for the many kind friends we everywhere found, although surrounded by bitter enemies. The boat did not design stopping until it reached Baton Rouge; but I wanted to stop at Plaquemine to get the little girl Matilda, previously mentioned, to take to her mother, who had made her escape a few years before.

After breakfast, dressing wounds was the order of the day. I kept off the flies during the process, as it was very difficult otherwise to keep them away, the stench being so great. Poor boys! there were all sorts of wounds among them,--saber-cuts and bullet-wounds in the head, neck, shoulders, arms, hands, body, legs, and feet, of all shapes and sizes. O what horrid mangling! Yet the same patience that so remarkably characterized the Union soldier everywhere was seen here. It was hard to restrain tears in their presence, but we gave vent to them when in our state-room.

I was unexpectedly called for at Plaquemine, as I was informed that Medical Inspector Stipp had ordered the Thomas to stop for me. They were already landing before they found me. I caught up my bonnet and shawl and threw them on while hastening through the cabin. Sister Backus ran with me to the plank, where we snatched a parting kiss. I jumped ashore, sister Backus, surgeons, and a few others waving good- by signals with their handkerchiefs. The Thomas pushed out into the channel, and the next moment found me without my official papers, pocket-book, or portfolio; all were gone on to Baton Rouge with my friend Letitia Backus. In my haste they had been forgotten. As I was inquiring for the name of Eliza's sister of a colored picket, he recognized me at once, being from Detroit. He said he had beard me speak in the colored church in that city, and urged me to speak for them the next evening in their confiscated Methodist Episcopal

Church. I consented, and found the two sisters, with little Matilda, almost wild with delight.

I soon had the pleasure of introducing my Detroit acquaintance, who called with a few other young men that knew me; and here, too, I was surrounded by friends, but they expressed fears of my not securing transportation to Baton Rouge, because their commander was cross and was known to issue but few orders for transportation. But I went to his office and told him what my business was in the army, and why I called there; that, on leaving the floating hospital in haste, I forgot my official papers, and consequently had nothing by which he could judge whether my statement was correct or not. I, however, had presumed to call on him to see if I could secure transportation for myself and that little girl of twelve years.

"Well, I think your motherly face will take you to Baton Rouge," he answered. "There is a regular packet running to that city, and I will send a note by you to the captain that will secure your passage, although it is not a government boat. The captain has received favors from me, and will gladly make this return."

He handed me a paper that requested a state-room and board for us, for which continued thankfulness filled my heart.

The friends of Eliza and of another escaped slave, Fleming, came in to inquire after them, and to tell long stories of the efforts put forth for their capture. But Bissel, Slaughter, and "Old Eaton," as they called him, only had the opportunity of gratifying themselves in threats.

The colored minister in the regiment took much pains in circulating notice of the meeting, and the church was well filled. We enjoyed the presence of the Lord Jesus in our midst. There were those there who had felt the bitter pangs of family separations, with cruel treatment, who wept for joy in speaking of the precious boon of freedom. Some of them were fearful that it would last no longer than the war; but I assured them, as officers and soldiers had done, that it was a fixed fact.

The packet Bank came in at five o'clock, P. M., April 21st, when we took leave of kind friends who accompanied us to the boat. After a pleasant trip, we were received with joy on our safe arrival at Baton Rouge. The next day we visited the Forty-eighth Illinois Regiment, and distributed a quantity of reading matter. We also attended the funeral of a deceased soldier, where the privilege was granted me of making some remarks. I endeavored to enforce the solemn truth, "It is appointed unto man once to die, and after this the judgment." I exhorted those present to prepare to live in friendship with God, as that alone would enable them to gain the victory over death.

On April 23d we visited the jail, in company with brother Merrifield, and distributed Testaments and tracts, which were gladly received. Here we met a rebel captain, who said he was a rebel of the strongest kind; had been fighting to establish his government, and should do it again if he lived to get to his regiment. I told him I had no hope in his case, unless he would accept the truth contained in the Testament, which I presented to him, and said that if he would read carefully and prayerfully, and drink in its spirit and practice its teachings, he would find a religion pure and undefiled.

"Madam," he answered, "if I thought reading that book carefully and prayerfully, and accepting pure and undefiled religion, would lead me to lay down arms in defense of the Confederate Government, I would never read a word in it or take one thought of religion; no, not to save my soul."

This he uttered with a change from a flushed to a blanched countenance. We afterwards learned he was a captain of a guerrilla band, and had been sentenced to be shot, but the sentence had been commuted. A Union man who was a citizen here knew him, and said he ordered a Union man out of his buggy, and shot him dead; then he bayoneted him through and through, in the presence of his wife and child; then ordered them out, took the horse and buggy, and left the distracted wife and child to wait by the mangled body, until a passer by hastened to the city and sent a hearse for the body. On the way to town for burial, the same band of guerrillas captured the team and hearse, and left again the distressed mother and child to get the mutilated body of the husband and father taken to burial as best they could. "Such horrible deeds," said a Union man of this city, "will continue until government takes a more decided policy."

On Sunday morning, April 24th, we attended the sunrise prayer-meeting among the colored people, and more earnest prayers I never heard for Union soldiers: never heard more earnest pleading for the triumph of liberty. God was truly overshadowing his own. Before the rising of the sun, there was a large congregation. At nine o'clock we were invited to make some opening remarks in brother Tucker's Sabbath-school of three hundred children. Then we were conducted to another Sabbath- school, where we were invited to make a few closing remarks. At 11 o'clock we attended a meeting led by Chaplain Berge. On returning to our boarding-place, we were called upon by brother Merrifield, who accompanied us into the fort to address the colored troops. Sister Backus referred to the importance of making themselves intelligent, so that when their rights were established as citizens, they would be prepared to vote understandingly. This brought smiles from the officers, and frowns from a few of the white soldiers. We also attended a meeting conducted by the chaplain of the general hospital, who preached a very appropriate sermon for officers as well as soldiers. He warned against the truckling, time-serving, and cotton- speculating manifestations in this war, and also the influence of Southern women in sympathy with the rebellion.

This was the sixth religious service we attended during the day, in four of which we had taken an active part. We retired to rest until the 6:30 o'clock meeting at the Methodist Episcopal Church, now turned over to Chaplain Brakeman, who was called away the previous day. He had left an urgent request for me to address the soldiers on Sabbath evening; but I told the chaplain who brought the word we could make no further engagements, as we were waiting hourly for a boat going up the river. Before six, a steamer stopped, and we took passage for Natchez, as we had business to see to concerning an orphan asylum. One of the chaplains said if we could realize the good it was doing the soldiers, we would visit them oftener; that there were more conversions during the week after we left than in many months previously. An exhortation from a mother reminded the soldiers of home and home influences.

We had a conversation with a colored captain, who had just resigned on account of the constant indignities heaped upon the colored troops. He was a man of wealth and intelligence, and gave us an account of a review by General Sherman, after General Butler left. When General Sherman came to him, he stopped to look at the bars on his shoulders, and gruffly asked, "Are you a captain?" "Yes, sir," was the reply. "O, you are too black for a captain," said the general. At Fort Hudson, when our troops were retreating under a galling fire, a colored captain, with his men, at the risk of his life, ran to bring out General Sherman, who was badly wounded, and would have died but for the daring feat of the colored soldiers. The colored captain lost his life, but General Sherman was rescued. Since then he has spoken highly of colored soldiers, and of the brave captains that led them.

My informant said that after General Banks assumed command they hoped for better treatment, but their hopes were vain. As the men in December and January were in want of shoes and clothing, he told General Banks that they were not in a suitable condition to work on the fortifications where the detachment was ordered, but no attention was paid to him. He inquired why his men could not be supplied the same as the white soldiers. The reply he received was, "Don't you know you are niggers, and must not expect the same treatment?" "From that moment," he said, "I resolved to resign; but after waiting a little, and seeing no better prospects, I did so, and shall not resume arms until we can be treated as men."

In New Orleans two regiments of free colored men were raised in forty-eight hours. They were officered by men of their color in grades as high as major by General Butler, who said they were as good officers as he held under him. We arrived in Natchez on the 26th, where we met rejoicing friends. We found a number of the missionaries sick, among them sister Burlingame.

The day following we spent chiefly in writing, and distributing Testaments and tracts among soldiers. In the evening we attended a protracted meeting, conducted by two sisters. They acquitted themselves nobly, and had three conversions. They exhorted earnestly and prayed fervently. They invited us to take part with them. One of the ministers told me they had worked in this meeting until they were tired out, and then gave it over to these mothers in the Church, whose labors the Lord was blessing in the conversion of precious souls.

We made an effort to secure a house for an orphan asylum.

Rebel sympathizers were making trouble all along the line of our work. They tried every plan that could be devised to drive the refugees back to their old plantations. An infamous "health order" was issued, compelling every colored person, not employed by responsible parties in the city or suburbs, to go into the "corral," or colored camp. Many were employed by colored citizens, who were doing all they could to find work for them. But on the day this order took effect soldiers were sent to hunt them out of all such places, as no colored party was deemed responsible; and all who were not actual members of these colored families were driven out at the point of Union bayonets.

They gathered two hundred and fifty, mostly women and children, and drove them through the streets of Natchez on a chilly, rainy day, and marched them into the camp of four thousand in condemned tents. One of the colored citizens told me that she was paying her woman wages, and allowing her to have her three children with her, but the soldiers drove her out into the rain. Men and women tantalized them as they were marching through the streets, saying: "That's the way the Yankees treat you, is it? You'd better come back to us; we never treated you like that." Many of the women went into camp crying. Said an old colored man: "Never min', thar's a better day a comin'. 'Twould be strange if Uncle Sam hadn't a few naughty boys." He was one of the group that was driven in.

We heard, April 30th, that there was a skirmish near our lines the evening before. A party of scouts had shot into the pickets, and they retreated; but we did not learn whether any were killed. News came to us of Calvin Fairbanks's release from the Kentucky penitentiary. We trusted that the same Deliverer would open the prison-door for the three thousand soldiers on the two islands in the Gulf.

At nine o'clock A. M., May 1st, we attended the organization of the fifth colored Sabbath-school in the city. At eleven A. M. we went to Wall Street Church, and listened to an interesting discourse by Chaplain Trask, of the Fourth Illinois Regiment. At two P. M., at the Colored Methodist Episcopal Church, we heard brother Burlingame. After a short exhortation by brother Fitzhugh, twelve came forward for prayer, and some were blessed with pardon. At six P. M. we attended a soldiers' meeting at Wall Street Church, in which we took a part; also a number of soldiers spoke and prayed. Between meetings I wrote a letter for a colored man to his wife, who is still a slave in Woodville, twenty miles distant.

I was sick with a chill and fever May 2d, and the nearest to being homesick since I left Michigan. The next day I was better. Here I met Joseph Warner, with whom I had been acquainted from his childhood. He was a lessee at Waterproof. He had a large plantation, and two hundred hands employed. He was twice taken by guerrillas. He told them they could hang or shoot him, but they might rest assured that forty of their men's lives would pay for his, and forty men stood ready to take his place; and they let him go each time. A distressed mother came to us to inquire for her two daughters, that her mistress had sent to Texas to elude the effects of the Proclamation of Emancipation. She had begged her mistress to allow them to remain in town, if she could not have them with her. The mistress said, "No you shall never have your girls with you again, not even to give you a drink of water if you are dying." This was at the retaking of Baton Rouge, when the mistress considered herself again in full power; but she was soon to suffer herself. When that city was retaken by Union men, the only son of the mistress was burned to death in the house at which he was boarding. Upon this she fell into fits. Yet, Pharaoh-like, she persisted in keeping the slave-girls in Texas.

A number of missionaries called on us, and urged me to remain with them a few weeks longer; but for two reasons I had to decline: First, those three thousand soldier prisoners were daily on my mind; and, second, my poor health made it a duty to return home.

Skirmishing four miles off took place May 5th, and we could see the blue smoke of battle. The shooting seemed near us. How little this terrible war was realized in our own free State homes!

I met on the street a mulatto girl seventeen years old, weeping, and inquired the cause of her grief. She said her owner, Mrs. Morehead, had been beating her.

"Why do you remain with her?" I asked.

"She keeps my baby locked up," was her reply; "and she says if I leave I shall never have him."

I told her that I could take her to the provost-marshal, who would give her an order for her child. At this she cheered up, and went with me, and received an order, in case she could not get it without. She said she would go back and pack her few things in her old trunk, and then watch her opportunity when the mistress was out to bring her baby to the freedmen's store. After the child was secured I sent a soldier with her, who brought her trunk, without letting any one in the hotel know of her movements. Only a short time elapsed before we saw Mrs. Morehead in front of the hotel, looking up and down the street for her Delphine, who kept herself hid in the freedmen's store with her little Charlie, about two years old. Just before the war Mr. Morehead had brought her away from her mother in St. Louis, Missouri, and the height of her ambition was to get back there. I secured transportation for herself and child to Cairo, and paid her fare to St. Louis. But she was in constant fear of her former owners.

Her history was a sad one. She was bought for their hotel fancy girl, and the father of her child was her own master. The child resembled his father so much that he was frequently taken by strangers to be the child of the mistress. The mother was two-thirds white; and the Roman, nose, straight hair, and white skin of the child would not give a stranger the least idea that he had even the sixteenth part of African blood in his veins.

As a boat was expected to arrive within an hour, we took leave of the many kind friends, and repaired to the wharf-boat. Soon Mrs. Morehead followed, and called for Delphine; but the trembling girl caught her babe and hid.

But as her mistress repeated the calls, she at length came to me with the child, asking, "What shall I do? I would rather throw myself and baby into the river than go back to her." Said her mistress, "I tell you, Del., I've got an officer to come and take you to jail for stealing." I told Delphine she could rest assured that none of the officers would trouble her, for they informed me they should not notice her mistress's complaints, let them be what they would, as they had had more trouble with that rebel family than a little ever since they occupied the city. I told her to leave Charlie on the boat, and go out on the levee and tell her mistress plainly that she was going to St. Louis to her mother, and not be so excited. She did so, and Mrs. Morehead kept her nearly an hour, trying to coax, hire, and frighten her, but without avail. Delphine all this while was trembling with fear. I believe if she had seen an officer coming with her mistress, she would have thrown herself and child into the river. Mrs. Morehead at length came upon the wharf-boat. When Delphine saw her coming she snatched up her child, and ran to the rear of the boat, and the mistress after her. Again she came to me with "What shall I do?" I replied, "Sit down here by me and hold your child, and she will not dare touch you." She trembled as if having an ague fit. Soon a her mistress stood before us in a rage, and turned to me:

"You came into my kitchen with an order, and took her, when she was doing better than you ever dare do."

"I never went into your kitchen," I said. "A soldier went with her for her trunk. I understood an officer called on you and called for her child, at her request, before she came to me."

"It's a lie. Delphine lied about me."

Said sister Backus, "I shouldn't think you would want such a person about you, if that is true."

"Well, the child seems so near to me. I've always had the care of it."

She left us at length with a threat that she would bring the officers to take her to jail for stealing.

The Kennet came in at 11 o'clock A. M., May 6th, bound for St. Louis, Missouri, and we went aboard. As we pushed out from shore, Delphine clapped her hands. "Now I know Mistress Morehead can trouble me no more; thank God, I've got my Charlie too! Nobody knows what I have gone through since I've been in this city." We arrived in Vicksburg May 7th, and took breakfast at the Soldiers' Home, where we met Ex-Governor Harvey, a soldiers' friend. Here was a lady who had charge of the body of her brother, killed up Red River, taking the remains back to Iowa.

After spending a little time in this large city of soldiers, whose tents whitened the adjoining fields, we left. On the day this city fell into Union hands, report said, there was an old man very confident of the success of the Confederate government, and he said that God could not let it fail; if he did, he would never believe there is a God. When, the gun-boats came in, and he was told the city was taken, he would not believe it, until he rose up from his chair and saw marching columns of soldiers, with their bayonets glistening in the Fourth of July sun. He immediately sank back in his chair in a faint, and soon died.

May 8th was a sort of a war Sabbath. The night before our boat ran aground, and it took three hours to get her off. Many of the passengers dressed, and made ready to escape at the first possible chance, in case she should become wrecked. We were told that at one time the water was three feet deep in her hull. By making great effort the men succeeded in pumping it out. She run slowly, being a very large boat. We had a variety of passengers on board, officers of various ranks, soldiers, missionaries, preachers, and a few secessionists. Major-general Hunter remained with us two days.

Quite an excitement arose over the arrest of a smuggler of goods through our lines. He was thought to be connected with the little steamer Baltic. There was a major and a provost-marshal, from Baton Rouge, who followed up the matter. When the prisoner was brought to the rear of the boat, with his hands tied, it created much feeling among a dozen colored people, until they heard the major ask him if he had taken the oath of allegiance. He answered gruffly, "No, and I never will."

This led the major to ask other questions concerning the trade of the Baltic.

"I will tell you nothing about it, if I stand here till I die, and you may go to--."

This brought the sympathy of the colored people, as well as of the rest of us, down below zero. Said one colored man, "Let him stand there, then, until he dies." But within an hour he consented to be sworn to tell the truth, and nothing but the truth, and the major examined him in the presence of many witnesses, Major-general Hunter one of them.

On Monday I introduced myself to General Hunter, as usual, by my letters.

"How long have you been in the army," he asked, "and how far?"

In reply to his queries I gave him a sketch of our work. I mentioned General Tuttle's refusal to grant us transportation, the wrongs of the colored soldiers, and the history of the three thousand prisoners on Ship Island and Dry Tortugas, and stated the fact that some missionaries and missionary teachers had advised me to say nothing of these wrongs, however flagrant. I also called his attention to the printed order placed in our hands, that we were not to report any movements in the army, either verbally or by writing, and asked his advice whether it was wiser to report or to keep silent.

"Mrs. Haviland," he replied, "I am glad you have been in the army so long, and I am glad you went so far, and I will explain that order.

"You have observed movements of troops from one place to another just on the eve of battle. These are the matters you are not to report; but the wrongs you have met you may proclaim on your arrival at home from the house-tops."

I thanked him for this advice, for it was to me a great relief. It seemed to trouble him. After pacing the cabin to and fro a few minutes, he came to me and said:

"Mrs. Haviland, we have had a good deal of sifting done in the army, and more must be done yet. Did General Tuttle see those papers you gave me?"

"He did," I answered.

"Copperheads have no business in the army in the exercise of such authority as this. General Tuttle ran for governor on the Copperhead ticket in Iowa last year. What right has a copperhead to be lifted up here, where loyal men are needed? I have never seen the least cause to abandon my first conclusion, that the only way to crush this rebellion was to emancipate and arm the slaves; and if I could have been permitted to carry out my plan of taking Kentucky into my field, as my rank and position entitled me to do, I should have proclaimed freedom to the slaves as fast as I reached them. The strength I could have gathered from the slave population would soon have been two hundred thousand men, and that number of stand of arms was all I asked. But the vacillating policy of the government would not permit it. I saw clearly that this was the only policy that would prove successful, and I thought every body else must see it when I first proc-laimed it in South Carolina. It seemed there were others who took a different view, and my order was superseded."

Said sister Backus, "You have the satisfaction of knowing that your policy had to be adopted before the nation could succeed."

"O, yes," replied he reluctantly; "but it is with regret that I think of the drafting of thousands, which might have been avoided just as well as not. There was no necessity for the draft."

Sister Backus remarked, "As a nation, we must suffer defeats until it reaches the right position, not only in arming colored men, but in paying them just wages; for they make as good soldiers as white men."

A bystander said, "I don't know that they make as good soldiers as white men, from the fact that they are not so intelligent. Here is General Hunter, and I presume he will say the same thing"--turning to him for an answer.

In a decided tone the general said, "I shall say no such thing. They make the best of soldiers; for, first, they are kind and docile; and, second, they are apt to learn. They learn military tactics very readily, and ought to have the same wages as any other soldier. All along this river I find one continued series of wrongs inflicted upon the negro."

We told him of the infamous order by Dr. Kelley, sanctioned by General Tuttle, and published under the specious guise of "Health Order," to drive the slaves back to their masters. He shook his head in disgust.

"Why does the head of this serpent rise up at almost every point? When it appeared in the department under my command I crushed it at once."

At the mouth of Red River three women came aboard, by permission of the gunboat officers stationed there. Their object was to hire men, whom they wanted to gather cane for working up into weaving reeds. One of them reported to Dr. Long that she had been watching a couple of ladies on our boat, and she believed them spies, for they seemed to have a great deal of writing to do. Dr. Long happened to know enough about the ladies reported as spies to allow sister Backus and myself to pass unmolested. But these ladies were themselves suspected of being spies.

We reached the city of Memphis May 10th. Sister Backus had been quite sick for three days, but was now a little better. We called at the Christian Commission Rooms, and got a market-basket full of reading matter for distribution.

The next day was quite cold and freezing. We stopped at Columbus a short time. Here we secured a paper giving an account of the terrible slaughter at Fredericksburg. Rumor had it that fifteen thousand were killed and wounded; that Lee was driven back thirty miles; Grant and Butler were said to be pushing on to Richmond, and were now within a short day's march of the rebel capital. General Hunter was quite sanguine in hope that Richmond would soon fall.

On May 13th we arrived at Cairo, and took leave of the friends whom our few days' acquaintance had made dear. We reached home on the 18th, amid the rejoicing of dear children and friends. It is no wonder the soldiers we met were delighted to see a Northern face, for it reminded them of their home associations. Intercession unceasing went up for the three thousand soldier prisoners banished to the Gulf Islands. The mail had brought nothing from New Orleans. By this I was to understand that nothing could be done for them there. Congress was still in session, and I immediately wrote a full account of their wrongs to congressman Beaman, and urged the presentation of the case to the war department.

Without giving myself time to rest, I hastened to Detroit, to report our work and give an account of the unjust sentences of those prisoners at Ship Island and the Tortugas. While making my statements in Captain E. B. Ward's office, he took them down to forward them to B. F. Wade, chairman of the Committee on the Conduct of the War; but he said, "You must go to Washington and report these facts to the committee in person." I told him I had written the full details to my friend, F. C. Beaman, member of Congress, and I thought he would do all that could be done. He answered, "I shall send these items to B. F. Wade, and our letters will make good entering wedges; but the living tongue will do more than the pen." I told him I was ready to go or do any thing I could for their release, but still hoped to hear from New Orleans. I would wait a week longer and rest. Then, if I had means, I would go. He said he would see to that, and I returned to my home.

Within a week I received a note from him, stating that he had just received a letter from B. F. Wade, requesting me to come at once and bring my extracts from the record I had examined on Ship Island. I was soon on my way to Detroit, and at nine o'clock, A. M., on the following day, I was in Captain Ward's office, ready to take the boat for Cleveland on my way to Washington. I waited but a few minutes when the captain came in with a letter, which he threw in my lap, saying, "There is a letter for you to read." The first sentence was, "The exhibition of these letters before Secretary Stanton has proved sufficient. Judge Attocha was dismissed immediately, and a committee is to be appointed to investigate and release those prisoners at once. There is therefore no necessity for Mrs. Haviland's presence on that score. General Tuttle is already relieved." On reading these glad words, I remarked that I never had been a shouting Methodist, but I felt more like shouting over these glad tidings than I ever had done in all my life. If I had not been spoiled for singing by being raised a Quaker, I would have sung the doxology.

I wrote an article for the Detroit Tribune containing these facts, and stating the prospects of the immediate release of the three thousand prisoners on Ship Island and Dry Tortugas. I sent the paper to Captain J. Noyce, and very soon received a reply that my letter, with the Tribune, was the first intimation they had received of any thing being done in their behalf. He said, "I sent the letter and paper to the prisoners, and they eagerly read them in all their companies, until I doubt whether a whole sentence can be found together." A few weeks later I received another letter from Captain Noyce, in which he stated that the committee was investigating, and that but one person in seventy-five was found unworthy of being released at once; but that very soon all would be restored to their regiments.

FREEDMEN'S AID COMMISSION

OUR Freedmen's Aid Commission was enlarged in June, 1864. Dr. George Duffield was made president; Drs. Hogarth and Chase, vice-presidents; David Preston, treasurer; and B. C. Durfee, secretary. The board of directors appointed me its agent, and allowed me a salary of forty dollars a month. This is the first remuneration I received for my labors; but seeing unfaithful officers dismissed, prisoners released, and the suffering and dying relieved, was a satisfaction far exceeding dollars and cents.

I received invitations to address congregations in large towns, where much was done in gathering supplies. At a Union thanksgiving meeting in Jackson, $97 was collected, and at a similar meeting at Grass Lake, the same day, $70; at Luce's Hall, Grand Rapids, $55; at Methodist Episcopal Church, Pontiac, $44; and at Leoni Wesleyan Methodist Conference, $68.65. Many other liberal donations were also received. Auxiliaries were organized, and I prepared to return to the field of desolation, whither duty seemed to be loudly calling me. I concluded to suspend Raisin Institute until the close of the war. I received propositions from a number of graduates of the Michigan University to take it in charge; but the care of preparing for another academic year was more than I could properly undertake, and do justice to the limitless field of mission work that was open before us.

In September I had a car-load of supplies ready, and $400 in money. Of this amount, $298 was placed in my hands by friends at Adrian, with the request of the donors that it should be retained in my own hands for disbursement on reaching the scene of suffering. At Chicago appeals were made to the Soldiers' Aid Society and Christian Commission for aid in the freedmen's department, and also to myself personally, on account of the great distress in Kansas after General Price's raid through Missouri, followed by Colonels Lane and Jennison, who drove thousands of poor whites and freedmen into that young State. I decided to hasten thither, with Mrs. Lee, of Hillsdale, as an assistant.

At Leavenworth we met J. R. Brown, half-brother of Captain John Brown, of Ossawatomie, who had charge of both white refugees and freedmen and a sort of soldiers' home, under General Curtis. He kindly offered me headquarters in his establishment, consisting of two large two-story frame buildings, with one hundred occupants each. I called on General Curtis, who telegraphed for my goods to be forwarded in preference to other army supplies, and gave me passes through the State to Fort Scott. My object was to investigate all intermediate towns where refugees and freedmen were congregated. He also gave me liberty to use an order he had given J. R. Brown, to call upon quarter-masters for half, whole, or quarter rations, wherever suffering for food existed. These investigations enabled me to judge of the amount of aid needed at each point.

As my supplies had not reached me, J. R. Brown filled two large trunks with sanitary supplies for the greatest sufferers. Thus supplied, I took the stage for Fort Scott. My first halt was at Quindaro, a small town built on rocky bluffs and in deep ravines. A few years previously it was designed by a few speculators to be an important landing on the Mississippi; and they built a few stone houses, a long wood store-house, and a number of small log-houses, which had been left untenanted, but were now filled with white refugees and freedmen, A large majority were women and children. The able-bodied men among the freedmen were in the Union army, but many of the men whose refugee families were here were in the Confederate army. General Price had made terrible havoc of all who were suspected of being favorable to the Union. Then followed Colonels Lane and Jennison, who made as great havoc of the remainder. Those who fled for their lives were crowded into every niche of available room.

In one open log-house I found twenty-three wretched inmates. Four of them were women, two of whom were sick from exposure in husking corn during cold, snowy weather. Eight of the children had the measles, and three of them died; two others seemed near death's door. Two women were hauling a small tree-top to their door to chop for night-wood. The feet of these poor women were exposed to the mud and snow, which was melting. O, what squalid wretchedness was here! Not a bed, chair, table, or whole dish in this gloomy abode! I inquired how they slept. I was shown a rag-carpet on the fence, which they obtained for washing for one of the neighbors. This was spread before a large fire-place, and all lay down upon that but two, who kept up the fire, and watched to keep those asleep from burning. They said the man who owned the adjoining wood-land kindly allowed them all the wood they needed that was on the ground. They borrowed an ax to chop it. I found the four women had husked corn on shares until two were sick with pneumonia; and the corn, boiled without salt, was all they had to eat during the five weeks they had been there. Now they were nearly out, and what to do they knew not, as they were forbidden to go into the field to husk more. I made out an order for rations, and measured their bare feet for shoes and stockings. I took one of the women to the post-office, where I had left my trunks, and gave her four army-blankets, six knit woolen socks, six pairs of drawers, four pairs of stockings, and two pairs of shoes, which were all I had to fit them. As I piled the above articles upon the shoulders and arms of the poor woman she wept for joy.

The postmaster said, "Is this your business here?"

On receiving an affirmative reply, he said, with tearful eye:

"To-morrow morning the ground will be frozen, and I will go with you where the most of these poor people are."

I procured lodging with a widow Johnson and her son, who was with Captain John Brown's party all through the border-ruffian troubles. My kind friend regretted my having made the mile and a half walk to the log-house in the field and back to the post-office before supper, as I had not taken refreshments since leaving Leavenworth, very early. But when I told her of the distress I found, she rejoiced with me at the partial relief I had given them.

After a good rest and an early breakfast, I went with the kind postmaster to visit the most wretched tenements of both white and colored, and found eighty-one to report for rations to the commander in Wyandotte. The postmaster and Mr. Johnson agreed to go with their team every week and distribute to the destitute; and if others were found equally needy they would report them to me on my return. After descending steep cliffs and climbing rugged rocks until past noon, we returned for dinner; but before it was finished the stage came along, and I took it for Wyandotte, where we arrived late in the evening. The weather for October was cold, and freezing quite hard.

When I informed Mrs. Halford, the landlady of the Garno House, of my errand, she was much pleased, and said that her duties forbade her to assist me, but she would do her part in giving me a welcome home while in their town. She introduced me to a family of benevolent ladies, who promised to aid me in my investigations, but did not think I would find the suffering in their city that I found in Quindaro. One of my new friends went with me to a neighborhood where there were new arrivals, and found many in a perishing condition with cold and hunger. From thence we went to old stables and sheds crowded with destitute human beings, both white and colored. The dear friend who volunteered to guide to these children of want wept herself sick as we listened to the stories of their flight from homes in Missouri and Arkansas. Here was a woman, named Melinda Dale, with six small children and a sick husband, who had to flee for their lives. A few pieces of old tent-cloth, picked up about an old camp, made their bed. Children were crying for bread, the mother was sick with grief, and the father had a high fever. A blanket was given them, with a few loaves of bread; and after the reading of Scripture and prayer we left for the relief of others.

Our next call was upon the wife and five small children of Lieutenant Miller, who was supposed to be in a rebel prison. The wife was in great distress, not knowing whether her husband was living or perishing by starvation. He was taken prisoner one year before and she and her children were in a starving condition. They occupied an old Sibley tent. These were also, with many others, reported for rations, and immediate relief was given. A few weeks previously rations were withheld, which caused great suffering with many. I gave rations to Barbara Stewart, with two sick children, whose husband was murdered by guerillas because he was known to be a Union man. I next called on Green F. Bethel, who left his Arkansas home with a large family, consisting of his wife, nine children, and aged mother. All except himself were taken down with the measles, soon after passing through Fort Scott. His mother soon died, and was buried by the way-side. A day later his wife and infant child died, and were also buried by the way. Not long after the last three children died, and were also buried by the road-side. He said, "O, what sorrow was mine! One-half of my family are gone! The light of my household seemed vanishing! Were it not for the help of my Lord I should have fainted under this sweeping affliction. My wife and mother were Christians many years. We were members of the Cumberland Presbyterian Church." We found the poor man in a hard chill. It came on every third day, and was followed with high fever. The two intervening days he was able to use his team in little jobs of hauling, and thus he kept his children and team alive. I inquired why he did not make his condition known to the citizens of that town. He said no one knew any thing about him, and there were so many making pretensions to loyalty who were not loyal, that none would know but he was of that class. "My wife's brother," he said, "came with his family when we did, and he also lost his wife on the way, following the Union soldiers. Our lives were threatened, and the rope was placed around my neck once, but by the entreaties of my wife and children the rebels concluded to let me go a day or two longer; then if I would not join with them in supporting the Confederate government, I was to be hung or shot. The same threat was made to my brother-in-law, and we hid in the woods three weeks, before we left in the night for the lines of the Union soldiers. We started with two wagons, and had nine horses and three cows. But they gave out one after another, and we had to leave them all on the way, except the youngest and best team, which I have yet. I have a good farm, and so has my brother-in-law; but if we are ever permitted to return to our homes, it is doubtful whether we shall find a building left."

He wept freely, as well as his children. The oldest daughter, Amy, of seventeen, leaned her head upon my shoulder, and wept aloud. She said, "We could all bear this furnace of affliction much better if our dear mother had been spared us."

With prayer we left this house of mourning, with a request for the afflicted brother to call at head-quarters for the rations I should report for the six in his family. Said he, on taking the parting hand, "One favor I ask of you, my dear sister; and that is, your continued prayers that the Lord may open a way for us where there now seems to be no way."

My friend who served as guide said, "My head aches with weeping, in witnessing these heart-rending scenes. I must decline going with you farther this afternoon. I shall be obliged to take my bed. I do not see how you live, as you meet similar scenes so frequently."

These visits made us quite late for dinner, but my kind hostess kept it waiting for me. With interest, she sat by my side to listen to a report of my morning calls. She was surprised to learn of so much suffering near them. After dinner I resumed my work. On my way I met a woman shivering in an ague chill, thinly clad, and weeping. I inquired for the cause of her grief. She said she had been hunting for washing or something to do, to purchase bread for her three little children, for they had had nothing to eat for a whole day. I told her I would call on her before night. I found a number in as great distress as in my morning calls. One man, who lost his wife, leaving him with six small children, had found work six miles away; but he returned at night to care for his little ones. The oldest child, ten years of age, was left during the day in charge of the five younger ones. For the sake of furnishing bread for his children, he walked the twelve miles back and forth daily. I found the woman whom I had met on the street in a high fever, with an infant of eight months in her arms, and two of her children crying for bread. I took them a few loaves, and gave her an order for rations. The husband had been pressed into service when they had been but two weeks from home, and was not allowed to see his wife and children to say good bye. She had heard nothing from him since. In the corner lay a crippled discharged colored soldier, who was also suffering for food. I stepped into a grocery and purchased sugar and crackers for the sick and for the children.

My next call was on another woman with six children.

Her husband had been in the army a long time, and she had not heard from him. She feared he was suffering in a rebel prison. Near this cabin was Agnes Everett, with five children between the ages of fifteen months and twelve years. Her two youngest children were in a starving condition--the baby, she said, had been too sick to allow her to do much in procuring food. Her boy of twelve years was her only dependence in getting little jobs of wood-sawing or doing chores for cold victuals, or a pint of meal which she made into porridge. The little emaciated baby was fed with the porridge. Its face was wrinkled like an old person's of ninety years. Its eyes were sunken and glassy; its hands looked more like birds' claws than like human hands. "Don't, Clarkie; poor little Fannie is so sick she must have this," said the mother to the little fellow who watched the mother when her attention was occupied for a chance to snatch a floating lump. As I looked upon these famishing children I could not refrain from weeping. Her husband and grown son were in the army. She had been looking for money from them for a number of months, but had heard nothing from them. I gave them two loaves of bread for their supper, and directed them to meet me at the post-office the next day at ten o'clock A. M., and I would give her an order for six half rations until she received help from her husband. This closed my day's work. On my return to the Garno House, Mrs. Halford informed me that the lady who went with me in the morning was sick, for she had hardly ceased weeping over those pitiful families we visited in the morning.

At the time appointed I met a number at the post-office, among whom was Agnes Everett, to receive orders for half, quarter, or whole rations, and gave out a few articles of clothing. As I gave Agnes the order for rations, I charged her strictly to give the two younger children no strong food for a few days, but only a little at a time and often, especially the youngest, as it would live but a few hours if she allowed it to eat all it craved. A number of gentlemen listened to my charge, and as the little group left the office one of them inquired where I was from. With my reply I gave them my papers from the governor and members of Congress of Michigan. After reading they introduced themselves,--Dr. Wood, Dr. Speck, Lawyer James, and others. Dr. Speck informed me of a family whose youngest child actually starved to death three days before. He was called when it was dying, but too late to save it. He said, "There were two other families who would have died soon if the citizens had not rendered the aid needed; and there would have been another death by starvation before we should have known it, here in our midst, but it took you to come from Michigan to find it out." Lawyer James said there was a family on the hill opposite the ferry he would like to see visited, but there were so many crowding in here of late that it seemed as if they had done all they possibly could. They were rejoiced to learn of the liberty granted, by General Curtis to issue orders for rations. Said Dr. Wood, "The freedmen are seeking for work, no matter what kind, but the white refugees are the most do-nothing set I ever saw." While I acknowledged his position true in most cases, yet there were noble exceptions and I mentioned the Bethel family and stated their condition. One gentleman said he would look after that family. In confirmation of his remarks I told of a family of poor whites in Quindaro who were asked to assist a neighbor in sickness. As there were the mother and two grown daughters, it was supposed one of them could be secured a few days with the promise of provisions or money; but the mother contemptuously tossed her head to one side and drawled out the reply, "I reckon we hain't come down so low yet as to work" I told them they must come up high enough to work before I could do any thing for them, and left them to sit in their own filth and rags.

My order from General Curtis was to report none for rations who could obtain work for wages. I passed on to other scenes of sorrow too numerous to narrate here.

One hundred and four rations I ordered in Wyandotte. This timely relief given, I crossed the river, and in Kansas City, Missouri, met brother

Copeland and wife, who were efficient agents and teachers in that field. I secured a pass to Lawrence, where, late in the evening, I was directed to a family that had suffered much in the Union cause. This was the important stamping ground of Captain John Brown. This city had passed through two terrible raids during the war. It is here that Quantrell rushed upon the unsuspecting citizens with a host of Confederate soldiers about daylight, and murdered men at their own doors, and when they could not call them out they rushed into their houses and made terrible havoc of human life. There was a woman here who was a spy. She had been in the city a few weeks taking horse-back rides two hours each morning, ostensibly for her health, but probably to report the most favorable time for attack. She was never seen after the raid. I attended the Methodist Episcopal Church, where seventy wounded, dying, and dead soldiers and citizens were brought in after that raid. The stains of blood were still left on the floor and some of the seats.

The house where I was kindly invited to make my home was entered, and the owner, brother Hockins, was demanded. His wife told them she saw him run up the hill a few moments before, which was true; but on seeing the Confederate soldiers entering the town he hastened back to his house and ran down to the cellar. A squad of them entered and placed the bayonet at his wife, and threatened her life if she did not tell the whereabouts of her husband; but she persisted in pointing up the hill. They went down the cellar, but returned without finding him, and set the house on fire. Then they ran up the hill after him. She succeeded in putting out the fire, and went into the cellar and called her husband. He answered from between the earth and the floor. This was his hiding-place until the Union soldiers rescued the city from further trouble. A strong Union force was now kept at this point.

I found fewer suffering for want of rations at this town than in other places I had visited, and took the stage for Fort Scott. We were advised to keep out of sight any appearance of watches or any sort of jewelry, as guerrillas were sometimes lurking in the woods and attacked the stages. We came in sight of Indians on horses who darted into the woods, fearing we were guerrillas, who had stolen or robbed them of their ponies. One man shouted, "We are all for the Union." This was on Price's track, where they lost their horses, and did not dare come in sight.

Late at night we reached Fort Scott. My first call was on Colonel Blair, commander of the post, who, with his wife, kindly offered me a home with them while I remained at that point. They introduced me to Dr. Slocum, who gave a sketch of the terrible destitution of the forty thousand refugees and freedmen, who passed through this great thoroughfare. Many of them had stopped here. He took me to a number of the destitute families, and gave directions to others, and left me to my work. Here was a great number of the poor whites, called "Clay- eaters," who complained about government dealing rations to colored people. I heard one of them, say that "if niggers would stay where they belonged, with their masters, they would have more white-bread and beef." I told them, I had learned that many of their husbands were fighting against the government while the husbands of many of the colored women were fighting to sustain it, and I should favor those who were on the side of the government. I asked them why they did not themselves remain in their old homes? "We came 'case our men was conscripted," they said. One woman and her daughter of eighteen had each a filthy, ragged bed quilt over her shoulders, and their faces were so swarthy that their eyes and teeth presented as great a contrast as those whose natural skin was of darker hue. As the little boy of four years had no shoes, and I had a pair left that would fit him, I told the mother to wash his feet and try them. "Sal, bring me that cup thar," said the woman. Their drinking cup with water was brought. "Han' me that rag thar," and she wet her hand and wet the feet, and was wiping off the mud, when I told her they were not washed; to look at the mud on the bottom of his feet and between his toes. "O, yez'm," she drawled out, and wet one end of the rag in the cup, and made a second effort. When the shoes were put on, he could not walk without holding to his mother or sister. They were probably the first he had ever had.

Most of the day was spent in visiting this class of persons--the most ignorant, listless, and degraded of any people I had ever met. On giving a description of the ignorance and filth, of the poor whites I called on, Colonel Blair inquired "What would you do with them?"

"I would keep body and soul together till Spring opens," I answered, "and then load up your great army wagons, and take them out upon the rich prairies and dump them out, giving them the homely adage, 'Root, pig, or die.'"

The greatest difficulty in managing this class was to get them to do any thing. Not so with colored people; they would do any thing they could find to do.

I found in this camp of two thousand, a colored woman of an earnest Christian principle. Colonel Blair gave her an excellent character. He said that I might place implicit confidence in any statement she would make. Her history was a novel one. She ran away from a cruel master to the Indians, and married an old Indian, and had four children. She said her husband came in great excitement and asked her if she wanted to run away to the Yankees? She said no, because she thought they were another tribe of Indians. He ran out, and soon came back, and said, "If you run, go quick. I am old; they can't rob me of many days, but they sha'n't have the children to punish." He threw them on a horse and ran off into the woods. She supposed her old master had found her out, and ran another way. Then she heard that her husband was dead, But the Lord hid her from the cruel master, though he broke up her family.

After spending three days in this place, including Sunday, I took the Monday morning stage for Leavenworth. In sending packages to all these places, to reliable friends with whom I had made acquaintance, I requested that no clothing be given to healthy men and women who refused to do work when they could get it.

In one of the hospitals at Leavenworth were two Confederates, one of whom had recently become a Christian. He said when he went into this army he knew not for what they were fighting, but when he learned the real cause, he was for the Union, and should do all be could for it.

During the month of December, we relieved four hundred and forty-four families. There were thirty children in both buildings under my care.

By request of J. R. Brown, the Freedmen's Aid Commission of Michigan consented to allow me to take charge of white refugees in connection with the freedmen. General Curtis detailed a sergeant for my assistant. Another important helper was a noble young woman, Amanda A. Way, who opened a school for children of inmates of the two buildings. I found it difficult to bring into school the white children, and only by a requisition could I accomplish it, or induce the mothers to wash the hands and faces, and comb the hair of their children, to fit them for school.

This, like all previous fields of army mission work, was a laborious one. Our Sundays were spent in teaching a large class in three Sabbath-schools, besides attending the public services and generally taking part in them. At the close of one of the meetings a deacon and his wife rushed through the crowd to me, and gave such an exhibition of joy that it drew the attention of the congregation. He gave a glowing account of my visit to Little Rock, Arkansas, and of my life-long work for their down-trodden people. The hand-shaking for half an hour made my hands lame for three days. The deacon bought himself when a young man, and acquired a property worth four thousand dollars. Slave-holders often said that he knew too much, and thought he was a damage to their slaves. If they lost any, they charged him with aiding them away. He was often lodged in jail and fines imposed upon him. At length he sold his property at half its value to come to Kansas, where he could breathe freely.

On New Year's day I found a poor woman in the last stages of consumption. She could not speak a loud word. I hired another poor woman to care for her, by giving bed and wearing clothes for herself and children. I left them in tears, saying, "We thank you, honey, and praise God. When my poor mother died in that old out-cellar, neither father nor one of us was permitted to give her a cup of cold water, but the last words she was heard to say was, 'I'm going home to die no more.'"

I visited ten families and sent four boxes more of supplies to Fort Scott. The next day I took a barrel of hospital supplies to Fort Leavenworth.

My supplies were now low, and the money nearly spent. I received a letter from the chairman of the committee having charge of preparations for the Ladies' State Freedmen's Fair, to be held in Detroit, soliciting relics of the war. J. R. Brown proposed that I should attend the fair and take his brother's sharp-shooter, that the captain carried through the border-ruffian conflict in Kansas, and during his movement at Harper's Ferry. After a few days' reflection I reached the conclusion to go. General Curtis gave me a pass to Detroit and return.

The John Brown gun created much interest. Besides this relic, the fifty pounds of slave-irons, which we picked up on deserted plantations in the far South, were exhibited in this fair. A petition from Lenawee County was sent to the committee having charge of the fair, to place the avails of our county, one thousand dollars, in my hands for distribution. This money relieved much suffering, and no doubt saved many lives.

During my visit home I sold Raisin Institute and ten acres of land, with an excellent orchard, to the State Freedmen's Aid Commission for an orphans' home. I donated three hundred dollars of the purchase money to this enterprise, stipulating that the premises were to be used for no other purpose. In my absence the friends gave the asylum the name of "Haviland Home for Homeless and Destitute Children." This home I intended as a nucleus for a State Orphan Asylum, as the war had increased the necessity for such an institution.

After two weeks' absence I returned with supplies. Spring was lessening the suffering, yet sickness from long exposures still prevailed. Miss Fidelia Phillips, a teacher, came with a letter from the Michigan Freedmen's Aid Commission, for us to locate and secure board, which duty fell upon me. I hired a conveyance and took her to Oskaloosa, Jefferson County, and found board for her in the kind family of Dr. J. Nelson, who proposed to assist the colored people in securing a house for the school at once.

I found here a poor sick woman with her five children, who was ordered out of her cabin, as she could no longer pay the rent. Dr. Nelson promised to see that she was not disturbed until she was able to be moved, when he would take the family to Leavenworth to go with me to our Home for Homeless Children in Michigan. Her husband was in the army, and she had not heard from him since he enlisted. On my return to Leavenworth I received an order from our Freedmen's Aid Commission, to send twenty-five children with five mothers to assist in caring for them. I accompanied them as far as Quincy, Illinois, with Mrs. Lee and a teacher who had been in the work a few months. They pursued their journey, and I went back.

On April 15th the sad news reached us of the assassination of President Lincoln! A nation in mourning! Every house of any note or size was draped with black.

We were now preparing to close the two refugee buildings before leaving for Michigan. I offered the women the best dresses for finding their own places for work, and by this means many found places, if only to work for their board till they could do better. A good old woman we called Aunt Phoebe came to us with her four grandchildren, and begged to go to

Michigan with me. She said the father of the children ran away to enlist in the army, and his master followed him. After an absence of three days, he returned with the report that he had got sight at him, and ordered him to come to him, but he refused, and he shot him dead. At this report his wife (the daughter of Aunt Phoebe), gave a scream and fainted. Both master and mistress were very severe, and whipped her severely for making so much fuss, as they called her grief. She sank under their severity, and died, leaving her infant, a week old, with her mother. Within a few days the oldest boy was taken with small-pox, but as he was not very near the other sick children, Dr. Carpenter thought the others would escape. I rolled him in a couple of quilts and sent him to the pest-house. Aunt Phoebe wept bitterly, as she said she should probably never see Jerry again, and he was such a good boy to help her take care of the other children. A few days later she was taken with a low type of lung fever. I had one of the colored women in the place nurse her.

The white refugee women took but little notice of my offer of best dresses, in finding homes for themselves. I found these women of the lowest class of humanity. I called on General Curtis, and told him I had expended my fund of lecturing material upon these white women in the refugee building, and now I had come to report to him as I had of late threatened them, that, while I was willing to do to the extent of my ability in relieving and improving the most degraded, I could not consent to keep under my charge a house of ill-fame. "I will give you a good honest guard day and night over that building," said the noble general. This did more than all things else to scatter them. They swore they would not be tyrannized over by that Yankee woman any longer, and left, very much to my relief.

Within four weeks our little small-pox boy was returned, but not as safe as the surgeon reported I took him into the wash-room and gave him a thorough cleansing, before taking him to see his grandmother, who wept for joy.

I spent a few days in revisiting Quindaro, Lawrence, Wyandotte, and Kansas City. I found seven homeless children, and a mother of three of them who wished to go with me to Michigan. During the day and night I was in Kansas City I was taken with a severe attack of pneumonia. I called on an army surgeon for mustard, of which, I placed a plaster over the seat of the pain, that had become so severe as to cut every breath. I could neither lie down nor sit still, but walked the room. Placing the children in charge of the mother, I telegraphed my sergeant to meet me at the boat with a hack. I took the boat for Leavenworth, where the carriage met me, and I was taken to our home, with a high fever, but the pain not quite so severe, as the mustard was serving its purpose. Dr. Carpenter said I could not go to Michigan under a month. Although my side remained very sore, yet I managed to sell the furniture. I took a hack to General Curtis's office, and managed to secure transportation for seventy-five, myself and Mrs. Lee included. There were three sick children, and I very much doubted the propriety of removing them. Dr. Carpenter said they would be more likely to live than if taken to the hospital, as I proposed.

We left the city May 28th, with a cloud resting over the nation. My health was still poor, and we had three sick children, whose mother was with them; three other children began to complain of chills and fever soon after leaving. These cases soon developed in measles, but my haste to reach home urged me to proceed against my better judgment. While it looked like presumption in others, I felt safe, as prayer for guidance was my daily bread. While waiting at St. Joseph, Missouri, for the train, I obtained rations for the company. Susan B. Anthony had provided a lunch-basket, well filled, for Mrs. Lee and myself, to serve for the entire journey.

While we were handing around rations, various remarks were made as to what I was going to do with all this company. Said one, "I reckon, she's got a big plantation to stock with a picked set of young niggers, she's going to train to her own liking." Said another, "I am going to ask where she is going with them." At length one ventured, "Will you please excuse me, madam, if I ask you where you are taking all this company?"

"Certainly," was my answer; "I am glad to inform you. I am taking these orphan children, who have been picked up on the streets, and out of freedmen's homes, to an orphan school in Michigan. By order of the State Freedmen's Aid Commission, they will be sent to school until good homes can be secured for them, where they will be taught habits of industry, as well as to improve their intellects. We of the North think they can learn, if an opportunity is provided."

At this he was much pleased, and, as it was communicated to other bystanders, a number came to congratulate me in my good work. One, who had a large number of slaves, said he wished they were with me, "as it would be a right smart of a while before it'll be settled here to have schools for 'em."

All stood ready to put the sick ones on the train. Mrs. Lee took care of the sick during the night, and I had them in charge during the day.

After our arrival at Quincy, Illinois, and our transportation papers were filled out for Chicago, with a little difficulty I secured the largest coach for the seventy-five passengers. By 9 P. M. all were in their beds. A few men were disposed to trouble us, because we did not allow them to enter. I called for the night policeman, and told him of four drunken men who were disposed to give us trouble, and as the train was not going out until eleven o'clock I appealed to him for aid. He assured me we should not receive further annoyance from them. We arrived in Chicago thirty minutes before the Michigan train left for Adrian. I bought tickets for four omnibus loads, but the drivers were determined to crowd them all into two. As they were putting little folks from four to eight years old on the tops I ordered them down. "We are capable of taking care of these children, madam," said they; "you take that one."

"So am I capable of taking care of them," I replied, "and of you too; I paid for four omnibuses and must have them." They had their own sport over their countermanded orders.

We arrived at Adrian June 1st, and met the superintendent of the "Haviland Home" with teams for the women and children. Here my heavy burden fell off, and I dropped into the home of my children to get the rest which I so much needed.

A few week's rest restored my health. Meanwhile I visited our State Prison, and one of the convicts, Thomas Lean, requested an interview with me, which was granted by the officer. He appealed to me to aid him in securing his pardon, as he had served seven years of his term of fifteen. He pleaded as earnestly in behalf of his wife and two little children as for himself. I told him I would do what I could, but as efforts had been made twice before, I thought success quite doubtful. I drafted a petition, and secured a letter of recommendation from Governor Blair, and a strong letter from Judge Ross Wilkins, who gave the sentence, and from the prosecuting attorney who acted in behalf of the United States in his case, and also secured fifty other names to the petition. With six hundred dollars placed in my hands by Mrs.

Campbell and Mrs. Pappineau, committee who had charge of the funds of the Freedmen's Fair, I left for Washington, D. C., August 3d. At Pittsburg I spent one night, and on the following day visited the State Prison at Allegheny City.

The next morning I took the early train for Baltimore, and from thence to Annapolis, to learn the result of Elizabeth L. Comstock's petition in behalf of fifteen convicts in the Maryland Penitentiary for aiding slaves to escape from bondage. I found ten of those men had been pardoned, but as four of them had used weapons in defending themselves, and one had taken a span of horses which the friends engaged in their behalf deemed theft, they were retained in prison. I found another on the governor's record for the same offense. I took the names of the six on my list, as the governor thought they were as worthy of release as the others, since the weapons were designed for self-defense, and the horses were only used to take them to the river, and were left to return to their owners. I saw the names of the friends who co-operated with E. L. Comstock on the petition, and called on James Bains, who introduced me to Judge Bond. The judge said he thought I was correct in my views as to the worthiness of the six men presented for his recommendation to the governor for clemency, and that he would attend to it soon. Said the Friend: "If thou feel'st easy to petition for their pardon I think thou hadst better remain with us until it is accomplished, as they have such an amount of business on hand at this time."

The judge seemed to think himself distrusted, and said: "Mrs. Haviland, I will attend to this within a week." With this assurance I told the judge and the Friend that I should feel easy to pursue my journey the first of the week.

From this office I was accompanied to the penitentiary and introduced to the warden, who sent a guide to conduct me through the shops and granted me the privilege of addressing the sixty-eight female convicts. A large majority of them were colored, placed there by their former owners for trivial offenses, the real cause being that of leaving them, but ostensibly for stealing a dress, a pair of shoes, or a dollar or two, etc. One smart-looking octoroon girl of eighteen years was about to be whipped by her mistress, but she had heard of the proclamation of emancipation and concluded that she had been whipped long enough, and snatched the cowhide from the mistress and whipped her. For this she was arrested, had a sham trial, and a sentence of nine years' imprisonment in the penitentiary. One man told me that the mistress reported that the girl half killed her, but he saw her riding out within four days after the whipping, and she looked as well as usual. I visited a very sick white woman in her cell, to whom I read a portion of Scripture, and at her request led in prayer. She said she was going to meet her Judge, in whom she trusted. Jesus hears the cry of a repentant sinner, and she was confident.

The following day was the Sabbath, and I accompanied my friend to the penitentiary, where he opened the Sabbath-school and invited me to teach a class of thirty men. There were nearly five hundred inmates in prison. As we were leaving the yard a request from the warden reached me to conduct the funeral service of the woman I had visited. She died within a few hours after I left. Three o'clock P.M. was the hour appointed. I met them in their chapel, that was well filled, some ladies of the city being present. Many of the convicts were much affected. They also manifested great interest at the meeting on the previous day.

On the following day I arrived at Washington. I found the White House perfectly besieged with pardon-seekers from ex-slave States. I called on a number of the officials, who said that the severity of Thomas Lean's sentence made the case look dark. I told them of one who had robbed the mail of five thousand dollars and was pardoned in three years, whose term was ten years. But he had wealthy and influential friends to intercede for him, while this man robbed the mail of forty- two dollars and had served over seven years of the fifteen, and was poor. Besides, his wife was in poor health, and was supporting herself and two small children. I was advised to take the letters, with petition, to Postmaster-general Dennison, from whom I secured a recommendation for his pardon. From thence I went to the capitol and secured the names of Hon. F. C. Beaman, Member of Congress, Senator Z. Chandler, and all other Michigan members of both Houses to my petition; and through Mr. Wade, the President's housekeeper, I secured an audience with the President, who took my letters with the petition and said he would refer them to the Attorney-general, and do what seemed best in the case. I then left him with his room crowded with Southern pardon-seekers.

While in the Postmaster-general's office the chief clerk said, "Come into this, office at nine A.M., next Wednesday, as I think that will be his pardoning day, and you will learn the result." I waited until eleven A.M., fearing for the worst. As I opened the office-door the clerk threw up both hands, crying, "Your man is pardoned! your man is pardoned! Come and see the notice in this morning's paper." A hearty hand-shaking followed the good news.

I told him I did not know that he had taken such an interest in my cause. He replied, "I have had an interest in this case from the first time you came into this office." A few days after I received a note from the pardoned man conveying his tearful thanks. Here was another burden laid aside, for which grateful thanks were tendered to the Healer of broken hearts.

I received a permit from Secretary Stanton to trade at the government store, where new goods were being sold at auction rates. For five hundred dollars I purchased two thousand dollars' worth of supplies to disburse among the sick, crippled, and aged, both colored and white. There were many in Washington and Georgetown relieved from great suffering. I learned of much suffering at Harper's Ferry, and took four hundred dollars' worth to that point.

On my way I called at the Baltimore penitentiary. As I entered the warden's office he informed me that our men had been released ten days before, except one, who was going out within a week. Another burden left me. These men were making efforts to free their families by flight, and were caught and received long sentences, according to the number in their families. Three men of the six had bought themselves, and in their efforts to free their families received from ten to thirty years' sentence, although two of these families were recovered by their owners. They all looked like intelligent men. I took an early train for Harper's Ferry. In the seat opposite sat a Presbyterian D. D., with his body-servant, who was very attentive in bringing him his coffee, books, or roll of manuscript "How far are you going on this road, madam?" inquired our dignitary.

On informing him he inquired, "Have you friends there?"

"I have," I said, "but I never saw them. They are the poorest of the poor, the sick, lame, and blind, of all classes, black, white, red, or yellow. I draw no lines of demarcation."

"Well, madam, that is a noble work, and God will bless you in it. I am now on my way to Vicksburg. I preached in that city a number of years. I own a plantation near that city, and had forty slaves. A little before Vicksburg fell I moved with them to Richmond, Virginia, and when that city fell I set them free, and they are now as free as myself. Madam, I will tell you what your duty is. It is to go to New York, Philadelphia, and Boston, and gather up fifty thousand dollars, and follow Sherman's track through to the Gulf. You will find plenty of suffering to relieve among both white and black; and you can do it. Those cities I have named are wealthy, I have been there myself. I spent a few months in New York, and I know you can gather up that amount easy, and it's your duty, madam; and God will bless you in it."

The consequential air be assumed would give one an impression that he, at least, considered himself, inspired with power from on high. He did not feel quite satisfied without repeating his command on our arrival at Harper's Ferry: "Do as I have told you, madam, and God will bless you; good by."

I found my goods had just arrived, and the commander of the post kindly offered to store the bales of supplies and furnish an ambulance and driver whenever I desired. My first inquiry was for a boarding place, as the house where the colonel was boarding was full. Mrs. Johnson was about opening a boarding-house, and I called on her for a few days' board.

"Where are you from?"

"From Washington," was my reply, "with supplies for the poor freedmen and whites who are in a suffering condition."

"Oh, you are a Bureau woman then. We don't have nothin' to do with Bureau folks. I can't board you."

After being directed to two others, who made like inquiries, and received like replies, I found I was going to have an all-day job on hand in feeling the public pulse at Harper's Ferry. After making eight calls, chatting a while at each place pleasantly, for I would talk in no other way, although I was told in nearly every place that no one in that town would disgrace himself by walking on the streets with a nigger teacher, or speaking to one, on my way to report my unsuccessful day's work to the colonel, it being after sunset, I found an army surgeon sitting on his front porch.

"Have you found no place for dinner?" he asked.

"O no," I said, "I have been amusing myself over Confederate fever that I find runs too high for health in your town."

"My mother-in-law is away," he answered, "but my wife and I will give you our room to-night, and we will see that you have supper at once."

At Mrs. Bilson's (the mother-in-law) I remained during the week.

At the close of the week I attended a quarterly-meeting of the Methodist Episcopal Church. When the minister invited all who loved the Lord Jesus to testify, I, with others, accepted and took part. At the close he came and inquired who I was. I introduced myself as usual. After reading my papers from the Governor, Members of Congress, and a few ministers of Michigan, I received a number of invitations to their houses, which gave me an opportunity to relate my first day's experience in their town. They made a number of excuses. Among them was the fact that Miss Mann (Horace Mann's sister), kept herself exclusively with the colored people. She not only taught their school, but boarded with them, and made no calls on white people. They acknowledged that those upon whom I had called were not in sympathy with the Union.

Here, as in other places, were those in extreme suffering, both white and colored. One blind man, and an old white man and his wife, were too sick to take care of each other. One sick woman, whose husband was in the army, had no fire, only as the little girl of three years old gathered old boots and shoes around an old camp with which to build it. All of these cases were relieved.

One day it rained too hard to be out. A little girl brought an umbrella with a request from her folks for me to call on them. I went and met about a dozen men and women, who wished to consult with me. The troops were liable to be withdrawn. If so, their lives would not be safe an hour. A few nights before a mob broke their windows and rushed into their grocery and took sacks of flour and meal, pies, cakes, and crackers, and strewed them over the street, in front of their grocery, and broke up their chairs and tables, and swore that no nigger should have a business place on Main Street. They threw stones and brickbats into their living rooms, and the men, women, and children ran to the soldiers for protection, with bleeding bruises that were bound up at the time of my call. A sad picture they presented with their broken furniture and injured bodies.

"What use is there in gathering more? Can you tell us what to do? You see our lives are in danger as it is. If the troops shall be withdrawn, what shall we do?"

There was a Free-will Baptist just arrived, who proposed opening a mission school in that town, and had just sent word that he wanted to meet them at their prayer-meeting. Of this I, as well as they, was glad to hear. I met with them, and was pleased with the Christian spirit of this brother, and the prospect of his school among them seemed like a silver lining in their dark cloud. We learned of his success in opening and continuing that school, which a few years after assumed the character of an academy.

The following day I took the train for Washington, and was accompanied to the depot by a number of the citizens, who manifested very kindly feelings, I was told by some to be sure to call on them if I ever visited their town again, and they would see that a weeks or a months board should cost me nothing. One man and his wife pointed to their brick house to which I could come, and be more than welcome. I left them, and soon met kindred spirits in Washington.

HOME MISSION WORK

THERE were many sick, crippled, aged, and blind sufferers in Washington to visit and relieve, but the severest trial I endured was encountering the virus of disloyalty wherever I went. Women were more outspoken than men, because they could dare be. Men were more subtle and appeared more pliant, only to hoodwink government. They said in secret, "We'll yet gain by the ballot, with the help of Northern sympa-thizers, what we failed to accomplish with the bullet." By order of President Johnson the colored soldiers were every where discharged and withdrawn from forts and garrisons, at the request of their former masters, only to be left to their unrelenting hate. One colored man returned to the plantation of his wife's master, and asked him if he could take his wife and children to himself, as he had means, after two years of service to support them. The only answer he received was the contents of a pistol, that took his life instantly! I heard of similar murders in this vicinity, of which no notice was taken by the State authorities.

I visited a number of large schools in Alexandria, September 14th, and was invited to address them. Two of these were kept in two of the largest slave-pens in the city. Alexandria was one of the greatest slave marts in Virginia. In the Avery slave-pen there was a dungeon-like room, designed for one standing, with iron staples to which the wrists were locked, and a sort of stocks for the feet, when a stream of cold water was pumped over the nude form of the refractory slave, from ten minutes to an hour or more, according to the offense. They told me they had known them taken down chilled to death. It was said to be one of the most cruel punishments. They showed me the stump of the whipping post, where hundreds of writhing victims had suffered this kind of torture. But it did seem as if the better day was coming, to see a hundred and fifty-three black children here so eager to learn, and to hear them read so well after only four months' schooling. I met a woman on the street in deep mourning who was weeping. I inquired the cause of her grief. She said: "I have been to visit the grave of my only son. His father died a few months ago, and this darling son was my only child. He died in the Union army; but what does all this terrible sacrifice amount to? President Johnson is giving strength to the rebels. Every rebel general has been pardoned, and the vast amount of land restored to them is increasing their power. You see, wherever troops are withdrawn they commit murders, and no notice is taken of it. I feel as though my son's life and thousands of other precious lives have been sacrificed for nothing." I could say but little to comfort that poor, broken-hearted, widowed, childless mother. I could only commend her to our Heavenly Father, who alone can console the widow's aching heart.

On September 15th I took a steamer for Richmond, Virginia, and arrived on the 16th at Fredericksburg. Here were standing many chimneys, showing us the waste places and burned houses in this small but quaint old city. I called at the teachers' boarding-house, kept by a good Union family, Wm. J. Jeffries. Mrs. King accompanied me to the soldiers' hospital. Here, as elsewhere, the poor suffering soldier seemed rejoiced to see and hear the representative of their mothers. After reading the Scripture and prayer I left a number in tears.

Here was the home of General Washington's mother. I visited the house, and a feeling of solemnity came over me as we passed through her sitting room into the large bed-room, where report said she died. Near by is her tomb. The pedestal only stands erect, but badly marred by the chisel in chipping off pieces, by hundreds of visitors Our teachers inquired if I would not like a chip from the tomb. I told them that no chisel or hammer should be applied for me; but I picked up a little piece at its base. We had gone but few rods before a carriage drove to the tomb, and the chisel and hammer were flaking off keepsakes for four men. The long block of marble designed to have been placed on the pedestal lay near it half buried in the ground where it had lain nearly or quite a century.

After inspecting the rebel earth-works and rifle-pits, I visited Miss Strausburg's school of 181 poor white children, quite unlike any colored school I had visited any where, as to order. They commenced to sneer at me the moment I entered, but their teacher invited me to speak to the school, and they became at once quiet and respectful. Little James Stone asked permission to sing for me, and he sang a religious hymn in which nearly all the school joined. To my surprise they sang the "Red, White and Blue" and "The Soldier's Farewell to his Mother," for which I thanked them. In passing along the street after the school was dismissed, many of the children came out with their mothers, pointing toward me. At two places I halted to speak to them and their mothers, which pleased them very much.

The next day I visited a few Union families, who gave some interesting facts concerning their trials. I left two dollars with one sick woman, who wept as I left her. I called at Major Johnson's headquarters. He was very anxious to send on an orphan baby one year old to Camp Lee orphanage, in Richmond. He gave me a paper that would secure its admission. On arriving at Richmond I left my charge at the orphanage. As no name was on the paper, or was given to me with the child, the matron, Mrs. Gibbons, named him Haviland Gibbons.

I visited the orphanage a number of times. The matron said the little fellow learned his name very readily. Here was a pair of twin boys, about two years old, very black and smart. As they quarreled so much of the time, Judge Fitzhugh proposed to name them Abe and Jeff, after the two Presidents. Though a strong Confederate, he said they were smarter than any white children he ever saw, and to prove his position he called them out to dance, as he had taught them to step the figure. He sang for them, and they danced to his music.

"There, I'll venture to say," he said, "you never saw two white children of their age do that. I tell you the negro race is naturally smarter than the Anglo-Saxon."

I told him I was surprised at this remark, when he had told me a few minutes before that the negroes would soon die out, because they could not take care of themselves.

"That is true," he rejoined, "and I have written a book in which I take the same position, and can prove it. They will do more work than white people can, but they lack calculation; hence the necessity of their being under the supervision of the whites." We have the planning faculty, and they have the ability to do the work. There is therefore a necessity for both races to work together to be a successful people. I repeat what I told you before, that we never shall prosper separated. The power of governing must remain with the Anglo-Saxon race, and God has so designed. The Yankees have made a sad mistake in freeing the slave, for in time they will become extinct; but God will never suffer this state of things to remain, and you will see the South in power in two years, and the North minus the power she now wields.

I cited him to black men in Canada, who had escaped from slavery and who had acquired wealth, and to one of the wealthiest livery men in their own city. I also referred to a shoemaker who had been free but a few months.

His credit was sufficient to purchase ten dollars' worth of stock, which he made up and sold, paying for his stock; he then made another purchase and was hard at work to purchase a little home. His wife was washing and house-cleaning, with the same object in view. They told me they allowed themselves meat but once a week, and lived on corn-bread, mush, and molasses, and that they intended to live and work in this way until they should succeed.

"Does not this look like calculation?" I asked.

"I admit," he said, "there are isolated cases, but it is not the rule."

He gave me his book to read, entitled "Sociology of the South, by J. Fitzhugh, Att'y." I found it a perfect bundle of inconsistencies. He goes into a labored argument against free-labor, free-schools, free- press and free-speech, as destructive to a prosperous people. He claimed to be a cousin of Gerrit Smith's wife, and said that they were crazy over slavery. He also claimed that President Johnson was doing all he could for them, and that through him they were going to have their rights restored. He knew of men who had gathered half a bushel of Confederate money, and said they should keep it until it would be worth as much as greenbacks. He also knew men who had bills of sale of negroes, a foot deep, that they were keeping to recover their slaves, or pay for them; and he was confident that it would be accomplished within two years. This I found to be a very general feeling among the most prominent Confederates.

On September 20th I visited a number of sick that I supplied with bedding and clothing. I walked six miles that day, and then went to the office of the Freedmen's Bureau, where I was furnished with an ambulance and driver to take things to the sufferers I had visited.

After spending several days in this work, visiting schools and giving attention to many sufferers, I returned, weary in body but restful in mind, and thankful that the friends of humanity had made me the almoner of their gifts.

On October 2d I spent some time in Libby Prison. My sanitary goods were stored in one apartment of it. The prisoners were under guards, and were permitted to assist me in opening, closing, and moving barrels and boxes, a portion of which I prepared to take to Ashland. One of the keepers took me to the long, deep tunnel which the Union prisoners had dug under the building to escape from their terrible sufferings. To look at the great risk they were running in their fruitless effort to escape, speaks loudly of the desperation to which they were driven. My guide gave me a few of the hand-cuffs that our officers removed from some of the emaciated prisoners when Richmond was taken. The doors of Castle Thunder and Libby were opened, and the hand-cuffs were placed on their cruel keepers, who had made a boast of killing as many Yankees in these prisons as their troops were killing in battle.

I went out some distance, October 3d, to an old camp, where a school was organized in an old slave-pen. Here was the stump of the whipping-post cut even with the ground. I was shown where stood the auction-block. As I listened to a history of cruelties inflicted here I did not wonder that our nation was compelled to pass through this baptism of blood. Pointing to a large plantation in sight, said one: "There lives my old master, who said in the beginning of this war, 'Before my children shall ever be disgraced with work I will wade in blood to the horse's bridle.' He did fight hard as long as the war lasted. But last week he told his two sons that they must go to work or die. He came into my shoe-shop the other day with his feet almost bare, and I took the best pair of boots I had and gave them to him. I know he thought of old days, for I did."

After talking to the children at school I visited the aged and sick. Anthony Wilson, very aged, said, "Dun kno' how ole I is. White folks say I's more'n eighty. Had heaps o' ups an' downs; good many more downs dan ups; my big family all tore to pieces two times." I gave him a whole suit of clothes. "Bress de good Lo'd," he exclaimed, "dis is de best suit I eber had; dis I reckon is my freedom suit." Mary Brackson, also very old, had two little grandchildren with her. Their mother was sold down the river when the youngest was a year old. Her life had been a sad one. She was crippled with rheumatism, and her arm had been broken by an overseer's club. I gave her a bed-tick, quilt, blanket, and a few clothes for herself and grandchildren. Then I visited and relieved four other families, to whom I gave advice, and with the most I read and offered prayer, which always seemed to be a great comfort to them.

Two days after I took a train with supplies for Ashland. I arrived in the afternoon and met an excellent Union family, formerly from England, Judge James, whose house was battered on each side with bullets and shells in the severe battle fought at that place. This town, the home of some strong political men, seemed dilapidated and forsaken. Judge James's wife and daughter were noble women, and I found a very pleasant home in this family. They directed me to the most suffering families and individuals. My first call was on Charlotte Boles, whose reply to the query for her age was, "I dun kno'; missus 'specks I's eighty, large odd." She had served three generations.

"I's had so many children," she said, "I can't tell till I call de names: Pomp, Jim, Tom, Sol, Sue, Dick, an' Dilcy; den some babies I's got in heaven. I seed heap o' trouble in my time. I nursed at de breas' eleven of my firs' massar's chillen, Isaac Wiston, and six of his gran'-chillen. I dress 'em firs', an' some on 'em for de grave. My secon' massar, William Winfield, Jun., da have six chillen, an' I dress 'em all firs', and most all at las' for de grave. O my God, I can neber, neber tell de trouble I's had. O how hard I prayed for freedom, an' de Lord come at las'. I's praise his name. De one dat I nurst when a babie ordered me whipped 'case I cried so much when da sole my chillen down de riber. But I hear dat de war free five of my chillen, an' I's prayin' God to sen' 'em to poor me."

Notwithstanding her great age her mind was unusually clear, and the frequent starting tear manifested strong maternal affection.

There was not a house, yard, or grove but bore the mark of shell or bullet.

An exciting scene passed before us October 15th. Young Mrs. Pollard, daughter of my host, who had became the wife of the noted Confederate editor of the most rabid paper in Richmond, had been forbidden to visit or even to correspond with her parents. Her husband said if she should attempt it, it would be at her peril. She found him to be inconstant, as he had become the paramour of a Cyprian in New York city, where he spent several weeks writing a book on the bravery of Confederate soldiers. "When she discovered these facts, with her heart full of grief, she told him the reports she had heard of his inconstancy. He acknowledged all, and entreated her pardon. But he soon became as cruel as ever. During his absence in New York she took her son of less than two years and came to her father's house, a poor, heart broken woman. A divorce was immediately sued for, and she received a summons to appear in court in Richmond. Although her father was there to receive her, she feared Mr. Pollard would take her life, also her father's, at their parting. She threw her arms around her mother's neck and wept upon her shoulders; then, sobbing, said, as she rested her head upon my shoulders:

"Mrs. Haviland, you won't leave me after our arrival in Richmond until I am with my father, will you?"

With an assurance that I would remain at her side until her father took her under his protection, she left her babe with her mother and we departed for Richmond. We met her father, with whom I felt she would be safe. I find these extremes of love and hate more prevalent in the South than in the North.

On the 18th of October, after visiting fifteen suffering families, I called at the office for an ambulance and driver to go to Libby Prison for supplies. These were obtained and distributed, and such gratitude from the recipients I never found elsewhere. Same of them wept aloud. A number of the women kissed my hands as I left them, and the hearty "God bless you, honey," was an everyday blessing from these poor-crushed spirits.

One of our officers came to me with the urgent request of two women, living in a large brick house, to see me. I obeyed the summons at once. As I rang the door-bell, a genteelly dressed lady in black satin met me at the door. I inquired if there were two ladies here who had sent for me? She replied in the affirmative. By this time the other lady appeared in the hall, also dressed in rich silk.

"What are your greatest needs," I asked, "that will come within my power to supply?"

"We want money, madam," they said, "and must have it."

"Are any of your family sick?"

"No, madam, but money we must have."

"Will rations answer your purpose?"

"No, madam, we want no such thing; we want money, and must have it."

I told them I had no money to disburse, and only supplied food and clothing to those who were suffering from greatest destitution, and left them without being invited inside their house. I saw at once they were most accustomed to the imperative mood.

The captain came to me a few days after and inquired if I found it in the way of my duty to relieve the wants of those two ladies? I told him I asked them a few questions and did not think it worth the money demanded. He said they had sent for him, and a number of other officers, making the same demand, and as they had not succeeded they sent for me, and he was not disappointed at the result.

As I was passing their news depot, I saw blazoned in red letters, "No New Nation sold here" I stepped in and inquired for their best paper. The Examiner was handed me, edited by Pollard, the whilom son-in-law of Judge James, one of the most rabid Confederate sheets in Richmond. I inquired where the New Nation was sold. They said nowhere, unless a few "niggers" might be found selling it on, the street. One of them poured forth a long catalogue of epithets: "Arrant liar," "reckless villain," and finally a "crazy scamp."

As I was passing the street one day, and saw "New Nation," I thought I would call on the "insane editor," Mr. Hunnicutt. I ascended to the third story, where I found the busy editor and his son. They were surprised to see a lady of sufficient moral courage to call on them. The editor exhibited a pile of anonymous letters, threatening his life. He was an outspoken Union man, and had received over one hundred of these nameless letters within three months. He was a native of Virginia, and said:

"The Union of the States is a fixed fact, and I will advocate it squarely, though it cost me my life, but Union principles must and will prevail."

I left a dollar for a subscription to the New Nation for six months. As I was about to leave, said he, with tearful eye:

"A select few in this city meet once a week for a prayer-meeting, but I can not attend it in the evening, as it is unsafe for me to be out after dark."

I told him I had received a secret invitation, and had attended each meeting since my first knowledge of this praying band. I told him it was one of the most solemn meetings I had ever attended. As in the days of the apostles, we met in an upper room at the hour of prayer, where I had heard the editor of the New Nation remembered.

"I know," he said, "that I have friends in this city, and some I know are secretly friends for fear of this bitter spirit that reigns to a fearful extent. Don't forget to pray for me and my family. I dare not bring my wife and daughter to this city."

My work kept me here many days. November 25th I spent mostly at the sanitary rooms in Libby Prison, with Miss Morris, a French lady, who served as a spy for the Union generals. Report had it that she was writing a book of her exploits. A soldier told me he saw her a prisoner in Southern hands before the fall of New Orleans. But she managed to make her escape from that city, and in disguise revisited it, and reported to our generals. She could speak French and German better than our own language. She often disguised herself most effectually. Her French politeness would have been quite annoying to me had it not been for the faithful assistance she rendered in seeking out the sick and dying, not hesitating to enter filthy alleys, dark, cold cellars, or with me to climb rickety flights of stairs into dark attics. I have found in almost every place one or more Christian women who kindly offered to assist me, but few would dare visit those filthy places, fearing contagious diseases. Having had the small pox, and all other common contagious diseases, with my very plain habits of living, I dared to visit the sick and dying in any of these loathsome places, many of which I found in Richmond.

The next day, being Sunday, was spent as usual in attending Sabbath-schools. I spoke in two of them, and in one meeting. At night I was at Camp Lee Orphanage with Annie Gibbons, the matron, who had an interesting group of little folks. As they gathered around the table, at the tap of the bell, with clasped hands and closed eyes, they repeated the verse:

> "Lord, teach a little child to pray,
> Thy grace to me impart," etc.

I met a colored man from Raleigh, North Carolina, who gave a few items of Andrew Johnson's early history, in regard to his apprenticeship in tailoring.

If there was a dance within reach, black or white, it was all the same to "Andy,"--he was sure to be there. His boss, Mr. Selby, lectured him about his late hours, and to evade these lectures he often "turned in" with Handy Luckett, a steady old slave man, whose bed was in the loft of J. O. Rork's carriage house.

At a shoe-shop, I met John Blevins, a noble appearing John Brown sort of man whose sentence was forty years in the Virginia Penitentiary in Richmond. His crime was, aiding slaves to their God-given rights. He had served sixteen years when Richmond was taken. The Union soldiers opened the prison door, and John Blevins, with four hundred other prisoners, walked out free men. His intelligence speaks of better days. He is sixty years of age, and hard treatment had added ten years to his appearance. During the first few years of his prison life he could tell when a master had lost his slaves, as they would then place him in the dungeon, where he was kept for weeks at a time, to compel him to give the names of other abolitionists, but they never succeeded. He was at this time teaching a colored school. Out of school-hours, he worked in the shoe-shop, and was trying to make enough to purchase for himself a suit of clothes, when he designed returning to his home in Philadelphia. He had just heard from a family that he assisted to their liberty, some of whom had become quite wealthy, and were trying to find him.

He had written to them and was expecting to receive assistance. Whenever he went out on the streets he was annoyed by half-grown boys hooting after him, "Old John Brown, nigger thief." At the time he was arrested, they took all of his money, amounting to five hundred and fifty seven dollars.

I visited a Baptist Sabbath-school where three thousand members were enrolled. Over one thousand five hundred were present. They were addressed by Professor Johnson, who introduced and invited me to address the school. They very cautiously discussed the coming holidays, as they had never held one there on their own account. They decided to observe Thanksgiving, Christmas, and celebrate the Proclamation of Freedom on New Year's day. Their minister advised his people to be very careful in word and deed, so as not to give the least occasion for misconstruing their motives. Some of the white people said it ought not to be allowed. They feared an "uprising," but our soldiers said they should have the privilege.

I visited Howard Grove Hospital, under the charge of Miss Marcia Colton, matron. She was a missionary among the Choctaw Indians nine years, and was a noble, self-sacrificing woman. The surgeon of the hospital was D. R. Browery. I found a little boy of about eight years, whose mother he said was "done dead." He knew nothing of his father. I took him to Camp Lee Orphanage. Here and there I find kindred spirits, but none more devoted to the cause of Christ than sister Marcia Colton. She gave herself entirely to the advancement of his cause during nine years of labor among the poor, despised Indians. During the terrible conflicts of the war she unreservedly gave herself to the suffering and dying soldier, and she said that when, no longer called for in that field her life was just as cheerfully given to uplifting the lowly among the freed slaves of the South.

On visiting the State Penitentiary, the keeper hesitated about allowing me admittance. Said he: "I am afraid you'll give a bad report of us, as did Miss Dix, who gave us a bad name, and I thought of her as you entered my office. You look like her, and I am afraid of you. You know we don't have our prisons like yours of the North, like grand palaces, with flower-yards; and I reckon I had better not let you in." I told him I perceived they were rebuilding the part burned awhile ago, and would make due allowance for bad house-keeping.

"Well, if you'll do that, I reckon I'll have to risk you, for you'll see we are whitewashing the old cells and other parts of the prison, and then you must make allowance for its age. It was built in 1800, and is the first penitentiary in the world, and you Northerners have had all these sixty-five years to improve in, and then your gardens about your prisons are all so grand that I am a little afraid of your report. But, steward, you may take her through, and well see what she'll do for us."

I discovered a contrast, it is true. But, as in other places in the South, they seem a century behind the times. I found here, as in our State prisons, a majority of the convicts were left orphans in childhood. The number of inmates was at that time two hundred and twenty-four. I called on the general in command to inquire for Oliver Williams, whose wife requested me to see if I could find him. She was in Washington, D. C., and had not heard from him for a long while. I found he had been sentenced to three months imprisonment to hard labor, with ball and chain, but the time had now expired. The general referred me to Fortress Monroe, as the military prisoners had been removed to that prison. He advised me to call on

Governor Pierpont, who gave the same reference, and gave me some interesting items concerning this State. He said that, but for slavery, Virginia would have been one of the richest States in the Union in mines. Colored men were then making a dollar a day in gathering gold dust without the facilities of enterprising men with capital. There were also silver, copper, nickel, and a fine quality of kaolin or porcelain clay. He exhibited a specimen of each metal, and two bowls made of the native kaolin, a very fine material. To show the absorbing interest in slave-dealing he gave the figures of income, as shown during the discussions in their State Convention in 1861. The Metropolitan Press reported that "the income from slaves for the last twenty years amounted to twenty millions of dollars annually, and from all other products eight million dollars annually." This Governor Pierpont believed to be a true estimate.

I called at Sarah E. Smiley's Teachers' Home. Here I found Rachel Snell, daughter of Richard Snell of Lockport, New York, my old childhood home. With this group of kindred spirits I spent a refreshing season during a hard rain.

New Year's Day, 1866, was long dreaded by a large majority of the white citizens of Richmond. Great excitement prevailed over its celebration by the colored people. Soldiers were seen in every direction. A few companies of colored men went on the common to organize for the day's procession. The citizens were excited over that, and said they were preparing for "insurrection." They had permission from the governor to form in front of the State House. In the park were rustic seats of ancient style, chipped off and notched here and there, yet a colored person had never been allowed inside unless as the body servant of his master. But now their banners of various devices were floating, interspersed with United States flags. Each society had its motto, such as, "Peace, Liberty, and Freedom with all Mankind;" "Union, Liberty's Protecting Society;" "Peace, Good Will to all Mankind;" "In Union there is Strength;" "In God we Trust." On a blue satin banner were initials of a Benevolent Protective Association. The religious exercises were opened in the morning by reading the eighth chapter of Deuteronomy and singing an appropriate hymn. The text of the minister's discourse was a part of the second verse, "And thou shalt remember all the way which the Lord thy God led thee forty years in the wilderness." The minister could read quite well, though his life had been spent in slavery. He presented the past and present prospects of his people in a clear and affecting manner, and the necessity of remembering the past, to be fully prepared to praise God for the precious boon of freedom he had bestowed upon their race. There were four very large congregations opened this morning in a similar manner, and songs of praise were heard from the marching multitudes wending their way to the State House Park. There was shooting from a hotel window. Two of the suspected men were taken to Libby Prison. With the soldiers on the alert, and an increased force of policemen, they had no further trouble.

At the meeting of fifteen thousand or more in the park good order prevailed. I passed along through the moving masses, a silent listener to many outburstings of joy, contrasting with past sorrows--a great change indeed. Editor Hunnicutt, of the New Nation, was called upon to make a speech, and he exhorted them to cultivate industry, honesty, and virtue. He was followed by a number of others. At three o'clock the crowds began to disperse, so as to reach their homes before nightfall. It is passing strange why the white people here were so much excited over this celebration. There were two colored Baptist Churches burned two nights before, and on the night previous threats were made that all who took part In the celebration would lose their places of business.

The Episcopalian rector came after ten P. M. the same night to advise the two teachers, Mrs. Starky and Miss Hicks, to continue their school, and persuade the scholars to remain, and take no part in it themselves whatever, as the white people said this rejoicing was over the fall of Richmond and the downfall of the Confederacy. This idea was dwelt upon to such an extent that the Committee of Arrangements printed circulars and scattered through town during the week previous, stating their object in full, "that it was only to celebrate the day that God gave freedom to their race, and nothing more." But "insurrection," "uprising among the negroes," had been household words since the days of Nat Turner. The rebel flag was carried past Sarah E. Smiley's Mission Home for Teachers twice that day. Had the fact been reported at head-quarters, the bearers would have found themselves in the military prison.

As the army was being disbanded, and rations curtailed, and the suffering for want of them equaled that for clothing, I was informed by the general in command that there were more calls for rations by white than the colored people since the fall of Richmond. Said he: "I will mention a few to show the importance of investigation. Daniel Lacy had nine houses and servants and applied for and drew rations for his whole family. John Kimbo had servants out at work and drew rations for all his family, and had a number of houses. Mrs. Mary Ann Moseby had a grocery store well supplied, and drew rations and sold them. Mrs. Elizabeth Hunt also kept a full grocery, and drew rations to sell. Mrs. Sophia Coach, whose husband was a plasterer, drew rations. Mrs. Miller represented herself as a widow, and drew rations all the season, but I found out that she had a husband at home all this time. Mrs. Houston had a husband, but represented herself a widow, and drew rations and wood, as did all the others. The whole of two blocks drew rations, and most of them wood. Joseph Mayo, who is mayor of the city, and was when it fell into Union hands, drew rations, and owns a number of houses, and has servants. Ten years ago his slave Margaret's babe died with the croup, and be charged her with choking it to death, and had her hung on the scaffold after being whipped almost to death. He sent one of his slave women to the penitentiary six months ago, for a trivial offense. I heard by one of her friends, that she said it was a relief, for she was treated better there than at her master's. She is so rejoiced to learn that when she comes out she will be a free woman, and never again be compelled to serve that cruel master. But what contrasts we find here in both races! I have never found as much lying, misrepresentation, and cheating, among the negroes as among the white people, in my experience in this four years of war. Our records show more rations, wood, and coal issued to the whites than to the blacks in the State of Virginia."

I was careful to take down these items, in writing, as he gave them, in his office. O, what changes, what reverses, were here experienced. A. R. Brooks, who bought himself fourteen years ago, was now a wealthy man, owned ten horses, and six fine hacks and carriages, and his former master, by the fall of the Confederate government, was reduced almost to beggary. A few months ago he sold his plantation of three thousand acres for Confederate money, and is now penniless. Last February his wife died, and his former slave, A. R. Brooks, bore the entire expense of her burial. He said he praised the Lord for giving him the ability to do it. But how greatly was that wealthy planter, Henry A. Winfy, now changed in his prospects, when, a few months before, he considered himself the owner of three thousand acres, "well stocked" with slaves to work it.

With every day come new scenes, and yet such a similarity; investigating, relieving, reading Scriptures, advising, and often by the cot of the sick and dying. I often felt myself a stranger in a strange land, and yet I was never alone. Although, boisterous waves dashed around me, yet the dear Savior was near at hand.

I learned of much suffering on the Peninsula, and decided to take the rest of my supplies down the James River to Williamsburg. While arranging my packages for leaving Libby, a multitude of people were thronging the street near the prison. I inquired for the cause of this excitement, and was informed that a Union soldier was about to be executed for murdering a man for his money, horse, and buggy. As he was led out of prison upon the scaffold I hurried away, trembling with the terrible thought that a young life was about to be taken. As it was impossible for me to speak to him I hastened to escape the sound of the drop, but did not succeed. The horrors of war no pen can describe, no tongue can utter, no pencil can paint. The demoralizing influence over the soldier is dreadful. No doubt desertion was this fellow's aim, and, to serve his purpose, he fell into this strong temptation and crime. Desertion cost the life of one whom I saw in Mississippi sitting on a white-pine coffin and followed by his armed comrades, who were soon to take his life. It was then as now, too late to speak a word to that soldier-boy. And I hastened to outdistance the report of the guns that took his life. But I failed, as in the present sad event.

I called on a number of friends and co-laborers in Richmond; for here, as in every place, I have found kindred spirits. I spent the night with dear sisters in Christ, who labored in his vineyard to uplift the lowly. Scripture reading and prayer closed this eventful day.

On March 3d, at six o'clock A. M., I left Richmond and took the steamer Martin at the Rockets, followed by my friend, Mrs. Morris, with a basket of fresh cakes, apples, oranges, and a bottle of wine. I asked her to excuse me for objecting to the bottle of wine, as I never drank it.

"O, indeed, you must take it; your royal highness may be ill, and you may find it quite proper to take a little wine for your 'stomach's sake.' Don't, my dear madam, refuse your most humble servant the privilege of presenting this basket and its contents, wine and all, to my royal madam."

And I saw by the starting tear that she would feel quite hurt if I refused her, and accepted her gift.

As we steamed down the river I saw many little hillocks where were buried the fallen soldiers who left their northern homes with high hopes of saving the nation's life from the hand of treason. Here they fell long before Richmond was taken. We passed Burmuda Hundred and City Point, upon which stood General Grant's headquarters. Next came Harrison's Landing, near President Harrison's birth-place, an ancient appearing building situated upon a high bluff.

At Wilson's Landing and Clarmount Landing there was a high bank, upon which lived one of the wealthiest men in the State of Virginia, William Allen, who adopted the name of his father-in-law for the sake of his immense wealth. William Allen, sen., had no son, but an only daughter, and he offered his entire estate to any young man whom his daughter might be pleased to accept, if he would assume his name; he cared not how poor he might be, if he was only respectable. The daughter had many suitors, but at length a young man won this bride and adopted the whole name--William Allen. At the death of the father- in-law he came into possession of thirteen plantations and over four thousand slaves. All these plantations were managed by overseers. One man told me he had seen him take a keg of gold and silver coins down to the sand-bank, with a company of his comrades, on a holiday spree, and when they were all thoroughly drunk he would take up a handful of gold and silver pieces, throw them in the sand, and tell them to scramble, and he that got the most was the best fellow. He, with the rest, "scrambled," as he called it. William Allen declared that the Yankees had robbed him of fifty thousand dollars worth of negroes under ten years of age, and more than one hundred and fifty thousand dollars' worth of slaves above that age.

At twelve o'clock we landed at Jamestown. In this old, dilapidated place were yet standing brick walls of three old buildings open to the birds and the bats. The brick of these half-torn down buildings were transported from England more than two hundred years ago. I saw a piece of a marble slab from the graveyard dated 1626, broken in pieces by soldiers for relics. We were soon met by the ambulance-driver, and he took us through a nice field of wheat owned by William Allen, just referred to, who was one of our passengers to the ancient city of Williamsburg. Here was a large insane asylum, built of imported bricks from England, with a marble front, erected, by Lord Bottetourt, governor of the colony. It was founded in 1688. The tower was ninety- six feet high, and the number of inmates one hundred and one, forty- two of whom were colored. Robert M. Garrett was the physician and superintendent. This is the oldest institution of the kind in the Union. In the front yard of this asylum stands, in life-size, the statue of Lord Bottetourt. As we were passing through the apartments we listened to a very sweet voice singing a hymn. Said my guide, "Mr. Scott is singing for you. He is General Winfield Scott's nephew. He bet both of his plantations that the Confederates would succeed in this war, and when Richmond fell he became insane and was brought here two weeks ago."

I was shown an old brick church in which was a colored school of one hundred and ninety-six scholars, taught by Miss Barton, of Connecticut, and a gentleman from Michigan. Here I found myself at home at once. There were here, previous to the late war, two institutions of learning--the William and Mary College at one end of the main street, and at the other, three and a quarter miles distant, the female seminary. The college was burned in the war of 1776, again in the war of 1812, and, for the third time, a few months before I was there. There was no school now in the female seminary, and it looked as if waiting for repairs. Here is the old ivy-bound church in which George Washington was married. The bricks of this building were also brought from England. This town was the capital of tins State previous to its removal to Richmond.

I walked nearly two miles to Fort Magruder, where I found a colored school of one hundred and fifty-eight members, taught by Maggie Thorpe and Martha Haines, of New York, under the auspices of the Society of Friends. To accommodate men and women who could not leave their work during the day they opened a night school, and had fifty of that class. Half of these did not know their letters when their school opened in February, and could then read quite fluently in the second and third readers. A few miles further there was another school of thirty scholars who had made commendable progress.

The teachers informed me that there were many very old people on the oldest plantation near King's Mill, who needed help. I was furnished with an ambulance, in which I took a bale of bedding and clothing, and went from cabin to cabin to visit twenty-seven aged people, from sixty to a hundred and five years of age. After learning their most urgent needs, I selected supplies for each. When I expressed my surprise at seeing the old plantation with such a grove of woods, Uncle Bob Jones, the oldest of them all, said:

"Missus, all dat woods on dat side I helped clar off when firs' woods was thar, beech, maple an' linn wood, only now an' agin a pine. Den we work it till it wore out, an' wouldn't noffin grow on it, an' we lef it to grow up to dose pines you see."

"Is this possible?" I said. "I saw men chopping sawmill logs as I came through that wood."

"Yes, missus," he answered; "shure's you are bo'n, my sweat lies dar under dem big tree roots. My Milla an' me was married when we's chillen, an' we's had a good many chillen, but de Lo'd knows whar da's gone to; da sole down de riber, many, many year ago. But we prayed to Lo'd Jesus to take keer on 'em all dese years, an' we'll go home to glory soon."

In answer to my query as to his age, he said:

"Massa Moses' book say I's a hundred an' five, an' my Milla's a hundred an' three. I might slip count a year or two, but I reckon not."

I never before met one couple living to this advanced age. I gave them the best new quilt I had, made by a class of Sabbath-school girls, from eight to fifteen years of age, in Wayne County, Michigan. The names of the little girls were written on the blocks they pieced. The old man was quite blind, but he felt of it; then he exclaimed:

"Missus, did you say little white gals made this? Lo'd bless the little angels! Honey, look at dis; we's neber had sich a nice bed- kiver in all our lives."

To this she assented:

"I see it's a beauty; we's neber had sich a kiver afore, missus; tell de sweet little angels we'll pray for 'em as long as we live."

"Yes, tell 'em we won't stop prayin' for 'em when we gits up yonder, in de mansions," rejoined the old man.

It seemed to them wonderful that white girls should make such a nice quilt for black folks, and they were in an ecstasy over the surprise. Aunt Milla could see to do considerable work in their little garden patch, that some of the younger men among them had spaded for her. Every thing about their little cabin was neat and clean, and their clothes were well patched. Uncle Bob had been off this plantation but twice in his life; then he went to Williamsburg. It was affecting to see these old, worn-out slaves rejoicing over freedom, but it seemed to be more on account of their children and of their race. They had passed through many hard trial but their faith was strong that they were soon going to rest with Jesus.

A colored man brought two cripples to me, in his cart, for relief and their wants were supplied. He said he wished I could see two old men who were living in the mill. One of them was an old soldier in the Jackson war. My ambulance friend took me to the old brick mill that was the first one built in that country, they said more than a hundred and fifty years ago. The roof was covered with thick moss. The cedar shingles, as well as bricks, were brought from England.

I found here an intelligent mulatto man of about sixty years who had had a fever sore a little above the ankle a number of years. He was the eldest of twenty seven children. His mother had thirteen pairs of twins and he the only single child, and they were all sold to slave- dealers of the lower States.

"When my mother died in the cold cellar' he told me 'I begged to see her but my old master said he would shoot me if I dared to set foot on his plantation case I'd been with Yankees and she died one year ago without a child to give her a sip of water. My wife and seven children belong to another man who said he would shoot my brains out if I dared to come on his plantation. But I pray God to help my wife to go to the soldiers before they are all gone and get them to help her to come to me with our children. I was one of the slaves that master promised freedom, at the close of General Jackson's war and the general promised us ten dollars a month besides during service which was one year and eight mouths. There were five regiments of colored men. Some got their freedom as promised but my master and many others were more severe than ever. On my return home I reminded my master of the promise of freedom by him and General Jackson but I found it unsafe to say any thing more about it. We thought General Jackson ought to have seen the promise made good, as long as he promised freedom as well as our masters. He gave us credit for being among the best soldiers he had. But we never would have fought as we did had it not been for freedom ahead. We pledged ourselves to each other, that we never would fight for white folks again, unless we knew our freedom was sure. And never would our people have gone into this war had it not been for the Proclamation of Emancipation from the President of the whole United States."

This man was the most intelligent and used the best language of any colored person of his age I met in this portion of Virginia. His mother's name was Maria Sampson. She lived and died in King William County, Virginia. There were twenty sons and seven daughters of her own. Yet, through wicked enactments, her master tore from her every one, and claimed her own body besides, as a valuable piece of property.

My next visit was to an old brick kitchen. In the "loft," lived two aged sisters of seventy-five and eighty years, whose youngest brother, of about sixty years, was insane. His sisters said about twenty years ago he "lost his mind." His wife and children were all sold from him down the river, and he grieved so long over it, he lost his mind, and never came right since. As I entered, I took him by the hand and inquired for the aged women in that house; he pointed to the stairway. As I was going up the stairs, he danced to and fro, slapping his hands, "Glory, hallelujah to the Lamb!" I paused to look at him. His sisters met me at the head of the stairs, and said, "Don't mind him, he has no mind, and is rejoicin' to see a white woman come up these stairs, for it's a new thing. I reckon there hain't been a white woman up here more'n twenty year, an' he don't know how to tell his gladness.". They said he was good to bring them wood and water, and take care of himself in washing and patching his own clothes. I presented him a suit, and when he found they would fit him, the dancing and singing were resumed. I should judge from the history his sisters gave of him, and from his high forehead, that he had been a man of more than ordinary talent. These sisters, too, had been made widows and childless by slavery's cruel hand. This I found to be the hard lot of all these old people. They told me of many cruel over- seers, that would take the life of a slave, to get their names up as "boss overseers." I told them I had heard of instances where an overseer was missing occasionally. One old man dropped his head, then looking up said, in a hesitating manner, "I's knowed that in my time, but massar keep it mighty still, an' say de overseer runned away, an' he git one right soon agin." I talked and read, and offered prayer with these stripped and lonely ones.

During my three weeks' stay in Williamsburg, Fort Magruder, and vicinity, I had a number of meetings with these newly freed slaves, three of them in those old slave-pens in which were large schools taught.

I took a stroll through the old graveyard which surrounded the old ivy-covered church. The marble slabs were mostly in a horizontal position, with quaint inscriptions. In these J, or I, was often found in place of the figure 1. The spelling, too, we should call badly warped. I copied a few of the epitaphs, as follows:

Here lyes the Body of Mr John Collett, who departed this life February 24th, 1794, aged 52 years

Sacred to the memory of James Nicholson, late stuard of William and Mary College. Was born in the Town of Invenck, North Britton, ano 1711, died the 22nd of January, 1773. Frugality--industry, and simplicity of manners and independence of Soul Adorned his character and procured universal esteem.

READER,

Learn from this example as the most exalted Station may be debased by vice, so there is no situation in life on which virtue will not confer DIGNITY.

Mrs. Catharine Stephenson died April 22; born in Nottinghamshire, 1778.

> Her body now slumbers along with the dead;
> Her Savior hath called, to him she has gone,
> Be ye also ready to follow her soon.

Under this marble lieth the body of Thomas Ludwell, Esq., Secretary of Virginia, who was born at Britton in of Summerset in the kingdom of England, and departed this life in the year 1678; and near this place lye the bodies of Richard Kerdp, Esq, his predecessor in ye Secretary's office and Sr.

Thomas Lunsford, Kt., in memory of whom this marble is placed by order of Philip Ludwell, Esq., nephew of the said Thomas Ludwell, in the year 1727.

As Yorktown was an important post, after three weeks' work in this section, I repaired to that ancient place. There I found two large camps. A few large freedmen's schools were established under the auspices of Philadelphia Friends, and of these Jacob Vining had supervision. Two others were under the supervision of the American Missionary Association. Both were doing a noble work for these people, who were like hungry children, grasping at the food handed them by these Christian teachers.

We had a very large meeting in the old barracks fitted up for school and meetings. There were more than could get inside, and groups stood at the door and outside the windows. Here I met two young men who had walked all the way from beyond Fort Magruder, eighteen miles, to attend this meeting. They were more intelligent than the larger portion of life-long slaves. They were encouraged in the future prospect of freedom. They said the white people declared they would soon have all their slaves back again, the same as they had before the war. Said one, "They talk it so strong it makes us trimble. For we-uns think they'd be harder on us than ever." I told them to look at that strong fort built by Confederates, which they had said "all the Yankees of the North could never take." "And where is it now?" I said. "You may rest assured it will be as I repeated to-day, 'Except the Lord keep the city the watchman walketh but in vain; except the Lord build the house they labor in vain who build it.' The Lord will never permit the house of bondage to be rebuilt, for the cup of our nation's wickedness has been filled to the brim. They will never again barter for paltry gold the bodies and souls of those whom Christ died to redeem with his own precious blood. No, never." They wept, while talking over the past, with new hopes before them of their future. They said they were well paid for their long walk, though they should work the next day with blistered feet. They were working for their old owner, as he had promised to pay them. They had sometimes felt fearful as to the final result of this war. If there were doubts, they would go as far North as they could while they were enjoying their present liberty.

A number lingered to talk with me on the prospect of freedom or slavery for them, telling me of the positive expressions of their former masters, and of their threats of having them all back again within a few months. They wanted to know what the prospect was in Washington.

"Do you think we are sure to come out of the wilderness?" said one.

"Will this sun of freedom, now peepin' troo de black cloud, come cl'ar out, an' make a bright day?" said another.

I found many of these people in trouble, because they saw plainly the old slave spirit reviving, and they were trembling with fear; but others had stronger faith. There was one poor woman, whose husband and four children were sold to a trader, to be taken down the river in a gang. When the news came to her master's home that Richmond had fallen, she said:

"Missus an' all was cryin', and say da catch Jeff. Davis. An' I hurried de supper on de table; an' I say, Missus, can Dilla wait on table till I go to de bush-spring an' git a bucket o' cool water?' She say, 'Hurry, Mill; an' I seed 'em all down to table afore I starts. Den I walks slow till I git out o' sight, when I runn'd wid all my might till I git to de spring, an' look all 'round, an' I jump up an' scream, 'Glory, glory, hallelujah to Jesus! I's free! I's free! Glory to God, you come down an' free us; no big man could do it.' An' I got sort o' scared, afeared somebody hear me, an' I takes another good look, an' fall on de groun', an' roll over, an' kiss de groun' fo' de Lord's sake, I's so full o' praise to Massar Jesus. He do all dis great work. De soul buyers can neber take my two chillen lef' me; no, neber can take 'em from me no mo';" and the tears fell thick and fast as she told me how she clung to her husband, then to her children, as the trader took them to the slave-pen to lock up till they were ready to start for the river. Her mistress ordered her to be whipped because she cried so long for her husband and children. I did not wonder at her ecstasy.

A poor old slave, called Aunt Sally, came to me April 15th; crippled with rheumatism, and walking as well as she could with two canes. She asked for a blanket or quilt, saying that one old blanket had been her only bed for seven years. I told her I should pass her home the next day, and would bring her some things. She said, "I mus' hurry back, or missus will fin' me out. You gib 'em to the man choppin' wood in de yard; he'll put 'em in de cellar for me. Missus is mighty hard on you alls;" and she hobbled back as fast as she could with two canes. But her mistress found out that she had been to see me, and told her she should never set her foot inside her yard again, neither should a Yankee. The day following I took a package for Aunt Sally, containing a straw bed-tick, quilt, blanket, and a good suit of clothes; for I had learned that Mrs. Pendleton, the daughter of ex-President Taylor, was a hard mistress. Aunt Sally had served her father, and helped bring up his children, and was now seventy-five or eighty years old. From the cold, damp cellar, with only one blanket to cover her, she had become badly crippled, and was left to die, like an old worn-out horse.

The colored man near the fence of the back yard told me I would find Aunt Sally in a little cabin he pointed out, with two old colored people. I found her crying. She said her mistress had turned her out, and told her she should never come inside her yard, nor eat a kernel of the corn that she had planted in ground all spaded by herself, and it was growing so nice. The old people very kindly offered to share with her. He was a cobbler, and made all he could, but he said they had but one bed. I furnished one for her, and gave the old people a quilt and a few needed garments for their kindness to Aunt Sally. They, too, had been stripped of all their large family, as well as Aunt Sally of hers.

As I passed Mrs. Pendleton's front yard I saw a large bloodhound on the door-step as sentinel. Even a look at him from the street brought a threatening growl.

Here, too, were William and Phillis Davis, over eighty years of age, they think. They had fourteen children, "all sold down the river," they said, "except those we's got in heaven. We's glad they's safe, an' we trus' de jubilee trumpet will retch their ears, way down Souf, we don't know whar. We's cried for freedom many years, an' it come at last," said the old, tottering man.

Eva Mercer, over seventy five years of age, had a large family. Her husband and all her children were sold twenty years ago. She has been left to perish alone, and had had no underclothes for seven years. She was supplied, and made more comfortable than she had been for years.

David Cary, one hundred years old, in great suffering, was relieved. He, too, had a large family. Three wives were sold from him, and his children, one, two, and three at a time, were sent down the river, never to be heard from again. He said he forgot a great many things every day, "but I can never forget the grief I passed through in parting with my good wives and chillens."

Pross Tabb, ninety years old, was turned out of his cabin, and came to the captain crying. He said, "Massar Tabb turn me out to die by de roadside. I begged him to let me build me a cabin in de woods, and he say if I cut a stick in his woods he'll shoot me." The captain informed J. P. Tabb that he would violate the martial law, and be fined and imprisoned, if he turned that old man out of his cabin, where be had lived and served him many years. The poor lone man was permitted to remain. J. P. Tabb owned twelve thousand acres of land, and had called himself master of one hundred and sixty slaves; now all had left him.

Sunday, May 3d, was a beautiful Sabbath. In the morning I attended service at the school-house, conducted by a Baptist minister, who examined nine new converts. Among them was a little girl, Susan Monroe, eight years old. The preacher asked her, "What have you got to say 'bout Jesus, sis?"

"He tuck de han' cuffs off my han's," she replied, "an' de spancels off my feet, an' Jesus made me free."

With a few other satisfactory answers he passed to the next, a man of forty, perhaps: "And what have you to tell us?"

"It 'peared," he said, "like I's so heavy here, on my heart. I could do nuffin but groan, 'Massar Jesus have pity on poor me;' an' as I was a walkin' 'long de road, he cum sure, an' poured hisself all over me, an' cover over my han's an' my feet, an' made me all over new. I say is dis me? Glory, hallalujah! dis is me. I went on an' met sis Molly. 'What's de matter o' me? it's all full tide here,' I says. 'Why honey,' she answered, 'you's got 'ligion; praise de Lord! Now keep de pure stuff, don't trade it off for de devil.' An' by de help o' de Lord, I don't do any sich tradin'."

The next was queried. "Ah, I's played de fool," he said, "in jist dat kind o' tradin'. I's an ole backslider. Ole Satan had me, sure, an' I cried, 'Massar Jesus, save me from dat horrible pit,' an' he fotch me out, an' put dese feet on de rock, and here I means to stan'."

Others were examined, and a season of prayer followed. Their prayers were marked for their originality and earnestness. Said one woman, "Oh Lord, do please hitch up your cheer a little nearer your winder--draw aside your curtain, an' look down 'pon us poor creturs, an' gib your table-cloth a good shake, dat we may pick up a few crumbs."

There were many of these much more intelligent than I supposed I should find them, and used as good language as the white people. House-servants and body-servants were more intelligent than those who lived only in the field. They were very imaginative, and talked with God. One woman in giving a sketch of slave life, said a young girl went to a night meeting contrary to orders, and for so doing was stripped naked and whipped in the presence of the other slaves, the master himself plying the lash. While she cried for mercy her master replied, "I'll give you mercy." "Good Lord do come and help me." "Yes, I'll help you" (and kept plying the lash). "Do, Lord, come now; if you ha'n't time send Jesus." "Yes, I'm your Jesus," retorted the inhuman persecutor, and he continued to ply the lash until thirty strokes were well laid on.

The colonel commanding this post called on me with a request to go to Gloucester Court-house, to look after the condition of the freedmen there. There were several very old, crippled people in Gloucester, in almost a nude condition. I agreed to go, and the colonel went to procure a buggy, as his own was broken; but he failed to get one, though more than a double price was offered, because he was a Yankee. He returned discouraged, as he was unwilling to send me in a Virginia cart, the only government conveyance. I told him I had frequently seen the wealthiest ladies sitting on straw, with no other seat in the cart. "O yes," he answered, "the F. F. V.'s ride in that way here. But you look too much like my mother to see you go in that style. I could not bear to have your children in Michigan know that I sent their mother out to ride thirty miles in that way;" and tears filled his eyes, as he referred to his own mother in his far off Northern home. I told him if I could accomplish any good by going, I was more than willing to take the cart-ride, as I could make a seat with my bale of clothing, and thus I went.

I crossed York River at Gloucester Point, and stepped into a store to wait for our soldier driver. Here a Southern brigadier-general addressed me in the following style:

"I reckon you are from the North, madam."

"I am from the State of Michigan," I said, "but more directly from Washington."

"You Northern people can not be satisfied with robbing us of millions of dollars in slaves, that were just as much our property as your horses and cattle, but you stole our sheep and horses, or any thing else you could get hands on; and yet that was not enough. Now you have a bill in Congress to rob us of our land, and of course it will pass. Then we'll go to work and mix up a little cake to bake for our families, and you'll come and snatch even that away from us."

"You probably refer," I said, "to the bill just introduced, to allow the leaders in this Rebellion no more than twenty thousand dollars' worth of real estate, confiscating the balance, to sell in parcels to the soldiers and poor people, black or white, on liberal terms, to liquidate the war debt. This debt would never have been contracted, had not the South brought on the war. You fired upon Sumter; you determined to sever the Union. It was a bargain of your own making. You determined to make slavery the chief corner stone of the Republic, but another stone, Liberty, has ground it to powder. We had better accept the situation as we find it, and not call each other thieves and robbers because your chief corner-stone is no more. God never designed that we should make merchandise of human beings. In the written Word we find that God made of one blood all the nations of the earth. We find there no lines of distinction because of color or condition. Now let us drop slavery and hold it no longer as the bone of contention, and live henceforward a united nation."

With flushed face and flashing eyes he said, "Never, NEVER shall we give up our rights. We acknowledge you have overpowered us, but you have not, and never will, conquer us; we shall yet in some way secure our rights as Southerners, notwithstanding all your Northern preaching."

"If you carry out your position," I rejoined, "you will unite with some foreign power to break up our government, or to grind its republican form into powder and scatter it to the four winds."

"Of course we should, and you can't blame us for doing that. It is just exactly what we shall do if we have the chance."

After a few minutes unpleasant talk of this sort our soldier drove in front of the door for me. We borrowed a little box, upon which a coffee sack of clothing was laid, and we thus made a comparatively comfortable seat.

We reached Gloucester, and, on May 10th, went to the office of Captain McConnell. He was engaged all the morning in hearing complaints on the part of the freedmen and in adjusting their wrongs. Some of them were pitiable cases of outrage, but we can not report them here. There were eight difficulties settled within the few hours that I remained in the office. I resumed visiting and supplying the wants of the destitute as far as my means would allow. There were some old and crippled people here in the same condition as those whom I had relieved in other places in this part of the State. As usual, I took with me my Bible, for these colored people had none, because they had never been permitted to learn to read. Many of them gave thrilling sketches of their experiences in slave-life.

On May 13th, at four o'clock P. M., I found myself back at Old Yorktown. Here I visited the cave in which General Cornwallis was found. The old wood house in which the treaty was signed is covered with thick moss. A two-story brick building was Washington's head- quarters after he took possession of Yorktown. It was also the head- quarters of the Union generals after it fell into their hands. Here was the stamping-ground of two great armies. The contention was not now with British red-coats, as in the Revolution, but with our brethren in gray. Richard Lee, an ex-slave-holder, undertook to whip a colored man with the help of his overseer, after the old style, but in the struggle he found himself cut in two or three places, and the blood was flowing pretty freely from the overseer. The colored man told them whipping days were past, and he came out of the affray with but few scratches. His offense was refusing to work on Sunday afternoon. They entered no complaint at the office of the Freedmen's Bureau, and the colored man went about his business unmolested.

After taking leave of many dear friends at this place, through the kindness of sister Ailsgood, the matron of the Teachers' Home, I was conveyed to the boat in Lieutenant Massy's carriage. We enjoyed a beautiful run on the Chesapeake. Among our passengers for Norfolk was a young lady who seemed bright and gay, but had nearly spoiled herself with affectation. She was going to visit her aunt previous to entering upon her new duties in teaching a school.

"I never did do any thing of the kind," she told me; "but pa says I must; now that we have lost all our servants by this awful war. But I don't know how I'll do. Do you think I can teach a small school?"

Receiving a word of encouragement, she went on:

"I reckon I'll have to try. We've always had a lady preceptress at our house, besides the nurse, to take care of us."

A few minutes after I saw her weeping bitterly, as if her heart was nearly broken. Placing my hand upon her shoulder I inquired if she had heard bad news that was grieving her? She sobbed and sighed with quite an effort in commanding her feelings to speak.

"No; do you see that man yonder with a light hat on?"

"Yes."

"Well, he winked at me, and I was never so insulted in my life."

And she burst again into tears.

"Don't grieve over that," I said; "I wouldn't look at him."

"But I never was so insulted. I'm so glad my brother ain't here; I tell you there'd be trouble."

"Never mind; don't notice him."

"Won't you stand by me?"

"Yes; I'll stand here," I answered. And she soon became calm, when I thought it safe to leave. But a few moments later I saw her weeping as hard as ever. I went across the cabin to her relief the third time and inquired, "What is the trouble now?"

"He winked at me again, and I never, never was so insulted. I know if my brother was here he'd shoot him, for he'd never stand this."

I stood by her this time till I saw her in the ladies' dressing-room, by her request remaining between her and the object of her fears, who was at least fifteen feet from us, sitting in the farthest end of the cabin. After she had washed and combed her hair she asked, "How does my hair look? I never combed my hair myself. Our nurse did that always, until six months ago our last servant left us, I don't know if it looks well anyhow, for I don't know how to dress it. And do my eyes look as if I'd been crying?"

"Not to be noticed," I said. "You look all right."

"Will you see if that fellow has gone out?"

On the report that he had left she returned. I inquired if she was alone.

"O, no, not entirely; pa put me under the care of a splendid man; I reckon he's on deck; O, he's such a beautiful gentleman; he was pa's overseer a good many years; pa thought he couldn't carry on our plantation without him; when I see him I'll be all right. I reckon you've heard of my pa. Everybody knows him--Mr. Hampton--in Gloucester County, one of the most splendid counties in the State. "Were you ever in Gloucester County?"

"I was there last week," I answered.

"Isn't it the most beautiful county you ever saw?"

I replied, "Nature has done enough to make it so."

"It was a grand county before the war," she said. "Everybody thinks it's the best county in the State of Virginia."

But my opinion widely differed from hers. It seemed to me one of the darkest and most God-forsaken corners of the earth. But the influence of slavery had its deleterious effects upon whites as well as blacks.

Laura Hampton knew nothing of self-reliance. All she knew was to be a consequential young lady of distinction, full of exalted qualifying adjectives in the superlative degree. But she was not so much to blame as her parents for her simpering and tossing the head with overstocked affectation. She was to be pitied for her unfortunate surroundings. Her "splendid man," a "beautiful gentleman," was a coarse, burly headed "Legree" in appearance.

I arrived at Norfolk at four o'clock P. M., and found a pleasant home at the Tyler House. Here, I met eighteen teachers, with whom I enjoyed a refreshing prayer-meeting, led by S. J. Whiting, a missionary, who gave an interesting sketch of his experience in the Meudi Mission in Africa. I gave an account of the work accomplished through the blessing of God in the Mississippi Valley, while I was accompanied by my dear sister Backus, and spoke of trials I had recently passed through. Here were kindred spirits, with whom we held sweet communion, and with our Heavenly Father, who is ever near at hand.

While in this part of the State, I saw a white woman who had been cruelly assaulted and beaten with a raw-hide by her sister and niece for associating with the teachers of our freedmen's schools. They thought she had disgraced the family; but she said she would not turn away from those Christian ladies, however her own kindred might treat her. O the wrongs and outrages which the spirit of slavery inflicted not only on the blacks, but also on the white people of the South!

EXPERIENCES AMONG FREEDMEN

I was told by General Armstrong, commander of the post in Elizabeth City, that twenty-five thousand inhabitants had been supplied with food, and that more whites than blacks had called for rations. There were six thousand freedmen in this district. Twenty-six hundred of their children were in schools; and thirteen hundred were half or entire orphans, that drew rations. They had had no civil court here since March 20th, and no justice was shown to freedmen. There was as much complaint here as elsewhere about their unwillingness to work; but the general said it was only because they got no pay. A few plantations were rented here by Northerners; but they made no complaint for want of hands, and had more applications for work than they could furnish.

General Armstrong secured a carriage, May 18th, to take his wife and myself to the Downey School, a few miles distant, to see what a noble work the two Stewart sisters were there doing. He took us to a large farm of eight hundred and six acres, rented by a Northern man by the name of Jackson, who said he had worked it three years, and had taken it for two years longer. He had no difficulty in keeping good help. "All these people want is fair and kind treatment" he said, "to make good and faithful hands the year around. I can not employ all who come for work. I have seen them leave weeping over their disappointment."

Near this place was the school conducted by the two sisters, Emily and Jennie Stewart, of South Hill, Steuben County, New York. They had one hundred and eighty-five scholars, and were doing a grand work among the white people in that community. Two young men were converted through their instrumentality, and were exerting a powerful influence over the white people. They were attending the school, to which a number of white families sent their children. It widely differs from all others I have visited In the South. These earnest Christian girls were emphatically teaching a school of Christ on week-days as well as on the Sabbath. The two young men referred to had the ministry in view, and were very earnest in their exhortations. I addressed the school, and conversed with those young white men, who seemed in a very tender frame of mind. These dear sisters urged me to spend a week with them; and General Armstrong kindly offered to send his conveyance for me at the close of the week, or whenever I might fix the time. But as my supplies were out, I wished to hasten back to Washington.

During the day's ride we passed the place of a large Sabbath school, which was first opened by a soldier, W. Badger, Jun., a faithful laborer in this work. It had flourished ever since.

We visited a number of plantations with which the general was unacquainted. He hailed a passer-by to inquire the distance to the Old Brick Church. "O, you're smash up to it," he said. I looked up to see it, when he continued, "'T ain't but two miles ahead." The general thought it was three miles, at least, before we reached the old colonial church, built one hundred and twenty-five years ago, out of brick brought from England.

We passed through, a forest of young pines that had been rented three years to colored people in five and ten acre lots. They were to receive one-fourth of all they raised, and pay the remainder as rent. Said the general, as we came opposite a ten-acre lot where a man, his wife, and daughter were all hard at work grubbing. "That man will hardly get a meager subsistence from one-fourth of that land." And he inquired of the man if he expected to get his living off the fourth of that lot.

"I reckon so," was the answer. "After we gets the crop in my wife and gal can tend it, and I'll get work by the day while its growin'."

Sunday, May 20th, was a pleasant Sabbath. I attended a large meeting, and listened to a very interesting discourse by a freedman. At the close he earnestly exhorted his hearers to purity of life in their new freedom. He wanted to see all filthy habits left behind with bondage. "Do not let us take with us," he said, "any habit of drinking--not even using tobacco. Let us search ourselves, and see if we are worshiping God with clean hearts and mouths."

Opportunity being offered, I made a few remarks from II Chronicles, xv:12, "And they entered into covenant to seek the Lord God of their fathers with all their heart and with all their soul." After meeting, minister and people gathered around me to shake my hands, until they were lame a number of days. Said one, "Da's took de bridle off our heads, an' let us loose to serve God." Near the place was the Zion Methodist Church, that had been used occasionally for auction sales of slaves. There were thirty acres here, purchased by colored people, laid out in two-acre lots. Most of them had built little cabins, but others were working out by the day to earn means to pay for their lots before they built.

In the evening I visited a school of twenty-five adults, who could not attend during the day. A number of them read for me very intelligibly. James Wright did not know his letters at Christmas, but could now read fluently. He was sixty years of age. Robert Bell, aged fifty, who did not know his letters in March, could now read in the second reader.

Captain Flagg and wife invited me to take another ride out in the country where colored people had rented land.

On our way we met five carts laden with F. F. V.'s. The captain inquired of one man how far it was to Providence Church. "Sir," he answered, "you are slap-jam on to it; only a mile and a half, sure." As usual we went twice the distance; the captain said he always calculated a Virginia mile to be double the length of ours. This church had been built one hundred years before with brick brought from England. We called on six families. Said one woman, "I tried hard to serve God forty years ago, but mighty idle; Massa's lash so sharp, 'peared like we poor creturs never rest till we drop in our graves."

We visited Ex-Governor Henry A. Wise's plantation of five hundred acres, with fifty cabins in the negro quarters. This was confiscated. There were many of his former slaves here, aged and helpless, and a successful school was taught in his dwelling-house. Here were seventeen schools under the charge of the American Missionary Association, which were taught by eleven lady teachers and six gentlemen. H. C. Perry was the superintendent of schools in Norfolk District.

The Taylor plantation was the next which we visited. It contained seventeen thousand acres, seven hundred acres of which were worked, and ready for renting to freedmen. In Captain Flagg's district there were three thousand four hundred and eighty-six freed children attending day-school, and five hundred and one scholars in the night- schools. One hundred and ninety-two of these were over sixteen years of age. The above included seven counties: Norfolk, Princess Ann, Nansemond, Isle of Wight, Southampton, Accomack, and Northampton, the last two on the eastern shore of Chesapeake Bay. It is well to note the income of these confiscated plantations, that had, up to May 25, 1866, been returned to original owners. There had been paid over by Captain Flagg to government toward liquidating the war debt, thirteen thousand dollars. All of this was the avails of negro help on the government farms, except the Wise and Taylor plantations, that were still occupied for the benefit of the aged, sick, blind, and crippled men, women, and orphans.

I returned to Washington, where I found a request that I should take fifteen colored orphans to our Home in Michigan.

The commissioners having charge of money sent here by all the Free States, for sanitary purposes, proposed to place five hundred dollars in my hands for the two orphan asylums in Michigan, out of the nine hundred dollars that came from our State. This was to be equally divided between Detroit Orphan Asylum and the one in Raisin Institute, known at that time as Haviland Home. A majority of the commissioners objected to its being placed in the hands of a woman, to select goods to be purchased at auction rates. Consequently, a young man was sent with me to see that wise selections were made for the little homeless waifs for whom the relief was designed. Being somewhat acquainted, with my work, he said he was ashamed of the vote of the board, in distrusting my ability to select goods for the little children of the asylums, when I had been at this work all my life, and constantly during three years past. But I told him I was thankful to get the five hundred dollars, and could waive their notions of woman's inability very comfortably. He assented to all the selections I made, and I arranged to return home with the fifteen orphans and forty laborers, who wished to go to Cleveland, Ohio, where their friends had gone for work and reported to them favorably.

I found in these people a strong attachment to their own color; hence the unwillingness for a few to go a great distance without a prospect of others to follow. It was a heavy pressure of persecution that could drive them from their old Southern homes to Washington for protection, and the heavy pressure of want staring them in the face that could induce them to leave for Northern States to find work. Fifteen thousand were then huddled in and about Washington. Hundreds could not get work at ten cents a day, besides rations. General O. O. Howard gave transportation for many car-loads to go to the States of New York, Pennsylvania, Ohio, and other free States. But the freedmen could not be persuaded to go into the former slave States, after having left them. General Howard said Northern humanitarians ought to have a share in this Christian enterprise of furnishing work for the able-bodied and assisting to care for these indigent children; and he urged me to bring as many as practicable.

Mrs. Ricks knew of fifteen who wished to follow their friends that had gone to Ohio, and said she would assist me in going through to Adrian, where Joseph McKenzie had spoken to me for eight or ten strong men for his brickyard. If they had families he said he would help them in building houses on his own land, and if both were suited he would eventually sell lots to them.

While calling on F. C. Beaman, member of Congress, and wife, I was urged to rest three or four days, at least, before leaving for home. But I told them I must hasten home to rest. Transportation was secured for fifty-five adults and fifteen orphans. Before we reached Altoona I found rations had not been provided for adults, and that we must purchase at least seventy-five loaves of bread at that town. As the train halted a few minutes, I left for the bakery, but found that it had been removed a block further. We went on a run, and secured the bread; and I sent the men running with it, so as to reach the cars before they should start. But I was left behind, with three young men who refused to desert me. The men with the bread reached the cars just as they were beginning to move. Mrs. Ricks being with them, I was easy as to their condition. I found I had better keep as quiet as possible, as I was threatened with an attack of dysentery. But transportation, with my official papers, had all gone on, and there was not a soul in Altoona that I ever knew. Yet I was not discouraged, but took the three young men with me to the railroad superintendent's office, and told the superintendent I had come on a queer errand, and told my short story. "And now I solicit the favor of a pass for myself and these three young men. But you do not know whether I have given you a truthful representation, for I have not so much as a scratch of a pen with me to prove it."

Said he: "You say your name is Laura S. Haviland. Did you not secure a pass to Chicago and return, three years ago, of Mr. Campbell, at Adrian?"

"I did," was my reply, "as I was going South with sanitary supplies."

"I thought I had seen you before," he said. "I was his chief clerk, and made out those passes for you; and I will give you a pass, as you request. Would you like to telegraph to the lady assistant?"

"I suppose," I said, "she will stop over at Pittsburg until I overtake them; but it would be a favor if their baggage could be properly rechecked at Pittsburg to stop over one train at Cleveland, as a portion of the adults are to stop there."

"I will telegraph the freight agent to take special care in rechecking their baggage, and request the operators to telegraph to railroad authorities at Cleveland that this car-load of blacks in charge of Mrs. Ricks are to wait over one train for you."

I told him if that could be done without fail it would be a great favor, as I was sick, and Mrs. Ricks would have time to send these colored people up town to their friends. He telegraphed all these directions, and also requested the ticket agent to meet me with the passes.

While waiting for the train I was furnished with a sofa by the kind matron who kept the ladies' waiting-room. I was met at the Pittsburg depot with passes, and conducted to the waiting-room for a few moments, when the young man came to assist me on the right car. By this time my fever ran high, but higher still on reaching Cleveland, and finding that all had gone on to Adrian. Here tickets to Adrian were waiting for me.

I met brother J. Berry at Adrian depot, who informed me that all were cared for. I left all with the Lord and the good people of Adrian, who knew nothing of my trying experiences.

My children were urgent to send for the doctor at once. I insisted on my water treatment, but promised to comply with their request if not materially better in twelve hours. A few days of rest and quiet restored my health.

Although Adrian was a little alarmed at this new experience of army stampedes, yet in due time places were found for all to work, and eventually many of them became owners of their own homes.

The children of soldiers and other homeless waifs, needed attention, and I found more than a dozen in our Orphans' Home without a shirt for a change. But sister Annie Berry donated forty yards of heavy sheeting, and within two weeks we had a hundred yards made up into substantial garments for these little homeless ones. My health being still too poor for hard work, I spent a few weeks with my son, Joseph B. Haviland, at Acme, Grand Traverse County.

On my return home, I found our commission had concluded to close the asylum work, and expend its means in supporting schools in the South. They had sold the West Hall, and it had been removed to Tecumseh, and they were about to sell the team and other property. I now stated the motive I had when I gave the deed with a proviso, and said that removing the building was a wrong step for our commission to take, in view of the proviso. I met the commission in Detroit, and laid before them my object, and my desire to make it a State asylum, for the children of soldiers and all others who were in our county poor- houses, that were mere nurseries for the prison. I had inquired of superintendents of penitentiaries, how many of the convicts had been left orphans in childhood; and the average in Virginia, Maryland, Pennsylvania, and our Michigan State Prison was more than three- fourths. Emma A. Hall, matron of the female prisoners in the Detroit house of correction, informed me that every girl and woman under her care had been left an orphan in childhood. In view of this record, and of there being a greater number of that class since the war than ever before, I had felt the necessity for this asylum.

George Duffield, D. D., the president of our commission, replied: "We know not but this check is of the Lord, for we are finding it hard work to secure homes for the forty children now in the Home who are under ten years of age." And he moved that a month be allowed me to make satisfactory arrangements according to my design. While I was endeavoring to secure ten-dollar subscriptions to effect this result, J. R. Shipherd, secretary, of the Western Division American Missionary Association, sent an agent to purchase the asylum and continue it in its present form. He stated the American Missionary Association could not take it with the proviso, but would pay me two hundred and fifty dollars of the five hundred dollars I had agreed to deduct out of the two thousand dollars purchase money, if I should relinquish the proviso. I feared the result, thinking the enterprise might be only an experiment, and might close at some future period, leaving these children a public burden. But J. R. Shipherd pledged his word that no child of whom the American Missionary Association should take control should become a public burden, and would further agree to expend on the building and grounds, at least from three thousand to five thousand dollars within a year and a half or two years at longest.

From the confidence I had in the association I yielded, though reluctantly. The agent desired me to take charge of the asylum as matron, ten days or two weeks, as Mr. Shipherd could secure a matron from Vicksburg, Mississippi, in that time. I agreed to do this free of charge. Mrs. Edgerton, whom se engaged as matron, arrived in four weeks.

It was now late in October, and my Winter cough began to trouble me. This the Southern Winters had melted away during three Winters past, and I concluded to resign my agency in our State Freedmen's Aid Commission and work under the auspices of American Missionary Association of the middle division. I secured transportation from General O. O. Howard to Atlanta, Georgia, and again left my dear ones at home for that field. I spent a few days with my dear friends, Levi and Catharine Coffin, at Cincinnati. As the secretary, brother Cravath, was on an investigating tour in the South, Levi Coffin proposed that I should go to work over the river, in Covington and Newport, Kentucky, as there were a few thousand freedmen congregated in those towns. He introduced me to a lieutenant, in whose charge the freedmen's department was left, who took me to a number of barracks, where the sick and suffering were occupying bunks with a bed sack that had, when possible, been filled with hay, leaves, or husks.

One poor woman had nothing in her sack, and that was all she had for her bed, aside from an old condemned blanket. She was suffering intensely with rheumatism. Her limbs and hands were all drawn out of shape, thus disabling her from dressing herself. I purchased some hay immediately and had her moved so as to have her bed-sack filled, and then furnished her with a warm quilt. I procured quantity of thick red flannel and made her a long-sleeved garment to reach over her feet, and made it before I slept. The next morning I took it to her and saw it on her. The poor woman could say nothing for weeping, but after commanding her feelings, she said, "This is more than I deserve. All the sufferin' I's had all the year is nothin' compared to the sufferin' of my Jesus for poor me." The colored woman who had the care of her said she never had seen such patience in all her life. The next day I took her another flannel garment, and relieved many others during the month I spent in this field.

Our lieutenant was an excellent man. One day he wished me to go with him to see his old building that he had ordered fitted up for a school for three hundred freed children in that part of his district. But he found that nothing had been done. "Upon my word," he exclaimed, "not a stroke, not a stone, not a window. O, I can't stand this red tape; I just want to leave every other duty and pitch into this house. I know I am too impulsive, but that is the way of an Irishman. I have often thought Peter was an Irishman, he was so impulsive."

I spent the greater portion of New-year's day, 1867, in calling upon twelve families and taking to the sick and aged ones, blankets and clothing. I walked nearly a mile to the ferry, and called at the mission-rooms, where I found the secretary, E, M. Cravath, just returned from his Southern tour. He thought my work was most needed in Memphis, Tennessee. I received from him my commission for that field. I met in his office Rev. A. Scofield and daughter, just driven from Camp Nelson, by returned secessionists. After a very busy New-year's day, I returned to Levi Coffin's for the night, and the next day left for Memphis, which I reached on the 6th, spending two days in Cairo.

In the evening I attended a large colored church, and at the close of the service introduced my work. The meeting, as usual, was very demonstrative. The home assigned me was a Mission Home, with thirteen teachers, Joseph Barnum, formerly of Oberlin, Ohio, being superintendent. It was a rich treat to meet several who had been co- workers in the field of clashing arms and roar of cannonading. But few can realize the strength of the tie that binds those who have labored together in the lion's den. One of the teachers being sick, at the request of the superintendent I temporarily took her place.

On my way to school, one morning, I was conducted to the place where lay twelve dead bodies till the third day after the terrible riot which occurred a few months previously. One of the bodies was half burned. I was shown another corner of the streets where lay six bodies more at the same time. O what horrible scenes were enacted then. My conductor pointed to a charred spot of earth where had stood a cabin in which lay a very sick woman, whose daughter of sixteen years stood in the door pleading with the infuriated mob not to burn their house for her mother was near dying, and it was impossible for her to carry her out. One fiend caught her up on his bayonet and tossed her into the midst of the flames of an adjoining cabin. In a moment her screams of agony were hushed by the crackling flames. Fire was then thrown into the dying woman's cabin, and both mother and daughter perished. Their charred bodies were taken out by their friends and buried with others slaughtered in the riot of May, 1866. In that riot there were forty-six negroes killed, seventy-five wounded, five rapes were committed, ten persons maltreated, and one hundred robbed, and ninety- one houses and cabins burned, besides four churches and twelve school- houses reduced to ashes. These facts were given me by white witnesses as well as colored, and they probably may be found in General Kiddoo's military record, as he was one of the officers with armed soldiers who quelled the terrible riot. I was soon relieved of school duty, and as I received a few boxes of goods, a portion of which were from England, I found constant employment in the ever-varying mission work.

The grandmother of a little girl who had died a few days before was very sick and in great distress of mind when I entered her cabin, she said imploringly, "O missus, do pray for poor me. Can God forgive sich an ole sinner as me? Can I fin' Jesus so quick as poor Mary Jane did afore she died? I knows she went so happy; I prayed all night, but 'pears like so dark; don't see de place o' de candle." I read to her of the readiness of Jesus to forgive, and how he forgave the thief on the cross, because he repented and looked to Jesus in faith even in his last moments. As I knelt by her cot I implored unbounded mercy in the Spirit's teaching this precious soul the way to enter in through the door. I left her more calm. She lingered a few days, but her mind became clear from the shadow of a cloud. She died in the triumphs of faith, leaving, she said, her little lambs with the dear Shepherd, "Dat hunted de lost sheep an' foun' her 'mid de wolves, dat scratch her mightily." The children were taken to the orphanage.

While pursuing this work our lives were daily threatened, and some had fears of another riot. One Union woman on our block told me that she had often spent sleepless nights on our account. She had heard such frequent threats that "Nigger teachers should be cleared out, as well as free niggers," that she expected every day would be our last, and every pistol shot she heard in the night, or the alarm of fire, she listened and looked in the direction of our Mission House. But I told her I did not believe we should have another riot; I believed the God of Daniel was able and willing to protect us, and that in him was my confidence.

"But you don't know these people as I do," she said, "for I have always lived here. I have sometimes thought I would not tell you. And then I made up my mind that I would, so you could be more on your guard; because they threatened, just as they do now, before that awful riot a few months ago."

The teachers who were my room-mates said they had heard of the same threats, but there were soldiers near at hand now, and when the riot broke out there were so few here they had to be called from other points to quell it.

On April 13th I visited the sick and relieved eight families. Then I went over old Fort Pickering and through the freedmen's hospital, containing one hundred and eighty-eight inmates, four of them cripples, and fifteen very old. Of one I inquired how old she was:

"I's goin' on two hundred," she answered. "Massa's book say I's one hundred and eight, an' dat is eight years for another hundred, ain't it? Dey name me Esther Jane. I was sole at sheriff's sale for debt to Massa Sparks. In de ole war Massa George Washington was a mighty kind man. He boarded wid Massa Sparks four or five weeks. He wore short breeches an' knee-buckles an' a cocked hat I kep' his room clar'd up."

She was not as blind as a number who were much younger. But her skin was full of fine as well as deep wrinkles, and of an ashen hue. I gave a little sugar and some crackers to many of them.

I returned to find a colored man who had been directed to me. He had made his escape the night before from his old master, who seemed to have no more idea of his leaving him than if there had been no proclamation of freedom. His wife had been sick a long time, and he stayed to take care of her till she died, then he watched an opportunity to bring his two little children with him. But his master he supposed was also watching, for he soon overtook him with help and took his children away from him, and his bundle of clothes that he was going to put on when he got far enough from the house to feel safe with his children. He said it was his best suit. The shirt and drawers he had on were good, and they constituted his entire wardrobe. I laid out a number of garments, and told him to go into the store-room and select a whole suit that would best fit him. The next thing to be done was to accompany him to Colonel Palmer's office, where he told his own pitiful story, and the colonel asked him if he could take care of his children if he got them.

"If you'll be so good as to help me get them, these hands," (holding them out toward the colonel) "shall take as good care of them as they do of me," and his eyes filled with tears. I left him with the colonel, who told him he would send with him an escort of soldiers the next morning, "and the master will not dare refuse to give up the children on reading the note I shall send him."

A little excitement existed over the murder of Mr. Errickson, a Union man, who fled to Memphis with his family for safety during the war. A few weeks before the present time, he returned to his home in Summerville. He had been home but a few days before he was shot dead in front of a store. His poor wife and two daughters were almost insane over his untimely death. He thought the country was becoming more quiet, and he could risk going quietly to their home. There was a very smart colored woman in town who witnessed his murder. She was at Memphis ostensibly to do a little trading; but her errand was to inquire of the real friends of the colored people which man they had better vote for--Parson Brownlow or the conservative candidate--for governor. The men did not dare to come, for fear they would be mistrusted; and she came to learn from Union men their choice for governor, to take back word, and report at Summerville.

I was one day passing the old barracks of soldiers, then occupied by freedmen. I heard distressing groans, and called to see whence they came. I found an old man of ninety-seven years, called "Uncle Philip," in great bodily distress. "How long have you been suffering like this?" I inquired.

"Only two years," he said.

"Two years must seem a great while."

"O no, it's only a little minute, compared with eternity of rest in glorious mansions Jesus went to prepare for me; for I knows I's got a home thar', missus, I knows it, 'case I's seen it, an' I feels it."

"How long have you felt this evidence?"

"I seen it cl'ar as sunshine when I was ten year ole. My massa was a mighty wicked, swearin', cruel man. An' his overseer was a mighty big wicked black man; his name was Munday. An' all the seventy-five grown han's on the plantation was mighty wicked too. I hear so much swearin' I had a bad ide' of God and Jesus; I reckon'd they's some great men, that sent people to a mighty bad place. One day a Methodis' minister stop to Massa Malachi's for dinner. When he lef' massa call me to bring his hoss to 'im. An' de preacher put his han' on my head an' say, 'Philip is a smart little boy. An' if you'll ask God to make you good he'll do it. Then when you die you'll go to that great, beautiful city up yonder, where it's all light and beautiful. Here little Philip has to go 'round among stubs and stones, barefoot; there he'll walk the golden streets in silver slippers. Here he wears his slip; there he'll be dressed in a beautiful white robe. Here he goes bareheaded; there he'll wear a beautiful crown, all glittering with stars. Wouldn't you like to go to such a beautiful city as that when you die?' 'Yes, sir,' I say. 'Well, ask God to make you good, and that will be your home; for Jesus loves little children.' An' he jump'd on his hoss and rode away, while I stood thar, wonderin' what sort of a man that could be, that knew so much 'bout God and heaven. Now I must fin' God, to ask 'im to make me good; an' f'om this man's 'scription, he must be settin' on some cloud. Day and night I watch for 'im; an' when I looked upon the stars I wondered if these sparklin' stars was what God put in de crowns he put on de heads of all good people an' good chillen.

"One day Aunt Milla, the cook, sent me to pick up an armful of wood for her. While I stood lookin' up to de clouds, huntin' for God, I hear a sweet soft voice say, 'Chile, pray.' I look all 'mong de tree- tops, to see who's thar, an' it say, 'Chile, pray,' again. An' I was sure somebody up in de tree-tops, an' I got scared, an' drop my armful of wood, an' run to Aunt Milla, all out o' bref. 'What ails you, Phil? What's the matter?' she said. 'Somebody's in de tree-tops, an' say, "Chile, pray."' 'Hush, chile,' Aunt Milla said, 'dat's God talkin to you.' 'No 't ain't. I's been huntin' for God a good many days, an' can't fin' im.' 'Honey, you can't see God wid de eyes you sees Aunt Milla. God is a great good spirit dat knows all 'bout what you want, an' what you're thinkin' 'bout. I wish I was a Christian, but I ain't. I's hearn Christians talk, an' I knows dat God's talkin' to you, honey. Now, you go by yourse'f, alone like, an' ask God to make you good, as you say you want to, an' he'll do it, sure.'

"Here was a new thought, dat I could fin' God, an' not see 'im. But I did as Aunt Milla tole me. It 'peared like I must fin' God. My heart ached like, all thro' me, I's so anxious. Only a few days after I was totin' an armful o' plates to the dinin'-room for Aunt Milla. All at once I's so happy I didn't know myse'f. I drop my plates, an' broke I don't know how many. But I didn't stop for plates; I shouted, 'Bless Massa Jesus! Glory! Glory hallelujah to God! I 'a foun' 'im; I knows it's God.' I got hold of my papa and mamma, an' tole 'em to ask God to make 'em good, an' he'd do it; an' took hold of my little mate July, 'bout my age, an' tole 'im he mus' pray, an' I'd pray for 'im. In a few days he got 'ligion too. An' two young white ladies, Massa Malachi's nieces, lived thar', an' learned us to sing the sweet hymn:

> "'My Savior, my Almighty Friend,
> When I begin thy praise,
> Where shall the growing numbers end,
> The numbers of thy grace?'

An' I tole July we'd have prayer-meetin's in our cabin of nights, an' de ole folks gathered 'round us, an' our cabin was full. Massa Malachi Murphy was angry 'bout it; sometimes he'd scold, sometimes make fun o' me, an' call me de 'big preacher, Howlin' Phil.' But as all dat didn't put me down, he call me to 'im an' say, 'You shall stop this prayin' an' singin' in your cabin, or I'll whip you to death,' an' he swore I was ruinin' his plantation. My papa an' mamma tried to get me to stop. They said, 'You know Massa Malachi will do jus' as he say.' 'O no, I can't stop prayin' to Jesus, he's so good to poor me. I can't stop prayin', I said. But we did stop our prayer-meetin's in our cabin, but we had our night meetin's in a deep ravine over a quarter of a mile away. Forty or fifty of our fellow slaves would, meet us thar to hear us pray an' sing. At las' massa set de overseer, Munday, to watch us, an' he found us out. He ordered Munday to bring July an' me to 'im afore sun up. When we come in sight of de yard we seen two ropes hangin' to a big tree limb, an' I stop an' look to July, an' to de woods, wid a half a min' to run. But July says, 'We knows we can't stop prayin', an' we knows what we'll take jus' as well firs' as las'.' Then I was 'shamed to think I was firs' in de cause, an' July stronger'n me. An' we went through de gate an' stood afore massa, settin' in de back door in his night shirt. He began to swear we was ruinin' his whole plantation, an' now he was goin' to have us whipped to death. 'Now you see you've got to die or stop prayin'; will you stop this d----d prayin'?' 'O massa, do please let me pray to God, do please.' 'Strip off your slip, tie 'im up thar, Mun, an' give 'im a full round.' It was done accordin' to order; twenty lashes with the bull whip, an' twenty strokes with the paddle. Turning to July, he said, 'Will you stop prayin' or die?' 'Massa, do please let me pray to God,' said July. With an oath, he was bidden to take off his slip, an' tied to the other rope with a rail at the lower end, nearly touching the ground. The paddle was an inch board four inches wide, three or four feet long, whittled at one end for the handle, having six or eight inches bored full of holes, each hole drawing a blister at every stroke. The full round was given to July as ordered, twenty lashes with the bull whip and twenty strokes with the paddle. With an oath he turned again to me, 'Now, have you got enough to stop your praying or will the devil die?' 'O massa, do please let me pray to God, he is so good,' I answered. 'Mun, give 'im another full round,' and twenty lashes with the whip, and twenty strokes with the paddle was again given. Again he queried July, who gave the same reply as before, and the full round was ordered and given again. Then he ordered him to be cut down, swearing that he would whip him to death the next time he heard of his praying. But he swore he'd have the little devil, Phil, whipped to death now, as he was first in this 'devilish' praying. As I expected to die, I prayed all through this terrible ordeal that Jesus would come near to help me endure it, in his name.

"I felt him like he was by my side," continued Uncle Philip, as the tears dropped thick and fast, often stopping a moment to find utterance. "Massa bid July go home an' behave, an' he order' de overseer to give me another round unless I'd promise to stop prayin'. But it 'peared like I felt stronger in de Lo'd, an' I give de same answer, and I can't tell how long I was whipped an' paddled, for when I cum to, I was cut down, and layin' in de blood on de groun'--I fainted away. Massa was lookin' at me thar in his night shirt; I see him as cl'ar as if't was done yesterday. He swore I should never cum in his sight again, or cum inside dat gate, pointing to it. I prayed in my heart for God to give me strength to git up and walk to de quarters, for the pain an' loss of blood made me so weak an' faint. But de good Lo'd was thar, an' I presently got strong enough to get up an' took my slip in han', an' staggered out dat yard, and cum up to July. He stop on de way to see if I was 'live. When we pass de quarters all along, de old men an' women stood at their doors cryin'.

When we got out o' sight of de great house, one ole man an' 'oman called us to 'em an' oiled our backs. Da said we was all cut up to a jelly, an' put soft cloth over de gashes. Our people tried harder'n ever to stop our prayin' an' singin', caze Massa Malachi sure to kill us.

"A few days after massa sent for me, an' I 'spected he'd finish me dis time sure. But I felt Jesus was close by me; I was weak in de body, but strong in de Lo'd. I obeyed, as I stood all trimbly afore 'im. 'Well, howlin' preacher, if you are boun' to preach you shall preach,' an' he swore I should have enough of it. 'Next Sunday, at eleven o'clock you shall preach; I'm going to invite all the white folks an' black people 'round here to cum to hear de big preacher. I'm going to have a pulpit built under that big tree' (pointing to one in the yard two rods from the one the ropes were tied to when we was whipped). 'Now we'll have a big meetin' to hear de big preacher. You understan', do you?' 'Yes, massa,' I say, an' he sent me away. I tol' July what massa said. 'Now we mus' pray to God to sen' a minister, an' pray God to soften massa's heart, to let 'im preach, for you knows Massa Malachi mil do jus' as he says he will, an' God will answer our prayer.' At nights I went to one plantation an' July went to another, an' we tried to git some Christian man or some Christian woman to promise to preach if massa would consent. But not one would promise. They all knew it was just for sport. Sunday morning came with a great parade of hauling boards, an' a pulpit was built."

Uncle Philip said it looked more terrifying to him than would a gallows if built for his own hanging. People gathered from all directions, both white and colored, and filled the whole yard. The hour of eleven brought the master to the door in his arm-chair, with his family Bible in his lap. Taking his watch from his pockets, he called out, "Come on, my big preacher."

"I obeyed the command," said Uncle Philip, "as I stood afore 'im. 'Now we are to hear this howling preacher,' he said, sneeringly, 'ad you can't preach without the Bible, an' I'll hold it wide open, an' you must look right at me when you preach. The time is up; go to your pulpit.' I asked July if he would go up with me and help me sing--

"'My Savior, my Almighty Friend'

Nodding an assent, we went on. It 'peared like I was too weak to go up four or five steps. I trimbled an' sweat all over. But once I was up my strength cum to me, and we sung so loud de people say da hear ev'ry word all over dat great yard. By de time we got to de las' line of third verse de people was cryin' for mercy an' down on dair knees crying, 'Lo'd, what shall I do to be saved? 'Lo'd have mercy on me, a sinner!' 'Be merciful to poor me, or I'm lost.' These cries we hear'n from every side. I never felt happier or bolder in my life, while tears of joy ran down as I faced my ole massa. He slam de door shut, an' da said he jumped between two feather-beds to keep from hearin' de cries of de people. I tell you, honey, de Lo'd made dat hymn my sin- killer on dat blessed day, long, long to be 'membered."

"And did you preach?" I asked.

"Preach, chile; de Lo'd did all de preachin' dat day. We finish' de hymn, an' we went down an' talked an' prayed wid de seekers, an' we staid dar all night, an' afore next mornin' twenty-three was converted an' praisin' God. Massa call for me, an' I 'spected my time cum now anyhow. But I was ready for death or life. I went without fear of any thing. He looked at me as mile as a lamb, an' said, 'Phil, my boy, you may preach, pray, or sing as much as you please, an' go where you please, an' you shall never be hit another lick as long as I live.' I bowed low an' said, 'Thanky, Massa Malachi; God bless you, massa.' I praised God as I turned away from, him who had caused me so much sufferin'.

"But God turned it into a great blessin'. He dismissed his overseer, an' never 'lowed one of his slaves to be punish' after that great day. In one year seventy-three on dat plantation was converted. Two nieces of massa's was 'mong 'em, besides a few other white folks. But Massa Malachi tried to git 'em to give up 'ligion, an' sent 'em to dancin' frolics. An' da come to me for advice as if I was deir brover. I tole em Massa Malachi took keer of 'em, 'caze day was orphans, an' de sin would res' on de uncle dat make 'em go agin deir will, and not on dem. Two years after one of 'em got married an' moved thirty miles away, an' she got leave of massa to let me go an' stay a week or two at a time. At las', poor gal, she died of consumption, and sent for me a month afore she died to stay wid her, an' she often asked me to pray wid her. O how happy she died, in full faith in de 'ligion she foun' on de blessed day massa compel me to preach, little thinkin' he was 'pointin' a meetin' for de Lo'd of hosts instead of little Phil. But my people on other plantations often sent for me to preach, but I never call it preachin', only 'ligious talks. Da would have me help organize Churches all 'roun' thar. In four years we organized seven Churches an' the cause prospered.

"At las' so many persecutions an' sufferin' was goin' on I got disheartened. I began to question whether it wan't me causin' all dis sufferin', an' I stop goin' to prayer-meetin' four months, an' de ministers an' Christian men an' Christian women come to see me an' say, 'Brodder Philip, why don't you come to meetin', as you use' to?' I tole 'em, 'caze I didn't feel like it. Said one man, 'I's feared de devil's got hold of you.' I tole 'im I 'spected he'd had hold o' me a long while, for I felt bad enough to be his work. I tole 'im Massa Malachi made me preach, an' God didn't have nothin' to do wid it, for he knew massa was a wicked man."

These doubts and fears seemed to follow Uncle Philip day and night, until, as, he said, his distress was great. Then, he fell into an insensible, lifeless state, in which he lay fourteen days. Said he:

"My mother dressed me for de grave; but as my limbs did not stiffen, Mada Malachi sent for a doctor who placed a glass before my face, an' moisture gathered on it. He tole 'em it was not entirely cole over de heart, an' da mus'n't bury me until decomposition took place, cuze it might be a trance. An' da kep' me in de kitchen wid Aunt Milla, de cook, to watch me. It 'peared like I's goin' down into a horrible place of awful soun's an' rattlin' of chains; an' I prayed mightily for help, an' Jesus reached down an' took my han' an' lifted me up to a glorious palace so beautiful, an' every thing was light. Steps seemed built out of light, somehow made into sub'sance, I can't 'escribe it. My guide tole me I was wrong to doubt, when God had been so good to me in all my hard trials. He showed me de windows dat let light down to dis earth, an' to de churches I helpt organize. It seemed like bein' led from place to place into a mighty big country. When I seen 'em all dress' in pure white robes an' singin' such splendid music, I look at myself and see how filthy an' ragged I look; I say to my guide, 'I can never go in dat company.' 'Yes you can when Jesus wash you in his blood. All you see was as filthy an' ragged as you. But da is made clean.' An' we crossed over a line like, an' firs' I know I's in de pure white robe too, an' singin' wid all dat great company. O I can't 'escribe, how happy I felt in rangin' wid my guide de fields of light an' sich glorious visions. At las' he said, 'You mus' go back to earth an' teach your people de way to dis glorious home, dat is your home if you be faithful in readin' dis book.' I said, 'I am a slave back thar, an' can't read.' 'But this book you can read,' an' he laid de open book on my outstretched lef' arm; de tip of de golden leaves reach the tip of my fingers, an' the other tip of the leaves touch my head. He took me two or three little steps, an' I thought I was back to earth, an' I ask Aunt Milla for a drink as I was so thirsty. And she said de bucket of water was on de bench, an' my little cup by it.

"When I cum to myse'f I was standin' by de bucket drinkin' out o' my cup. But nobody was in de house but Mina, a little gal 'bout eight year ole, massa bought out of a drove was passin' by de kitchen door, and run to the fiel' shoutin' all de way 'Phil's alive! Phil's alive!' An' all de han's on de plantation cum runnin' to de house, an' my mother caught me firs', 'Praise God, my chile's alive.' De firs' I said, 'I's been wrong to doubt God, I never, never will doubt him any more.' I never can, for I's had a glimpse of hell, and have been in dat beautiful world of light."

I have given Uncle Philip's narrative in his own language as I took it down in my note-book at the time of my interviews with him. His was indeed a green old age; his mind remarkably clear, and his memory retentive. From time to time, as I read a chapter or a psalm, he often referred to certain passages that he had dwelt upon since I had left him. In relating his history be often shed tears; at one time with his elbows resting upon his knees, and face buried in the calico 'kerchief until it was wet. At another time he was just raising himself up from the kneeling position--when I came in. "I's jus' bin prayin' for you," he said. "I did't know as you's so near, but I felt your spirit. It sort o' lifs me up to talk wid you. I prayed dat de good seed you's sowin' 'mong our people may lodge in good groun' an' bring a hundred fol'. De men you talked to on de bridge 'bout swearin' never'll forgit your words. You's doin' more for our poor, ignorant people dan you knows on."

He lived about a year after I left Memphis, Tennessee. I sent him occasionally two or three dollars, through Superintendent Barnum or his wife, who often called to see his wants supplied. The last words he uttered were a few lines of one of his favorite hymns, "Give me wings," and his happy spirit took its flight; having faithfully read the book he said he had always kept in his heart. I was often forcibly impressed while conversing with that aged saint. How manifest is the power of our Wonderful, in his dealing with his followers, just according to their needs. That poor ignorant man could not read the written Word, but God took his own way to lead and instruct him, to fit him for an instrument in his hand of turning many souls to the knowledge of the truth as it is in Jesus.

On May 11, 1867, I took the cars for home. Having instructions from the American Missionary Association and transportation, I took fifteen homeless orphans to our asylum in my former school, Raisin Institute. I left this field of arduous toiling, often passing the former residence of John P. and Thomas K. Chester, who had so often threatened my life. Both closed their earthly career by untimely deaths. I reached home on the 14th, praising the God of Daniel for his keeping power in the lion's den.

"STATE PUBLIC SCHOOL"

AFTER my return my health gave way, as did also that of our worthy agent, Catherine Taylor. She endured great suffering from inflammation of the sciatic nerve, and was entirely disabled from labor for months. Late in the Autumn our supplies ran very low, and our self-sacrificing president was also in poor health. She, with a few other members of the board, visited the asylum, and found nothing on hand but corn-meal and turnips, which, with a little milk that was made into a gravy, was all there was to keep the children from starving. Our president ran in debt twenty-six dollars at the mill and grocery; but on Thanksgiving-day a collection of sixty-six dollars was taken for the asylum. This liquidated the debt, and furnished the necessary food for the time being. But Winter was approaching, and the failing health of the workers seemed to forebode the necessity of closing our asylum work.

Mrs. Catherine Rice corresponded with friends of the work in Grand Rapids, asking them to unite with us in a petition to the State Legislature to establish a State manual labor school in Grand Rapids, as the friends in that city were arranging for a local orphan asylum. The subject was discussed in the board, but a small majority voted against uniting their local interests with the State work. During this time, all new material sent in for clothing was exchanged for food, and Jane A. Smith and our faithful teacher applied to a few friends and received temporary aid. On December 15, 1870, we found the provisions too short to last for two weeks. The question came up, What shall be done for the twenty children for whom no homes are provided? Under the circumstances, there seemed no alternative but to return the children to their respective county infirmaries. When this decision was reached by the board of managers, and made known to the matron and teacher, on the evening of their week-day prayer-meeting, the matron informed the children of it. Eleven of them had made a profession of religion, and had given evidence of having found Him who said, "Suffer little children to come unto me, and forbid them not" Each of these offered earnest prayer for God to help them live so faithfully that he would make friends for them, to bring them something to eat, "so we won't have to go back to the county poor-house."

All this time my children and friends had not allowed me to know the condition of the asylum. Our firm friend, Rebecca Bennett, and our president called on my physician to ask permission to see me for advice as to whom they could write for aid. He replied, "With your calm and judicious manner, I can risk you." But they came far short of making a full revelation of the true state of things. I advised them to write the superintendent of the Congregationalist Sabbath-school at, Franklin Center, and to the pastor of the Methodist Episcopal Church in Tecumseh. They proposed that I should dictate to my daughter what to write. This was done, and my appeal was read in their respective congregations. Within a week two sleigh-loads, containing grain, flour, meal, and beef, and a whole dressed sheep, came from those places. The drivers rolled in barrel after barrel from each of the sleighs, and said they would bring more before this was gone. One little boy of eleven years said:

"Mrs. Smith, don't you think God sent all this 'cause we prayed so hard the other night?"

"My child," she answered, "the Lord has heard our prayers, and has answered; and, although it is snowing hard, yet you must hurry, and hitch Jack to the buggy as quick as possible, so that we can let Mrs. Haviland know this; for I have been afraid she has been worse since she learned we were so nearly out."

Soon she came into my room with the glad tidings: "Do not take another anxious thought over our asylum. We had more supplies come to us to- day than we have had for two months--two heavy sleigh-loads." We clasped each others' hands and wept for joy, and praised God, from whom all blessings flow.

This news revived the spirits of those whose hands were hanging down, and gave them courage to reappoint officers. Rev. Dr. Asa Mahan's wife served as president, with other officers, duly elected. A petition to the Legislature was drafted and industriously circulated, and printed copies were sent to a number of the superintendents of counties who had favored our project. Though the Legislature was in session, and there was not time to circulate it as extensively as desirable, yet Dr. Mahan and others thought it might succeed, although there were heavy drafts upon our Legislature of 1870-71. The State Prison was to be enlarged, the Insane Asylum to be improved, and additions to Ann Arbor University made, while there were still other calls for appropriations. All these made the success of our scheme look doubtful to many. All I could do was to continue in prayer that senators and representatives might feel the importance of looking after the pressing wants of our future men and women, soon to fill our vacated places. I found many children in the county poor-house through the debauchery of their fathers, and occasionally mothers.

The improvement, both in conduct and in morals, of the neglected little waifs whom we had gathered into our asylum, urged us on in our work; for we realized that our experiment was a success. Our friends were thus encouraged to press forward with the petition.

Dr. Mahan and his wife, our president, went before the Legislature with the view of pressing our claims. Members of the Senate and House proposed to grant Dr. Mahan one evening in representing the project, and left it in the hands of the Committee on Petitions. Senator Randall, of Coldwater, put it in the form of a bill that covered the spirit and requests of the petition. Being chairman of the Committee on Bills, he presented it in the Senate. It was passed in that body, to our great joy, and soon after was passed in the House, and received the governor's signature, making it a law.

Though only thirty thousand dollars were appropriated by the Legislature with which to commence operations, yet I knew the State would carry on the work hereafter. The site for the new asylum was to be selected at whatever desirable locality offered the most liberal donations. As Coldwater offered thirty thousand dollars toward the new enterprise, it was located in that city. While the buildings for the State school were being erected, our asylum was moved into the city of Adrian, as at that point it was more convenient for the sisters composing the board of managers to care for it. When the "State Public School" should be opened, all in our asylum not provided with homes were to be transferred to it.

My health improved sufficiently to enable me to make a few appeals to bring up arrears in our work. The matron and myself had received but very little, as all went to the support of the children. I cared but little for myself; but for sister Smith, who had been such a faithful, mother to these poor children, I was more anxious. At length I secured permission of my tender care-takers--my two daughters--to go among my friends in Detroit. To most of them I appealed by letter, and made but one personal call. That was more particularly in the interest of a prisoner for whom I solicited a pardon.

This was at length granted. Governor Baldwin had known of my asylum work, and inquired after its interests. He gave me twenty dollars towards it. Mr. Crapo's son gave me twenty-five dollars, and Captain E. B. Ward fifty dollars. Others responded to my letters, and I obtained over two hundred dollars.

The great fires in Chicago and Northern Michigan stopped farther work of this character; but we did what we could toward canceling arrearages, being confident that were it not for the continued and faithful toiling of Jane A. Smith the asylum would have died during my long and serious illness. It must have died, even after its removal to Adrian, had it not been for a faithful few.

A few months after the State Public School was opened at Coldwater, in charge of Professor Truesdell, superintendent, and Miss Emma A. Hall, matron. I went into the school as seamstress and nurse, and remained there nearly two years. Instead of overhauling, cutting, and making over second-hand clothes for the three hundred little homeless waifs we had cared for in our orphans' home, we were now well supplied with bolts of substantial new material, out of which we made comfortable bedding and clothing. Here we had no care about furnishing, and no anxious fear for their support. With pleasure we saw the vast contrast in conveniences and supplies compared with our little rill in which we so long paddled our own canoe, and in which faithful laborers were still at work. It matters not by whom this great work was accomplished; it matters not by what agencies our prayer of more than four years long, previous to the adopting of this work by the State, was answered. Through an overruling power clouds and icebergs vanished, and in lieu thereof the massive brick buildings of the State Public School in Coldwater were raised, instead of the old Raisin Institute, where it drew its first breath.

CHRISTIAN LABOR AND RESULTS

IT seemed refreshing to meet with sympathizing friends after toiling for months among false brethren. It was a relief to enjoy a few days of freedom from care. After asking a few friends to sign an article of agreement to pay one dollar a year during five years for the orphan asylum, and mailing a couple of letters to Levi Coffin and Rev. E. M. Cravath, of Cincinnati, I took from the office a drop-letter from Mr. Burton Kent, County Superintendent of the Poor, containing the following notice:

"MRS. LAURA S. HAVILAND,--Many persons transported by you last year have become a county charge, and it has become an intolerable burden to the tax-payers. Any person bringing a child or indigent person into this county without being legally indentured, shall be prosecuted to the full extent of the law."

Within five minutes after reading the above notice I was on my way to our County Poor-house, three miles from town. To my surprise I found that no colored child had been there, and of the fifty-one inmates but three were colored, and only one man (Mr. Morris Brown) who came with me the previous Summer had been received. He was discharged in a short time. A stay at the infirmary for two months and a half was a burden, but was it "intolerable to the tax-payers" of our county?

I felt that I must search diligently to discover all the facts. I called on Mr. Helms, who said there was widow with four or five children that was sick a couple of weeks, and he had supplied her with a load of wood and groceries. I asked for the cost, but as it was not convenient for him to give the figures then, he said he would furnish them the following Tuesday. Mr. Young had told him that he had buried a family. I called to learn what family it was in his ward. He gave the name of the man who died after a short illness, and to whom he had taken a load of wood, a small sack of flour, and some other groceries. I inquired if he had taken these things to them more than once. He said he had not, as his wife was all there was to look after, and she took care of herself after her husband's death. He gave me the expenses--eight dollars and ninety-six cents. I called on Mr. Helms at three appointed times, and failed to get his precise figures, but, placing them at highest rates, from all I could gather it could not have been more than thirty-five dollars. I wrote an article for the Adrian Times, in which I stated the figures, and informed the citizens and tax-payers of Lenawee County that this orphan asylum was under the auspices of the American Missionary Association, which was responsible for its support. I solicited some mathematician to give us the fraction of a mill to each taxpayer as his share of this "intolerable burden upon the tax-payers."

Our county superintendents of the poor, Burton Kent and Alice Warren, the officials from whom I received the notice, were surprised to learn that the American Missionary Association was the responsible party. But all these threats sprang from prejudiced parties, and clearly indicated the necessity of a few strokes of the reconstruction brush north of Mason and Dixon's line, as well as south of it, to obliterate the color-line. Friends here and there paid me a dollar on their pledge of a dollar a year, and our colored friends in the city of Adrian--Sarah Lewis, with her brothers and Mr. Wilson, managers of a festival--realized thirty-two dollars and sixty-one cents, cash, and fifty pounds of meat, beans, fruit and clothing, valued at fifty dollars.

July the Fourth was a merry day for the forty little folks at the asylum. At dark fire-crackers, torpedoes and sky-rockets flew in every direction for an hour, when all were arranged in a semicircle and sang "John Brown," "Red White and Blue," "Rally 'Round the Flag, Boys," and a few temperance songs, in great glee. It was a happy group. We had a few visitors, who left us the happier for seeing the children and listening to their sweet voices in song.

I was often engaged in procuring good homes for these orphans. A few homes were found that were not suitable, and the children were withdrawn and placed in other homes.

On September 19th I met Mrs. Edgerton, the matron of our asylum, with T. D. Allen, of Kalamazoo, agent under J. R. Shipherd, secretary of the American Missionary Association, who were authorized to build a schoolroom for the asylum. Heretofore the children's play-room had been used for the school during the warm season. As the American Missionary Association was doing a great work in the late slave States in maintaining freedmen's schools, the officers concluded to solicit aid, in the State of Michigan for the building of the much needed school-room. They urged me to engage in this work, but I thought that I had done my share, in giving the time I had to soliciting money for the purchase of supplies. Besides Elizabeth L. Comstock had given one thousand dollars in money, with which to enlarge the little farm to thirty-five acres, buy a horse, and furnish the little folks with hats, etc. Then I wanted to look for a home, as I was becoming rather weary of singing the old song,

> "No foot of land do I possess,
> No cottage in this wilderness."

This had been my condition for nearly three years; but with all my pleading, I failed to be released. As it was already cooler weather, and Winter would soon overtake us, T. D. Allen said I had worked long enough without reward, save that of blessing these little homeless waifs, and now, if I would take hold of this enterprise, I should be paid the same amount he was receiving.

At length I agreed to spend a week or two at least, and took from him the bill of all the kinds of lumber needed, and left for Detroit. Judge F. C. Beaman furnished me with a letter of introduction, indorsed by Rev. Dr. George Duffield, of Detroit. I called, as he advised, on Samuel Pitts, who subscribed one hundred dollars in lumber. I selected out of my bill what was first called for to enable the carpenters already engaged to commence their work. I then called on Mr. Cooper, freight agent, to secure, if possible, free transportation to Adrian; to him I gave my introductory letter. When he glanced at the heading, without reading it, he gave it a toss on his table toward me, with a look of disgust, saying, "I've seen that thing before, and I've nothing to do with it."

"That is a mistake," said I; "that paper is from F. C. Beaman, and not a week old."

"If I'm not very much mistaken I've seen it before."

"Well, you are very much mistaken, for I brought it to this city with me yesterday, and I have not been in your office until this minute. But I am not soliciting money. I only called to see if I can secure free transportation for one hundred dollars' worth of lumber to Adrian for an orphan school-room, as forty little homeless waifs, under our care, have no school-room, except a wood-house and play-room. The cold weather will soon overtake us."

He listened patiently to my short speech, and said he had no authority to grant such a favor; that I would have to write to C. H. Hatch, then in Chicago.

"I know he would grant it," I said, "for he granted this quarter pass on his road for my mission work," showing the pass.

He turned it over and spent double the time in examining it that he did on my introductory letter, and said, slowly, "I think I will risk sending this car-load," and wrote an order to his assistant to send it forthwith to Adrian.

I thankfully returned to my duty of calling on the list of the benevolently inclined wealthy persons whose names Dr. Duffield and J. F. Conover had furnished. Rev. Dr. Hogarth, Mr. Raymond, the book-merchant, and Rev. Dr. Duffield gave sufficient to pay the cartage of the lumber to the depot. Soon it was on its way. I dined at Moses Sutton's, who gave $5, and his sister Annie $1. Mr. Brooks gave me $25 in lumber. Mr. Bronson gave five thousand shingles; another gave $2.50 in shingles.

After a few days at home I returned, October 25th, to Detroit, and toiled, like the fishermen, nearly all day, and caught nothing. Weary, and almost discouraged, I was about to retire to my resting-place at Augustus Leggett's, when one gave $5, another $2. The following day I called on C. Merrill, who gave $5; another gave $5; Mr. R. C. Renuick gave $10; Mr. Whitney gave $5. Weariness coaxed me to another sweet resting-place, the home of my dear friends J. F. and Hannah Conover. I called on a few persons whose names had been given me by Mr. Palmer, from whom I received $17; and from a few others I received $15. John Bagley gave $10; another gave $5; Rev. J. A. Baughman, $5; and Mr. King, his son-in-law, $5. I also called on Governor Crapo, who gave $5. Others gave $5, $2, and $1, until I had forty dollars more to aid in constructing our school-room.

We secured sufficient means to build our school-room. In all, with the favors granted by the Michigan Southern and Lake Shore Railroad, we received about four hundred dollars.

Through the kindness of my friend, L. Tabor, Esq., who purchased a house and small lot for me, I again had a place for my children to occupy, which I could call my home; for which I praised the Lord, from whom all blessings flow.

As our orphan asylum was now in a good condition, Mrs. Edgerton, the matron, said the secretaries of the three divisions of the Missionary Association, Chicago, Cincinnati, and New York, met and voted her one hundred dollars a month, with which to carry forward this asylum. She deemed this an ample supply, with what had been raised on the place. She said it was then on a more substantial basis than it had been during the year she had had it in charge.

Through General O. O. Howard I learned that mission work was much needed in Charleston, South Carolina, and received from him transportation to that city by way of Washington, District of Columbia.

My health being now restored, on January 29, 1869, I left my sweet home and loved ones at three o'clock P. M., and spent the night in Toledo, with my old friends, William Merritt and wife. I attended with them the prayer-meeting in the new colored church. I arrived at Pittsburg with but little detention. Passing through the mountains, we found the snow deeper than when I left Michigan. At seven A. M. we passed the wreck of three cars which had run off the embankment and were still burning. Among the killed taken from the wreck was a woman partially burnt. I did not learn the number of killed and injured. Among these dead and dying I should probably have been had I not spent the night in Toledo, as this was the train, I would have been on had I remained on the one I left. O, how sad to look upon this smoldering wreck, from which I had so narrowly escaped! This was the third accident of this kind which I had thus providentially missed in my travels by river and rail of three thousand miles. Many are the dangers, seen and unseen, through which I have passed, and the remembrance of this disaster calls forth a renewed song of deliverance and praise for the Guiding Hand that preserves through the vicissitudes of this ever-changing life.

I arrived in Washington early in the morning, and took breakfast with my friend Dr. Glenan. Here I found my brother, Harvey Smith, and his son, who were teaching freedmen's schools, and with them I spent the Sabbath, In the evening I attended the Colored Methodist Episcopal Church, and was invited to address the large meeting. I spoke half an hour, and told the history of Uncle Philip, and how, amidst the persecutions and sorrows to which his slave-life subjected him, he had kept his hand in the hand of his Savior all these ninety-seven years.

While speaking of his being whipped until he fainted, a few wept aloud, and after meeting a number came to tell me of their being whipped for praying. One woman was whipped until she fainted, and one man was kept in the stocks all night after being whipped, and came near dying. His master told him he "would whip the praying devil out of him," using the same words that Uncle Philip's master used to him.

The surgeon-in-chief, Dr. Reynolds, wished me to remain in Washington another day, and thought General Howard would permit me to stay there for a time, to engage in sanitary work. I had an interview with the general, who thought I was most needed in Washington, during the Winter season at least. He gave me authority to visit the free soup- houses, and investigate the sanitary work generally. After reading my commission, I told him I had a request to make, and that was that the authority with which I was vested, might be kept secret. To investigate to the best advantage was my object. I was also appointed to examine, as far as practicable, the condition of applicants for charity, and the manner in which the charity was applied. My office was furnished, and board was allowed me at the head-quarters of the freedmen's hospital in Campbell Camp.

On February eth I called at Josephine Griffin's relief office before 10 o'clock A. M. Between sixty and seventy persons called on her, mostly for work. I followed a number of the applicants for soup- tickets to their homes. In visiting twenty families during the day, I found a number of persona in squalid wretchedness. One man was very sick with a high fever, and unconscious. He had received no help, because unable to make personal application, and he had no family to intercede for him. His bed was a pile of rags in the corner on the floor. I called for the Bureau physician and saw that he had suitable bed-clothing and food. The physician said he must have died within two or three days in that condition. Among the applicants for relief was an Irishwoman, who had a brick house she was renting, except the back room, which she occupied, and had another nearly finished. She and her family for whom she was begging soup, lived in good style.

The fourth day of my investigations revealed great deficiency in properly looking after applicants for aid. The greatest sufferers were often too diffident to ask for help. The soup-houses were generally well managed. I called as one whom curiosity had drawn into the motley crowd, and was treated to a taste of fine soup, even at the "Savage Soup-house," where I saw two caldrons of soup. The one from which I was served might well tempt the palate of an epicure, but the other looked too forbidding for a human stomach. I soon found the good soup was being given to the white applicants, who were first served, while the colored people, standing in the yard, were waiting their time. Policeman Ross told a shivering colored man to go inside and put his pail on the farther block for soup.

"I shall be sent out," he replied.

"I tell you to go in," said the policeman; "I'll see to that."

He obeyed the order, only to receive curses: "You know better than to come yet; another thing you know, this soup is for white folks, the other is for niggers."

At this, Policeman Roes canoe in: "I have seen," said he, "fish made of one and flesh of another long enough. Here are women and children standing out on the ice and snow, waiting all this afternoon for you to serve the white people first. Another thing I'd like to know, why is this difference in the soup? That black stuff is hardly fit for pigs to eat, Mr. Savage, and you know it."

"Our citizens furnish material for this soup," replied he, "and our citizens shall have it."

"Doesn't General Howard furnish a hundred pounds of beef and two hundred loaves of bread each day? and on Saturday it is double. Another thing I'd like to know--are these not our citizens?" pointing toward the yard full of colored people.

"There are ten thousand too many of 'em, and it's none of your business; I shall do as I please."

"I will let you know; I shall make it my business to report you to General Howard."

Mr. Savage poured out a horrid volley of oaths at him, adding that all his reporting would make no difference with him. One Irish woman received three loaves of bread, four quarts of soup, and a large piece of meat. After nearly all, both white and colored, were served, the lieutenant policeman left, but Mr. Ross remained until the end of the disbursing. I was tempted to cheer the policeman for his bravery, but thought silence the better part of valor.

When Aunt Chloe's "cl'arin' up time" was come, I took my departure. I saw the policeman standing near the gate, and said in low tone, as I passed out, "I thank you for your words."

"Stop; do you live here?" he said.

"Temporarily."

"Go slowly till I get my club, so I can catch up. I want to see you."

He soon overtook me, and inquired whether I was one of the visiting committee. I told him that I was authorized by General Howard to inspect the soup-houses. He asked whether I was going to report Savage "I am on my way," I said, "to the general's office for that purpose." "I will give you my name and number," he replied, "and will run to see the lieutenant of police, who will give his name and number for reference also; I'll overtake you by the time you reach Pennsylvania Avenue" And off he ran. As I wished to inspect the poor soup more thoroughly, I called at a cabin, the home of the poor man that the policeman compelled to go in and demand the good soup. I found his quart of excuse for soup, on the stove to cook the half raw bits of turnips and potatoes. I tasted of what the policeman said was hardly fit for pigs, and fully agreed with his assertion, for the man said it made them sick to eat it without cooking it over. This man had been sick with pneumonia, and his mother very sick with it at this time I hurried to the nearest grocery, where I bought crackers, sugar, rice, bread, tea, and mustard for a plaster to put on her side. The man had received only a slice of bread with his quart of soup, for the seven reported in his family, four of whom were sick.

When I reached the avenue, I met the policeman who had nearly run himself out of breath. He was delayed in hunting for the lieutenant, who sent word that he would call on the general to confirm my report if necessary, and gave his name and number. The result of the report was, that a notice was sent at once to Mr. Savage that there must be no difference in giving to the poor, either in quality or quantity at his soup-house, and that the difference mad between white and colored, as reported to him, could not continue. In reply, Mr. Savage denied having made any difference in his soup-house, and charged the reporter with being an arrant liar, and he also made the same statement in the Daily Chronicle.

I wrote a confirmation of my report, using his own words in connection with the remarks of policeman Ross, and took it to Dr. Reyburn, Burgeon-in-chief in the sanitary work. The doctor approved my statement, and wrote a few lines of preface himself. As I used Mr. Boss's name, I called on him, who also approved, and referred to the lieutenant of police, who was present; and both sanctioned my report. This was published in the Chronicle.

At this Savage raved, and swore he would arrest me for defamation. Neither did the policeman whose name I used as reference go unscathed. The chief of the police force requested Mr. Ross to see me and learn by what authority I was acting, as there seemed to be none indicated in my article in the Chronicle. Mr. Ross said the chief of police did not doubt my authority, but would like to know, if I had no objection. I presented my paper, with a request that the matter should be held as confidential, as I did not wish to make it public.

After reading the paper he said: "I think you are authorized to inspect the work of the whole of us; I see in this the whole field is included. Would you object to my taking this to the chief of police, if I bring it back within, an hour or two? We may in some cases render you assistance."

I had no objection, and he took it. I found their assistance in a few cases very important, as well as convenient. But with all the Savage threats, nothing was done, and not even a reference was made to the subject in either of the papers. Surgeon Reyburn told me, as he was passing a corner where a group of secessionists were discussing the subject quite freely, that one man said, "Why don't Savage do something about that soup-house affair, and not be a numb-head, and let that woman wind him around her finger like that?" Another said, "If I'd lied once over that old soup-house, I'd lie again, before I'd hold still and take all that" He changed his soup-house policy for a little while; but the complaints among secession friends and white customers caused him soon afterward to backslide.

Mr. Carpenter, treasurer of the Provident Aid Society, wrote a letter to George Savage that he thought might improve him. But Surgeon Reyburn sent for me, and requested me to prepare for running the Fourth Ward soup-house, as he had heard they were going to discharge George Savage. I called on Mr. Shepherd, the proper authority to discharge him. He said that in a week or two all the soup-houses would close for the season, and, as Savage had received letters that he thought he would improve by, he would release me from the task of running the soup-house. I therefore continued visiting and relieving the sick and suffering.

I met in my rounds Dr. Cook, who said there was a child frozen to death in Kendal Green Barracks, nearly two miles away. Neither the doctor nor myself knew who had charge there. I went, and found a child of ten months old that had chilled to death. The mother said hers was the fourth child in that row of cabins that had died; and that none of them were allowed more than two four-foot sticks of fire-wood for twenty-four hours. I called at the other cabins, and found them without fire, and all told the same story of lack of wood and no coal. There was neither bedding nor clothing enough among them all to make a single family comfortable. The mother of the dead child had been to see the superintendent of the poor of the city to get a coffin. With shoes but little better than none, she had waded through melting snow until her dress was wet four inches, at least, around the bottom. I inquired who the superintendent of this camp and barracks was, and they said, Major Thompson. I went to his head-quarters, but found that be and his family had gone to the Capital to learn how President Johnson's impeachment trial was likely to end. I repaired to General C. H. Howard's office, and reported the condition of these families. He sent me back in his ambulance, with fifty loaves of bread, a coffin for the dead child, and two quilts and a few blankets for the destitute, with instructions to give the bread, except one loaf to each of the four families I had visited, to Major Townsend, a man that I had met in the Sabbath-school he superintended. He was surprised to find those families under his care in such a condition. The general furthermore requested me to make a thorough investigation of Kendal Green Barracks and camp.

The following day I visited forty families, and found twelve sick, and not sufficiently supplied. I listened to many sad stories by a white man, who had been one of Major Townsend's police guards while he had charge of Campbell Camp, before I went to Washington. I was informed that the major had charged his two police guards to bring the woman that was interfering with his camp to his office till he returned, if she should come again in his absence. Although they were quite cross, they did not take me to the major's head-quarters, as I told them I was calling by request. The major had no more idea of who the intruder was than I knew who the superintendent was until I made my report to the general, when he informed me that it was not Thompson, but Major Townsend, to whom I had been introduced in a colored Sabbath-school. But as he knew by the supplies which I took to the families that they came from head-quarters, he called on General Howard, and from him learned who the inspector was, and he told the general he would aid me in calling on the poor who needed aid. While he spent most of the day in calling at my office and going to see the general, I was visiting the barracks.

For sundry misdemeanors while in office the major was relieved, and another appointed in his stead. Though I did not think he was the right man for the place, yet I felt sorry for his excellent family. His wife and two young lady daughters I had called on, and was much pleased with their self-sacrificing Christian spirit.

There was much excitement in Washington during a portion of May, on account of the impeachment and trial of President Johnson. At length, on the 16th of the month, the news spread that he was acquitted of the high charges made against him by the House of Representatives, and that his power was left uncurtailed. But he had turned his back upon our brave soldiers, who bled and died to save the nation's life, and made no serious effort to put an end to the Kuklux outrages in the Southern States. For this reason many demanded that he be removed from his office. With them his acquittal foreboded ill; but we hoped for the best.

Uncle Dodson, aged sixty-five years, a plantation preacher and a resident of Campbell Camp, caused great excitement when he found his long-lost wife and she found her long-lost husband. Twenty years before the husband and wife were torn apart by the unrelenting slave- master. Weeping and begging to be sold together, while kneeling at the master's feet, they were only answered by a kick and the lash. Now they met again. In the front yard the wife came running to him crying out, "O Ben Dodson, is dis you? I am your own Betty." And she clasped him closely. "Glory! glory! hallalujah! Dis is my Betty, shuah," he said, pushing her away to look at her face. "I foun' you at las'. I's hunted an' hunted till I track you up here. I's boun' to hunt till I fin' you if you's alive." And they both wept tears of joy. "Ah, Betty, we cried harder'n dis when da sole us apart down dar in Egyp'." And another, outburst of joy followed. They were soon happily living together in their own little cabin.

The old man had some queer Scripture quotations. One he recited in meeting twice before I had an opportunity of correcting him, and that was, "Adam called his wife's name Eve because she was the mother of all evil." As Uncle Dodson often wished me to read a chapter in their chapel meetings "an 'splain it to us," I took occasion to read the third chapter of Genesis, and when I read,

"Because she was the mother of all living," he called out "ebil, ebil, sistah Hab'lin." Uncle Dodson was learning to read, and could read easy words in the first reader. I placed the Bible before him and pointed to the word "living." "Dat is so in dis place," he acknowledged, "but it's some place in de Bible." "Father Dodson," I said, "I have read every word in this Bible a number of times, and there is no such sentence between the two lids that Adam called his wife's name Eve because she was the mother of all evil," and a smile ran through the entire congregation. I added that it was not a wonder that these poor people should misquote Scripture, as a few years ago many of them were not allowed to learn to read. At this three of that company testified to being punished severely for learning their letters of a little white boy. I told them it was a greater wonder that they had passed through such privations and retained as much intelligence as they possessed. "O yes, well do I 'member when I was punish' too," said another, "for tryin' to learn to read." Turning to a young exhorter sitting by him, Uncle Dodson said, "Brodder Davis, I've labored in de Gospel mor'n forty years wid de white ministers and wid de black ministers, an' I neber foun' one so deep in de Scriptur' as sistah Hablin." We continued our exercises with good satisfaction.

Another of Father Dodson's comforting passages was, "Blessed is the corpse that the rain falls on." If the departed one had left no other evidence of being, prepared for the great change, then a rain on the day of the funeral was sufficient. I found this was quite generally accepted as a sure evidence with many of them.

As I was passing through the hospital yard a number of the convalescents were in a group discussing the subject of charity, thinking that some one had been too harshly judged. Said one man, "Paul said faith, hope, and charity. An' de greates' of 'em all was char'ty. An' I knows what a bigger man nor Paul said, better man too."

"An' who dat, an' what he say?" rejoined another. "He say, 'Judge not an' ye shan't be judged.'" "An' who said dat?" "'T was George Washington."

On inquiry I found his parents lived many years in the vicinity of Mount Vernon, and probably the colored people heard George Washington repeat that text, and it was handed down among them as an original saying of the Father of his Country, in their minds a greater and better man than Paul.

While engaged in my work, as the weather became very warm, I often rested an hour or two in the capitol to listen to the many witnesses who testified to the awful condition of our soldiers at Andersonville Prison, under Henry Wirtz. At the statement made concerning his stabbing and shooting the soldiers for leaning against the "dead line," the guilty man, Wirtz, shook as he arose from the sofa upon which he was reclining, and swore "that was a lie;" but General Auger, the president of the court, told him that he had nothing to say, and bade him sit down, which he did with cursing in great excitement. I some-times spent two or three hours in listening to the tale of the heartless cruelties that unprincipled wretch had committed. One woman, whose son died in that prison, was listening one afternoon. She stood in the corridor, and as he passed with his guards for the ambulance, which was to bear him back to the prison, she followed with her best weapon, a large umbrella. This she nimbly used, thrusting the pointed end into his side or back, or wherever she could hit him, saying, "You rascal, you villain, you murderer, you murdered my son in Andersonville." Her thrusts were in such quick succession that he begged the guards to protect him; but they did not interfere with the bereaved woman until they got the prisoner into the ambulance.

While I did not feel like following her example because of his murdering my cousin, yet I told General Auger that it was well for Henry Wirtz that his case was not tried by mothers and sisters of the thousands who had suffered and died under his cruelties. Said the general, "I do not know but it would be the best thing for him if mothers and sisters were his judges." But if they were the ones to give the decision, justice and mercy would never kiss each other over him. I never was an advocate of capital punishment, but I must acknowledge I did feel at times, while listening to Henry Wirtz's trial, that I would like to see that tiger in human form take a hemp swing. But when at last he received his sentence and swore he "always thought the American Eagle was a d--- buzzard," I had no desire to mingle with the multitude to witness the execution, though he well deserved the execration of all.

On May 14th I received a note from Mrs. Edgerton, stating that a peremptory order from Rev. J. R. Shipherd, secretary of the American Missionary Association at Chicago, had been received, to close the asylum immediately. From her note I learned that this was the day for the auction sale of the asylum personal property. I was confident that forty or fifty little folks could not at once be properly situated in compliance with such an order, and wrote J. R. Shipherd a proposition, reminding him of his verbal pledge and proposed terms on which we could reopen the asylum for all for whom no suitable homes might be found. I also wrote an appeal to Rev. Geo. Whipple, of the New York Division, and sent with it a copy of the proposition I had made to J. R. Shipherd. I received in reply a request to remit to that division the reply I should receive from J. R. Shipherd, or a copy, by the first mail, for they thought my proposition would be accepted. I wrote them they should have whatever reply I might receive from J. R. Shipherd, but I did not look for any word whatever from him. In the mean time I received a letter from Adrian informing me that four of the little children were already in the county poor-house, and that others would soon be taken there, that four of the younger ones were left in the streets of Adrian to find their own homes among colored people, and that four were left with a poor colored family who were promised pay for keeping them until other homes could be found. Four more were also left with a white family in Palmyra, with the promise of pay until other arrangements were made. One little girl of ten years was left with a woman of ill-fame and of drinking habits, and the little girl had been seen drunk.

I wrote to Rev. E. M. Cravath, secretary of the Middle Division, at Cincinnati, and to Levi Coffin, and learned in reply that eight of the little children were found one morning sitting on the stone steps of the office of the American Missionary Association, with a note in the hand of the oldest, aged ten or eleven years, the purport of which was, "These children were sent by you to the asylum near Adrian, Michigan. It has closed. You must take care of them." They said that Mrs. Edgerton brought them from the asylum, and sent them here in the express wagon. The office being locked, the driver left them on the steps at 6 o'clock A. M. As they had eaten nothing during the night, Levi Coffin furnished them with food, while Rev.

E. M. Cravath went to the colored orphan asylum of the city, and made arrangements by paying the board of managers one hundred dollars for their admittance. The letter from Levi Coffin contained the following queries: "What ails Michigan, that she can not care for thirty or forty of these poor little homeless orphans, when we have had a few thousands to look after in this great thoroughfare? Where is the Christianity and philanthropy of your great State, to send these children back to us, who took them from those crowded camps, where there was so much suffering and dying, for the purpose of their being properly trained, and fitted for usefulness, amid humane surroundings?" They soon found the whys and wherefores in my letter and appeal to allow the asylum to be reopened.

After writing a number of letters to the New York Division, containing a full account of the condition of the children, and sending them a copy of the letter from Adrian, I inquired whether as a Christian body they could allow these children over whom they had assumed control, and for whom they were responsible, to be turned out into the streets, to be lodged in the county poor-house, and to be left in the house of ill-fame, and appealed to them as Christian men to make some suitable arrangements for them. Their reply was: "We can not afford to allow this condition of those children. We have not received a communication in this office that has produced the deep feeling that your last letter has. We have telegraphed Mr. Shipherd to dispose of nothing more connected with that asylum. How long would it be before it could he reopened, should we replace it in the hands of its friend?" I answered, "It shall be re-opened as soon as I receive official authority from your association to do it, and I will resign my position in this work." In reply to this, the Rev. Mr. Smith, a member of the New York Division, came to Washington and authorized me to secure a part of the asylum building, and reopen it for the children that were in improper houses. I secured a pass by way of Cincinnati, in accordance with the request of Levi Coffin and Rev. E. M. Cravath, of the Middle Division. They had secured good homes for two of the children. I took the others home.

The secretaries and a few other members of the three divisions met in Oberlin to consider further concerning the asylum that had been so unwisely closed. At the close of this consultation I received a letter from Mr. Whipple, of New York, in which he stated that there was much sympathy expressed for me in behalf of the asylum by all except Mr. Shipherd, who said be had done nothing of which I or any one else had any right to complain. He was ordered to return twenty-three boxes and packages of asylum goods to me, as I was acting under their orders in reopening the home; and they sent me fifty dollars for supplies. I gathered in between twenty-five and thirty children that had previously belonged to the home, and bought back what furniture I could that had been sold at a great sacrifice. The corporation appointed me general superintendent of the asylum, and engaged me to devote my whole time to it.

Although to provide means to carry it on was no small task, yet the burden to me seemed light compared with its importance. It had cost great anxiety and effort to accomplish what we had already done. I secured a horse, repaired the buggy, and employed our soldier, Charlie Taft, whose health was much impaired from service in the army. He offered to spend the Winter with us, and render what assistance he could, for his board. Just now our prospects were brighter than at any period since Raisin Institute was converted into a home for harmless little people, to train for useful citizens, instead of tramps, or inmates of prisons.

But, alas! we were doomed to a heavy draft upon our faith. After a very busy day of measuring, cutting, and fitting garments for the little ones, I went in haste to place a bundle of patches in the box in the hall room. It was now dark twilight, and I mistook the cellar door for that of the hall. Passing through, I fell headlong seven feet against the corner of a hard-wood beam. I received many bruises, and the concussion fractured both the inner and outer layers of the left temporal bone, and severed the temporal artery. I was taken up insensible, and it was supposed that life was extinct; but in a few moments signs of life appeared, and a physician was immediately sent for. Great consternation prevailed among the children, and much sympathy was expressed, as well as many prayers offered by them in my behalf.

Brother Smart, pastor of the Methodist Episcopal Church in Adrian, was then holding a series of meetings; and being told of the accident at the evening meeting, he said: "Elder Jacokes informs me that sister Haviland is supposed to be in a dying state from a dangerous fall in the orphan asylum this evening. I propose to pursue my subject no further, but to turn this meeting into a season of prayer for her restoration, if in accordance with the Lord's will; if not, that her mantle may fall upon another, to carry forward that enterprise. The Lord can hear and answer here as readily as by her bedside." He then led in fervent supplication, followed by a few others. Said a friend present: "The announcement fell upon us like an electric shock, and I never heard brother Smart, or those who followed, pray with such power. Then brother Bird arose and said, 'I feel confident that we shall have an answer to our prayers, that sister Haviland will be restored or another take her place.'"

My dear sister in Christ, Elizabeth L. Comstock, was at that time laboring in the Master's vineyard in Chicago. Hearing of the accident by means of the telegram sent to my daughter residing in that city, she mentioned it at the Moody noon prayer-meeting, and requested prayer for my restoration, if it were the Lord's will. I was made the subject of prayer also at Pittsford Wesleyan Methodist protracted meeting.

A letter came from Rev. E. M. Cravath, of Cincinnati, addressed to me. In answer, my daughter, L. J. Brownell, wrote that "mother is unconscious from a dangerous fall, and we (her children) are earnestly praying for her restoration. If our Heavenly Father sees meet to grant our petition, you will receive a reply from her when practicable." The immediate reply was: "You may rest assured our All-wise Father will restore your mother if he has further work for her to do. You may also be assured that her friends in this city are uniting in prayer with her children for her recovery."

I was so nearly conscious at one time that I heard some one say, "She will never speak again." The thought struck me forcibly that I was going to get well, and yet I had no sense of being ill. But I reflected that my children must be very sad at the thought of giving me up, and I would try to say, "I am going to get well." With all the effort I could command I could not utter a syllable. Then I tried to see if my children were present; but I seemed to be in a pure, soft, white cloud, such as we sometimes see floating in the ethereal blue, where I could discover no countenance of those moving around my bed. Consequently I gave over the effort, and was again lost to all consciousness until three days and nights had passed. Then the first returning consciousness was the passing away of that beautiful white cloud, and I recognized my three daughters standing before me. One of them said, "Mother looks as if she knew us." Why, yes, I thought, they are my daughters; but what are their names? and what is my name? Then I surveyed the room. The papered wall, maps, pictures, and furniture all looked familiar; but where am I? Am I in some large city, or in a country place? I am advanced in years; and what have I done in all my life? But I could recall nothing.

While in this mental soliloquy, it came to me what my name was, and that this was the orphan asylum.

"Do you know me, mother?" said my daughter Jane.

It was a matter of reflection before I could utter the word "yes," and then a study to give her name. At length I pronounced it. Another daughter made the same query, and I had the answer, "yes," ready, but it seemed a hard study again to recollect the name Mira. The same effort brought to my lips the name of Esther when she addressed me.

"Don't have the least anxiety or care," she said, "about this orphan asylum, for the friends have brought gram, flour, meal, meat, and groceries in abundance." O what a relief these words brought! Surely the Lord is the Father of the fatherless.

After studying for words I said, "What is the matter?" for I felt that my head was very sore, and my face swollen. When told that I had fallen down cellar and was badly hurt, I was surprised, for I could recall nothing of the fall. After calling to mind the various residences of my daughters, and words to inquire how they knew of the accident, I was told that my son-in-law telegraphed them. At length I reached the conclusion that I became stunned by the bruise on my head, and fell asleep and slept my senses all away, and that was the reason I did not know any thing. I thought, must I learn to read again? Shall I ever know any thing? How sad it will be not to know how to read or do any thing; but I will leave all in the hands of the dear Savior. They gave me medicine that I knew I had taken. Did I not take this an hour ago? "O no, mother, not since yesterday." What day of the week is to-day? "Monday." Then to-morrow will be Tuesday. "Yes." I have got so far, I will remember that, thought I. Again another dose of medicine was given. Did I take this yesterday? "You took this two hours ago." It is certain that I do not know any thing. How sad it will be when I get well of this hurt (as I had no doubt but I should) and not know any thing. But, then, the second thought of leaving it with the Lord was a resting-place. But consciousness was gradually restored. The next day my son Daniel came; but he did not dare to approach the front door, fearing that a tie of crepe on the knob would be the first to tell him the sad story of his mother's departure He was met at the back door by his three sisters, one of whom informed him of a faint hope of my recovery, as there was evidence of returning consciousness.

A day later the fourth daughter, Anna H. Camburo, arrived. I was thus permitted to meet all my children save one, whose infant son had died the day after the news reached him of my fall. But as the children daily informed their brother Joseph of increasing hope of my recovery, he, of my six children, was the only absent one. Through their tender care and the blessing of God, in answer to many earnest prayers, I was spared to toil on a few years longer. To him alone be all the praise! My Savior never seemed nearer.

It was January, 15, 1869, when I fully realized that consciousness was restored. I renewed my entire consecration to the service of my Lord and Master. All was peace and quiet within. The inmates of the asylum, between twenty-five and thirty, were so quiet that it seemed as if no more than my own children were moving around me. During the second week, through my dear friend Elizabeth L. Comstock, seventy-five dollars was sent to us from friends in Chicago. A few days later thirty dollars came from the same city. The fourth week after the fall I was removed to my home in the city of Adrian, accompanied by my five children, three of whom then returned to their homes. In four months I had so far recovered as to be able to do moderate asylum work, and in one year I solicited and received one thousand dollars for the asylum, aside from the means sent during my inability to labor. This kept the asylum in supplies, we hardly knew how, only as it came from the Father of the fatherless. Within ten days after my arrival at home I received three checks of fifty dollars each from the Cincinnati Branch of the American Missionary Association, from the Friends' Sabbath- school, in Syracuse, New York, and from John Stanton, Washington, D.C.

In all this severe trial I had no regrets in making this scheme another specialty in my life-work. I visited nine county poor-houses, learning the number of children in each, and noting their condition, with the view of reporting to our next Legislature. In three of the county houses were girls, half idiotic, who had become mothers. In one there were twenty children of school-age, sent to school four hours each day. As I followed the matron through the dormitory and other parts of the house, I saw by the filthy appearance of the sheets and pillows, as well as a want of order generally, a great need of system. As I was about to leave I remarked to the matron, "You have many unpleasant tasks to perform here."

"La me, I guess we do," she said.

"You have plenty of vermin to deal with, I suppose?"

"Indeed we do. You can scrape up quarts of 'em."

I added her testimony to my report. Then, after visiting many of the infirmaries on April 6th, I attended meetings of our county supervisors and superintendent of the poor. I reported our work, and presented an order for dues for the previous month. Having arranged my monthly report, I presented it to the monthly meeting of our asylum association.

I retired weary, and awoke to see Dr. Pearsall about to leave my room. He was giving directions to my two anxious daughters. To my surprise my son-in-law remarked, "Mother is so much better, I will return home." Here was a mystery I was unable to solve, and I insisted on knowing why the doctor was there, now nearly 2 o'clock in the morning. I was informed that I had suffered an attack of apoplexy. I was not the least startled, but told them if I had had a fit of that character, I was liable to go at any time, and I wished to say a few things and then I would sleep: If I should be taken away in an unconscious state for them not to have the least uneasiness about me, as my way was clear. I wished my children to live nearer the Savior, and meet their mother in a fairer clime than this, and I requested them to tell my dear absent children the same. I then directed how my little effects should be divided among my six children, and rested well in sleep until the usual hour of waking, and was able to dress in the afternoon.

Within ten days I rode to the asylum, made arrangements to rent the land of the asylum farm for the coming season, and wrote to brother G. A. Olmstead to take my place in looking after its interests for a few months, as my physicians told me it was unsafe for me to continue mental labor, and I must rest at least six months. This was another heavy drawback upon our faith and work, as we had designed to circulate our petition during the remainder of the year, so as to have it ready to present to the next Legislature. Rev. G. A. Olmstead undertook the work of soliciting, and kept the asylum comfortably supplied until his health failed. Then a devoted and self-sacrificing sister, Catharine Taylor, took the field, while I spent six months visiting my children. The severest prescription I ever took from physician, was to think of nothing. But I succeeded admirably, and spent much time in drawing bits of clippings and rags of diverse colors through canvas, making domestic rugs for each of my children. I called upon various physicians, who gave it as their opinion that I could safely accomplish one-fourth of my former work, but I did not even reach that amount of labor. In a little over a month's work, with a petition to the Legislature in my pocket, and at the home of Anson Barkus and wife, I was taken with another midnight fit, and was much longer unconscious than before, but I returned home the following afternoon, accompanied by brother Backus. Twenty-five miles ride on the car and a mile in the hack did not improve the strange pressure in my head. Within a week I had five terrible spasms, lasting at times from five to twenty minutes; during consciousness I was not able to speak a word. When I appeared more comfortable, and my head more natural, greater hopes of my recovery were entertained by my physician and children.

I thought these fits were faintings; for I felt as if I had waked out of sleep each time. But the purple fingernails on the last day led me to suppose that I would die in one of these faints. Between the fits I most earnestly prayed that, if it was the Lord's will, I might be restored to work for him a little longer; but, if otherwise, I would praise him still for taking me over the beautiful river. O what a mistake to call it a dark, deep river, when it is only a bright, rippling stream, just across which all is peace and joy for ever-more! This was the constant breathing of my soul all day; and it vividly flashed upon my mind that fifteen years were added to Hezekiah's life in answer to prayer. This prayer, followed by these words, ran through my mind during all that happy day. Can death, that is called the last enemy, look pleasant? It did look pleasant to me. Praise filled my soul.

That day will never be forgotten as long as memory and reason endure. In the evening I slept three minutes, they said, by the watch, and when I awoke I could talk as easily as ever. From that day I improved in health. These spasms were caused by the pressure of blood in reopening the temporal artery, or forcing its way through a new channel. I again received the tenderest of nursing on the part of my four daughters, and praise is due only to him who is the prayer- hearing God. With the fervent prayers of that memorable day come the words of the poet:

> "'Tis a glorious boon to die,
> A favor that can't be prized too high,"

because of an abundant entrance to be administered to us into the glorious mansions prepared by our Lord and Savior Jesus Christ.

PRESENT CONDITION OF THE FREEDMEN

OUR investigations have proved to the friends of the former slaves that their emigration from the South was not instituted and put into operation by their own choice, except as the force of circumstances, in their surroundings, pressed them into this remarkable movement. Monthly reports of the Kansas Freedmen's Relief Association have also proved satisfactory to thousands of donors toward their relief. The increasing intelligence among the four millions and a half of slaves, declared free by the nation's pen in the hand of her President, Abraham Lincoln, they found did not bring with it the glorious sunlight of freedom the proclamation promised in its dawn. After fifteen years of patient hoping, waiting, and watching for the shaping of government, they saw clearly that their future condition as a race must be submissive vassalage, a war of races, or emigration. Circulars were secretly distributed among themselves, until the conclusion was reached to wend their way northward, as their former masters' power had again become tyrannous. This power they were and are made to see and feel most keenly in many localities, a few incidents will show.

Elder Perry Bradley left Carthage, Leek County, Mississippi, in January, 1880, and testifies to the following facts:

"In October, 1879, twenty-five or thirty masked men went into Peter Watson's house, and took him from his bed, amid screams of 'murder' from his wife and seven children; but the only reply the wife and children received at the hands of the desperadoes was a beating. Their boy of twelve years knocked one down with a chair. While the fighting was going on within, and in their efforts to hold their victim outside, he wrenched himself from their grasp--leaving his shirt in their hands--and ran through the woods to my house, around which colored men gathered and protected him. Although twelve gun-shots followed him in the chase, yet none hit him. By the aid of friends he took the first train he could reach, which, to his surprise, took him twenty-five miles southward, instead of in a northern direction. At Cassiasca, Attala County, Mississippi, not knowing whether they were friends or foes, he told them he wanted to go to

Kansas. They told him he should swear that he could not make a living there, before they would allow him to go North. As he found they were all Democrats at that depot, he consented to their demand; consequently they brought the Bible, and he took his oath 'that he could make a living there, but could not get it.' The Democratic 'bull-dozers,' who had sworn they would hang him if they ever caught him, took his span of horses, wagon, three cows, and his crop of cotton, corn, sugar-cane, and potatoes (all matured), and gave his wife money with which to pay the fare for herself and seven children, the twenty-five miles on the cars to meet her husband. The colored men were told 'that if they would be Democrats they could stay; but Republicans and carpet-baggers could not live there.'

"Austin Carter, a Methodist preacher, was an earnest temperance worker, and was prospering in that part of his work. He was also a strong Republican. He was shot dead in August, 1878, near New Forest Station, Scott County, Mississippi, on the railroad running east and west between Jackson and Meridian, Mississippi, while on his way home, between the hours of six and seven o'clock P. M. He received four shots in the back of his head, which instantly took his life. His wife and children knew nothing of it until the shocking tidings reached them the following morning. Thomas Graham, a wealthy merchant at Forest Station, reported that the man who shot him had gone to Texas and could not be found or heard from; and nothing was done to find the murderer or to bring him to justice."

Elder Perry Bradley was told by a number of this class of Democrats, at various places where he was accustomed to preach, that he could not live there and preach unless he would vote the Democratic ticket and teach his people to do the same. Said he, "In the town of Hillsboro, at one of my meetings, the bulldozers came into the congregation and took me out of the meeting, held in a school-house one mile from Hillsboro, on April 15, 1879, at ten o'clock P. M., where I had preached during our day meetings without disturbance. Captain Hardy, leading the band, took me into the woods to an old deserted house, in which was their general or chief commander, Warsham, who asked the following question: 'Will you stop preaching to your people that Christ died to make you all free, body, soul, and spirit?' 'I can not stop preaching God's truth as I find it in the Bible,' was my answer. 'I want you to understand now that you can't preach such doctrine to our niggers,' was the rejoinder. He then directed them to give me two hundred lashes. They took me out in the front yard and drove four stakes in the ground, to which each wrist and foot was fastened. After being disrobed of my clothing and fastened, face downward, two men were selected to do the whipping, one on each side, alternating their strokes, while the rabble stood around until the two hundred lashes were given. Then they were told to stop and let me up. Too weak and trembling to stand, I was again queried whether I would not now preach the Democratic doctrine and vote that ticket? I replied, 'I can not conscientiously make such a promise.' 'Why not? 'Because I do not believe there are Democrats in heaven.' Said their general, Warsham, 'We'll turn him loose with this brushing; may be he'll conclude to behave himself after this.' Turning to me he said, 'Remember, this is but a light brushing compared with what you'll get next time; but well try you with this.' I returned to my home with my back cut in many deep gashes, the scars of which I shall carry to my grave. Yet I praised God in remembrance that my loving Savior suffered more than this for me, and that this suffering was in his cause. As soon as I was able to continue my work for my Lord and Master among my people I was again enabled to proclaim the riches of his grace. A few weeks after resuming my work I preached on the Dan. Lewis' place, in Scott County, where I had held meetings undisturbed. But the same company sought me out, and took me out of an evening meeting into the woods about three miles distant to hang me. After due preparations were made they passed their whisky around, of which they all drank so freely that in their carousings they got into a fight, and while drawing pistols at each other young Warsham, the acting captain, in whose charge I was left, cut the rope that bound my hands behind me, and told me to 'go.' And gladly I obeyed the order and left them engaged in their fight and too drunk to notice my escape. I left that land of darkness as soon as possible for this free Kansas, and I have my family with me, for which I thank my Deliverer from the jaws of the lion of oppression, and praise the Lord of hosts for a free country, where I can vote as well as preach according to the dictates of my own conscience without the torturing whip or the hangman's rope."

Professor T. Greener, of Howard University, Washington, D. C., who has been prominently identified in the new exodus lately returned from a trip to Kansas, where he visited the colored colonies, and gathered information regarding the black emigrants. He reports them as doing well, constantly receiving accessions to their numbers, and well treated by their white neighbors. He says: "Indications point to a continuance of emigration during the Winter, and increase in the Spring, not in consequence of any special effort on the part of those who favor this solution of the vexed Southern question, but because the emigrants themselves are proving the best agents and propagandists among their friends South." Professor Greener is warm in his praise of Governor John P. St. John and the people of Kansas.

A staff correspondent of the Chicago Inter-Ocean, writing from Topeka, Kansas, December 31, 1879, says: "During four weeks' travel through the State, I estimate the number of colored emigrants at fifteen, or twenty thousand. Of these one-fifth probably are able to buy land, and are making good progress at farming. Most of the others have found, through the Freedmen's Relief Association, places as laborers, and are giving good satisfaction; and in no county are they applying for aid, nor are burdens upon corporate charities. The demand for laborers seems stretched to its fullest capacity, as the accumulation of refugees at the barracks (now nearly seven hundred), for whom no places can be found, clearly indicates. Judging from what I learn from the refugees themselves, and from the increasing numbers, now from twenty-five to fifty arriving every day, we predict that the movement to Kansas will soon assume such proportions as to astonish the country, and unless the tide can be turned, or the charity of the North be more readily bestowed, the suffering which the relief committee, although laboring faithfully with the means at their command, has not been entirely sufficient to relieve during the past cold weather, will soon be turned to general destitution and great suffering among the pauper refugees."

The greatest crime in many portions of the South is being a Republican. This has added largely to the emigration, and the tide has reached not only Kansas, but the older States of the North. It has entered Indiana, Ohio, and Illinois, and soon will find its way into Wisconsin, Iowa, and Michigan. We find no political chicanery of the North in this universal uprising of the colored people of the South in leaving the home of their birth. But it is the mistaken policy of the South that is driving their laborers northward; that is, compelling them to flee to more congenial surroundings. It is among the wonders that they waited so long and so patiently for the better day to come. Not long ago one thousand arrived in Parsons, Kansas, in the south-western part of the State. Governor St. John gave them a temperance speech with other good advice. Two hundred and twenty-five arrived in Topeka, and while I was at the barracks over seventy came in from Texas. Hardly a day passed while I was there but we heard of fresh arrivals. Eleven wagon-loads came into Parsons, and two of the men came to Topeka and reported the condition of many of them as very poor. We relieved within three weeks over one thousand persons.

The crime of being a Republican, in many portions of the South, is shown by the following testimonies. I interviewed an intelligent colored man, John S. Scott, of Anderson County, South Carolina. He came well recommended as a well qualified teacher. He had taught twenty-eight terms of school in South Carolina and six terms in Georgia; but if he succeeded in collecting half his pay he did well. He handed me a package of certificates and commendations. His friends were about to run him for office, but his life was threatened, and he was informed that they were determined to have a "white man's government," and gave him to understand that if he got the office, his life would be worthless.

Abbeville district, in that State, was Republican, and John Owen was an influential colored Republican. During the election he was arrested and placed in jail, under the charge of selling forty-eight pounds of twisted tobacco without license. When arraigned before the court it was proved that he had no such article, yet they fined him fifty dollars. He had raised tobacco, but it was still in the leaf. The fine was paid, and after the election he was released.

In the Seventh Congressional District, on Coosa River, September 24, 1877, a white man by the name of Burnam offered to purchase a small cotton farm near his, owned by a colored man, and offered him forty dollars for it. The owner replied, "I will sell to no man for that amount." Nothing more was said on the subject, and the colored man purchased a few pounds of bacon of Burnam and left for home. As he had to pass a little skirt of woods, Burnam took his gun, crossed the woods, and came out ahead of the colored man and shot him dead! He remained at his home two weeks, when the excitement over the cold- blooded murder became unpleasant for him, and he left the neighborhood, and had not returned in March, 1878, the date my informant left the country. The murdered man was a Republican.

Sanford Griffin was an honorably discharged soldier, and he testified that Columbus Seats was shot dead by Frank Phillips, in Clarksville, Tennessee. Griffin made an effort to have the murderer arrested, but failed. No difference was known to exist between them, except on the subject of politics. Seats was a Republican, and could not be induced to vote the Bourbon ticket.

In the autumn of 1878 Vincent Andersen was brought into Clarksville, Montgomery County, Tennessee, at eleven o'clock A. M. The following night a mob took him out of jail and hanged him on a locust tree on the Nashville Pike, near Clarksville. This case Griffin made an effort to bring before the court, but failed. The jailer, Perkins, said the men who brought Anderson to the jail, came in the night, and having overpowered him, forcibly took the jail key. But a girl of thirteen years testified that she saw the men in conversation with the jailer, and was confident they paid him money. Vincent Anderson had purchased ten acres of land, and had paid every installment promptly, and was on the way to the railroad station to make his last payment, when the mob took him to jail, until the darkness of night favored their wicked purpose of taking his life. He could not be prevailed upon to vote the Bourbon ticket.

One more incident this intelligent ex-Union soldier gave to which he was a witness: A young white woman, Miss Smith, purchased a pistol and remarked, "I am going to kill a nigger before the week is out." During that week her father and Farran, a colored man, had a dispute, but Farran had no thought of any serious result from it. But as Lydia Farran, the wife of the colored man, was on her way to the field to help her husband, Miss Smith, the white girl of eighteen or twenty years of age, took the pistol she had purchased a day or two previously, and followed Lydia and shot her dead! She left two little children, then a colored family got to their distracted father, who escaped for his life. He had not known of any difficulty between his wife and Miss Smith, or any other of the family, and could attribute the cool calculating murder of his wife to no other cause than the little difference of opinion that was expressed a few days previous to the fatal deed! Sanford Griffin succeeded in bringing this case before the court. But the charge of the judge to the jurors was, "You must bear in mind that Miss Smith was the weaker party, and if the shooting was in self-defense, it would be justifiable homicide." The jury so returned their verdict, and the case was dismissed.

The Freedmen's Aid Commission in Kansas relieved the wants of many of these refugees from the South; but the number of colored people was so great that, until they could find places to work for others or for themselves, the Commission had difficulty to care for them. A circular letter was issued, appealing to the friends of the cause for help. To this letter, sent out in December, 1879, these few telling words, from our dear friend and Christian philanthropist, Elizabeth L. Comstock, were added: "The treasury is nearly empty; city and barracks very much crowded; refugees coming in faster than we can care for them; money urgently needed for food, fuel, and medicine, and also to provide shelter." We take pleasure in announcing that our appeals from time to time met with responsive chords in many hearts, and relief was sent to the perishing.

It is needless to speak further of the causes for emigration, so clearly set forth in the foregoing facts; but we give a late one, which in its section of country caused considerable anxiety and stir among this oppressed people. About the close of July an article appeared in the Mercury, edited by Colonel A. G. Horn, at Meridian, Mississippi, in which occurs the following: "We would like to engrave a prophecy on stone, to be read by generations in the future. The negroes in these States will be slaves again or cease to be. Their sole refuge from extinction will be in slavery to the white man." Do not forget, dear reader, that though ignorant, as a large majority of ex-slaves are, yet their children read these sentiments, which are more outspoken than that which characterizes Southern Democracy; yet re-enlivened treason is nevertheless the true sentiment and ruling power of many places in ex-slave States. It is so accepted by the negroes, who, to avoid extinction or slavery, seek refuge amid physical and pecuniary hardships. Indeed, this exodus from the South, is not ended--a move for freedom is not easily extinguished.

To aid the reader fully to understand the needs of these poor people in the southern portion of Kansas, I insert an appeal of a constant and self-sacrificing worker for them, Daniel Votaw, of Independence, Kansas: "It appears that the southern portion of this State is having a larger share of emigrants than any other part of it. For this reason I ask the philanthropist to send aid quickly. I believe clothing will come; but who will send money to buy bread? Most of them say, 'Just give corn-bread, and we are satisfied.' I have never seen nor heard so much gratitude come from any people as flows from the hearts of these poor colored refugees. Our granaries are full, our groceries groan with the weight of provisions; but these sufferers have nothing to buy with. My blood almost runs chill when I remember that there are two excessive luxuries used by persons who call themselves men, that would, if rightly applied, fill this crying bill of want; namely, tobacco and whisky. Come, erring brothers, to the rescue. Can you not donate these expenses to this good cause? Do it, and Heaven will bless you. Those who may send provisions, clothing, or money, will get a correct account, if a note of donor or shipper is found inside the package, to enable us to respond with a correct receipt."

I have a letter from a colored man in Mississippi, addressed to Governor John P. St. John, which he turned over to me to answer. I give an extract: "Please advise me what to do. The white men here say we have got to stay here, because we have no money to go with. We can organise with a little. Since the white people mistrust our intentions, they hardly let us have bread to eat. As soon as we can go on a cheap scale, we are getting ready to leave. Some of us are almost naked and starved. We are banding together without any instruction from you or any aid society. We are all Republicans, and hard-working men, and men of trust We have to keep our intention secret or be shot; and we are not allowed to meet. We want to leave before the matter is found out by the bulldozers. There are forty widows in our band. They are work-women and farmers also. The white men here take our wives and daughters and serve them as they please, and we are shot if we say any thing about it and if we vote any other way than their way we can not live in our State or county. We are sure to leave, or be killed. They have driven away all Northern whites and colored leaders. A little instruction from you will aid the committee greatly in our efforts in getting away. Hoping to hear from you soon in regard to the request, we remain, Very truly yours," etc.

The foregoing from which I purposely omit the name and address of the writer is a sample of many hundreds of letters received by Governor St John. Many of them he placed in our hands to reply. But neither the governor nor our association could do any thing to bring these poor people to Kansas. Our sole object is to relieve them after their arrival. Consequently, it is but little encouragement we could give these sorrowing hearts as to any preparations for leaving that poisoned land. One family told us "We were compelled to lay our plans in secret, and we left our bureau and two large pitchers standing in our cabin and took a night boat." What a misnomer to call our former slave States "free!"

The cry has been, "The sooner Northern carpet-baggers leave the South, the better for them, and the sooner the nigger finds his proper place, and keeps it the better for him." The following incidents will serve as data from which we have a right to judge of the manner used to bring the colored people into what they deem their proper place. But they are becoming too intelligent to endure subjugation when they can evade it by flight.

Robert Robinson on the road between Huntsville, Alabama, and Cold Springs hired a colored man for three months, and he called at his store for his pay "All right," said Robison, "step back and we'll look over the books and pay you." After entering the room the door was locked, and Robinson placed a pistol at his head, while his brother beat him with a pine club, which disabled him from labor for three weeks. This was his pay.

Giles Lester was taken to jail, and was in the hands of Bailiff Dantey. A mob of fifteen or twenty men took him out on Friday night, to a piece of woods, and hanged him--not so as to break his neck at once; but they were three hours in beating him to death. A white man living near by said he never heard such cries and groans of agony in all his life as during those three hours. These atrocities were committed within two years past.

During the Mississippi riot that fiercely raged during 1875-6, the object of which was to secure a solid Democratic vote at the presidential election, innocent men, without the shadow of provocation, were hauled out of their houses and shot, or hanged; and no legal notice was taken of the murderers, for they were men of property and standing. General J.R. Chalmers was a leader in one band of these rioters, and is now honored with a seat in Congress. The mob took Henry Alcorn out of his house to the woods and shot him, leaving the murdered man to be buried by his friends, who mourned over his sad fate. But there is no redress where this corrupt public sentiment takes the place of law. This band of rioters called up Charlie Green to cook for them all night at one of their places of rendezvous. At early morn, Charlie being tired, fell asleep sitting on a dry-goods box. One of the party said he wanted to try his gun before starting, and discharged its contents into Green's body, taking his life instantly!

One or two instances of Southern malignity and outrage were reported to me by one of these refugees. A woman residing near some of those whom I interviewed during my stay in Kansas, in 1879-80, was called out by the "Bourbons" or "Regulators" who were in pursuit of her husband, and questioned as to his whereabouts. Suspecting that their object was to take his life she refused to tell. Upon this a rope was placed around her neck and tied to a horse's tail, and she was thus dragged to the nearest wood and hanged to the limb of a tree until she was dead. Her husband made his escape as, best he could with his mother-less babe.

There was a plantation in Mississippi rented to six colored men, three of them with families. At Christmas they called for a settlement. Morgan, the proprietor, brought them into his debt, and swore "every nigger had eaten his head off." He took seven hundred bushels of wheat that they had raised, and fourteen fat hogs, the corn, and even the team and wagon they brought on the place. They concluded to resort to the civil authorities, hoping to recover a portion of the avails of the season's hard work. But Morgan gained the suit. At this the colored men told him just what they thought of this wholesale robbery. Within a week after the six men were taken out of their beds in the dead of night, by a company of masked "Regulators," who stripped the bedsteads of their cords, with which they were hanged and then lashed to boards and sent floating down the Mississippi River. A white cloth was fastened over their bosoms, upon which was written: "Any one taking up these bodies to bury may expect the same fate." They were taken out of the river one hundred miles below. Two of the widows sent for the bodies of their husbands, and a number whom I conversed with attended the funeral and read the notice on the linen, which had not been removed from their persons. Surely we have a right, and it is our duty to ventilate these facts, though we may be deemed sensational. We can not be charged with political wire-pulling, as they are beyond our reach. But I ask, in the words of Elizabeth H. Chandler, who has long since gone to her rest and reward--

> "Shall we behold unheeding
> Life's holiest feelings crushed?
> When woman's heart is bleeding,
> Shall woman's voice be hushed?"

Is it a wonder the freedmen flee by hundreds and thousands? They are still coming into Kansas. There are many sick and dying among them. Let every man, woman, and child arise and work for the refugees, who are suffering for food, fuel, and clothing. There is great necessity for immediate and vigorous effort, in taking the place of the Good Samaritan in caring for the robbed and bruised stranger, who find many priests and Levites passing by. During the Winter all money and supplies for Kansas refugees should be directed to Elizabeth L. Comstock, North Topeka, Kansas.

Our work is by every possible means aiding these poor people to help themselves, which they are doing wherever work can be found. But Winter season overtaking them on the way to Kansas, and no work to be obtained, the philanthropy of our North will not withhold her liberal hand. It is a debt which we owe to this people. Comparatively few call for assistance who have been in the State a year, and most of these are aged grandparents, the sick, and widows with large families of small children.

Of those who came early in the Spring of 1879, many have raised from one hundred to four hundred bushels of corn each year, but they divide with their friends and relatives who follow them. Some raised a few acres of cotton in their first year, and they are jubilant over their future outlook. They say, "Kansas prairies will blossom as the rose, and whiten her thousands of acres with their favorite staple." One old man whose head was almost as white as the few acres of cotton he produced, said, "We'll 'stonish the nation wid thousands of snow-white acres of cotton in dis yere free Kansas, raised wid black hands." I find they are writing back to their relatives and friends in the far off South, that they can raise cotton as successfully in Kansas as in Mississippi, Alabama, and Louisiana. In this prospect the door of hope is opening before them, as if by the Almighty hand, which they accept as having led them to the "land of freedom," as they often express themselves.

They are coming in larger numbers again, notwithstanding every possible effort of planters to keep them back, and false reports from their enemies in this State that the exodus had ended, but we who are in communication with other portions of the State know to the contrary, and all who come report more to follow. These poor people who, between March, 1879, and March, 1881, have made their escape from an oppression that seems almost incredible, and have come to Kansas to live, now number more than fifty thousand, and still they come. Like a great panorama, the scenes I witnessed in this State sixteen years ago, amid clashing arms, come back to me. Suffering and dying then seemed the order of each day. True, there is a great deal of suffering and ignorance among these field hands still, but there is a marked improvement, both as to the intelligence of these masses and their personal comfort. Are they not as intelligent as were the children of Israel when they left Egypt? They made a golden calf to worship after Moses had left them a few days. All ignorant people are prone to depend upon leaders instead of relying on themselves.

Joseph Fletcher, who came into Kansas July 8, 1879, I found by his papers to be an honorably discharged soldier from Mississippi. He testifies to the following facts: "I saw one hundred men killed by shooting and hanging during the two years, 1878 and 1879; and my brother was one of them; I can point to their graves to-day in the two parishes I worked in. This was in the Red River section, Mississippi. Their crime was their persistence in voting the Republican ticket." A number of the representative men from those parishes were interviewed, and they testified to the same things A number of them had been soldiers.

Andrew J. Jackson, directly from Waterproof, Mississippi, says: "Fairfax was a smart, educated man. He owned his house and land, and gave a lot to the colored Baptist Church and mostly built it. But the bulldozers burned both house and church. He rebuilt his house. The Republicans nominated him for Senator, and the Bourbon Democrats found he would be elected. They threatened his life, and as he found snares were laid to entrap him, he made his escape to New Orleans for safety. When, they learned as to his whereabouts, a number of men wrote for him to come back, and they would drop the matter and let the election go as it would; but he heeded neither their letters nor telegrams. One of his friends was fearful that he would heed their persuasions and went to see him, and told him not to listen to their sweet talk, for the bulldozers only wanted him back so that they might take his life. The white Democrats continued to write to him to come back and advise the colored people not to go North, and they would promise to protect him, for every body wanted him to return and none would molest him. As he did not return for all their pledges, one man, who had always appeared very friendly with him, went to see him, and told him that all who had opposed him pledged their word and honor that he should not be disturbed in the least if he would only return and persuade the colored people not to go to Kansas, as he had more influence over them than any other man. He assured him so confidently that he concluded to trust them, and returned to the bosom of his family on Saturday; but before Monday morning he was shot dead. The heart-rending scene can better be imagined than described."

Said one intelligent man, "We can do nothing to protect the virtue of our wives and daughters." Near Greenville, Mississippi, a colored woman was passing through a little skirt of woods, when she was attacked by two white men, who violated her person; then, to prevent exposure, they murdered her in the most savage manner. They tied her clothes over her head and hanged her by her waist to a hickory sapling, and ripped open her bowels until a babe, that would within a few weeks have occupied its place in its mother's arms, fell to the ground. Just at that juncture two colored men came in sight, and the white men dodged into the woods. This drew attention to the awful scene of the dying woman weltering in her gore. They hastened to cut her down, and just as she was breathing her last she whispered, "Tell my husband." One watched the corpse while the other went to inform the husband. This barbarous murder, which took place in April, 1879, was twice related to me in the same way by different women from the same neighborhood, who attended the funeral. As I related this to our friend, W. Armour and wife, of Kansas City, he remarked that the same incident had been told to him by some of the new arrivals. We repeat, Who can wonder at their flight?

On July 12th and 13th two boat-loads more of refugees, numbering four hundred persons, landed in lower Kansas City. I heard it again repeated, "What shall we do? Here in Topeka are two hundred poor people waiting to go somewhere to get work, and only two hundred dollars in our treasury!" What shall we send them? More than fifty men and women were then out hunting work; many found it and rented cabins. We waited for a reply from the railroad authorities, to see if they would take two hundred passengers for that money to Colorado.

This association met and reached the conclusion to telegraph Mr. W. Armour and his co-laborers, at Kansas City, to send the four hundred at that place to other points, as it was impossible to receive them in Topeka until those already there were furnished with homes, or more money should come to our aid. I returned to Kansas City, and found their hands and hearts full also, and heard the query repeated, "What are we to do for these poor people? We can not send them back, and they must be fed until we hear from places to which we have telegraphed." Favorable replies came for seventy-five families to Colorado. The colored minister, Elder Watson, was to take them away, and visited St. Louis to request the friends in that city to send no more in this direction for the present.

A white woman called to see some of these poor people, and brought chicken broth for a very sick man. She said she was born in Virginia, raised in Georgia, where she had taught school, and also taught in Mississippi and Alabama. Because she contended for the rights of the colored people, as they were free, she was ostracised and compelled to leave the South. Said she, "I have seen them hung and shot like dogs. They can not tell you the half of what they suffer. I know it, for I have seen it."

While I was still visiting among these people, the steamer Fannie Lewis landed with one hundred and four more refugees from Mississippi. Here they had nothing for their covering except the open sky. We feared that, unless other States should rally to the rescue, nothing but suffering and death would be before them. Kansas had domiciled about what she could for the present, unless further aid should be given from without. This State had hardly recovered from the sweeping devastation of war when drought swept over her rich prairies, and scarcely had she recovered from that drawback when the grasshoppers came and desolated her again. Then the Macedonian cry, "Come over and help us," was heard and answered. Again we raise this cry in behalf of this oppressed people, and it will meet a generous response.

When forty thousand dependents were thrown into young Kansas by Price's raid through Missouri, followed by Colonels James Lane and Jennison, I received from General Curtis the report that twenty thousand poor whites and as many freedmen were here to be cared for by government and the benevolence of the North. At that time of sore need Michigan placed in my hands two thousand six hundred dollars in money, and from seven thousand to eight thousand dollars in supplies to relieve the perishing and dying of that day. The lesson is not forgotten, that it is more blessed to give than to receive. He alone who knows the end from the beginning can tell the future of our country, and of the five million of its inhabitants of African descent. Yet eternal right must and will triumph. The debt our nation owes to the ex-slave should be paid. The hundred thousand colored soldiers who fought as bravely to save our nation's life as did their paler-faced brethren, and faced the cannon's mouth as fearlessly for the prize above all price--liberty--are worthy of consideration. They were ever true to our soldiers. Many of our prisoners escaping from rebel dungeons were piloted by them into our lines. Many black "aunties" took their last chicken and made broth for our sick Union soldiers, as did the one I met in Natchez, Mississippi. She had been free a number of years, and had her yard full of geese, ducks, and chickens; but all went for Union soldiers. She was a noble Christian woman. She said, "I feels so sorry for a sick soldier, so far from their home. I feels happy for all I kin do for 'em. I knows Jesus pay me." Another colored woman whom I met at Gloucester Courthouse, in Virginia, did the same.

An ex-soldier wrote in a note, found in a box of valuable clothing sent to the refugees in Kansas: "I send this as a small token of the gratitude I owe to the colored people for saving my life when I was sick and escaping from a loathsome rebel prison. They took care of me and conducted me safely to our Union camp. This goes with a prayer that God will bless that suffering people."

We have the testimony of many witnesses. Among them is J. C. Hartzell, D. D., of New Orleans, editor of the Southwestern Christian Advocate. He says, "The cruelties endured by the colored people of the South can not be overdrawn." He knew of a number of families that took homesteads on government lands and were doing well for themselves, but masked "Bourbons" went in a company and drove them off, telling them they "had no business with homes of their own. The plantation was their place, and there they should go." One man undertook to defend himself and family with his gun, but receiving a serious wound from one of the Bourbons, he hid from his pursuers. One of his white friends heard of what had befallen him, and took him to New Orleans for safety, as he knew him to be an industrious and peaceable man. Here he employed a skillful surgeon to treat him. Our informant saw the bullet taken from his body, and thought his life could be saved. But he is sure to lose it if he returns to his own home. Rev. J. C. Hartzell said he had received letters from various places all over the South, written by intelligent colored ministers, that their Churches were closed against them until after election. The same thing was told me by many of those I interviewed.

The Bourbons said their meetings were the hot-beds of emigration and Republicanism. In some places they were forbidden to meet in their private houses for prayer-meetings, as their enemies said they met to make plans to go to Kansas. Is there no guarantee for life, liberty, and the pursuit of happiness? What a state of society is this for a free country? Our first duty as a government is protection. But if it is too weak for that, the second duty is to welcome the fleeing refugee and point him to work, or to the thousands of acres of good government land, and help him where he needs help to keep body and soul together during the few months it may require to make himself self-sustaining.

From Daniel Votaw's report from Independence, Kansas, I extract the following: "Thomas Bell, of Dallas County, Texas, was hanged about October 5th for attempting to go with his family and a few neighbors to

Kansas. Blood and rapine mark the fugitive. After supper, from meal furnished them for this purpose, they gave us a history of their trials in Texas, which was truly sorrowful; and with the notes, mortgages, and credits given--to the whole amount, two thousand five hundred dollars--for their farms, they were compelled to leave and flee for their lives, as David did before Saul."

Shot-gun rule still continued. Philip Fauber, recently from near Baton Kouge, Louisiana, testifies as follows: "I rented land of Bragg and James McNealy, and was to have one-third of the crop and furnish team and seed. I took three bales of cotton to the weigher, who read my contract, and set aside one bale for me. But the McNealys claimed the three bales, and I referred the matter to the Justice of the Peace, who, after reading the contract, sanctioned the decision of the weigher. But the McNealys brought another officer, who asked to see the contract I handed him the paper, which he read and tore up and threw away, and McNealy took possession of the last bale of cotton, which I told them was my only dependence for my family's support for the Winter. On my way home through a little woods I received the contents of a shot-gun in my face, both eyes being put out. In great distress I felt my way home. The doctor took a number of shot out of my face, but he couldn't put my eyes back. I can now do nothing but depend upon others to feed and clothe me till God takes me from this dark world to that glorious world of light and peace. The old man, McNealy denied shooting me, but he never said he did not know who did. But he and his two sons died within a few months after I was shot In the last sickness of Bragg McNealy he sent for me to tell me for the last time that he did not shoot me. Still he would not tell who did." The industrious wife of this poor man whose face is speckled with shot scars, is anxious to get four or five acres of land to work herself, and support herself and blind husband.

A. A. Lacy, an intelligent colored man from New Orleans, who came to us indorsed by a number of others from the same city, testifies to the facts related by him as follows: "May 5, 1880, I called at the custom- house to report for duty to General A. S. Badger, collector of customs, by whom I had been employed. He directed me to Captain L. E. Salles, the chief weigher, to whom I had reported a number of days, but failed to get work, and as I failed this time I asked if I had better continue calling for work. He replied, 'You had better call again.' As I was passing out of the door his partner, Michael Walsh, came to me (in a gruff, commanding tone), 'What is that you say, Lacy?' 'Nothing to you,' I replied; 'I was speaking to Captain Salles.' At this he gave a stab, and as I turned to see what he was hitting me for, he added two stabs more with cursing. As I was going down the steps I felt the warm blood running down my side, not yet realizing that I had been cut. I opened my vest and saw the flowing blood. I stepped into Mr. Blanchard's office, the assistant weigher, who was a Republican, and showed him my side, with clothes saturated with blood. He was so shocked and excited that he was taken ill and died in just two weeks. He advised me to enter a complaint against Michael Walsh, which I did, and he was placed in jail in default of thousand dollar bond. I was sent to the hospital. As there were many friends and reporters calling on me, the surgeon forbade callers except immediate attendants and my wife. He said the deepest wound reached the left lung, and an eighth of an inch deeper would have produced instant death. On the tenth day I was allowed to be removed to my home, and pronounced to be convalescent. Michael Walsh was released from prison with no other mark of displeasure resting upon him for this attempt at murder than a few days' imprisonment. As soon as I was able to walk about I took a boat with friends whose lives had been threatened for Kansas, where we arrived July 15, 1880. I am only able to light work, for which I am thankful. Yet it seems hard to lose all this time from the assassin's stab in a custom-house that belongs to the government I fought two years to sustain."

Uncle Peter Cox, an aged man of eighty-eight years, has a wen on the back of his neck, running between his shoulders, larger than a two- quart bowl, that has been over thirty years coming. It was caused by heavy lifting and continued hard work during his slave-life. He came to Topeka, Kansas, in July, 1880, with his aged wife and deaf and dumb grandson of eighteen years. His advanced age and deformity induced me to inquire more closely into the cause of leaving his State (Louisiana). After giving the sad history of his slave-life--the common lot of that class of goods and chattels--he said: "Missus I stay'd thar as long as I could, when I seed my brodder in de Lo'd hangin' on a tree not more'n a hundred rods from my house, near Baton Rouge. A sistah was hanged five miles off, on de plank road, in West Baton Rouge, in a little woods. Her sistah followed her beggin' for her life, and tole de bulldosers she couldn't tell whar her husban' was that da's gwine to hang. But da swore she should hang if she didn't tell." Giving his head a shake, while tears dropped thick and fast down the deeply furrowed cheeks, he continued: "O, Missus, I couldn't live thar no longer. I's so distressed day an' night. De chief captain of dis ban' of murder's was Henry

Castle, who wid his ban' of men was supported by Mr. Garrett, Mr. Fisher, an' Mr. Washington, who were merchants in Baton Rouge."

But that poor grandfather's heart was filled with grief to overflowing when the faithful grandson was walking alone in the railroad track, and was run over by the cars and instantly killed. Although the warning whistle was given the poor deaf boy heard it not. As he was all the aged pair had to depend upon for their living, it was to them a heavy stroke. No one can look over these testimonies without exclaiming, with David, "Is there not a cause" for the flight of this persecuted people? We find many among them, like Lazarus, begging for the crumbs that fall from the rich man's table; but let us not allow them to die in this land of plenty.

Yet, through all these dark clouds, we perceive the silver linings. The heaven-born cause of temperance is gaining a foothold in our Southern States. A crusade against the liquor-traffic commenced in Ohio, and has swept over Michigan and other neighboring States, and is still going on conquering and to conquer.

PROSPECTS OF THE FREEDMEN

OUR last chapter contains the dark side of our picture. In this we present the brighter prospects for a long and sorely oppressed race. We first note what has been and is being done for the fifty thousand who have emigrated to Kansas As I have been a co-laborer with Elizabeth L. Comstock more than two years in rescuing the perishing in their new homes, I speak from personal knowledge.

During the first Winter--1879-80--as mild as it was, more than one hundred refugees were found with frozen feet fingers. Five were frozen to death coming through the Indian Territory with their teams. Through faithful agents, with supplies forwarded from other States, and even from friends in England in response to appeals sent out by Elizabeth L. Comstock, very many sufferers were relieved. The goods from England were forwarded mostly by James Clark, of Street. Over seventy thousand dollars' worth of supplies have passed through my hands for the relief of the refugees between September, 1879, when I commenced working for them, and March, 1881 Thirteen thousand dollars of this amount came from England, having been sent by Friends or Quakers Besides money, we received new goods, as follows,

Warm, new blankets	2,000
New garments for women and girls	5,000
New garments for men and boys	3,000
New garments for babies and small children	5,000
New knitted socks and hose, five hundred dozen pairs	6,000
Large quantity of sheets, pillow-cases, bed-quilts, towels etc	3,000
Queensware--Six large crates, one hundred and nineteen dozen plates in each	8,568
Cups and saucers, nearly	6,000
Bowls and mugs	4,000
Platters, pitchers, and chamber wares	3,500
Scissors	6,000
Sets of knives and forks	4,000
Spoons	8,000

Needles	15,000
Knitting needles	2,500
Rags, with sewing materials	2,500
Papers of pins, six hundred and fifty dozen, and tape	350,
	1,000
Tin-cups and basins	6,000
Bed-ticks	1,500
Wash-dishes and pans	2,000
Woolen dresses for women and girls, valued at	$1,680
New overcoats for men and boys, valued at	$650
Three whole bolts of Welch flannel (seventy-two yards each)	$150
Two bolts heavy broadcloth, for overcoats, valued at	$144
Women's cloaks and shawls, valued at	$2,250
New red flannel, valued at	$150
Muslins, valued at	$150
Gray flannel and three hundred pairs mittens, valued at	$500
Buttons, hooks and eyes, cotton thread, silk, etc.	$500
New pieces goods, chiefly cotton, valued at	$5,000

Over ninety thousand dollars in money and supplies were distributed by the Kansas Relief Association, until it was disbanded in May, 1881, and its head-quarters removed to Southern Kansas, where thousands of these Southern emigrants are congregated. That locality is more favorable to cotton raising. Many of the refugees know but little of other business; hence the necessity for an agricultural, industrial, and educational institute, of which Elizabeth L. Comstock is the founder. At the present date (August, 1881) eight thousand dollars are invested. This includes the Homestead Fund. To meet the crying need of this people she, in connection with her daughter, Caroline DeGreen, are untiring in their efforts to establish a permanent or systematized work. They have established this much needed institution on four hundred acres of good land, which is tilled by colored people, who receive pay for their work in provision, clothing, or money until they can purchase cheap land for their own homes.

It has been no small task to disburse wisely the large supplies sent from every Northern State and England in various portions of the State of Kansas. It has been done through the instrumentality of self- sacrificing men and women. The noble women of Topeka did their full share. They districted the city, appointed a large investigating committee, and gave tickets calling for the articles most needed in the families found in a suffering condition. By this plan impositions were avoided.

While we have entered bitter complaints against our Southern ex-slave States, we ought to call to mind many persecutions endured by the opponents of slavery in our own States of the North. I have still in remembrance the many mobs to which abolitionists were exposed for discussing their views. I have not forgotten the burning shame and disgrace upon our whole North because of the treatment it allowed to an earnest Christian philanthropist, Prudence Crandall, of Windham County, Connecticut. She opened a school in Canterbury Green for girls, and was patronized by the best families, not only of that town, but of other counties and States. Among those who sought the advantages of her school was a colored girl. But Prudence was too thorough a Quaker to regard the request of bitter prejudice on the part of her other patrons to dismiss her colored pupil. But she did not wait for them to execute their threat to withdraw their children. She sent them home. Then she advertised her school as a boarding school for young ladies of color.

The people felt insulted, and held indignation meetings and appointed committees to remonstrate with her. But she stood by her principles regardless of their remonstrance. The excitement in that town ran high. A town meeting was called to devise means to remove the nuisance. In 1833 Miss Crandall opened her school against the protest of an indignant populace. Another town meeting was called, at which it was resolved, "That the establishment of a rendezvous, falsely denominated a school, was designed by its projectors as the theater to promulgate their disgusting theory of amalgamation and their pernicious sentiments of subverting the Union. These pupils were to have been congregated here from all quarters under the false pretense of educating them, but really to scatter firebrands, arrows, and death among brethren of our own blood."

I well remember the voice of more than seven thousand, even at that day, who had never bowed the knee to the Baal of slavery that was raised in favor of the course pursued by the noble woman. Against one of these young colored girls the people were about to enforce an old vagrant law, requiring her to give security for her maintenance on penalty of being whipped on the naked body. Thus they required her to return to her home in Providence. Canterbury did its best to drive Prudence from her post. Her neighbors refused to give her fresh water from their wells, though they knew their own sons had filled her well with stable refuse. Her father was threatened with mob-violence. An appeal was sent to their Legislature, and that body of wise men devised a wicked enactment which they called law, which was brought to bear upon her parents on this wise: An order was sent to her father, in substance, as follows: "Mr. Crandall, if you go to visit your daughter you are to be fined one hundred dollars for the first offense, two hundred dollars for the second offense, doubling the amount every time. Mrs. Crandall, if you go there you will be fined, and your daughter, Almira, will be fined, and Mr. May,--and those gentlemen from Providence [Messrs. George and Henry Benson], if they come here, will be fined at the same rate. And your daughter, the one that has established the school for colored females, will be taken up the same way as for stealing a horse or for burglary. Her property will not be taken, but she will be put in jail, not having the Liberty of the yard. There is no mercy to be shown about it."

Soon after this Miss Crandall was arrested and taken to jail for an alleged offense. Her trial resulted in an acquittal, but her establishment was persecuted by every conceivable insult. She and her school were shut out from attendance at the Congregational Church, and religious services held in her own house were interrupted by volleys of rotten eggs and other missiles. At length the house was set on fire, but the blaze was soon extinguished.

In 1834, on September 9th, just as the family was retiring for the night, a body of men with iron bars surrounded the house, and simultaneously beat in the windows and doors. This shameful outrage was more than they could endure. Prudence Crandall was driven at last to close her interesting school and send her pupils home. Then another town meeting was held, a sort of glorification, justifying themselves, and praising their Legislature for passing the law for which they asked. All this abominable outrage I well remember, and am glad to see it called up in Scribner's Magazine for December, 1880. A scathing denunciation of the outrage was published in the Boston Liberator, edited by William Lloyd Garrison.

Prudence Crandall did more for the cause of freedom by her persistence in the "Higher Law" doctrine of eternal right than the most eloquent antislavery lecturer could have accomplished in molding public sentiment of the whole North. Her name became a household word in thousands of Northern homes. When we see the changes forty and fifty years have wrought in the North, surely we may look forward in strong faith for like changes to take place over the South. It may take longer, but come it will.

We note with pleasure the rapid strides of education among the colored people in sixteen years. In 1864-5 I visited large schools in slave- pens that had become useless for the purposes for which they were designed. The stumps of their whipping-posts and the place of the dreaded auction block was vacated. Although many of their public schools are not all that could be desired, yet they have them, and they are doing a good work. In Virginia, beginning with 1871, the colored children enrolled for successive years numbered as follows: 38,554; 46,736; 49,169; 54,945; 62,178, 65,043; 61,772; and 35,768. In South Carolina the enrollment from 1870 was, 15,894: 38,635; 46,535; 56,249; 63,415; 70,802; 55,952; 62,120; and 64,095. In Mississippi, beginning with 1875, the enrollment was 89,813; 90,178; 104,777; and 111,796. At the present we foot up the astonishing number of 738,164 pupils. Maryland has appropriated two thousand dollars per annum for the support of normal schools for the training of colored teachers. An ex-Confederate and ex-slave-holder of high degree subscribed five thousand dollars toward a college for colored people under the patronage of one of the colored Churches in the State of Georgia. All honor is due such noble deeds. May there be more to follow his good example.

From the best authorities we have the figures of over a million communicants among the colored people in the United States. Of those in the Southern States we have as follows, at this date, 1881:

African Methodists,	214,808
Methodist Episcopal Church (Colored)	112,000
Colored Baptist Church	500,000
Methodist Episcopal Zion Church	190,000
Methodist Episcopal Church	300,000

Almost every Church in the North has contributed to educational purposes in the South, but they are doing none too much. The Friends have done much toward supporting a school in Helena, Arkansas, under the supervision of Lida Clark, an untiring worker for that people. But we have not the figures of amounts. But the Methodist Episcopal Church has done, and is still doing, a great work, as our figures will show, in building commodious schoolhouses in various States.

Schools of the Freedmen's Aid Society of the Methodist Episcopal Church for 1880-81:

CHARTERED INSTITUTIONS

	TEACHERS.	PUPILS.
Central Tennessee College, Nashville, Tenn.	12	433
Clark University, Atlanta, Ga.	7	176
Chiflin University, Orangeburg, S. C.	9	388
New Orleans University. New Orleans, La.	4	200
Shaw University, Holly Springs, Miss.	8	277
Wiley University, Marshall, Texas	6	323

THEOLOGICAL SCHOOLS.

Centenary Biblical Institute, Baltimore, Md.	4	118
Baker Institute; Orangeburg, S. C.	...	.....[1]
Thompson Biblical Institute, N. Orleans, La.	...	.....[2]

MEDICAL COLLEGE.

Meharry Medical College, Nashville, Tenn.	8	35

Institutions NOT CHARTERED.

Bennett Seminary, Greensburg, N. C.	5	150
Cookman Institute, Jacksonville, Fla.	5	166
Haven Normal School, Waynesboro, Ga.	2	60
La Grange Seminary, La Grange, Ga.	2	96
Meridian Academy, Meridian, Miss.	3	100
Rust Normal School, Huntsville, Ala.	2	112
Walden Seminary, Little Rock, Ark.	2	60
West Texas Conf. Seminary, Austin, Tex.	3	101
La Teche Seminary, La Teche, La.	3	100
West Tennessee Seminary, Mason, Tenn.	2	75

---

[1] Pupils enumerated in the other schools
[2] Pupils enumerated in the other schools

We must here put in our claim for the fifty thousand emigrants in Kansas from the South. The Freedmen's Relief work in Kansas has been thoroughly organized and officered, and the contributions received for the refugees judiciously distributed. An agricultural and industrial school was established some time ago, and is meeting, so far, with good success. It will, if properly sustained, prove to be a blessing not only to the colored race, but to the State. From a circular issued in June last, by Elizabeth L. Comstock, one of the superintendents of this work, I extract the following paragraphs:

"Our first object is to employ those who come for work or for aid. We are strongly advised by their best friends, and the kind donors both sides the Atlantic, not to give any thing (except in return for labor) to those who are able to work, especially during the warm weather. Wages are paid regularly every Saturday, and they come with their money to buy and select from the stock on hand what will suit themselves. Second-hand clothing and bedding have a price affixed almost nominal. Coats, 10 cents each to $1, very few at $1; pants, drawers, shirts, and vests, 5 cents each; shoes, 5 cents a pair; stockings and socks, two pairs for 5 cents; women's dresses, 10, 20, 30, and 40 cents each; children's clothes, 5 to 10 cents a garment; bed-quilts, comforters, and blankets, 20 to 50 cents; new ones, $1 each, if very good. New shoes and other articles, provisions, etc., that we have to purchase we buy at wholesale, and try to supply them below the market price, some of them at half the retail price. Thus what little is gained on the old clothes makes up in part what we lose on the new. We could employ more laborers if we had more money. The state of the treasury is low now. It seems hard to turn away any poor people who want to work. We should be very glad of help just now in the way of seed for sowing, money to provide food and shelter, and to finish up our buildings. We greatly desire to start several industries before Winter, as blacksmith's shop, carpenter's shop, broom factory, etc., etc., that they may have work during the cold weather. We hope to have our school-house soon ready and to educate the children, and have an evening school for adults.

"An important part of our work will be to train the women and girls in the various branches of household work, and sewing, knitting, etc. Nor do we lose sight of the spiritual garden while providing for the intellectual fields and the physical wants. We greatly desire that this long-oppressed race, who have been kept in darkness and ignorance, should have the light of the glorious Gospel, and should have the Bible put into their hands, and be taught to read and understand it. Of course we meet with some opposition in our work, as many a brave soldier has done before us, in battling for the right and for the colored race."

We extract an item from the Columbus Courier (Kansas): "We are proud of the work of the 'Agricultural, Industrial, and Educational Institute,' and earnestly desire its success, and we feel proud of these good men and women who are led on by Mrs. Elizabeth L. Comstock at their head, and Mrs. Laura 8. Haviland, their secretary. Characteristic spirits of the broad philanthropy of our beloved land, they need no commendation to sustain them. This has been their life-work, and they now select our State for their field of labor. J. E. Picketing was chosen from a body of eighteen directors as its president, because of his experience in this kind of work, having at one time been a conductor on the 'Under Ground." He does not receive or ask for salary. He only presides at meetings of the Board of Directors, and has general oversight of the work in progress. His son, Lindly, was selected by the Board according to the expressed wish of Mrs. Comstock as superintendent. His wife is acting in the capacity of matron, but neither of them receives a salary, and they are to be paid by some friends of the work when it is established. But now pay is a matter of no consideration. Charity does not require that these people should leave their comfortable homes and devote their time and energies to the laborious duties of their positions without some reward. "Forty acres of the four hundred upon which the institute is located was purchased of Lindly M. Pickering, at one hundred dollars less than he could otherwise have obtained for it. It was selected for its improvements and its fine location, unsurpassed in the country. In conclusion, we desire to refer to the good management with which without ostentation its affairs are vigorously pushed forward, believing that the ever-living, ever-aggressive principle of right will sustain them and secure the success which so commendable an enterprise deserves. May heaven prosper the work of the nation's truest spirits and best and most respected citizens!"

From the financial statement from April 15th to June 13, 1881, we find that there has been received fur this industrial institute, in cash, $6,931.96. Two large consignments of goods were received about the last date at Columbus by Elizabeth L. Comstock for the same object. We appeal to the Christian public to give us at least one school in Kansas for the refugees.

"Sow thy seed in the morning, and in the evening withhold not thy hand, for thou knowest not whether this or that will prosper."

"Sowing the seed with an aching heart
Sowing the seed while the tear-drops start,
Sowing in hope till the reapers come,
Gladly to welcome the harvest home.
O what shall the harvest be?"